12.50

# Miraculous Stories from the Japanese Buddhist Tradition

HARVARD-YENCHING INSTITUTE
MONOGRAPH SERIES
VOLUME 20

Keikai, comp.

# Miraculous Stories from the Japanese Buddhist Tradition

## The *Nihon ryōiki* of the Monk Kyōkai

Translated and annotated with an introduction by

KYOKO MOTOMOCHI NAKAMURA

HARVARD UNIVERSITY PRESS   CAMBRIDGE, MASSACHUSETTS

1973

# Translator's Preface

In the various publications of the "new religions" in Japan, many stories about the miraculous karmic retribution of good and evil are reported side by side with sophisticated discussions of the doctrines and management of the organizations. Some intellectuals tend to condemn these stories as vulgar expressions of a concern for material benefits; however, one cannot deny the fact that the miraculous events related in the stories often generate and deepen faith in those who have witnessed, heard, or read them. Why do such stories appeal to so many minds in this century? Is the world of the miraculous totally foreign to us who live in the nuclear age?

To put great trust in a literal statement and little in a mythological one is a prejudice, which, although increasingly being challenged, is still very strong. In the field of the history of religions, insufficient work has been done on the folk piety that is oriented around the miraculous in different religious traditions, and this tendency leads to a misunderstanding of both the medieval world and contemporary man.

Recently I had a chance to observe the reaction of some Catholics when the list of approved and recognized saints was revised. The Vatican released the new calendar which had dropped or reclassified about two hundred saints, including such popular ones as St. Nicolas and St. Christopher, in an attempt to drop historically obscure saints, thus separating pious legends and local devotions from the central tradition of the saints of the Church. Even if few Catholics literally believed in the historicity of all the saints, many were dissatisfied with the way Vatican authorities had handled these matters relating to their faith. Not only the lay people but also representatives of the Eastern Catholic churches criticized the move to reclassify the saints. Such an example suggests that there is common ground between the folk piety of Catholics in a modern Western city and that of Buddhists in a medieval Asian village. My interest lies in this common human experience, understood within its different historical and cultural settings.

The present work consists of two parts: an introductory essay followed by an annotated translation of the *Nihon ryōiki* 日本靈異記,[1]

1. *Nihon (Nippon) reiiki* is the alternative reading. Its full title is *Nihonkoku genpō zen'aku ryōiki* 日本國現報善惡靈異記 (Miraculous Stories of Karmic Retribution of Good and Evil in Japan) [hereafter *Nihon ryōiki*].

which was compiled in the ninth century in Japan. I chose this collection of legends for several reasons. First, it offers illustrations of religious phenomena whose interpretation is helpful for a better understanding of human experience. Second, the *Nihon ryōiki* is the earliest collection of Buddhist legends in Japan, and its influence on later literature is significant. Third, it is a key document for understanding how Buddhism was accepted by the Japanese in the first few centuries after its introduction. In other words, this document was produced through the interaction of the Buddhist tradition with the Japanese indigenous tradition. And, finally, these legends have a charm of their own; apart from their doctrinal significance, they are both enjoyable and informative.

The *Nihon ryōiki* is a product of the Buddhist tradition as it took root in Japanese soil. The author Kyōkai 景戒[2] was moved to compile these stories both by a sense of awe of the Buddhist *dharma*[3] and by a sense of the wonder of the world. He lived a monastic life at a temple called Yakushi-ji 藥師寺, one of the great state temples in Nara,[4] during a period of political change when the capital was in the process of being moved from Nara to Nagaoka and then to Kyoto. His work served as a source from which his fellow monks might draw "true stories" to illustrate their popular preaching. It has also become the source of later legendary literature in Japan, many of its motifs reappearing in more elaborate and polished forms. It is quoted by historians and folklorists in their attempts to reconstruct the history and popular Buddhism of the Nara period. So far, however, insufficient attention has been given to interpreting the work as an illustration of how people in early Japan oriented themselves in the world. For this reason I have attempted in the introduction to place these tales in their cultural and historical context and have emphasized their cosmic orientation rather than their specific doctrinal significance.

The *Nihon ryōiki* is divided into three *kan* or volumes. Although no complete manuscript of the work has been preserved, several critical editions of the text have been published since the nineteenth century, most of which are based on the first critical text made by Kariya Ekisai 狩谷棭齋 (1775–1835).[5] In the recent work by Takeda Yūkichi

---

2. Keikai is the alternative reading, according to the *kan'on* or so-called Han pronunciation.
3. Skt., meaning elements of existence, universal law, the teaching of Buddha. Hereafter *dharma* is treated as an English word.
4. Located at present Nishinokyō-machi, Nara-shi 奈良市西京町. See Chap. I(1)c.
5. *Kōhon Nihon ryōiki* 校本日本靈異記 (1816); *Nihon ryōiki kōshō* 日本靈異記攷證 (1821); reprinted in the *Gunsho ruijū* 群書類從, XVI, Book 447 (1894); *Kariya Ekisai zenshū*, 2 vols. (1925); *Shinkō gunsho ruijū*, XIX (1932, 1939).

武田祐吉,[6] and in the joint work of Endō Yoshimoto 遠藤嘉基 and Kasuga Kazuo 春日和男,[7] a forward step was made by using a newly discovered Kōfukuji manuscript as the basic text for the first of the three volumes.[8]

The *Nihon ryōiki* was introduced to the West in 1934 through Herman Bohner's elaborate and scholarly German translation,[9] but because of the outbreak of the Second World War, Bohner's work received only limited attention. His translation is faithful to the text of Kariya's critical edition. I have chosen the most recently edited text of Endō and Kasuga, for I find it the most comprehensive and critical.[10] A bibliography of the many excellent works of specialists in textual criticism and philology appears at the end of this work. Without these works I could never have undertaken this translation.

I am responsible for all paragraphing and punctuation since the original text lacks any division beyond that into stories. Sanskrit, Chinese, and Japanese words are retained in cases where translation might lead to misunderstanding. Chinese characters are generally given after the first transcription of a particular noun, a title of a quoted work, or an important term. English translations of technical terms are explained in the footnotes or identified in Appendix C. Difficulties in determining the actual pronunciation used in the age of the *Nihon ryōiki*[11] have prompted me to follow the readings given by Endō and Kasuga for personal and local names, and the *Bussho kaisetsu daijiten*[12]

---

6. *Nihon ryōiki* (*Nihon koten zensho* 日本古典全書, 1950).

7. *Nihon ryōiki* (*NKBT*, 70, 1967).

8. The Kōfukuji manuscript discovered in 1922 has only the first volume, but is the oldest (904) of all the extant manuscripts. See Chap. I(1)b, n. 26.

| Vol. | Kariya text | Nos. of tales | Takeda text | Nos. of tales | Endō & Kasuga text | Nos. of tales |
|---|---|---|---|---|---|---|
| I | Kōyasan ms. | 31 | Kōfukuji ms. | 35 | Kōfukuji ms. | 35 |
| II | Shinobazu-bunko ms. | 42 | Shinobazu-bunko ms. | 42 | Shinpuku-ji ms. | 42 |
| III | Shinobazu-bunko ms. | 39 | Shinobazu-bunko ms. | 39 | Shinpuku-ji ms. | 39 |
| | total | 112 | total | 116 | total | 116 |

9. "Legenden aus der Frühzeit des Japanischen Buddhismus," 2 vols., *Mitteilungen der Deutschen Gesellschaft für Natur- und Völkerkunde Ostasiens*, XXVII (1934–35).

10. As to the first volume, the choice falls on the Kōfukuji ms. due to the fact it is the oldest and best preserved; while, as to the second and third, the Shinobazu-bunko ms., a critically edited text of the Shinpukuji ms., was adopted by several scholars, and the recent work of Endō and Kasuga is a new attempt to adopt the Shinpukuji ms. as its basis. Endō and Kasuga, who had found the Shinobazu-bunko ms. unsatisfactory, followed the established practice of textual criticism, adopting the manuscript closest to the source.

11. Tsukishima Hiroshi 築島裕, *Heian jidaigo shinron* 平安時代語新論, 404–410.

12. Ono Genmyō 小野玄妙, ed. 佛書解説大辭典, 12 vols. (1933).

for titles of Buddhist scriptures. Japanese words are transcribed according to the system adopted in *Kenkyūsha's New Japanese-English Dictionary*,[13] and Chinese words, according to *Mathew's Chinese-English Dictionary*.[14] All historical dates in this work follow the lunar calendar. For full information concerning the works referred to in the notes, see the bibliography.

I hope that this work will serve as a clue to the better understanding of the Japanese tradition which has partly survived even to this day in various spheres of life.

13. *Kenkyūsha's New Japanese-English Dictionary*, ed. by Senkichiro Katsumata (1954).
14. *Mathew's Chinese-English Dictionary* (American Revised ed., 1943), ed. by R. H. Mathews.

# Acknowledgments

I began my study of the *Nihon ryōiki* when writing a thesis at the University of Tokyo. If my work displays any merits, credit should be given to the professors in the Department of the Study of Religion there, as well as in the Department of the History of Religions at the University of Chicago, where I spent two stimulating years, 1960–1962, under the guidance of Professors Mircea Eliade and Joseph M. Kitagawa.

I am grateful to the Radcliffe Institute for providing a fellowship grant, 1968–1970, and in particular to the late Dean Constance E. Smith for her encouragement in preparing this work for publication. I am greatly indebted to Professor Masatoshi Nagatomi of Harvard University and to Dr. Glen W. Baxter, associate director of the Harvard-Yenching Institute, who encouraged me to carry out this project and offered valuable suggestions. My sincere thanks go to Professor Burton Watson of Columbia University who kindly read the entire manuscript and made numerous suggestions and corrections; to Professors Virginia Corwin of Smith College and H. Byron Earhart of Western Michigan University who read portions of my draft to help me improve it. I owe much to Dr. and Mrs. Minor Rogers for their constant help in my struggle to write in English. Also, I should like to express my gratitude to Miss M. Rita Howe, editor at the Harvard University Press, whose patient work greatly improved my manuscript. Without the help of my friends I could not have completed this work.

This work is dedicated to my father, Tetsunosuke Motomochi, who passed away in 1962 before I could return from Chicago.

Tokyo, Japan                    Kyoko Motomochi Nakamura
Spring 1972

# Contents

Part One    Introduction to the *Nihon ryōiki*

Abbreviations    2

Chapter I    Background    3
    (1) Kyōkai, the Author    3
        a. His Life and His Motive
        b. Date of Compilation and Authorship
        c. Yakushi-ji and the Six Nara Schools
        d. State Control of the Samgha and Popular
           Buddhist Movements
    (2) Influence of Earlier Writings    29
        a. Doctrine of Karma and Samsara
        b. The Influence of Chinese Buddhist
           Literature
        c. Japanese Legendary Literature

Chapter II    World View Reflected    45
    (1) Cosmic Order    45
        a. Rites of Cosmic Renewal
        b. Symbolism of the Visit to the Other World
        c. Paradise and Hell: Good and Evil
    (2) Man and Power    60
        a. What Makes Man Human
        b. Woman as a Cosmic Symbol
        c. Ideal Image of Man
    (3) Miraculous World    80
        a. Belief in the Spirits of the Dead
        b. Wonder of the Three Treasures

Part Two    Annotated Translation of the *Nihon ryōiki*

Volume  I    Contents    95
            Preface    99
            Tales 1–35    102
Volume II    Contents    153
            Preface    157
            Tales 1–42    158

# Contents

Volume III    Contents    217
              Preface    221
              Tales 1–39    223


Appendix A.    Chronology    289
         B.    Imperial Family Lineage    293
         C.    Translated Ranks and Titles    294
         D.    Buddhist Scriptures Quoted or Referred
               to in the *Nihon ryōiki*    295
         E.    Chronological List of Major Japanese Works
               of Legendary Literature during the Heian-
               Kamakura Periods    298
Selected Bibliography    301
Index    319

# PART ONE

# Introduction to the *Nihon ryōiki*

# ABBREVIATIONS

| | |
|---|---|
| *DBZ* | *Dainihon Bukkyō zensho* 大日本佛教全書 |
| *ERE* | *Encyclopaedia of Religion and Ethics* |
| *HJAS* | *Harvard Journal of Asiatic Studies* |
| *IBK* | *Indogaku Bukkyōgaku kenkyū* 印度學佛教學研究 |
| *JAOS* | *Journal of the American Oriental Society* |
| *JRAS* | *Journal of the Royal Asiatic Society* |
| *NKBT* | *Nihon koten bungaku taikei* 日本古典文学大系 |
| *SBE* | *Sacred Books of the East* |
| *SGR* | *Shinkō gunsho ruijū* 新校群書類從 |
| *SPTK* | *Ssu-pu ts'ung-k'an* 四部叢刊 |
| *SZKT* | *Shintei zōho kokushi taikei* 新訂增補國史大系 |
| *Taishō* | *Taishō shinshū daizōkyō* 大正新脩大藏經 |
| *TASJ* | *Transactions of the Asiatic Society of Japan* |
| *TPJS* | *Transactions and Proceedings of the Japan Society* |
| *ZGR* | *Zoku gunsho ruijū* 續群書類從 |

| | |
|---|---|
| Ch. | Chinese |
| Ja. | Japanese |
| Skt. | Sanskrit |

Chap. I(1)a A cross-reference to Part One, referring to chapter, section, and subsection.

I.1      A cross-reference to Part Two, referring to volume and tale.

CHAPTER I

# Background

## (I) KYŌKAI, THE AUTHOR

### a. *His Life and His Motive*

The *Nihon ryōiki* compiled by Kyōkai, a monk of Yakushi-ji, is the earliest collection of Buddhist legends in Japan. Nothing is known of his life except what is revealed in this single work. Although his biography is found in the *Honchō kōsō-den* 本朝高僧傳 (Biographies of Eminent Monks in Japan) compiled by Shiban 師蠻 in 1702, all that is said about him is:

> The birthplace of the monk, Kyōkai, is not known. He lived at Yakushi-ji, and espoused the teaching of the Yuishiki 唯識 School as his doctrinal base. In addition to Buddhist studies he compiled the *Ryōiki*, in the preface of which he says. . . .[1]

As the passage which follows consists of a quotation from the *Nihon ryōiki*, it will be seen that this "biography" fails to reveal even the birth and death dates or the birthplace of the subject. Some scholars assume that he came from Kii 紀伊 province, because that is the location of several legends recorded in his work, those which can be dated approximately within his lifetime and which offer precise local names of the area.[2] Probably we would be safe in surmising that he was from a province in or near Kinai 畿內, where most of the legends originated.[3] His signature, "Kyōkai, a monk[4] of Yakushi-ji on the West Side of Nara," is found at the beginning of each volume and at the end of the third volume. Only the last of these signatures specifies his clerical rank, *Dentō jū-i* 傳燈住位, next to the lowest of the five clerical ranks.[5]

1. Shiban, *Honchō kōsōden*, VI (*DBZ*, 102), 125–126.
2. Hashikawa Tadashi, "*Ryōiki no kenkyū*," *Geibun*, XIII (No. 3, 1922), 194.
3. Takase Shōgon, *Nihonkoku genpō zen'aku ryōiki* (*Kokuyaku issaikyō*, Shiden-bu, XXIV), 19–23. Kinai is the area comprising the five home provinces of the Yamato court; they are Yamato 大和, Settsu 攝津, Kawachi 河內, Izumi 和泉, and Yamashiro 山城.
4. Skt. *śramaṇa*, transliterated as *sha-men* 沙門, 桑門, etc., in Chinese and *shamon* in Japanese, originally means "ascetic, recluse," and is later used in the same sense as *biku* 比丘 (Skt. *bhikṣu*), a (Buddhist) monk. In this work the Japanese terms *shamon*, *sō* 僧 (see below, n. 17), and *biku* are all translated as "monk," since they are used interchangeably in the *Nihon ryōiki*.
5. *Dentō daihōshi-i* 傳燈大法師位 (Rank of the Great Master of Transmission of Light), *Dentō hōshi-i* 傳燈法師位 (Rank of the Master of Transmission of Light), *Dentō man-i* 傳燈滿位 (Senior Rank of Transmission of Light), *Dentō jū-i* 傳燈住位 (Junior Rank of Transmission of Light), and *Dentō nyū-i* 傳燈入位 (Initiatory Rank of Transmission of Light) correspond, respectively, to court ranks from three to seven (see II.35, n. 7). The clerical ranks were instituted in 760, in the reign of Emperor Jun'nin. See *Shoku Nihongi* 續日本紀, XXIV (Tenpyō hōji 4:7:23).

Shiban must have assumed that because Kyōkai lived at Yakushi-ji, he studied the Yuishiki teachings since Yakushi-ji had been the center of the Yuishiki School.[6] By Kyōkai's lifetime, however, the sectarian administrative structure was still rudimentary. Temples were not yet affiliated with particular sects but were, rather, Buddhist institutes for the study of several different doctrines. On the other hand, Kyōkai might well have witnessed a sectarian consciousness growing among scholar monks at Yakushi-ji in response to the challenge of the new Buddhist teachings introduced by Saichō 最澄 (767–822)[7] and Kūkai 空海 (744–835),[8] who were favored by the court. Kyōkai seems to have been interested in the new teachings as offering a more comprehensive way to happiness (III.38). In any event, he chose not to identify himself with the eminent monks at Nara, who attempted to maintain their leadership by revitalizing the traditional doctrinal learning in the face of these two new schools.

Kyōkai's autobiographical passages, which are found in the latter section of Tale 38 in Volume III, were unavailable to Shiban because the Kōyasan manuscript of the Nihon ryōiki, which Shiban used, lacked Tale 38 and eleven other stories. Shiban's knowledge of Kyōkai was limited, therefore, to the few lines quoted above. We may conclude that the only dependable information on Kyōkai's life is to be found in the Nihon ryōiki, primarily the autobiographical sections, the three prefaces at the beginning of each volume, and the postscript at the end of Volume III. What do these passages tell us about his life? In the second half of Tale 38, the following dated events are mentioned:

| Year | Era | Event |
|---|---|---|
| 787 | Enryaku 6:9:4[9] | He was stricken with remorse in the evening and dreamed at night of a novice monk[10] named Kyō-nichi 鏡日. |

6. Skt. *vijñaptimātratā*, "consciousness only," is the tenet of the Yuishiki or Hossō 法相 School which asserts that all phenomena are produced from seeds stored in the *ālayavijñāna*, a sort of "reserve consciousness." The founder of this school in China is Hsüan-tsang 玄奘 (c. 596–664); the Japanese monk Dōshō 道昭(照) (629–700), who studied under Hsüan-tsang in China, is considered the founder in Japan (I.22).

7. Founder of the Tendai 天臺 School, known posthumously as Dengyō Daishi 傳教大師. He was sent by an imperial decree to study at Mt. T'ien t'ai, the headquarters of the T'ien t'ai School in China for one year (804–805).

8. Founder of the Shingon 眞言 School, known posthumously as Kōbō Daishi 弘法大師. He studied in China for two years (804–806) and advocated esoteric Buddhist teachings.

9. The numbers mean 6th year, 9th month, 4th day of the Enryaku era. See Appendix A.

10. *Shami* 沙彌, transliterated from Skt. *śrāmaṇera*, means a monk below the age of ordination who keeps the ten precepts (see Chap. I(1)d, n. 87); the Nihon ryōiki also uses the term to mean a monk who leads a householder's life and does not strictly follow the precepts, regardless of age.

| 788 | Enryaku 7:3:17 | He dreamed of his own death. |
| 795 | Enryaku 14:12:30 | He was awarded Junior Rank of Transmission of Light. |
| 797 | Enryaku 16:12:17 | His son died. |
| 800 | Enryaku 19:1:12, 25 | His horses died. |

One autumn evening in 787 Kyōkai reflected on his poverty-stricken life filled with cravings and burning desires, and lamented his past *karma*.[11] He sighed with remorse, dozed off, and dreamed what he took to be a revelation from the Buddha. In the dream he was called on by a mendicant named Kyōnichi. The mendicant showed him a huge flat board on which were marked the heights of several men, their stature being indicative of their relative merits. According to Kyōkai's interpretation, the mendicant was none other than an embodiment of Kannon 觀音,[12] who had come to teach him that man possesses the Buddha-nature, and that, by adding to it wisdom and practice, he can erase past karma and thereby gain happiness. The mendicant, whose begging was an expression of the great mercy of Kannon, gave him an anthology of Buddhist scriptures in order that he might cultivate wisdom, and then disappeared.

In the following year Kyōkai had a second mysterious dream in which he died and was cremated while his spirit observed the whole procedure as an onlooker. Kyōkai did not interpret this dream, but simply remarked that it might be an omen indicating the attainment of long life or a particular rank since dreams sometimes depict the opposite of what is to follow. We do not know whether he lived a long life, but eventually, in 795, he was honored with the second lowest clerical rank.

From these accounts Kyōkai must have entered the priesthood sometime between 787 and 795, perhaps near the time of his second dream in 788, since several years must have passed in the priesthood before he received even the second lowest rank. That Kyōkai did not give any specific information as to when and how he entered the priesthood is in strange contrast with the exact dates and detailed description given for his dreams and for the death of his son and of the

11. Skt. meaning deeds: it is a common Hindu-Buddhist belief that each individual existence is conditioned by past deeds and that every action must bear fruit for the doer. See Chap. I(2)a. Hereafter *karma* is treated as an English word.

12. Or Kanzeon 觀世音 (Ch. Kuan-yin or Kuan-shih-yin), the equivalent of Skt. Avalokitasvara, which means "the one who hears the sounds of the world"; another name, Kanjizai 觀自在 (Ch. Kuan-tzu-tsai) is equivalent to Avalokiteśvara, which means "the onlooking lord," or "the lord who is manifested." Hindu and Iranian influences are evident in the development of the cult of Kannon, who appears in many Mahayana scriptures as a *bodhisattva* (hereafter this will be treated as an English word) of great mercy, and who has been continuously popular among Mahayana Buddhists. See Chap. II(3)b.

horses. However, since Tale 38 of Volume III was given the heading "On the Appearance of Evil and Good Omens Which Were Later Followed by Their Results," and as it is likely that this section was written not as autobiography but to illustrate the interrelationship between Heaven and human beings, he may have deliberately omitted details irrelevant to the theme.

Since our sources are limited, these two dreams must serve as the primary clues to Kyōkai's decision to pursue the spiritual life. The first dream seems to have roused him from the "web of delusion" by widening his vision from a self-centered love to a universal love for all sentient beings. As a result of what Kannon revealed to him, he came to understand the working of the principle of karma. It is possible that he remained silent about the second dream, refraining from interpreting it in Buddhist terms, because it expressed symbols not uniquely Buddhist but universal in character. In many religious traditions the reduction of the body to bones symbolizes the death and rebirth of man, that is, the total transformation and mystical rebirth of a new man. By being reduced to bones, man can be liberated from the human condition. In the Buddhist tradition, the symbol of death, rebirth, and initiation are prominent: "Buddha taught the way and the means of dying to the human condition, to bondage and suffering, in order to be reborn to the freedom, the bliss, and the unconditionality of nirvāṇa."[13]

In 787, the year of his first dream, Kyōkai was still a layman, but he must have been familiar with the Shokyō yōshū 諸經要集 (Essentials of All Sūtras),[14] which was given to him in his dream by the mendicant Kyōnichi. This means that his spiritual pilgrimage must have begun earlier.[15] We have assumed that he entered the priesthood in the following year, soon after the second dream, and it seems that entering the priesthood represented a way for him to seek a happier life by gaining knowledge of the law of causation.

"Aspire to wisdom, and guide all sentient beings" is an important Mahayana Buddhist maxim which Kyōkai espoused. It was believed

13. Mircea Eliade, *Yoga: Immortality and Feedom*, 166. In his *Birth and Rebirth* (p. 105), he says, "In another Tantric meditation, the novice imagines that he is being stripped of his flesh and finally sees himself as a 'huge, white, shining skeleton.'" Hereafter nirvāṇa will be treated as an English word.

14. Tao-shih 道世, *Chu-ching yao-chi* (*Taishō*, LIV, No. 2123), 81–194.

15. Kurano Kenji, "*Nihon ryōiki kō*," *Bungaku* II (No. 12, 1934), 751–766; reprinted in the *Koten to jōdai seishin*. He asserts that the *Nihon ryōiki* was compiled by Kyōkai in 787, and that sections dated later than this were added by others. Although the text as we have it now was most likely compiled during the Kōnin era (810–824), it is agreed that 787 was an epoch-making year in Kyōkai's life, and it might indicate the beginning of the compilation of the *Nihon ryōiki*.

that enlightenment could be attained by devotion to Buddha and mercy for all fellow beings. Thus, he brought together the tales of the *Nihon ryōiki* as a step toward such enlightenment:

> By editing these stories of miraculous events I want to pull people forward by the ears, offer my hand to lead them to good, and show them how to cleanse their feet of evil. My sincere hope is that we may all be reborn in the western land of bliss, leaving no one on the earth, and live together in the jeweled palace in heaven, abandoning our earthly residence [III.Preface].

Although Kyōkai belonged to Yakushi-ji, one of the greatest centers of Buddhist studies, and was honored with clerical rank, he was conscious of a gap between scholarly monks and common devotees with whom he often identified himself. He showed great sympathy for lay devotees whose simple, direct faith he admired, and he was determined to "guide all sentient beings" to the western land of bliss[16] in spite of his own limitations.

By the time Kyōkai came to live at Yakushi-ji, state control of the Buddhist *saṃgha*[17] had gradually been strengthened. Emperor Kōnin (r. 770–781) exiled Dōkyō 道鏡, who had been appointed *Dharma King* 法王[18] by Empress Shōtoku[19] in 766 and who almost usurped the throne after the empress died (III.38). Emperor Kanmu, who had succeeded Emperor Kōnin, transferred the capital from Nara to Kyoto in order to sever traditional ties between the court and the temples in Nara. During the twenty-five years of his reign he issued more than fifty decrees concerning Buddhist temples and monks, a number unparalleled in Japanese history. More than thirty of these decrees were apparently intended to correct the evils and injustices found in the samgha. One decree issued in 798 states that there were many temples

16. Skt. *sukhāvatī* translated as *gokuraku* 極樂, *jōdo* 淨土, *anrakukoku* 安樂國, etc.; Amida's pure land in the west where devotees are reborn after death and live happily free from any desires. For the details of this land of bliss, see the *Larger and Smaller Sukhāvatī-vyūha, Buddhist Mahāyāna Texts* (*SBE*, XLIX). Also see A.K. Reischauer, "Genshin's Ojo Yoshu: Collected Essays on Birth into Paradise," *TASJ*, Second Series, III (December 1930), 68–94. For Amida, see Chap. II(3)b, n. 132.

17. Transliterated as 僧伽, which is shortened into 僧; originally the community of Buddhist monks and nuns united by wisdom and practice for the purpose of reaching Buddhahood. It has both historical and transcendental aspects as one of the Three Treasures (Skt. *triratna*). In the Mahayana tradition it includes not only monks and nuns but also lay brothers and sisters. Hereafter *saṃgha* will be treated as an English word.

18. Skt. *dharmarāja*, originally an honorific title for the Buddha; in Japan *hōō* is used only for Prince Shōtoku (574–622) and Dōkyō. See *Jōgū Shōtoku hōō teisetsu* 上宮聖德法王帝說 (*DBZ*, 112), 43–48; *Shoku Nihongi*, XXVII (Tenpyō jingo 2:10:20). Hereafter *dharma* will be treated as an English word, both as a title and a term.

19. Empress Kōken (r. 749–757) resumed the throne as Empress Shōtoku (r. 764–770) after banishing Emperor Jun'nin. Cf. Nakagawa Osamu, "Shōtoku-Dōkyō seiken no keisei katei," *Nihon rekishi*, No. 196 (1964), 41–55.

in the former capital of Heijō (Nara) where monks and nuns did not keep the Buddhist precepts.[20] Another decree issued in 804 notes that many monks in all provinces had failed to keep the precepts, and that some had maintained their family life after they were appointed to the high Buddhist position of lecturer.[21]

When we read the passage on the death of Kyōkai's son, one decree seems particularly relevant: "From now on all monks who have sons shall return to lay status so that they may set an example to future generations."[22] It was issued to correct the evils of the loose monastic life and to avoid giving special favors to the sons of high-ranking monks. Two years later a monk named Kyōkoku (Keikoku) 景國 of Yakushi-ji sought to conform to the spirit of this decree, and he petitioned to be allowed to return to lay status on the grounds that he was innately dull and incapable of studying.[23] Perhaps Kyōkai knew of Kyōkoku's petition and departure since they had lived at the same temple about the same time. How did Kyōkai feel about himself, a monk of a clerical rank, who was not separated completely from his family? He might well have wanted to clarify his motivation for joining the samgha and to maintain his clerical position free from family ties. The brief glimpses of his life end with the note that his horses died in 800, and we recall an article of the Sōni-ryō 僧尼令 (Ordinances concerning Monks and Nuns) which states that monks and nuns shall not receive any slaves,[24] horses, oxen, or weapons as offerings.[25] It is difficult to know how conscious he was of these laws and how desirous of living up to them, but there is evidence in the Nihon ryōiki that he intended to make his renunciation complete and to clarify his status as a member of the samgha. The detailed description of his dreams suggests that he was led to renounce lay status by the revelation of the great mercy of Buddha.

The Nihon ryōiki gives no information on his latter years, but he

20. Ruijū kokushi 類從國史, 186 (Enryaku 17:7:28).
21. Ibid., 186 (Enryaku 23:1:11). The position of lecturer, kōji 講師, was instituted in 795, replacing that of provincial preceptor, kokushi 國師, a mature and venerable monk who expounded dharma and who was in charge of discipline for monks and nuns; also a learned monk who was appointed to lecture at court ceremonies. See Ruijū sandaikyaku 類從三代格, III (Enryaku 14:8:13, 24:12:25).
22. Ruijū sandaikyaku, XIX (Enryaku 17:9:17).
23. Ruijū kokushi, 187 (Enryaku 19:8:15).
24. Nuhi 奴婢; one category of the unfree people, mostly manual workers or farm laborers, prescribed in the Yōrō-ryō 養老令 as hereditary status with no property rights but protected by law against injury (Yōrō-ryō, "Ko-ryō," Article 35). See Yoshida Akira, Nihon kodai shakai kōsei shiron, 297–364.
25. Ryō no gige 令義解, "Sōni-ryō," Article 26. See Chap. I(1)c; G.B. Sansom, "Early Japanese Law and Administration," Part Two, TASJ, Second Series, XI (December 1934), 117–147.

must have lived until the reign of Emperor Saga (r. 809–823), at which time the narrative of the *Nihon ryōiki* ends.

## b. *Date of Compilation and Authorship*

No single extant manuscript of the *Nihon ryōiki* contains the complete text of all three volumes. There are four manuscripts; the Kō-fukuji manuscript of the first volume,[26] the Shinpukuji manuscript of the second and third volumes,[27] the Maeda (-ke) manuscript of the third volume,[28] and the Kōya manuscript of the three incomplete volumes.[29] They seem to have been transmitted independently of each other, and most of them appear to have been edited from different manuscripts.[30]

The most controversial passage in the *Nihon ryōiki* is the first part of the preface to the third volume, which is known as "Maeda (-ke) -bon itsubun" 前田 (家) 本逸文 (Unknown Passage of the Maeda Manuscript). It gives an exact date for the compilation of the *Nihon ryōiki* in the course of outlining a Buddhist eschatological view of history.

> The Inner Scriptures show how good and evil deeds are repaid, while the Outer Writings show how good and bad fortunes bring merit and demerit. If we study all the discourses Śākyamuni made during his lifetime, we learn that there are three periods: first, the period of the true dharma (*shōbō* 正法), which lasts five hundred years; second, the period of the counterfeit dharma (*zōbō* 像法), lasting a thousand years; and third, the period of the degenerate dharma (*mappō* 末法), which continues for ten thousand years. By the fourth year of the hare, the sixth year of the Enryaku era, seventeen hundred and twenty-two years have passed since Buddha entered nirvana. Accordingly, we live in the age of the degenerate dharma following the first two periods. Now in Japan, by the sixth year of the Enryaku era, two hundred and thirty-six years have elapsed since the arrival of the Buddha, Dharma, and Samgha.

26. Ōya Tokujō, ed., *Kōfukuji Nihon ryōiki* (1934): oldest and most accurate of all the manuscripts, which can be dated in 904, although it was recopied later.

27. Koizumi Michi, ed. and annot., *Kōchū Shinpukuji-bon Nihon ryōiki, Kuntengo to kunten shiryō*, suppl. No. 22 (June 1962): dated in the Kamakura period (1192–1333) and less corrupt than the Maeda and Kōya mss., although some errors crept in since it was copied more than three times.

28. A photostatic copy of the Maeda ms. was published in the *Sonkyōkaku sōkan* 尊經閣叢刊 (No. 19, 1931). The manuscript is dated 1236, and was discovered in 1883. The first section of the preface to the third volume is found only in this manuscript.

29. Also known as Sanmaiin 三昧院 ms., dated 1214. Although it has three volumes, it is incomplete and corrupt; it was lost in the 1930's or 1940's. See Nagai Yoshinori *Nihon Bukkyō bungaku kenkyū*, 139–146.

30. Koizumi Michi, *Nihon ryōiki* (NKBT, 70), 8–21.

This passage offers a basis for the theory that Kyōkai wrote this preface and compiled the *Nihon ryōiki* during the Enryaku era (782–805), probably in the sixth year (787); accordingly, the stories dated later must be interpolations by others.[31] Scholars who assert that Kyōkai's compilation took place during the Kōnin era (810–824) regard the "Unknown Passage of the Maeda Manuscript" as an interpolation made by Kyōkai himself or a later forgery.[32] Therefore, the theories for the date of compilation and the authorship of the "Unknown Passage" are intricately entangled, and neither has been documented convincingly. If we assume that the passage was written by Kyōkai himself in the sixth year of the Enryaku era, this becomes the first reference to Buddhist eschatological ideas in Japan.

That the text of the *Nihon ryōiki* suffers from poor editing is shown by the confused plots in some tales (II.16, 25, 42), the combination of two independent tales into one (I.4; III.1), the irrelevance of the editor's note to the story (I.4), and the inappropriateness of the quotations from the scriptures (II.13, 22). If, indeed, it was written by Kyōkai himself, it represents the accumulation of more than thirty years' effort, but it lacks unity. Some scholars point out that the term "mappō," meaning degenerate dharma,[33] is found in only one passage of the Maeda manuscript and does not occur in the rest of the work. Therefore, they conclude that *mappō* consciousness was alien to Kyōkai, and that the "Unknown Passage" is a later interpolation. It is further argued that *mappō* consciousness became prominent only toward the end of the Heian period, while the *Nihon ryōiki* was compiled at the beginning of this period. These arguments do not, however, rule out the possibility that Kyōkai wrote the controversial preface or that the passage reflects his knowledge of the concept of *mappō*.

The argument that *mappō* consciousness was alien to Kyōkai is called into question by evidence presented in the *Myōhōki* 冥報記.[34] This text, which influenced Kyōkai, does not use the term *mappō*, in spite of the author's obvious respect for Hsin-hsing 信行 (540–594), who

---

31. See Chap. I(1)a, n. 15.

32. The theory of a later forgery originated with Itabashi Tomoyuki, "*Nihon ryōiki no senjutsu nenji ni tsuite*," *Kokugo to kokubungaku*, VII (No. 2, 1930), 132–142; "*Ryōiki Enryaku yonen izen gensensetsu ni tsuite*," *Bungaku*, III (No. 6, 1935), 757–764. The theory that the interpolation was made by Kyōkai himself is advocated by Sakaguchi Genshō, *Nihon Bukkyō bungaku josetsu*, 95–103.

33. In English, it is usually known as "the decline," "the end," or "the latter period of the law."

34. T'ang-lin 唐臨, *Ming-pao chi* (Records of Invisible Work of Karmic Retribution; *Taishō*, LI, No. 2082), 787b–802a. It begins with the story of Hsin-hsing (788a–c), which is followed by that of his disciple, Hui-ju 慧如 (788c).

founded the Sect of the Three Stages.[35] Hsin-hsing stressed the teaching of the three stages of dharma and preached a Buddhist eschatological message to the common people. There is also ample evidence against the general argument that *mappō* consciousness became prominent only in late Heian times. Clearly, a Buddhist eschatology was known to many monks in both the Nara and Heian periods, even though it did not become a social force until the late Heian period. Kyōkai, being a monk, would surely have known of it.

In the "Unknown Passage," the author specifies five hundred years of true dharma and one thousand years of counterfeit dharma. He miscalculates when he says that seventeen hundred and twenty-two years have passed since the date of Buddha's nirvana which was widely thought to be 949 B.C. in the Chinese tradition,[36] since the sixth year of the Enryaku era, 789, falls on the seventeen hundred and thirty-sixth year. On the other hand, as he says that two hundred and thirty years have passed since the arrival of Buddhism in Japan, it becomes evident that he adopted 552 A.D. as the date of the introduction of Buddhism, for which the only source is the *Nihon shoki*.[37] Historians have speculated why the writer of this section of the *Nihon shoki*, probably Dōji 道慈,[38] chose 552 instead of 538, the latter date being generally accepted in the older traditions.[39] Some concluded that 552 was chosen because it was the first year of the age of degenerate dharma, assuming that Dōji adopted 949 B.C. as the date of Śākyamuni's nirvana and used the same time spans for the two periods, as did the author of the "Unknown Passage."

But, why was the first year of degenerate dharma chosen as the beginning of Buddhist history in Japan? According to Tamura Enchō, Dōji wanted to demonstrate the strength of Japanese Buddhism in overcoming the age of degenerate dharma, and to contrast it with Chinese Buddhism, which was showing signs of serious deterioration.[40] However, such an interpretation of Dōji's motivation is questionable when we consider his treatise "Gushi" 愚志 (A Fool's Idea), in which he deplored the condition of Buddhism in Japan as

35. Cf. Yabuki Keiki, *Sangaikyō no kenkyū*.

36. Concerning the date of Śākyamuni's nirvana there are two theories in the Chinese tradition: the *Chou i shu* 周異書 gives 949 B.C., while the *Li-tai san-pao chi* 歷代三寶記 gives 609 B.C.

37. *Nihon shoki* 日本書紀, XIX (Kinmei 13:10) gives 552 as the year of the formal introduction of Buddhism, but contemporary scholars agree on the earlier date of 538. See W. G. Aston, "Nihongi, Chronicles of Japan," *TPJS*, suppl. I (1896), II, 65–67.

38. Inoue Kaoru, *Nihon kodai no seiji to shūkyō*, 189–258.

39. See "Gangōji garan engi narabini ruki shizaichō," *Nara ibun*, ed. by Takeuchi Rizō, I, 383, *Jōgū Shōtoku hōō teisetsu* (*DBZ*, 112), 47.

40. Tamura, *Asuka Bukkyōshi kenkyū*, 166–177.

he found it when he returned from China after seventeen years of study.[41] In the *Shoku Nihongi*, there are passages indicating that the Tenpyō era was regarded as the age of counterfeit dharma, the second of the three ages,[42] and Dōji might have been hoping for the restoration of dharma when he set the date of Buddhism's introduction to Japan in the first year of the third age, that of degenerate dharma. Kyōkai might have shared the view held by Dōji, who was known for his anti-Confucianism.[43] He had witnessed the effects of anti-Buddhist propaganda spread by Chinese Confucian scholars during his stay in China, but it had only deepened his great respect for the scholarship and discipline of Chinese Buddhists. He must have hoped that Japan as a country would achieve the Buddhist ideal.

In India, sectarian struggles and violations of precepts led to serious self-examination within the samgha. The theory of the three stages of dharma was formulated as a warning to monks against the danger of violating the precepts, which was believed to cause the destruction of dharma. In China, persecution of the Buddhists led to a similar process of self-examination.[44] Thus, a more deterministic view of history arose, which was gradually combined with the theory of the three stages of dharma. This is why the time spans allotted to each period vary in the different scriptures. They may be summarized as:

| Theory | True dharma (years) | Counterfeit dharma (years) |
|--------|---------------------|----------------------------|
| A | 500 | 1,000 |
| B | 500 | 500 |
| C | 1,000 | 1,000 |
| D | 1,000 | 500 |

Among the four theories, A and C were popular in China.[45]

These ideas were transmitted to Japan in the scriptures and through the accounts of student monks who studied in China. The *Daihōdō daijik-kyō* 大方等大集經,[46] one of the scriptures from which the author

41. The work is no longer extant, but an outline of it is given in the *Shoku Nihongi*, XV (Tenpyō 16:10:2).

42. *Ibid.*, XV (Tenpyō 15:1:13): "The age of counterfeit dharma is revived . . . "; XXIII (Tenpyō hōji 4:7:22) "Now the age of counterfeit dharma is coming to the end . . . ."

43. Inoue Kaoru, *Nihon kodai*, 205–208.

44. Major persecutions took place in 444–446 (in the reign of Emperor Wu of Northern Wei), and 574 (Emperor Wu of Northern Chou), while minor ones occurred in 626 and 713. See Nomura Yōshō, *Shūbu hōnan no kenkyū*.

45. In China, theory A was adopted by Hui-yüan 慧遠 (334–416), Tao-ch'o 道綽 (526–645), K'uei-chi 窺基 (632–682), and others. Theory C was adopted by Tao-hsüan 道宣 (596–667). See Takao Giken, *Chūgoku Bukkyō shiron*, 54–96.

46. *Mahāvaipulyamahāsaṃnipātasūtra* (*Taishō*, XIII, No. 397), 1–408.

of the *Nihon ryōiki* may have derived the Buddhist eschatological concept, focuses on the age of degenerate dharma when monks fail to live up to the precepts and laymen lose faith, but at the same time stresses the eternal presence of true dharma which can be maintained with the help of *dhāraṇī*.[47] According to the *Daihōdō daijik-kyō*, Buddha preached on the subject of the five periods, each lasting five hundred years: the first is the period of enlightenment; the second, that of meditation; the third, that of reciting and hearing scriptures; the fourth, that of building temples and pagodas; the fifth, that of disputes and the disappearance of dharma.[48] This periodization parallels theory C, which allots one thousand years to both the age of true dharma and the age of counterfeit dharma. There is a possibility that Dōji accepted this theory of five periods, along with theory C. If so, then 552 A.D. would mark the beginning of the fourth period, which fits well with the historical situation of the Nara period. Chikō 智光 (II. 7) and Zenshu 善珠 (III. 35, 38), two eminent monks whose lives are recorded in the *Nihon ryōiki*, adopted theory A, although neither wrote explicitly on the age of degenerate dharma. Saichō was the the first Japanese monk to discuss the eschatological idea explicitly in terms of its relation to human existence.[49]

When Kyōkai, their contemporary, read the scriptures predicting the coming age of decadence of dharma, he understood it in the Japanese historical context of his time and must have felt a desire for salvation, which he states clearly in the prefaces and autobiographical sections. Throughout the Nara period there were power struggles, intrigues, and murders around the throne. The imperial patronage of Buddhism encouraged corruption among monks and embroiled them in politics, as in the case of Dōkyō. Flagrant violation of the precepts led to the promulgation of many decrees to bring about order. Since the *Nihon ryōiki* is full of the stories of men killing, stealing, and cheating, it is evident that Kyōkai recognized the decadence of his times. Such recognition did not, however, necessarily mean that he believed in the Buddhist eschatological theory. The sinfulness of human nature appeared to conflict with his fundamentally optimistic world view. At the end of his work he says:

47. 陀羅尼, mystic syllables which sustain the faith of their reciters; later this power expanded and was regarded as a talisman instrumental in achieving desires, a charm to bring about miracles, a means to attain Buddhahood; it was analogous to *mantra* 眞言. See L. A. Waddell, "The *Dhāraṇī* Cult in Buddhism," *Ostasiatische Zeitschrift*, I (No. 2, 1912), 155–195; M. Eliade, *Yoga*, 212–216; Toganoo Shōun, *Mandara no kenkyū*, 429–468. Hereafter *dhāraṇī* will appear in its English form.
48. *Daihōdō daijik-kyō* (*Taishō*, XIII), 363. Cf. Kazue Kyōichi, *Nihon no mappō shisō*, 17.
49. Tamura, *Nihon Bukkyō shisōshi kenkyū*, 277–308.

By conferring the merits obtained in writing this work on all beings who are going astray, I pray to be born in the western land of bliss with them all [III.Postscript].

He believed that man would be saved if he repented of his past and aspired to Buddhahood, and he compiled the *Nihon ryōiki* to accumulate merits in the hope that he and his fellowmen might be saved from evil and misfortune.[50] In another passage he says:

Kyōkai, however, has not studied the *yin-yang tao* 陰陽道 of Huang Ti 黄帝, nor understood the profound truth of the Tendai Sage 天台智者, and he is stricken with disaster without knowing how to evade it, worrying and grieving without looking for the way to do away with disaster [III.38].

For Kyōkai, the sophisticated Buddhist doctrines of the Tendai Sage,[51] as well as the Chinese cosmological theories[52] lead to the secret of the cosmic law. He was convinced that the good way of life could be taught to all. In this respect he differed from those monks who became prominent toward the end of the Heian period, for they professed faith in the pure land and affirmed that man is too sinful to attain any merits on his own.

We can conclude, tentatively, that the *Nihon ryōiki*, including the "Unknown Passage," is the work of Kyōkai and that it was compiled over many years but was left incompletely edited. Kyōkai seems to have accepted Buddhist eschatological ideas and the notion of the decadent age, but these concepts did not change his basic world view. The inconsistencies that resulted do not prevent us from concluding that Kyōkai is responsible for the *Nihon ryōiki*, for he seems to have been an ordinary monk, little interested in doctrinal studies and the writing of a systematic work. His aim, rather, was to guide people to salvation by transferring the merit gained in the compilation of a collection of Buddhist legends. He intended to show how dharma was at work in the history of the whole Japanese people, whether or not they knew of the teachings of Śākyamuni, and to demonstrate that dharma is neither Indian nor Chinese, but universal.

50. The Buddhist idea of karma cannot be understood apart from the belief that Śākyamuni attained enlightenment after long, unflinching efforts, through a series of many births, toward the maturing of good stock (Skt. *kuśalamūla* 善根) and accumulation of merits (Skt. *puṇyaskandha* 功徳).

51. Refers to Chih-i 智顗 (538–597), founder of the T'ien t'ai School in China, who formulated the T'ien t'ai doctrines. Cf. Leon Hurvitz, "Chih-i," *Mélanges chinois et bouddhiques*, XII (1962), 1–372.

52. A cosmology which presupposes that all phenomena result from the interplay of male and female principles; it was customarily regarded as the creation of the mythical Huang Ti 黄帝 (traditional dates 2998–2598 B.C.), often called the Yellow Emperor, who was believed to be the founder of the Chinese Empire and to symbolize the ancient golden rule. Cf. Fung Yu-lan, *A History of Chinese Philosophy*, II, Chap. 2. See III.38, n. 50.

## c. *Yakushi-ji and the Six Nara Schools*

Kyōkai compiled the *Nihon ryōiki* in the precincts of Yakushi-ji, which was originally built in the central part of the capital known as Fujiwara-kyō 藤原京.[53] Yakushi-ji was one of the four great temples in the capital, together with Asuka-no-tera 飛鳥寺 (Hōkō-ji 法興寺), Ōtsukasa-no-ōtera 大官大寺 (Takechi-no-ōtera 高市大寺), and Kawara-no-tera 川原寺 (Gufuku-ji 弘福寺). In 680 Emperor Tenmu made a vow to build Yakushi-ji as a meritorious act of petition for the recovery of his consort's health,[54] but he died before making much progress. His consort, who succeeded him as Empress Jitō, continued the construction, and it was almost completed by 698, during the reign of Emperor Monmu, her grandson.[55] After the transfer of the capital to Nara, Yakushi-ji was removed to its present site in 718, the original temple becoming known as Moto-yakushi-ji.

During the first stage of Buddhism in Japan, most temples were built by influential families; after the acceptance of Buddhism at court, emperors built temples which functioned both as private temples for the imperial family and as official temples for the state cult. In the capital of Fujiwara the four great temples were designated as state temples by Emperor Tenmu and given financial support.[56] The capital of Nara was built on a larger scale, with state temples being added one after another.[57] The erection of Tōdai-ji with its colossal Buddha statue marks the high point of the Nara period (710–774). It was built as the headquarters for all provincial temples, and, at the dedication ceremony of the Great Lochana Buddha,[58] ex-Emperor Shōmu declared himself to be the "slave of the Three Treasures."[59]

53. The original temple was located at present Kidono-machi, Kashihara-shi, Nara-ken 奈良縣橿原市木殿町. Fujiwara-kyō was the first permanent capital situated in the Yamato plain, although it was short-lived (694–710).

54. *Nihon shoki*, XXIX (Tenmu 9:11:12): "The empress was unwell. Having made a vow on her behalf, the emperor began the construction of Yakushi-ji and made one hundred persons enter the priesthood. In consequence of this she recovered." See Aston, "Nihongi," II, 348.

55. *Shoku Nihongi*, I (Monmu 2:10:4): "The construction of Yakushi-ji being nearly completed, an imperial command was given to the monks to occupy their quarters." See J. R. Snellen, "Shoku Nihongi," *TASJ*, Second Series, XI (December 1934), 176.

56. *Nihon shoki*, XXXIX (Tenmu 9:4). See Aston, "Nihongi," II, 356.

57. Possible dates for the transfer and erection of new temples are:

   710 Kōfuku-ji 興福寺 (former Yamashina-no-tera 山階寺) and Daian-ji 大安寺 (former Ōtsukasa-no-ōtera) transferred.

   718 Yakushi-ji and Gangō-ji (former Asuka-no-tera) transferred.

   749 Tōdai-ji 東大寺 erected.

   759 Tōshōdai-ji 唐招提寺 erected.

   765 Saidai-ji 西大寺 erected.

58. Vairocana Buddha of the *Kegon-gyō* 華嚴經 (*Avataṃsakasūtra*) and *Bonmō-kyō* 梵網經 (*Brahmajālasūtra*), a cosmic Buddha symbolizing the oneness of the universe.

59. *Shoku Nihongi*, XVII (Tenpyō shōhō 1:4:1): "This is the word of the sovereign who is the slave (*yakko* 奴, same as *nuhi*) of the Three Treasures. . . ."

One indication of the wide acceptance of Buddhism among the common people is the fact that more than thirty stories out of a hundred and sixteen in the *Nihon ryōiki* originated in his reign. By that time about four hundred temples had been built throughout the country, almost ten thousand scriptures had been brought from the continent and copied, and about fifteen hundred monks and nuns had been officially recognized.[60]

Buddhism was transmitted to Japan mainly from Korea, and Korean monks and immigrants played a significant role in its acceptance.[61] During the century following its introduction, the need for direct contact with China was felt, and many student monks were sent to China to pursue the study of Buddhism there. One of their missions was to bring back as many scriptures as possible to build up Buddhist libraries in Japan. Soon after Buddhist scriptures were translated from Sanskrit into Chinese, they found their way to Japan, stimulating the rise and development of Buddhist study groups, which eventually became Buddhist schools during the Nara period.

The first reference to Buddhist schools is found in a decree issued in 718 by the chancellor (*daijōkan* 太政官), which mentions that "the studies of the five schools and the teachings of the Three Baskets (Skt. *tripiṭaka*) differ in theory and argument. . . ."[62] The Six Nara Schools[63] came into existence between 747 and 751, and they were well represented at Tōdai-ji; there each had its own facilities including a library, an altar, and an office, and each had its own officials who administered funds.[64] The situation seems to have been different at older temples, but unfortunately their history is so poorly documented that it has been little studied by scholars. Only recently has the existence of the pre-Nara tradition transmitted in those temples been discussed and assessed.

The *Nihon ryōiki* contains some passages relevant to this problem. There are three stories about the funds of the Sutara-shū 修多羅宗(衆), a school or seminar which existed at Daian-ji from the late Nara

---

60. Ishida Mosaku, *Nara jidai bunka zakkō*, 2.

61. The *Nihon ryōiki* gives records of Korean monks such as Kanroku 勸勒 (I.5), Ensei 圓勢 (I.4), Gigaku 義覺 (I.14), Ta(ra)jō 多(羅)常 (I.26), and of monks of immigrant families such as Soga 蘇我 and Kuratsukuri 鞍作 (I.5). The *Shinsen shōjiroku* 新撰姓氏録 (Newly Selected Records of Family Names and Titles) compiled in 814–815 gives the proportion of immigrant families as 326 to 1,059, or about 30 percent of the registered families.

62. *Shoku Nihongi*, VIII (Yōrō 2:10:10).

63. They are Kusha 倶舍, Sanron 三論, Jōjitsu 成實, Hossō 法相, Ritsu 律, and Kegon 華嚴. Cf. J. Takakusu, *The Essentials of Buddhist Philosophy*.

64. See Ishida, *Nara jidai*, 136–149; Inoue Mitsusada, "Nanto rokushū no seiritsu," *Nihon rekishi*, No. 156 (1961), 2–14.

period to the early Heian period (II.24, 28; III.3).[65] It seems that each seminar had its officials: senior dean (*daigakutō* 大學頭), junior dean (*shōgakutō* 小學頭), and provost (*ina* 維那). In addition to the Sutara School, the Ritsu, Sanron, Betsu-sanron, and Shōron 攝論 Schools were represented at Daian-ji.[66] At Gangō-ji there were three seminars: Sanron, Jōjitsu, and Shōron, the history of which can be traced back to Fujiwara no Kamatari 藤原鎌足 (614–669)[67] who donated building funds.[68] At Hōryū-ji 法隆寺 there were four seminars: Sanron, Betsu-sanron, Hossō, and Ritsu.[69] No record exists concerning Yakushi-ji.

It is evident from this material that at large temples there were several distinct seminars, called *shū*,[70] devoted to the study of particular scriptures. The names of at least nine such seminars which once existed in several temples are known to us,[71] and the great state temples, where various seminars were represented, thus served as institutes for Buddhist studies. These seminars, each of which centered about the study of a scripture, existed in the eighth century. They were gradually reorganized and eventually institutionalized as six officially recognized schools. The *Nihon ryōiki* employs the phrase, "deans of the Six Schools" (II.28), and we may conclude that the idea of the Six Nara Schools had become widespread by the beginning of the Heian period, which coincided with Kyōkai's lifetime. This was

65. Tamura, *Asuka Bukkyōshi kenkyū*, 113–133. As there had been no such school in either China or Korea and no document reveals its nature in Japanese history, there is ample room for arguments and theories as to its identity. Tamura asserts that it is a school established by Dōji for the study of the *Dai hannya-kyō* 大般若經, while others identify it with one of the Six Nara Schools. Inoue Mitsusada ("Nanto rokushū," 11–12) equates it with Jōjitsu; Ishida Mosaku, with Hossō (*Shakyō yori mitaru Narachō Bykkyō no kenkyū*, 67).

66. "Daian-ji garan engi narabini ruki shizaichō," *Nara ibun*, ed. by Takeuchi, I, 299. Two Sanron Schools were found at Hōryū-ji and Kōfuku-ji as well as Daian-ji. According to Inoue, one is the school of Chi-tsang 吉藏 (549–623), and the other is that of the followers of Bhāvaviveka (or Bhavya) 清辯 (490–560/570), whose works were transmitted to China by Hsüan-tsang ("Nanto rokushū," 8–10). Shōron is a shortened title of Asaṅga's *Mahāyānaparisaṃgraha*, *Shōdaijōron* 攝大乘論, a major text for the Yuishiki School till the seventh century; hence the name of a school devoted to its study (*Taishō*, XXXI, No. 1592, 97–112b; No. 1593, 112b–132c; No. 1594, 132c–152a).

67. Also known as Nakatomi no Kamako no muraji 中臣鎌子連 who helped Prince Naka no Ōe 中大兄皇子 overthrow the Soga family and carry out the Taika Reform.

68. "Gangōji garan engi," *Nara ibun*, I, 390; "Kaden," *ibid.*, II, 880.

69. "Hōryū-ji garan engi narabini ruki shizaichō," *ibid.*, I, 347. The founding of Hōryū-ji is ascribed to Prince Shōtoku who lived close to its precincts at Ikaruga (I.5); the original temple building was destroyed by fire in 670 (*Nihon shoki*, XXVII, Tenchi 9:4:30). See Aston, "Nihongi," II, 293; also, J. H. Kamstra, *Encounter or Syncretism*, 312–315.

70. As to the use of two characters 衆 and 宗 for *shū*, Ishida thinks that the former character stands for seminar groups; the latter, for organizations made up of the seminars devoted to the study of the same scriptures at several temples. The two are structurally different (*Nara jidai*, 105). Inoue, however, says that the former character is not found after 747 and that the latter character replaces it in later documents. Considering other factors as well, he concludes that the latter means an officially recognized school of Buddhism ("Nanto rokushū," 3, 11).

71. Inoue, "Nanto rokushū," 13.

brought about partly by the natural development of Buddhist studies, and partly by the government's eagerness to standardize and promote such studies.

### d. *State Control of the Samgha and Popular Buddhist Movements*

As soon as Buddhism spread beyond India, where the samgha enjoyed an authority independent of the state, the problem of the relationship between samgha and state was raised. In China a central supervisory system was instituted during the fourth century, but not much is known about it. Generally speaking, state control was stronger in the north than in the south. Under the northern dynasties samgha officials independently administered the affairs of its members, but secular officials were appointed to oversee samgha properties. Under the southern dynasties, however, no secular officials were appointed as samgha officials.[72] The Sui dynasty (581–618), which united northern and southern China, followed the legal system of the northern dynasties, and secular officials were appointed to oversee samgha officials. The T'ang dynasty (618–907) adopted a similar system, and the autonomy of the samgha was weakened.

In Japan the relationship between samgha and state was regulated by the institution of the *Sōgō-sei* 僧綱制, a supervisory system for monks and nuns, and its legal code laid down in the *Sōni-ryō* 僧尼令, a collection of ordinances concerning monks and nuns. The former was established in 624, when Empress Suiko made appointments of *sōjō* 僧正 (Ch. *seng-cheng*), *sōzu* 僧都 (Ch. *seng-tu*), and *hōzu* or *hōtō* 法頭 for the control of monks and nuns.[73] These titles reflect the influence of the southern Chinese tradition. The *sōgō*, samgha supervisors, were charged with the discipline and punishment of monks and nuns. A story in the *Nihon ryōiki* tells how a Korean monk, Kanroku (Kwalleuk), stressing the importance of the autonomy of the samgha, ap-

72. See Yamazaki Hiroshi, *Shina chūsei Bukkyō no tenkai*, Part II. In Liu Sung (420–479) and Ch'i (479–502) times, the chief executive was called *seng-chu* 僧主; under the Liang (502–557) and Ch'en (557–589), he was called *seng-cheng* 僧正. Assistant executives were termed *seng-tu* 僧都 or *wei-no* 維那. Inoue Mitsusada believes that the Japanese system was more influenced by the southern tradition than by the northern tradition or the later Sui and T'ang systems. See his *Nihon kodai kokka no kenkyū*, 324–327.

73. According to the *Nihon shoki*, XXII (Suiko 32:4:3): "There was a Buddhist monk who took an axe and struck his grandfather with it. Having heard of this, the empress summoned ministers and gave a command, saying: 'The man who has renounced the mundane world should be devoted to the Three Treasures, and cherish devoutly the Buddhist precepts. How can he recklessly cause a crime? We have heard that a monk struck his grandfather. Therefore, let all the monks and nuns of temples be assembled and an investigation made. Let severe punishment be inflicted on any who are convicted of offences.'" See Aston, "Nihongi," II, 152–153.

pealed to the empress to prevent secular officials from punishing monks and nuns and to leave this responsibility to samgha officials (I.5). Eventually he was appointed *sōjō* with two laymen for *sōzu* and *hōzu*.[74] Of the three samgha officials, *sōjō* and *sōzu* had precedents in China and Korea, even though a layman had never been appointed *sōzu* in China. The office of *hōzu*, a secretary in charge of samgha properties, was created in Japan. As the first three appointees were all related to the Soga family, the leadership seems at first to have been in their hands.

In 645, when the Soga family perished, the reformed government established fundamental policies and appointed ten eminent monks as leaders of the samgha.[75] These appointments were politically motivated to smooth over the transition of leadership from the Sogas to the court, and, after this objective was fulfilled, no further appointments of this kind were made.[76] The new Sōgō system was firmly established in the reign of Emperor Tenmu by replacing *hōzu* with *risshi* 律師, preceptors, and by excluding lay officials from the Sōgō system.[77] The function of *hōzu* was taken over by the bureau for the administration of alien relations and registry of monks and nuns, Genbaryō 玄蕃寮, which was probably established by Empress Jitō about 690.[78] Theoretically, the samgha officials were subordinate to the Genbaryō, but the autonomy of the samgha was respected in the Kinai region, while in the rest of the country a provincial magistrate (國司) and a provincial preceptor (國師) were in charge of samgha

74. *Ibid.*, XXII (Suiko 32:4:17): "Monk Kanroku was appointed *sōjō*, and Kuratsukuri no Tokosaka 鞍作德積 was made *sōzu*. On the same day Azumi no muraji 阿曇連 was made *hōzu*." See Aston, "Nihongi," II, 153.

75. *Ibid.*, XXV (Taika 1:8:8).

76. The Chinese precedent for this system occurred during the T'ang dynasty when ten virtuous monks were appointed to control the samgha in 619. This autonomous system did not last long, however, and secular officials took office again. See Yamazaki, *Shina chūsei*, 602–607.

77. *Nihon shoki*, XXIX (Tenmu 2:12:27).

78. Tamura, *Asuka Bukkyōshi*, 90. The following is adapted from his table on p. 94 to show the chronological development of the Sōgō system. The numbers in parentheses indicate the number of appointees, and the offices in italics were filled by laymen.

| Year | Reign | Appointive offices in the Sōgō system | | | |
|------|-------|------|------|------|------|
| 624 | Suiko 32 | sōjō (1) | sōzu (1) | *hōzu* (1) | |
| 645 | Taika 1 | jusshi (10) | | *hōzu* (3) | |
| 673 | Tenmu 2 | sōjō (1) | dai-sōzu (1)<br>shō-sōzu (1) | *hōzu* (1) | sakan (4) |
| 683 | Tenmu 12 | sōjō (1) | dai-sōzu (1)<br>shō-sōzu (1) | risshi (1) | sakan (4) |

affairs.[79] This system must have been influenced by the T'ang's bureaucratic rule of the samgha, but the appointment of a provincial preceptor, a new position created in Japan, revealed that the samgha maintained some autonomy in Japan in spite of apparent state control.

The *Sōni-ryō*, a compilation of ordinances concerning monks and nuns, was aimed at more direct control over the samgha, although in reality it represented a compromise with the already established tradition of the Sōgō system. The *Sōni-ryō* is contained in the earliest extant legislative code, the *Yōrō-ryō* 養老令, which was promulgated in 757,[80] although there are a few earlier codes such as the *Ōmi-ryō* 近江令 (668?), *Kiyomigahara-ryō* 淨御原令 (689), and *Taihō-ritsuryō* 大寶律令 (702). It is probable that the T'ang laws influenced the *Sōni-ryō*, but the T'ang codes do not include a specific chapter of ordinances concerning monks and nuns. There are, however, some temporary and subsidiary laws called *Tao-seng ko* 道僧格, or laws concerning Taoist and Buddhist monks.[81] The Japanese government, after careful study, adopted the T'ang laws after making certain modifications necessary to meet political and social conditions at that time.[82] The *Sōni-ryō* consists of administrative, substantive, qualifying, and penal administrative laws. It is assumed that the *Sōni-ryō* was an independent set of laws that originated in the autonomous rules of the samgha and was later incorporated into the code.[83] The severest punishment prescribed for monks and nuns was reversion to lay status. For instance, article 14 of the *Sōni-ryō* says:

> For the office of the *Sōgō* it is essential to select a man of virtuous conduct, who can guide the people wisely. It is necessary that he be respected by both clergy and laity, and be competent in management of samgha affairs. Those who wish to recommend someone shall notify the authorities with collected signatures, . . .

79. *Shoku Nihongi*, II (Taihō 2:2:20): "A provincial preceptor was appointed and assigned to every province." See Chap. I(1)a, n. 21.

Chibushō 治部省 —— Genbaryō ⟨ (Kinai) sōgō sango (officials at each temple) / (outside of Kinai) kokushi sango (provincial magistrate, provincial preceptor)
(Ministry of Civil Administration)

80. See Chap. I(1)a, n. 25.
81. Cf. Futaba Kenkō, *Kodai Bukkyō shisōshi kenkyū*, Part II, Chap. 2.
82. Inoue Kaoru asserts that the *Sōni-ryō* was first compiled in the *Taihō-ritsuryō*, basing his assertion on the passage in the *Shoku Nihongi*, II (Taihō 1:6:1): "Michi no kimi Ofutona 道君首名 was made to expound the *Sōni-ryō* to the congregation of monks at Daian-ji." See his *Nihon kodai*, 238. On the other hand, Futaba believes it originated in Emperor Tenmu's reign. See his *Kodai Bukkyō*, 137. Emperor Tenmu achieved the centralization of the state by establishing many new systems to consolidate it. The *Sōni-ryō* is regarded by Futaba as one of these measures.
83. Nanba Toshinari, "*Sōni-ryō no kōsei to seiritsu ni tsuite*," *Bukkyō shigaku*, XIII (No. 2, 1967), 104–120.

The samgha supervisors in the central office who managed all monastic establishments with the help of officials at each temple[84] were recommended by the monks and appointed by the chancellor.

Although this system of recommendation and election sounds quite democratic, throughout the Nara period the ordination of monks and nuns was in the hands of the Genbaryō, a bureau of the central government. When a free citizen wanted to renounce lay status, he had to obtain a permit from that bureau in order to exempt himself from taxation and the rule of local authorities. For those taxed heavily, entering the priesthood brought a considerable degree of relief. Accordingly, the government carefully checked the activities of any itinerant peasants in an effort to detect laymen pretending to be monks and to return them to their original status (III.14). Those who attempted to obtain immunities by fraudulent means or to deceive the public by wearing clerical robes and begging with a bowl were punished (Article 22). Those who had once pretended to be monks and nuns could never be ordained, even if they had led a disciplined life (Article 24). State control of ordination through the Sōgō system was not challenged until the arrival of Ganjin 鑑眞 (688–763), an eminent Chinese monk who was invited to Japan to establish the orthodox platform for full ordination. A later protest was lodged by Saichō, the founder of the Tendai School and the Mahayana platform for ordination.[85]

To become a monk, a man customarily passed through the following stages: he renounced lay life at an early age to serve as an acolyte to a monk; in his teens he underwent ordination, *tokudo* 得度, and became a novice. Before this could be done, however, a recommendation for ordination had to be sent to the Genbaryō, which examined the applicant's personal character and his knowledge of essential requirements.[86] Once ordained, novice monks were issued permits from the bureau, and they were expected to observe the precepts.[87]

84. *Sangō* 三綱 consists of *jōza* 上座 (Skt. *sthāvira*), president, *tera-ju/-nushi* 寺主 (Skt. *vihārasvāmin*), director, and *(tsu) ina* (都)維那 (Skt. *karmadāna*), provost. In smaller temples there was one official for each office, while in larger ones there were two directors and provosts, a junior one and a senior one. See Ishida, *Nara jidai*, 101–102.

85. See Satō Tetsuei, "Dengyō Daishi no Daijō sōdan," in *Bukkyō kyōdan no kenkyū*, ed. by Yoshimura Shūki, 351–396.

86. Horiike Shunpō, "Ubasoku kōshinge to shukke nyūshisho," *Nihon rekishi*, No. 114 (1957), 25–32.

87. The first five of the ten precepts were binding on all lay devotees, lay brothers and sisters; novice monks and nuns were required to keep all ten precepts. Many different versions of the precepts are found in Buddhist scriptures. According to the *Khuddakapāṭha*, II, they are: no killing, no stealing, no adultery, no lying, no drinking, no eating at wrong hours, no worldly amusements, no ornaments, no sleeping in a large bed, and no possession of gold and jewels. Mahayana scriptures such as the *Kegon-gyō* and *Bonmō-kyō* give the ten precepts for a bodhisattva. See Tsuchihashi Shūkō, "Jukai girei no hensen," *Bukkyō kyōdan no kenkyū*, 205–282.

After a few years of disciplined life, novices received the full list of some two hundred and fifty precepts, *jukai* 受戒, and became full-fledged monks. In the Buddhist tradition three masters and seven witnesses, all qualified monks, had to be present to give the complete set of precepts to a novice and to consecrate him as a monk. Before the arrival of Ganjin, there were so few monks qualified to perform this rite that it was practically unknown. However, the texts of the Hinayana precepts continued to be studied by some monks.[88] Ganjin was invited by Emperor Shōmu to initiate the traditional rite of giving the complete precepts to Japanese monks. For example, Saichō, who followed the standard procedure, left home to serve a provincial preceptor at the age of twelve. After two years he was examined for ordination as a novice, and he received the complete precepts to become a monk at the age of nineteen, a little earlier than the standard age of twenty.[89] On the other hand, Kyōkai was ordained in middle age, after marrying and begetting a child. Those who renounced the householder's life in middle age were, after a few years of discipline, ordained as lay brothers or sisters. For example, Kūkai, who first intended to become a government official and who went to the university[90] in order to study the Chinese classics, changed his course as the result of an encounter with a Buddhist monk. After following ascetic practices in the mountains as a lay brother,[91] he renounced lay status at the age of twenty-four and was ordained when he was thirty-one, before sailing for China.

The official ordination system was aimed not only at controlling the number of monks but also at setting minimum standards for their doctrinal education. When Buddhism was first introduced, it was organized largely as a system of religious rites for the benefit of influential families. Many persons were ordained so that their masters might obtain merit and recover from illness. By the early eighth century, however, a minimal standard of learning was required for ordination. A decree issued in 734 states that no one was to be ordained

---

88. Ishida Mizumaro, *Ganjin*, 25–33; *Nihon Bukkyō ni okeru kairitsu no kenkyū*, 25–31.

89. Sonoda Kōyū, "Saichō to Kūkai," *Nihon Bukkyō shisō no tenkai*, ed. by Ienaga Saburō, 33–57.

90. *Daigaku* 大學, a state college for the study of the Chinese classics, established to train the sons of men of the fifth rank or higher for official careers. See *Ryō no gige*, "Gaku-ryō," Articles 2, 5, etc.

91. *Ubasoku* 優婆塞, transliterated from Skt. *upāsaka*; a layman who professes faith in the Three Treasures and keeps the five precepts. In Mahayana Buddhism lay brothers form one group in the samgha.

without first memorizing a chapter of the *Hoke-kyō* 法華經[92] or the
*Saishōō-kyō* 最勝王經,[93] learning to perform Buddhist rites, and living
under monastic discipline for at least three years.[94] According to the
record of the recommendations for ordination during the period from
732 to 745, the number of years spent under discipline ranged from
four to fifteen, and the age of those who had undergone discipline,
from thirteen to forty-eight.[95] After that period the names of scriptures memorized and the number of years of discipline were not
recorded, but evidence of participation in the construction of a temple,
particularly Tōdai-ji, or the fact of being related to an official or a
monk was noted. There was a tendency toward lowering the age and
qualifications of monks as their numbers increased.[96]

Monks and nuns were expected to maintain disciplined lives of
study, instruction, and the performance of rites in the temples, except
when they were allowed to go for meditation in the mountains
(Articles 5, 13). They were not permitted to own land, buildings, or
other forms of wealth, nor could they buy and sell for profit or lend at
interest (Article 18). They could not set up unauthorized establishments and preach to congregations, nor falsely expound on the karmic
retribution of good and evil (Article 5). They were not permitted to
practice fortune-telling or to attempt curing illness by exorcism or
magic. However, healing by the recitation of Buddhist formulas[97]
was practiced (Article 2).

These articles of the *Sōni-ryō* were often ignored, even by officially
ordained monks in state temples. In spite of the government ban there
were many self-ordained monks, and descriptions of them can be
found in the *Nihon ryōiki* (I.19, 27; III.10, 15, 17, 33). Retreat to the
mountains was such a popular practice among ascetics that eventually,
in 770, the prohibition against living in the mountains was relaxed.[98]
Both Saichō and Kūkai emphasized withdrawal to the mountains,
aiming at a meditative and rigorously disciplined life. The samgha
and monks are well known for their economic activities in the cultiva-

92. *Myōhōrenge-kyō* 妙法蓮華經 (*Taishō*, IX, No. 262, 1–62c; No. 263, 63a–134b; No. 264,
134b–196a). H. Kern, trans., *Saddharmapuṇḍarīka or the Lotus of the True Law* (SBE, XXI);
Bunnō Katō, trans., *Myōhō-renge-kyō: The Sutra of the Lotus Flower of the Wonderful Law*.
93. *Konkōmyō saishōō-kyō* (*Suvarṇaprabhāsottamarājasūtra*), (*Taishō*, XVI, No. 665, 403–456.)
94. *Ruijū sandai-kyaku*, II (Tenpyō 6:11:20).
95. "Chishiki ubasoku tō kōshinbun," *Nara ibun*, ed. by Takeuchi, II, 508–531.
96. *Shoku Nihongi*, XIV (Tenpyō 13:10:16), for an example of a mass ordination of 750
lay brothers.
97. *Ju* 咒 (incantation, spell, oath), though it originated in pre-Buddhist China, denotes
Mantrayana dharani. See Chap. I(1)b, n. 47.
98. *Shoku Nihongi*, XXXI (Hōki 1:10:28).

tion of land (III.30), money lending (II.24; III.3, 4), and brewing (II.32), thus violating the ban (Article 18). Originally money lending had been instituted at Chinese monasteries as a social welfare measure, but it soon turned into a profit-making business conducted by unscrupulous monks.[99] One story in the *Nihon ryōiki* reveals a popular belief that one could escape the messenger of death by being engaged in business with a loan from the temple fund (II.24).

Although Buddhism in the Nara period served the state and was often referred to as "Buddhism for the welfare of the nation," the concept "nation" did not exclude the common people. The *Nihon ryōiki*, as stated above, has been considered one of the earliest sources for popular Buddhism in Japan, and it has been quoted to illustrate that Buddhism was popularly accepted. However, the distance that separated state Buddhism from popular Buddhism should not be unduly exaggerated. A helpful illustration of the situation that existed is seen in the case of Gyōgi 行基 (668–749), the person most venerated by the author of the *Nihon ryōiki*. At the age of fifteen, he renounced the world.[100] In spite of being condemned by the court because of activities outlawed by the *Sōni-ryō*, he continued preaching.[101] Emperor Shōmu sought his cooperation in building the statue of the Lochana Buddha at Tōdai-ji in 741 and appointed him great chief executive in 745.[102] According to tradition, he lived for some time in Yakushi-ji, a state temple.[103] He traveled and preached (II.2, 7, 8, 12, 29, 30), and directed the construction of bridges and canals and the establishment of ferries (II.30). Wherever he went, thousands of followers gathered to hear him. Lay brothers over sixty-one and lay sisters over fifty-five who followed him were allowed to enter the priesthood in 731,[104] and these lay devotees played an intermediary role between the clergy and the common people.

Gyōgi was not the first monk to carry out such projects on behalf of society. Dōshō, the founder of the Hossō School in Japan and Gyōgi's master, had also traveled, preached, and built bridges and ferries while on journeys in later years (I.22). Evidently such activities worked against the government's intention to confine monks to the

99. Michihata Ryōshū, *Tōdai Bukkyōshi no kenkyū*, 514–545.
100. Inoue Kaoru, *Gyōki*, 7.
101. *Shoku Nihongi*, VII (Yōrō 1:4:23): "These days the streets are filled with an ordinary monk named Gyōgi and his followers, who preach the karmic retribution of good and evil irresponsibly and mislead people by organizing groups and burning fingers and elbows as they abuse the Buddha's teaching to ask for donations."
102. *Ibid.*, XVI (Tenpyō 17:1:21). See II. 7, n. 18.
103. *Ibid.*, XVII (Tenpyō shōhō 1:2:2).
104. *Ibid.*, XI (Tenpyō 3:8:7).

temple precincts (*Sōni-ryō*, Articles 5, 13), but Dōshō was greatly respected by Emperor Monmu.[105] Although Gyōgi was condemned by the court, it is clear that he was neither exiled nor persecuted, for he actively organized devotees and established many private temples and retreat halls for nearly forty years. Finally Emperor Shōmu compromised by sanctioning his leadership in the popular Buddhist movements, while asking for his help.

The *Sōni-ryō* aims at having Buddhist monks serve the state, thus preventing them from gaining leadership among the common people. There were reasons why Buddhism could not be confined to the monastic establishments, however. First, there were a number of immigrants and their descendants who had participated in the Buddhist tradition even before it was officially introduced from the continent. Eminent monks such as Gyōgi, Dōji, Dōshō, and Saichō were descendants of immigrants. Secondly, the imperial family and many influential families such as the Sogas gradually accepted Buddhism and built family temples, *uji-dera* 氏寺 (I.5, 7, 17; III.23, 30, for example). The idea of "state temples" evolved in the reign of Emperor Tenmu as part of the third phase of the development of Buddhism in Japan.[106]

In the early stages the ruling class was mainly responsible for building temples, promoting Buddhist art and sculpture, copying scriptures, and carrying out regular or occasional Buddhist ceremonies. This practice, however, did not continue for long. The *Sōni-ryō* includes an article prohibiting the building of private establishments (Article 5), but, far from its being enforced, state officials and influential families were actually encouraged to build temples.[107] In addition to state and provincial temples, there were "licensed temples," *jōgaku-ji* 定額寺, which were built with private means but officially recognized and financially supported by the state.[108] The decree issued in 783,

105. *Ibid.*, I (Monmu 4:3:10): "On his return home from China he built and lived in a hall for meditation in the southeastern corner of the Gangō-ji precincts. Seekers from all quarters came to learn meditation under his guidance. In his later years he traveled widely, dug wells by the roadside, provided boats at each ferry and built bridges. Thus the Uji Bridge in Yamashiro is his construction. As the Venerable Dōshō had traveled for more than ten years, the emperor asked him to return, and he came back to live at the hall for meditation." For details of the relationship between Gyōgi and Dōshō, see Inoue Kaoru, *Gyōki*, 30–34.

106. Tamura, *Asuka Bukkyōshi*, 34–53. On the basis of his analysis of the period from the introduction of Buddhism to its establishment as state religion, he postulates a first stage covering the reigns of Kinmei, Bitatsu, Yōmei, and Sushun, when the court adopted a noncommittal policy, although Buddhism was accepted by some emperors privately; a second stage covering the reigns of Suiko, Jomei, Kōgyoku, Kōtoku, Saimei, and Tenchi, when the state control of the samgha was instituted and Buddhism was established at court; and a third stage coinciding with the reign of Tenmu, when Buddhism was established as a state religion.

107. *Ruijū kokushi*, 180 (Tenpyō 7:6:5); *Shoku Nihongi*, XVII (Tenpyō 19:11:7, 19:11:14).
108. *Shoku Nihongi*, XVII (Tenpyō shōhō 1:4:3, 1:7:13).

which stated that even in the smallest districts there were temples, stressed the need to limit their numbers.[109]

From the *Nihon ryōiki* we learn that there were many private temples whose buildings and statues were more modest than those of the state temples. They were often named after the village or hamlet where they stood, and were called *dō* 堂 rather than *tera* 寺. They were centers for the religious activities of the villagers, whereas mountain temples were for the retreat of disciplined monks. These village buildings were erected and maintained by villagers organized into *chishiki* 知識[110] by a monk or local official. [111] The *chishiki*, made up of lay devotees of considerable education and means, not only built private temples, made images, and copied scriptures, but they also sponsored monks to expound Buddhist teachings. It was through their activities that the common people came into contact with Buddhist teachings. In the case of the erection of an *uji-dera*, the *uji*[112] functioned as a *chishiki* and the temple symbolized the organizational unity of that *uji*.

The *Nihon ryōiki* records the story of the Ōtomo 大伴 family in Shinano 信濃 province. They built an *uji*-temple, and, after it was completed, an ordained member of the *uji* lived in the temple until he was killed by one of the patrons, a member of the same *uji*. We are told that the monk went to hell because he made private use of the temple property (III.23). This story suggests a decree issued in 716:

> It is reported that in all provinces even if temples have been constructed, there are neither monks nor nuns in residence, no Buddhist rites are performed, and descendants of the donors take over the rice paddies of the temple to support their families. . . .[113]

According to the records of recommendations for ordination, many monks and lay devotees came from the families of local magistrates.

109. *Ibid.*, XXXVII (Enryaku 2:6:10).

110. A translation of Skt. *kalyāṇamitra*, a friend of virtue, good counsellor, or name of Śākyamuni; donation of fields, grains, money, labor for the Three Treasures; hence, an organization of devotees who share the same faith and participate in the same project.

111. References of *chishiki* in the *Nihon ryōiki*:

| Vol. | Tale | Date or reign | Organizer | Project |
|------|------|---------------|-----------|---------|
| I | 35 | ? | nun | making image, saving life |
| II | 31 | Emperor Shōmu's reign | local official | building temple |
|    | 39 | 758 (Tenpyō hōji 2) | monk | building hall, making image |
| III | 13 | Empress Kōken's reign | local official | copying *Hoke-kyō* |
|    | 17 | 771 (Hōki 2) | monk | making image |

112. Naoki Kōjirō, *Nihon kodai no shizoku to tennō*, 101–135. *Uji* is defined as families grouped around a powerful family with a position in the hierarchical structure of the court.

113. *Shoku Nihongi*, VII (Reiki 2:5:15).

These magistrates, who had once been members of the ruling class in the provinces, were appointed to occupy lower ranks in the hierarchy after the centralization of the ritsuryō state.[114] They were made aware of the plight of the peasants, who suffered constantly from heavy taxation, famines, natural disasters, and civil war. Some of them turned to Buddhist teachings for some answer to their problems (II.2), while others utilized the temples as an institutional base for solidifying their power.[115] For example, the head of an uji built a temple by organizing his family group into a chishiki, and made one member of the same uji a monk in charge of the temple.

Several stages in the interaction of Buddhism with the native tradition can be traced in the Nihon ryōiki. The first instance is found in the story about an ancestor of a district magistrate of the seventh century. In gratitude for the protection given him in battle, he built a temple[116] to enshrine all the kami 神 of heaven and earth (I.7).[117] This early story omits any reference to the relationship between kami and Buddha. There follows a story illustrating the conflict between indigenous and imported traditions (I.28). E no Ozunu 役小角, legendary founder of the Shugendō 修験道,[118] was slandered by Hitokotonushi no kami 一言主神[119] and exiled to Izu[120] by the court. This story is unique in the Nihon ryōiki, for it contains numerous Taoist phrases, in spite of the fact that E no Ozunu is pictured as a Buddhist lay ascetic and practicer of Buddhist dharani.

In ancient Japan there were religious practices associated with mountains where kami lived and ascetics practiced austerities. When

114. In the eighth and ninth centuries Japan showed many characteristics of an imperial state due to the fact that the legal codes, ritsuryō, were patterned after those of T'ang China. See Sogabe Shizuo, Ritsuryō o chūshin toshita Nichū kankeishi no kenkyū.

115. Shoku Nihongi, XVII (Tenpyō 19:11:7). One way to secure the status of district magistrate was by building a temple.

116. Garan 伽藍 being the shortened transliteration of Skt. saṃghārāma, originally a monastery or convent, later meaning a temple which consists of buildings for religious rites and residential quarters.

117. Kami denotes the divine in the Shinto tradition and cannot be translated by any one English word. It refers to various deities of heaven and earth as well as their spirits, or to human beings, animals, trees, mountains, etc., which exhibit extraordinary powers; also it denotes the functional divinity affiliated with such natural phenomena as birth, growth, change. See Tsuda Sōkichi, "The Idea of Kami in Ancient Japanese Classics," T'oung Pao, LII (No. 4–5, 1966), 293–304. Hereafter kami will be treated as an English word.

118. Shoku Nihongi, I (Monmu 5:4:24); Snellen, 179. See H. Byron Earhart, "Shugendō, the Traditions of En no Gyōja, and Mikkyo Influences," in Studies of Esoteric Buddhism and Tantrism, 297–317. E is a family name which is often pronounced En in an elision with no; he is also known as E (or En) no gyōja (or ubasoku).

119. Kojiki 古事記, III, 132; Nihon shoki, XIV (Yūryaku 4:2). During the reign of Emperor Yūryaku, Great Kami of Kazuraki (or Katsuragi) Hitokotonushi no kami [Lord of One Word], who dispelled evil and incurred good with a charm, revealed himself to the emperor on Mt. Kazuraki. See D. L. Philippi, Kojiki, 360–361; Aston, "Nihongi," I, 341–342.

120. 伊圖嶋; Shoku Nihongi, I (Monmu 5:5:24) 伊豆島; identified with present Izu Ōshima.

Buddhist ascetics went to the mountains, they prayed for the protection of the kami. Even scholar monks sent to China for Buddhist studies prayed to native kami for their safe journey. The prosperity of Buddhism was sought through the protection of kami. Many Hindu deities found their way into Buddhist scriptures as guardians of the dharma, and, in similar fashion, Japanese deities were considered protectors of dharma. Emperor Shōmu, a noted patron of Buddhism, paid homage to the Grand Shrine of Ise during a rebellion in 740,[121] and, in the following year, he sent copies of the *Saishōō-kyō* and *Hoke-kyō*, monks, and horses to the deity Usa Hachiman 宇佐八幡, and built a pagoda attached to the shrine.[122] This is the beginning of the practice of building a *jingū-ji* 神宮寺, shrine-temple, which represents the institutional merger of a shrine and a temple. There developed at the same time the idea that kami were among the sentient beings and therefore in need of enlightenment. The story is told that in the Hōki era (770–780) the Great Kami of Taga 陀我 asked a monk to read the *Hoke-kyō* for him so that he might be liberated from *saṃsāra* (III.24). From the eighth century it became a common practice to read Buddhist scriptures before the altar at which a kami was enshrined.[123]

When Saichō challenged the traditional Buddhism at Nara, he insisted on establishing the Mahayana samgha, based on the Mahayana precepts expounded in the *Hoke-kyō* and independent of state control.[124] However, in declaring that the aim of the samgha was to protect the state, his teaching differed little from the traditional position which upheld the *Hoke-kyō, Saishōō-kyō*, and *Ninnō hannya-kyō* 仁王般若經[125] as a trilogy of scriptures with power to promote the welfare of the state. However, his teaching was distinct in stressing that initiation into the Mahayana samgha—that is, transmission of the Mahayana precepts—should symbolize the immediate attainment of Buddhahood. Since Saichō was a prominent advocate of the new Buddhist teachings and a contemporary of Kyōkai, it is highly possible that Kyōkai knew Saichō.[126] Kyōkai was apparently interested in Saichō's fresh approach to Buddhist teachings. He was particularly

121. *Shoku Nihongi*, XIII (Tenpyō 12:9:11, 11:3). Nishida Nagao says that Gyōgi went to the Ise Shrine as an imperial messenger at that time. See his *Jinja no rekishiteki kenkyū*, 87–149.

122. *Shoku Nihongi*, XIV (Tenpyō 13:3:24).

123. Tamura, *Asuka Bukkyōshi*, 190–216. Hereafter *saṃsāra* will be treated as an English word.

124. Asai Endō, "Dengyō Daishi to Hokke shisō no renkan," *Hokke-kyō no shisō to bunka*, ed. by Sakamoto Yukio, 569–597.

125. *Ninnō hannya haramitsu-kyō* 仁王般若波羅蜜經 (*Taishō*, VIII, No. 245. 825a–834a).

126. In 801 and 802 Saichō invited several eminent monks of the great temples in Nara to his lectures on the *Hoke-kyō* and Tendai doctrines. In 815 he lectured on the *Hoke-kyō* at Daian-ji in Nara. This occasion marked the beginning of the debates between Saichō and Tokuichi 德一 (749–824) of the Hossō School in Nara which lasted for several years.

impressed with the bodhisattva ideal of working for the salvation of all and acquiring mystical knowledge as a means for attaining Buddhahood. Saichō's insistence on the Mahayana precepts and teachings for men in the decadent age met a ready response in an ordinary monk such as Kyōkai, who was keenly conscious of his limitations.

Although the Sōgō system and Sōni-ryō never fully realized their goals, they did achieve a fundamental aim in making Buddhist monks and nuns serve the state. Both suffering and happiness were understood as a communal experience to be shared within the family, village, province, and state. Such a tendency, which emphasizes group participation and identity is a recurrent theme in the Japanese tradition. On the level of popular practice, there was little differentiation in the roles of Buddha, bodhisattva, and kami in helping people to lead happier lives. In spite of the fact that their symbolic forms differed, they referred to faith and happiness here and now.

## (2) INFLUENCE OF EARLIER WRITINGS

### a. *Doctrine of Karma and Samsara*

Karma is a notion fundamental to the world view of Hindus and Buddhists alike. Karma, which etymologically means "action," "deed," is moral law, which is taken for granted by most Hindus as the basis on which the cosmos operates. The doctrine teaches that every human action takes place in a sequence of the moral law of cause and effect and each individual's existence is conditioned by the idea of samsara, transmigration. Man's life is neither limited to one lifetime nor to the human species. Man's existence is believed to transmigrate through numerous lives in different species, such as deities, animals, hungry ghosts, hell beings.[127]

This world view underlies Śākyamuni's teachings. The doctrine of interdependent causation[128] is interpreted by some Buddhists in close association with the idea of karma. Tradition says that Śākayamuni allowed a man who accepted the Buddhist interpretation of karma to join the samgha, for karma was probably regarded as a popular expression of the central doctrine of interdependent causation.[129] Bud-

---

127. The six modes and places of existence of animate beings are *naraka* (hell), *preta* (hungry ghost), *tiryañc* (animal), *asura* (furious spirit), *manuṣya* (man), and *deva* (heavenly being). The idea of the five modes and places of existence, excluding *asura* from the above six, was more popular in China and Japan. Although *asura* is never mentioned in the *Nihon ryōiki*, the terms "six destinies" (I. 21, 35) and "five destinies" (III. 38) are found in the *Nihon ryōiki*.

128. Skt. *partityasamutpāda* (縁起), chain of causation, or dependent origination. See Edward J. Thomas, *The History of Buddhist Thought*, 58–70.

129. Mizuno Kōgen, "Gō-setsu ni tsuite," *IBK*, II (No. 2, 1954), 463–473.

dhists thoroughly adopted this pre-Buddhist notion of karma and samsara in the Jātaka literature, the tales of Buddha's numerous past lives, which appealed particularly to lay Buddhists.

When the Buddhist tradition entered Tibet, China, Korea, and Japan, the teaching of karma and samsara proved to be most novel and appealing to those who were taken by surprise by the subtle, metaphysical doctrines of Buddhism. This doctrine, although presented as a highly speculative cosmology, found some points of contact with the Chinese tradition because of the universality of the moral law of cause and effect. In China, where the idea of Heaven presiding over the universe was tenacious, however, the idea of fortune as a result of past deeds did not develop. Confucian scholars actively criticized this Buddhist doctrine on the basis of their concept of the "Mandate of Heaven" (*t'ien-ming* 天命),[130] which they regarded as determining man's fate. But the idea of the moral law of causation was not entirely absent among the Chinese, for in the Mandate of Heaven theory there was a common belief that good fortune comes to a family which does good deeds over a period of time, and misfortune to a family which does evil ones.[131] The difference lies in the fact that Buddhism combines the doctrines of karma and samsara and postulates a residuum that persists through many lives as a consequence of karma. The Chinese had difficulties with the doctrine of samsara in the beginning, but later interpreted it by using their concept of *shen* 神, soul, as an entity for transmigration and stressing its immortality, though this is somewhat contrary to the original Buddhist teachings.[132]

A clear understanding of karma was evidenced as early as the fourth century by Hsi Ch'ao 郗超 (336–377), who emphasized the function of the mind as subject to karmic retribution and stated that the effects of karma are borne by an individual.[133] His contention was further expounded by Hui-yüan 慧遠 (334–416) who wrote "San-pao lun" 三報論 (Treatise on the Three Ways of Karmic Retribution) in order to defend the doctrine of karma before those contemporaries who doubted the validity of the law of karmic retribution. He argues that people fail to recognize the effects of karma, because they confine

130. The theory of the "Mandate of Heaven" asserts that Heaven is accountable not only for human affairs but for natural phenomena; the cosmos is a self-contained, harmonious organism and it is the duty of rulers to maintain the state of equilibrium between man and nature.

131. Uchiyama Toshihiko, "Kandai no ōhō shisō," *Tokyo Shina gakuhō*, No. 6 (1960), 19.

132. Walter Liebenthal, "The Immortality of the Soul in Chinese Thought," *Monumenta Nipponica*, VIII (1952), 327–396; Kajiyama Yūichi, "Eon no hōōsetsu to shinfumetsuron," *Eon kenkyū—kenkyūhen*, ed. by Kimura Eiichi, 89–120.

133. Hsi Ch'ao, "Feng-fa yao," *Hung-ming chi* 弘明集, XIII (*Taishō*, LII, 86a–91b). See Erik Zürcher, *Buddhist Conquest of China*, Appendix B to Chapter III, 165–176.

their consideration to their present existence. In order to convince them of the invisible function of karmic retribution, he introduces a new theory of *san-pao*, or three ways of karmic retribution.

The scripture says that karma is worked out in three ways: *hsien-pao* 現報, *sheng-pao* 生報, and *hou-pao* 後報. In the first, good and evil deeds originate and receive responses in the same lifetime. In the second, the effects of deeds will visit the person in the next lifetime. In the third, consequences will come in a second, third, hundredth, or thousandth lifetime. Nobody controls the function of karmic retribution, and only our mind is responsible for it.[134]

Hui-yüan may have taken this theory from the *Abhidharmasāra-hṛdaya*[135] which was translated for him in 391/392 by Saṃghadeva.[136] His treatises popularized the theory of karmic retribution and contributed to its influence on later generations.

According to the *Kao-seng chuan* 高僧傳 (Biographies of Eminent Monks), Hui-yüan introduced an innovation into the routine of the Buddhist ceremonial meeting by opening it with stories on karmic causation.

Whenever there was a ceremonial meeting, he himself would ascend the high seat and personally take the lead in preaching, first elucidating the work of causation in the past, present, and future, and then discussing the significance of the particular occasions. Later generations continued this practice until it became a standard for all times.[137]

This is the beginning of *ch'ang-tao* 唱導, the practice of preaching, and the stories used as illustrations treated the theme of the law of karmic retribution. Tradition says that Kumārajīva (344–413) wrote a work called "Treatises on the Past, Present, and Future" (通三世論 inextant) and also emphasized the law of karmic retribution.[138] Chinese Buddhist writers are fond of asserting that a result follows a deed in the same way that a shadow follows a form or an echo follows a sound.[139]

134. Hui-yüan, "San-pao lun," *Hung-ming chi*, V (*Taishō*, LII, 34b); *Eon kenkyū—ibunhen*, ed. by Kimura, 70–71. See W. Liebenthal, "Shih Hui-yuan's Buddhism as Set Forth in his Writings," *JAOS*, LXX (1950), 243–259.
135. *A-pi-t'an hsin lun* 阿毘曇心論 (*Taishō*, XXVIII, No. 1550, 814b). 若業現法報次受於生報後報亦復然 餘則說不定.
136. *Eon kenkyū—ibunhen*, ed. by Kimura, 314. See Zürcher, *Buddhist Conquest of China*, 230.
137. Hui-chiao 慧皎, *Kao-seng chuan*, XIII (*Taishō*, L, 417c).
138. *Ibid.*, II (332b).
139. Hsi Ch'ao, "Feng-fa yao," (*Taishō*, LII, 87c). See Zürcher, *Buddhist Conquest of China*, 169. Hui-yüan refers to this cliché in his "Ming pao-ying lun," 明報應論 (*Eon kenkyū—ibunhen*, 76) and uses it himself (*ibid.*, 85). It is also found in an anonymous treatise, "Cheng-wu lun," 正誣論, *Hung-ming chi*, I (*Taishō*, LII, 8b), dated in the early fourth century and in Taoist scriptures.

They stressed that karmic retribution is based on the law of nature, and Kyōkai adopted their idea and cliché. It was about this time that several Buddhist scriptures expounding this doctrine were translated into Chinese.[140] People accepted a new cosmology in which the world was enlarged from the present to include the past and future, and at the same time from human beings to other modes of existence such as deities, animals, and ghosts. In contrast to the Confucianists, the Taoists did not attempt to refute the doctrine of karma and samsara. In fact, they used it to supplement their teachings, though it took several centuries for the Chinese indigenous idea of the other world to fully combine with the Buddhist cosmological conception.[141]

Hui-yüan's concept of karmic retribution is repeated in the preface of T'ang-lin's *Ming-pao chi*, a collection of Buddhist legends compiled between 650 and 655.

> It is taught that there are three ways [of karmic retribution]. First, one receives in the present existence what one's good or evil deeds have caused. This is called *hsien-pao*. Second, what one's deeds have caused is not received in this existence, but determines the next life according to good and evil deeds. This is called *sheng-pao*. Third, if good or evil deeds in the past have not brought the results and one has gone through many lives and still created karma without any consequences, one will receive them in a second, fifth, or tenth lifetime. This is called *hou-pao*.[142]

T'ang-lin was a government official who received a Confucian education and espoused the Buddhist faith. He collected stories throughout China, presenting a Sinicized interpretation of the doctrine of karmic retribution. As the title and theme of his work, he chose *ming-pao*, "invisible function of karmic retribution," which is a general concept blending the three ways into one. In China, Buddhists tried to demonstrate the profundity of Buddhist doctrines by stressing the fact that they revealed future responses that were not even considered in Confucian teachings.

On the other hand, Kyōkai used the word *genpō* (*hsien-pao*), which in T'ang-lin's preface refers to consequences that are manifested in this life, as the main theme for the collection of Japanese Buddhist

140. *Kako genzai inga-kyō* 過去現在因果經 (*Taishō*, III, No. 189, 620c–653b), *Zaifuku hōō-kyō* 罪福報應經 (*Taishō*, XVII, No. 747, 562b–564c), *Funbetsu gōhō ryak-kyō* 分別業報略經 (*Taishō*, XVII, No. 723, 446b–450c), and others.

141. Akizuki Kan'ei, "Rikuchō Dōkyō ni okeru ōhōsetsu no hatten," *Hirosaki daigaku jinbunshakai*, No. 33 (1964), 26–60; reprinted in *Chūgoku kankei ronsetsu shiryō*, I (1964), Part One, 386–403.

142. T'ang-lin, *Ming-pao chi* (*Taishō*, LI, 788a).

legends. This may reflect his emphasis on present existence, even though he did not exclude stories dealing with the effects of past deeds upon a future life. He was uninterested in subtle arguments concerning the meaning of karma and samsara, or the question of whether there is something about man which is immortal. Rather, he compiled the *Nihon ryōiki* as an aid for monks in their preaching, should they wish to follow the fashion initiated by Hui-yüan in China, and as a guide for lay Buddhists. Kyōkai's primary concern seems to have been in the salvation of his fellow beings and himself, which he hoped would be accomplished as a result of the merit accumulated in the compiling of the collection. He understood karmic retribution as a universal principle and stated that its operation was also discernible in the Chinese classics and in the pre-Buddhist age in Japan (I. Preface).

Kyōkai's task differed from that of the Chinese monks who tried to demonstrate the profundity of Buddhist teachings in comparison with those of Confucianism and Taoism. Many fundamental questions concerning Buddhist teachings were asked and answered in the debates and writings of eminent Chinese monks obliged to delineate their positions in the face of anti-Buddhist propaganda and occasional persecutions. Japanese monks, on the other hand, were free from both the good and bad effects imposed by such a competitive situation. Their task lay in choosing the most effective scriptures or doctrines from the vast accumulation of materials in the Buddhist tradition. They accepted the Buddhist doctrines expounded by Chinese monks, and their concern was to apply them meaningfully to themselves, the people, and the state.

In the *Nihon ryōiki*, nirvana is mentioned only once in reference to Śākyamuni (III.30). Kyōkai's ideal is the bodhisattva who makes a vow to stay in this world in order to work for the salvation of all. By means of "maturing good stock and accumulating merit" the bodhisattva practices love for others in the world of samsara. The common goal is rebirth in this world, heaven, or the land of bliss. According to Kyōkai, some emperors and princes had been virtuous monks in their previous lives and had accumulated enough merit to be born into the imperial family. For this reason they deserved to be revered and obeyed (III.39).

In contrast to the understanding of the law of causation as the law of nature, the *Hoke-kyō* gives another interpretation which may have influenced Kyōkai. The *Hoke-kyō* is the scripture most frequently quoted in the *Nihon ryōiki*, and it has been extremely popular throughout the history of Japanese Buddhism. Although the *Hoke-kyō* makes many references to karma (Chaps. i, ii, vii, x, xii, xv, xvi, xix, xxv),[143] the main emphasis is on overcoming karma and obtaining salvation, rather than on the doctrine of karma itself. The recitation of the *Hoke-kyō* or even the invocation of its title, when done with faith, constitutes an act of merit which will overcome all other karma. Further, it says that dharani and mantra (Chap. xxvi), a remembrance of Kannon, or the calling of Kannon's name (Chap. xxv) also transcend time and space, making possible the immediate attainment of Buddhahood. This message of the *Hoke-kyō* may be considered as a warning against a mechanical, static, or deterministic understanding of karma. Faith is the basis for salvation here and now, which is the work of the dharma-body Buddha, both transcendent and immanent.

b. *The Influence of Chinese Buddhist Literature*

Japanese literature was gradually shaped under the influence of the Chinese classics which were brought to Japan in the fifth century, and the vast amount of Buddhist writing that followed the official introduction of Buddhism in the sixth century (I.Preface). The earliest works of literature which have been preserved are the *Kojiki*[144] and *Nihon shoki*,[145] historical records written in the early eighth century, and patterned on Chinese historical works such as the *Han shu* (History of Former Han Dynasty), *Hou-Han shu* (History of Later Han Dynasty), and *Shih chi* (Records of the Historian), which clearly show that the influence of Buddhist literature is readily apparent in them.[146]

Since the *Nihon ryōiki* is the first collection of Buddhist legends in Japan, the heavy influence of earlier Chinese literature is to be expected in almost every aspect of its style, form, content, motif, and arrangement. As to the depth and extent of the influence, however, scholars differ in opinion. Some maintain that most of the legends were borrowed directly from the Chinese tradition and simply rephrased.[147] Others hold that the legends must have been accepted and believed by the people who transmitted them, concluding that, in spite of their partial foreign origin, their popularity stamps them as Japanese.[148]

Kyōkai stated his editorial principles as follows:

My work is comparable to a rough pebble. . . . Its source in the

---

143. Kamimura Shinjō, "Chūgoku Tendai to Hokke shisō no renkan," *Hoke-kyō no shisō to bunka*, ed. by Sakamoto, 550–555.

144. *Kojiki* (NKBT, 1), ed. by Kurano and Takeda; D. L. Philippi, *Kojiki*.

145. *Nihon shoki* (NKBT, 67–68), ed. by Sakamoto Tarō and others; Aston, "Nihongi."

146. Kojima Noriyuki, *Jōdai Nihon bungaku to Chūgoku bungaku*, I, 241–255.

147. Haga Yaichi, *Kōshō Konjaku monogatarishū*, I, 3.

148. Hori Ichirō, *Nihon jōdai bunka to Bukkyō*, 187.

oral tradition is so indistinct that I am afraid of omitting much [I.Preface].

However, I cannot suppress my passion to do good, so I dare to write down oral traditions [at the risk of] soiling clean paper with mistakes [II.Preface].

According to what I had heard, I selected oral traditions and put down miraculous events, dividing them into good and evil [III.39, Postscript].

It is evident from his repeated references to an oral tradition there were many stories circulating among the monks in Nara and that some of these stories had already been written down. The fact that Kyōkai's quotations from scriptures are not faithful to the letter of the text suggests his dependence on previous writings and a frequent use of anthologies rather than the original texts.[149] We cannot trace the source of all these quotations because of the vast body of writings in the Buddhist Canon and because some of the works extant in Kyōkai's lifetime are no longer available.[150] However, a list has been prepared of the Chinese Buddhist literature that might have influenced Kyōkai in compiling the *Nihon ryōiki*. It consists of two categories of works: anthologies of scriptures and biographies edited by monks, and legends collected by lay Buddhists. The aim of the *Nihon ryōiki* was to combine these two types of literature.

The quotations from scriptures in the *Nihon ryōiki* may be divided into four categories: first, direct quotations from the original texts; second, indirect quotations which match passages in anthologies rather than the original texts; third, rephrased quotations; fourth, apparent quotations whose sources cannot be located. As the second category is the largest (13 out of 44 cases), it is evident that Kyōkai was more familiar with anthologies than with the original texts of scriptures, except in the case of the *Hoke-kyō* and probably the *Nehan-gyō* 涅槃經,[151] which are quoted several times. The inclusion of materials from the third and fourth categories suggests that some legends were transmitted orally before they were compiled by Kyōkai.[152] Many scriptures in the Buddhist Canon are filled with colorful Indian leg-

149. See Appendix C.
150. Kariya Ekisai wrote a pioneer work tracing quotations to their sources (see his *Nihon ryōiki kōshō*). Recent works done by Tokushi Yūshō ("*Nihon ryōiki ni inyō seru kyōkan ni tsuite*," *Bukkyō kenkyū*, I [No. 2, February 1937], 51–65) and Haraguchi Hiroshi ("*Nihon ryōiki shutten goku kanken*," *Kuntengo to kunten shiryō*, No. 34 [December 1966], 53–67) are to be noted.
151. *Mahāparinirvāṇasūtra* 大般涅槃經 (*Taishō*, XII, No. 374, 365–604; No. 375, 605–852).
152. Uematsu Shigeru, *Kodai setsuwa bungaku*, 116–142.

ends about deities, men, and animals depicted in Buddhist terms. These legends incorporated the Buddhist teachings of karma within several types of stories such as *jātaka, avadāna,* and *nidāna*.[153] Their influence was great not only on later Buddhist literature but on the development of lay Buddhism in particular. The translation of the Buddhist Canon in China led to the compilation of many anthologies of legends taken from the scriptures. They were arranged thematically in order to serve as handbooks for Buddhist studies.

Among them, the *Shokyō yōshū (Chu-ching yao-chi)* was decisive in its influence on Kyōkai's life and work.[154] Kyōnichi, the mendicant who appeared in Kyōkai's dream, gave him a copy of it, saying that it was an excellent scripture for instructing the people (III.38). The *Shokyō yōshū,* compiled in 659 by the Chinese monk Tao-shih (d. 683), consists of important passages from the scriptures arranged thematically. Its purpose was to instruct monks; the author gives an exegesis of doctrine at the beginning of each section, followed by illustrations. The major themes of this work are karmic retribution and the veneration of the Three Treasures. As far as themes are concerned, the *Nihon ryōiki* followed the priorities of the *Shokyō yōshū*.[155] The latter was compiled to summarize Buddhist teachings in a systematic way using scriptural passages as illustrations, while the former arranged the stories from the Japanese tradition, both oral and written, in historical sequence. The style of the headings of the stories is similar.[156]

In addition to the *Shokyō yōshū,* two other works seem to have been favorites of Kyōkai. In the preface he says:

> In China, the *Myōhōki* (Record of Invisible Work of Karmic Retribution) was compiled, and, during the great T'ang dynasty, the *Hannya kenki* (A Collection of Miraculous Stories concerning the *Kongō hannya-kyō*) was written. Since we respect the docu-

153. *Jātaka* is a story which tells how Śākyamuni accumulated merits in his former lives; *avadāna* is a type of story about a hero who is a disciple or follower of Śākyamuni, and whose past karma is described by Buddha; *nidāna* is a tale of how a Buddhist precept originated. See Iwamoto Yutaka, *Bukkyō setsuwa kenkyū josetsu,* 26–43; Edward J. Thomas, *The History of Buddhist Thought,* Appendix I, 261–287.

154. See Chap. I(1)a, n. 14.

155. The headings of the *Shokyō yōshū* are as follows: (1) Three Treasures: Veneration of Buddha, Dharma, and Samgha; (2) Veneration of Pagodas; (3) Meditation; (4) Renunciation; (5) Adoration; (6) Incense and Lamps; (7) Receiving Invitations; (8) Starting a Fast; (9) Ending a Fast; (10) Wealth; (11) Poverty; (12) Advocating the Way; (13) Repaying Kindness; (14) Saving Life; (15) Attaining Merits; (16) Selecting Friends; (17) Thoughtfulness; (18) Six Virtues (Donations, Keeping Precepts, Perseverance, Hard Work, Meditation, and Wisdom); (19) Karmic Causation; (20) Desires and Illusions; (21) Four Kinds of Birth; (22) Receiving Consequences of Retribution; (23) Ten Evils; (24) Deception; (25) Falling into Pride; (26) Liquor and Meat; (27) Divination; (28) Hell; (29) Funerals; (30) Miscellaneous.

156. Katayose Masayoshi, *Konjaku monogatarishū no kenkyū,* I, 404–413.

ments of foreign lands, should we not also believe and stand in awe of the miraculous events in our own land? [I.Preface].

By the beginning of the Heian period the *Myōhōki* was known to Japan, where its three volumes have been preserved.[157] Except for five stories in the third volume, most of the stories seem to be based on the Chinese oral tradition. In the preface to the work, T'ang-lin says that he also followed earlier works of Buddhist literature.[158] The *Hoke-kyō* is the most popular scripture in the *Myōhōki* as well as in the *Nihon ryōiki*. In both works the stories begin with the date and name of the central figure and teach the law of causation through the interpretation of miraculous events. Both T'ang-lin and Kyōkai were Buddhists, but the fact that the former was a layman while the latter was a monk may explain several differences between their respective works. Kyōkai dealt sympathetically with self-ordained monks who had not studied Buddhist doctrine and who violated Buddhist precepts and the *Sōni-ryō*. At the same time, in spite of his identification with the common people, he was aware of his status as a monk of a great state temple with a clerical rank. T'ang-lin, on the other hand, was critical of the corrupt clergy. T'ang-lin records the source of each story at its end, while Kyōkai concludes each story with a note (*san* 讚) or his comment which is often accompanied by scriptural quotations to draw a moral from the story.[159]

The "Hannya kenki" mentioned in the preface quoted above may have introduced the style of a note following a story. It is known in full as the *Kongō hannya-kyō jikkenki*,[160] a collection of miraculous stories about the *Kongō hannya-kyō* thematically arranged.[161] We do

157. The original text does not exist in China, for it was probably lost soon after its transmission to Japan. Extant manuscripts in Japan are incomplete, but nearly eighty stories have been reconstructed from quotations in other works. See *ibid.*, I, 350–385.

158. They are the *Kanzeon reigenki* (*Kuan-shih-yin ling-yen chi*) 觀世音靈驗記, *Sengenki* (*Hsüan-yen chi*) 宣驗記, and *Myōshōki* (*Ming-hsiang chi*) 冥祥記.

159. In the *Nihon ryōiki* there are fifteen stories accompanied by a concluding remark which begins with "The note says . . . ." Their distribution is as follows:

I.5, 6, 14, 18, 22, 25, 33

II.2, 21, 42

III.1, 4, 10, 12, 30

In Chinese historical writings a passage known as a *tsan* (san) is appended to a biography and used to summarize the writer's opinion of its central figure. Hui-chiao adopted this device in his *Kao-seng chuan*. Since the note is generally written in four-character phrases, it may indicate Kyōkai's desire to conform to Chinese style and his dependence on preceding literary works. Sometimes Kyōkai adds his comment after the note; this has given rise to the speculation that the note was not written by Kyōkai at all but that the story, along with the note, was borrowed by him from an earlier work.

160. Iwabuchi Etsutarō, "*Nihon ryōiki* ni mietaru *Hannya kenki* towa nanika," *Kokugo to kokubungaku*, XII (No. 8, 1935), 61–67; Katayose, *Konjaku monogatarishū no kenkyū*, I, 388–389.

161. It consists of three volumes, each divided into two sections: Vol. 1: (1) Salvation and Protection; (2) Protection. Vol. II: (1) Making up for Sins; (2) Divine Power. Vol. III: (1) Merits; (2) Sympathy for the Faithful.

not know when it was introduced into Japan, but by the early Heian period, when the *Nihon ryōiki* was written, it was popular and known as the *Hannya kenki*, although it was no longer mentioned in China. It contributed a story to the *Nihon ryōiki* (II.24), and also suggested the idea for a separate preface for each volume. Its popularity lasted throughout the Heian period.

Kyōkai's dependence on these three works as his models is proved by a comparison of the content of the stories in them. It reveals that the *Myōhōki* furnished eight stories, the *Shokyō yōshū*, four, and the *Kongō hannya-kyō jikkenki*, one story in the *Nihon ryōiki*, where all are retold as Japanese stories.[162] A study of these earlier Chinese works shows that their main theme was karmic retribution, particularly in the works written by lay Buddhists. There is little doubt that the *Nihon ryōiki* was influenced by and patterned on them, and in this sense was dependent on the Chinese Buddhist tradition. However, there are differences which should be noted. Kyōkai's chronological arrangement of Japanese stories[163] was probably influenced by Japanese historical works such as the *Kojiki, Nihon shoki*, and *Shoku Nihongi*, for the Chinese works discussed above are not chronologically arranged. However, we must admit that Chinese stories are presented in a historical fashion by indicating the sources, even though they are thematically classified. Kyōkai, on the other hand, did not give the sources for his stories. The *Nihon ryōiki* has the quality of a chronicle, but at the same time much of the content is legendary. It is not factual history, but history seen from a Buddhist viewpoint, even though it lacks the consistency of a causal narrative and remains a collection of separate stories. It became the precursor of a new genre of narrative history which eventually in the tenth century replaced the court chronicles that had been modeled on the Chinese pattern.

In addition to the established sources mentioned above, there are numerous other possible sources. Recent studies in comparative literature suggest an increasing number of correlations between Japanese and foreign literature and the oral transmission of legends from the continent to Japan. It is extremely difficult to document the latter, but

162. The *Myōhōki* offers the plots to the following stories of the *Nihon ryōiki* (I.7, 10, 18; II.5, 10, 19; III.10, 13). *The Shokyō yōshū* gives four, of which two (I.4; III.1) are originally from the *Kao-seng chuan* (Biographies of Eminent Monks); one (I.17) is from the *Hsiao-tzu chuan* (Biographies of Filial Sons); and one (II.3) is from the *Zōhōzō-kyō* 雜寶藏經. The *Kongō hannya-kyō jikkenki* offers one (II.24) which is also adopted in the *Myōhōki*.

163. The first volume begins with a story from Emperor Yūryaku's reign (late fifth century) and ends with a story from Emperor Shōmu's reign, dated in 727. The second volume comprises stories which range from 729 to 763. The third volume covers the period from Empress Kōken's reign to Emperor Saga's reign, 749–822. See Appendix A.

there are two significant cases worthy of note. One is the legend centering about Prince Shōtoku while the other concerns E no Ozunu.

The *Nihon shoki* obviously mythologized Prince Shōtoku as the Dharma King, and the *Nihon ryōiki* contributed a story which is not found in the *Nihon shoki*. On a golden mountain Prince Shōtoku was given a jewel of the elixir of life by a monk in order that he might go back to the world of the living to propagate Buddhist teaching (I.5). The note following the story identifies this golden mountain with Mt. Wu-t'ai 五臺山 in Shansi province in China, a sacred mountain traditionally regarded as the place of Mañjuśrī's descent.[164] He was reborn a century later as a great patron of Buddhism, Emperor Shōmu. Tradition says he is an incarnation of Mañjuśrī. The same type of story is also found in the Korean Buddhist legends, compiled in the *Samguk yusa* 三國遺事. One of these tells of a Korean preceptor named Chanjang 慈藏 of the seventh century, who met Mañjuśrī on Mt. Wu-t'ai in China. Mañjuśrī advised Chanjang to return to Silla and visit Mt. Odae where they would meet again. Another story concerns two princes who withdrew to Mt. Odae and met Mañjuśrī.[165] These legends are used to help legitimize Korean Buddhism and to make Silla the land of the eternally present Buddha. We conclude that the Mt. Wu-t'ai legends in China and Korea had great influence on the formation of the early Japanese legends, including that of Prince Shōtoku's encounter with Mañjuśrī. Each played, respectively, the same role of establishing Buddhism firmly on the native soil in the three lands.

A similar resemblance is found between the E no Ozunu legend in the *Nihon ryōiki* and the Hui-yüan legendary cycle as it is documented in "Lu-shan Yüan-kung hua" 廬山遠公話, discovered at Tun-huang.[166] Both Hui-yüan and E no Ozunu are said to have had an encounter with the local deity of the mountain where each one resided. As the "Lu-shan Yüan-kung hua" cannot be dated, it is impossible to prove its direct influence on the E no Ozunu legend. However, we may assume that these legends originally had little to do with Prince Shōtoku, E no Ozunu, or Hui-yüan, but that folk piety incorporated

164. Mt. Wu-t'ai is also known as Mt. Ch'ing-liang 清凉山. Tradition says that the Bodhisattva Mañjuśrī (Monju-bosatsu 文殊菩薩) descended on its peak to convert the Chinese. Cf. Étienne Lamotte, "Mañjuśrī," *T'oung Pao*, XLVIII (1960), 54–61; Ennin 圓仁, *Nittō guhō junreiki* 入唐求法巡禮記 (*DBZ*, 113), III, 237–238, 243; Edwin O. Reischauer, trans., *Ennin's Diary*, 246–247, 266.

165. Iryŏn 一然, *Samguk yusa* (*Taishō*, XLIX, 590a). See Peter H. Lee, *Lives of Eminent Korean Monks*, 9–10.

166. Stein, No. 2073. For a critically edited text, see Makita Tairyō, *Chūgoku kinsei Bukkyōshi kenkyū*, 287–311.

these historical figures as heroes into the various legends. Immigrant monks and student monks who had studied abroad probably transmitted such legends to Japan orally. We will discuss the symbolism of these legends more fully in the next chapter.

### c. *Japanese Legendary Literature*

By the early ninth century, when the *Nihon ryōiki* was compiled, many works of Japanese literature had already been written. The *Nihon ryōiki*, following the *Manyōshū* 萬葉集,[167] begins with the story of Emperor Yūryaku who reigned in the fifth century (I.1). The idea of the land of the dead, *Yomi no kuni* 黄泉國, and a taboo on eating food cooked in that land (II.7) is probably drawn from the *Kojiki*, which was compiled in 712. The *Nihon ryōiki* is the earliest work to support the *Nihon shoki*'s date of 552 for the official introduction of Buddhism, as against the traditional dating of 538. Kyōkai closely followed the tradition of the court histories, although there is some doubt about his familiarity with the *Shoku Nihongi* which was compiled in 797. If the *Nihon ryōiki* was compiled in 787 (Enryaku 6) as some scholars assert, it would have been impossible for him to have consulted the *Shoku Nihongi*. However, if the *Nihon ryōiki* was compiled during the Kōnin era (810–824) as we have concluded, he might have made use of it. When we compare passages on E no Ozunu and Gyōgi in these two works, we find that the story in the *Nihon ryōiki* is a development of the one in the *Shoku Nihongi*. Since Kyōkai sought to make his work a history of dharma existing in Japan, he must have been interested in the newly compiled history which covers approximately the same historical period. On the other hand, it may be argued that he simply used older private records, which differed in some instances from the sources for the court history. This hypothesis is supported by a few references made by Kyōkai to records otherwise unknown.

> According to a record, in the reign of Emperor Bitatsu, sounds of musical instruments were heard off the coast of Izumi province [I.5].

> According to a record, in the second month of the ninth year . . . , an imperial order was given to the officials . . . [I.25].

There seem to have been some historical documents apart from the court tradition. The former passage differs from the *Nihon shoki*, which dates that event in the reign of Emperor Kinmei.[168] No passage corresponding to the latter can be found in the court history.

167. *Manyōshū* (*NKBT*, 4–7), ed. by Takagi Ichinosuke, Gomi Tomohide, and Ōno Susumu. See the *Manyōsū*, trans. by J. L. Pierson.
168. *Nihon shoki*, XIX (Kinmei 14:5:7). See Aston, "Nihongi," II, 68.

The following passage implies that a private record of a miraculous event was in circulation.

As Hirokuni visited the land of the dead and saw the karmic retribution of good and evil, he recorded it for circulation [I.30].

A close comparison between the descriptions of the same historical figures in the *Nihon ryōiki* and the *Shoku Nihongi* may illuminate the degree of Kyōkai's dependency on the court histories. Princes and nobles who appear in the two works are those who were involved in rebellion and political intrigues.[169] Although Kyōkai tries to explain the violent death of the rebels as being the result of their evil deeds in the past, he concurs with the judgment in the court history except in the case of two men (III.36, 37). These two are not rebels but loyal courtiers who are praised in the court history but condemned by Kyōkai as sufferers in hell because of their offences against the Three Treasures. However, they were eventually saved. The adaptation of these two stories illustrates Kyōkai's intention to preach the inescapability of suffering in hell. Tale 38 of the third volume closely parallels accounts in the *Shoku Nihongi*. The same is true with the *Nihon shoki* and *Nihon ryōiki*. Therefore, it seems clear that Kyōkai was familiar with the *Nihon shoki* and the *Shoku Nihongi*, depended on them for historical dates and events, but interpreted them according to the law of karmic causation.

It is extremely difficult to learn about the oral tradition before the compilation of the *Kojiki, Nihon shoki,* and *Fudoki* 風土記 (Topographic Records).[170] However, many myths and legends in these early writings reflect the rich local traditions that had existed throughout Japan for several centuries before they were written down. Some found their way into the court histories and poetry, while others served as the basis for stories of the founding of shrines and temples, the genealogy of families, folk etymology, and folk tales. The *Nihon ryōiki* shares with other early texts such ancient motifs as divine marriage, descent of deities, marriage between a human being and an animal, or visits to the other world. For instance, the section of the *Suminoe no taisha jindaiki* 住吉大社神代記 (Ancient History of the Great Shrine of Suminoe)[171] which deals with legend, written in part in 659

169. Prince Nagaya (II.1), Prince Uji (II.35), Princes Funado, Kifumi, and Shioyaki (III.38); Tachibana no Naramaro (II.40), Fujiwara no Nagate (III.36), Saheki no Itachi (III.37), Fujiwara no Nakamaro and Tanetsugu (III.38), etc. Fukushima Kōichi, "*Nihon ryōiki* ni arawareta Kyōkai no kangaekata," *Heian bungaku (Kokubungaku ronsō,* 3), 99–138.

170. They were compiled between 713 and 733, and five of them are extant: Hitachi 常陸, Izumo 出雲, Harima 播磨, Bungo 豊後, and Hizen 肥前. Several others exist only in fragments. See *Fudoki (NKBT,* 2), ed. by Akimoto Kichirō.

171. Tanaka Takashi, *Sumiyoshi taisha shi* (History of Great Shrine of Sumiyoshi [originally Suminoe]), Vol. I, Appendix I.

and 702, gives a local version of the mythological tradition which differs from the corresponding section in the *Nihon shoki*. Many Buddhist temples have in their historical records "origin tales," which are found to be of the same genre as the *Nihon ryōiki*. For instance, "The Founding of Hase-dera" 長谷寺緣起,[172] compiled in 741, gives an origin tale structurally similar to some stories in the *Nihon ryōiki*.

The *Nihon ryōiki* is the earliest collection of such legends selected to clarify the Buddhist teaching of karmic retribution. It includes origin tales, anecdotes of saints, and folktales, which are partly historical and partly fictional. Out of twelve origin tales, seven refer to temples (I.5, 7, 17; II.5, 21, 31, 39), three to painted or sculptured images (I.33; III.17, 30), one to a hill (I.1), and one to a family (I.2). There are many anecdotes about historical figures, for Kyōkai wanted to show dharma working in human history.

As stated above, Kyōkai used as his sources not only the oral tradition of his time but also written traditions both Japanese and foreign. According to Uematsu, nearly 90 percent of the stories had been handed down by monks or local people before they reached Kyōkai. He was by no means a creative writer, but rather an editor and commentator on the tradition he worked so faithfully to document.[173] Although isolated legends had existed for several centuries, Japanese legendary literature was not born until a special set of conditions came into existence. It is clear that the corpus of Buddhist legends that had originated in India, developed in China, and been transmitted to Japan greatly stimulated and influenced the development of indigenous Japanese legends.

Thus the *Nihon ryōiki* created a form of literature called "legendary literature," and served as the fountainhead for later writings. In legendary literature the author neither expresses his ideas nor describes society as directly as he does in other genres. The object of his interest is man, and he selects a motif which matches his creative purpose from among extant legends in order to explore the nature of humanity. The *Nihon ryōiki* was followed in the same century by the *Nihon kanryō-roku* 日本感靈錄 (Japanese Record of Miraculous Events),[174] which is indebted to the former in both content and form.[175] The next two centuries may be called the golden age of legendary literature, during which the great popularity of the *Nihon ryōiki* continued.

172. "Hase-dera engi," *Shoji engi-shū* 諸寺緣起集 (*DBZ*, 118), 326–333.
173. Uematsu Shigeru, *Kodai setsuwa bungaku*, 141.
174. *Nihon kanryōroku* (*ZGR*, XXVB, Book 717).
175. Nagai Yoshinori, *Bukkyō bungaku kenkyū*, I, 147–154.

In the tenth century the *Nihon ryōiki* tradition is represented by two works which are somewhat dissimilar in nature. One is the *Sanbō ekotoba* 三寶繪詞 (Notes on Pictorial Presentations of the Three Treasures) written for a princess by Minamoto no Tamenori 源爲憲 in 984[176]. It consists of three volumes, which correspond to Buddha, Dharma and Samgha, and it incorporates seventeen stories from the *Nihon ryōiki*. The other work is the *Nihon ōjō gokurakuki* 日本往生極樂記 (Biographies of the Japanese Who Were Born in the Land of Bliss) compiled by Yoshishige no Yasutane 慶滋保胤 between 985 and 987.[177] In a note the author explains why he included Prince Shōtoku and Gyōgi among those who were born in the land of bliss. Originally he had not intended to do so, but he altered his intention in order to comply with the last wishes of Prince Kaneaki. He distinguished Prince Shōtoku and Gyōgi from the others he described by identifying them as "appearances of the two incarnated bodhisattvas,"[178] and making Prince Shōtoku's biography several times longer than other biographies. Since these two men were not known for their belief and rebirth in the pure land, the author must have hesitated to include them.

The function of the *Nihon ryōiki* as a casebook for preachers was carried on in works such as the *Uchigikishū* 打聞集 (Collection of Sermons)[179] and *Hyakuza hōdan kikigakishō* 百座法談聞書抄 (Summary Notes of One Hundred Lectures on Dharma)[180] in the twelfth century. The faith in the *Hoke-kyō* was singled out as the subject for the *Dainihon Hoke-kyō kenki* 大日本法華經驗記 (Records of Wonders Related to the *Hoke-kyō* in Japan).[181] The narrative aspects of the *Nihon ryōiki* found their fullest expression in the *Konjaku monogatarishū* 今昔物語集 (Collection of Tales Present and Past)[182] and *Uji shūi monogatari* 宇治拾遺物語 (Tales from the Later Gleanings of Uji),[183] the most famous and admired works of the legendary literature.

Kyōkai's custom of adding personal comments and morals after each story developed into the genre of moralizing legends which

176. Yamada Yoshio, ed. and annot., *Sanbō ekotoba ryakuchū*.
177. Yoshishige no Yasutane, *Nihon ōjō gokurakuki* (*Gunsho ruijū*, IV, Book 66; *SGR*, III).
178. *Ibid.* (*SGR*, III, 726a). 披國史別傳等 入二菩薩應迹之事焉.
179. *Uchigikishū* (photostat ed.), Koten hozonkai.
180. *Hyakuza hōdan kikigakishō*, ed. by Satō Akio.
181. Chingen, *Honchō Hokke kenki* (*ZGR*, VIIIA, Book 194).
182. *Konjaku monogatarishū* (*NKBT*, 22–26), ed. by Yamada Yoshio, Tadao, Hideo, and Toshio. For a selected translation of thirty-seven stories, see E. O. Jones, *Ages Ago*. It is also called *Konjaku monogatari*.
183. *Uji shūi monogatari* (*NKBT*, 27), ed. by Watanabe Tsunaya and Nishio Kōichi. For a selected translation of fifty-five tales (out of one hundred and ninety-four), see John S. Forster, "Uji shūi monogatari," *Monumenta Nipponica*, XX (No. 1–2, 1965), 135–208.

flourished in the Kamakura period and produced introspective works such as the *Hosshinshū* 發心集 (Collection of Tales for Awakening Faith)[184] and *Shasekishū* 沙石集 (Collection of Sand and Stone).[185] They fit well into the genre of essays. Kyōkai's interest in writing a history was carried on partly in the biographical writings such as the *Ōjōden* series, [186] and partly in interpretative histories such as the *Fusō ryakki* (Concise Chronicle of Japan)[187] and the *Gukanshō* 愚管抄 (Miscellany of Ignorant Views).[188]

It is evident that later works surpass the *Nihon ryōiki* in literary refinement, historicity, and depth of introspection. However, the merit of the *Nihon ryōiki* lies in its simple affirmation of faith and its diversity of interests and views. Though no one would deny the influence of Chinese tradition, the *Nihon ryōiki* is, nonetheless, Japanese in the sense that it was not only accepted by the people at the time of its compilation but also helped to shape the later Japanese tradition.

184. *Hosshinshū* (*Kamo no Chōmei zenshū*), ed. by Yanase Kazuo.
185. Mujū 無住, *Shasekishū* (*NKBT*, 85), ed. by Watanabe Tsunaya.
186. See Shigematsu Akihisa, "*Ōjōden no kenkyū*," *Nagoya daigaku bungakubu kenkyū ronshū*, XXIII (1960), 1–124; *Ōjōden no kenkyū*, ed. by Koten isan no kai. The following seven works are classified as *Ōjōden*: *Nihon ōjō gokurakuki* (see n. 177); *Dainihon Hoke-kyō kenki* (see n. 181); *Zoku honchō ōjōden* by Ōe no Masafusa (*Gunsho ruijū*, IV, Book 66, *SGR*, III); *Shūi ōjōden* and *Goshūi ōjōden* by Miyoshi no Tameyasu (*ZGR*, VIII, Books 196, 197); *Honchō shinshū ōjōden* by Fujiwara no Munetomo (*ZGR*, Book 199); and *Sange ōjōki* by Renzen (*ZGR*, Book 198).
187. Kōen, *Fusō ryakki* (*SZKT*, XII).
188. Jien, *Gukanshō* (*NKBT*, 86), ed. by Okami Masao and Akamatsu Toshihide. For a partial translation, see J. Rahder, "Miscellany of Personal Views of an Ignorant Fool," *Acta Orientalis*, XV (1936), 173–230; XVI (1937), 59–77.

# CHAPTER II

# World View Reflected

## (1) COSMIC ORDER

### a. *Rites of Cosmic Renewal*

In ancient Japan the religious life of the people frequently found expression in a variety of cyclical rites performed at court, at local shrines, and in private homes. The state cult performed at the court consisted primarily of communal agricultural rites at times of planting and harvest, and prayers for the protection of the crops and the community in spring and summer. On the last day of the sixth and twelfth months, the rite of purification (*Ōharae* 大祓) took place, during which the law prescribed that both native prayers[1] and formulas of Chinese origin should be recited to expiate defilement and insure happiness.[2]

The introduction of Buddhism did not affect the observance of these rites. At first Buddhist rites were performed on behalf of the sick and the dead, while traditional rites continued to be observed at the New Year, at planting and harvest, and in prayers offered for the community. Such a division of function gradually disappeared, and monks were invited to the court to pray for the nation's protection from natural disaster.[3] Buddhism increased its claims by adopting indigenous rites, reinterpreting them, and providing them with a new symbolic meaning. For example, from the time of Śākyamuni the confession of sins had been one of the most important rites in the samgha, and many scriptures taught the merit of confession and repentance.[4] Beginning in the seventh century the rite of repentance (*keka* 悔過) was held in the Japanese court on various occasions.[5] This rite usually took the form of a devotional service which centered on a Buddha or bodhisattva mentioned in a particular scripture. In the eighth century a rite of repentance based on the *Saishōō-kyō* (*Kichijō-*

1. *Norito*, ed. by Takeda Yūkichi (*NKBT*, 1, 422–427). See Philippi, trans., *Norito: A New Translation of the Ancient Ritual Prayers*; E. Satow and K. Florents, "Ancient Japanese Rituals," *TASJ*, reprint, II (December 1927), 5–143.
2. *Ryō no gige*, "Jingi-ryō," Articles 2–9, 18. See Sansom, "Early Japanese Law," Part Two, 123–126.
3. *Shoku Nihongi*, IX (Jinki 2:1:17).
4. See *Sharihotsu keka-kyō* 舍利弗悔過經 (*Taishō*, XXIV, No. 1492) for its full exposition.
5. *Shoku Nihongi*, XXV (Hakuchi 2:12:30, 3:12:30).

*keka* 吉祥悔過)[6] was celebrated at all provincial temples during the first week of the year to pray for the prosperity of the state.[7]

This practice gradually spread, accompanied by the belief that the sins of the outgoing year should be confessed and expiated. It fulfilled the same function as the traditional rite of *Ōharae*, although Buddhism emphasized the internal significance of the ceremony. The *Nihon ryōiki* gives an example of a man who wanted to atone for his sins by holding a ceremony of repentance at the end of the year (I.10). He invited a monk to recite a Mahayana scripture[8] and to officiate at the ritual of repentance. Eventually it was discovered that the deceased father of the man had been born as an ox and had suffered as a consequence of his past karma. Owing to the merit of the man's faith in the Three Treasures[9] and the monk's helpful guidance, the father was released from such a life of suffering. The rite of repentance, which aimed at removing anything that might hinder meditation and the enlightenment of monks in the Indian samgha, became a meritorious act for those who sponsored the ceremony in China or Japan.

Another prominent change was introduced with Buddhism: dread of defilement by the dead was replaced by a sense of veneration for the dead. In contemporary Japan, the visit of the dead to their former homes is popularly celebrated at the *Bon* festival, July 15,[10] but in the *Nihon ryōiki* there are indications of a belief that the dead visited the living on New Year's Eve and that it was customary to make offerings for a ceremonial meal with them at the family altar.

> Dōtō, a Buddhist scholar of Koryö 高麗, was a monk of Gangō-ji. . . . Once, when he was passing through the valley . . . , he saw a skull which had been trampled by men and animals. In sorrow, he had his attendant Maro 萬侶 place it on a tree.

6. Or *Kisshō-keka*; in the *Konkōmyō saishōō-kyō* (VIII, 16, 17; IX, 22) Kichijōten 吉祥天 (Śrīdevī or Lakṣmī), female deity of felicity, promises to bestow wealth and prosperity to the followers of that scripture. Cf. Gerda Hartmann, *Beiträge zur Geschichte der Göttin Lakṣmī*.

7. *Shoku Nihongi*, XVII (Tenpyō shōhō 1:12:18, 25); XXII (Tenpyō hōji 3:6:22); XXVIII (Jingo keiun 1:1:8), etc.

8. *Hōkō-kyō* 方廣經; since the term is used for Mahāyāna scriptures in general it is impossible to determine what particular scripture is meant; possibly the reference is to *Daitsū hōkō sange metsuzai shōgon jōbutsu-kyō* 大通方廣懺悔滅罪莊嚴成佛經 (*Taishō*, LXXXV, No. 2871) forged in China during the Sui dynasty. The forgery attests to the popularity of this rite in China; the rite was transmitted to Japan before 731.

9. See Chap. II(3)b.

10. A shortened form of *Urabon* 盂蘭盆. (In many rural areas it is still celebrated according to the lunar calendar.) For the latest theory on the etymological and historical origin of the cult of *Urabon*, see Iwamoto, *Mokuren densetsu to Urabon*, 225–245. According to Iwamoto, the term *Urabon* comes from *urvan*, which is "soul" in Avestan; it came to denote an agricultural rite in honor of ancestral spirits which was celebrated in the Central Asia, northern India, and China. In China the cult was assimilated into Buddhist and Taoist traditions. For the traditional theory, see Ashikaga Enshō, "Notes on Urabon," *JAOS*, 71 (1951), 71–75.

On the New Years's Eve of the same year, a man came to the temple gate, saying, "I would like to see the Venerable Dōtō's attendant Maro." When Maro came out to see him, he said, "Thanks to the mercy of your master, I have been happy and at peace. And I can repay your kindness only on this evening" [I.12]. There is another version of this story (III.27). These two stories share the motif of "the grateful dead" which is found in folktales elsewhere.[11] The dead man appears in a human form and asks his benefactor to join the ceremonial meal at the end of the year to help rectify evil deeds. New Year's Eve is the time for repentance and the renewing of the cosmic and moral order, and the family altar is prepared for the ceremony. It is a chaotic time when barriers between the dead and the living, present and future, this world and the world of the dead, dissolve.[12]

This renewal of the cosmos may take place not only annually but daily, seasonally, and at the beginning of every era or emperor's reign. For example, there are two stories in which the hungry ghosts[13] or wicked spirits come to devour the living at midnight (I.3; II.33). The notion of cosmic renewal was reflected in the ancient custom of building a new palace and changing the name of the era every time a new emperor was enthroned. The ceremony at the enthronement symbolized cosmic unity and renewal, and is similar in form to the harvest festival; in addition, it emphasizes the emperor's union with the ancestral spirits.[14]

The practice of using era names, which was initiated in 645, was obviously influenced by the Chinese system. During the Asuka and Nara periods covered by the *Nihon ryōiki*, the naming of the era took place so often that in one instance the same year was named twice.[15] We may ascribe this practice to the great influence of Chinese cosmological thought, which was so highly systematized during the Han dynasty. All natural phenomena and human affairs were believed to be governed by two principles, *yin* and *yang*, which complement each other and follow the unchanging law of Heaven. A mysterious cor-

11. According to Stith Thompson's *Motif-Index of Folk-literature*, this type of folktale is indexed E. 341.

12. Cf. Eliade, *Cosmos and History*, 54.

13. *Gaki* 餓鬼 (Skt. *preta*); frustrated spirits wandering among men and hells without means to gratify their desires. See Chap. I(2)a, n. 127.

14. See Orikuchi Shinobu, "Ōmube matsuri no hongi," *Orikuchi Shinobu zenshū*, III, 174–240; Robert Ellwood, "Harvest and Renewal at the Grand Shrine of Ise," *Numen*, XV (No. 3, November 1968), 165–190.

15. The year 749 is the twenty-first year of the Tenpyō era, and the first year of the Tenpyō-kanpō and Tenpyō-shōhō eras.

respondence between nature and man was recognized in all phenomena as a consequence of the interaction of these two forces. Seasonal vicissitudes, a man's life and death, human relationships, and history were all explained in terms of *yin* and *yang*, and any disharmony and abnormality in the human world inevitably stirred Heaven to manifest corresponding abnormal phenomena in the natural world.[16] Such phenomena were known as "visitations" (*tsai* 災) or "prodigies" (*yi* 異)[17] and were interpreted as Heaven's warnings to the ruler, while the appearance of unusual birds and animals or events were considered to be signs of Heaven's sanction and blessing. Accordingly, whenever and wherever such occurences took place, the court was notified and sometimes the unusual animals and birds were presented to the court. On such occasions the emperor might wish to change the name of the era, naming it after felicitous omens such as a white pheasant (Hakuchi 白雉), a vermilion bird (Akamidori 朱鳥), a sacred tortoise (Reiki 靈龜), a divine tortoise (Jinki 神龜), or symbolical phrases or events such as universal peace (Tenpyō 天平), universal peace and excellent treasure (Tenpyō shōhō 天平勝寶), universal peace and precious script (Tenpyō hōji 天平寶字). The emperor's decision to change the name of the era represented the abolishment of the past and the initiation of a new period.

With such a cosmological frame of reference, praying for the dead and praying for the welfare of the nation were not separate actions. In the Asuka and Nara periods political intrigue and murder took place frequently, and people feared that natural disasters and epidemics were caused by the curses of the victims. Those in authority longed to return to a state of primordial unity by destroying the past and renewing life. This unity was realized in the ceremonial meal of the living and dead, in which the moral and cosmic order was renewed and re-established. Since Buddhism had been able to incorporate the ancestral cult and also taught a life after death, it seemed to offer a more comprehensive way to ensure happiness and prosperity. It was only natural that Buddhism should be patronized by emperors and empresses who keenly felt the need for peace and harmony provided by rites of cosmic renewal. Buddhist rites were performed in the traditional pattern and with similar aims.

The persistence of a symbolism of cosmic renewal in the Japanese

16. See Sawada Takio, "Tong chang-shu tenjin sōkansetsu shitan," *Nihon bunka kenkyūsho kiyō*, III (1967), 293–312; reprinted in the *Chūgoku kankei ronsetsu shiryō*, VIII (1967), Part One, 428–438. Ikeda Suetoshi, "*Tendō to tenmei*, Part I," *Hiroshima daigaku bungakubu kiyō*, XXVIII (No. 1, 1968), 24–39; reprinted in *Chūgoku kankei*, X (1968), Part One, 68–75.

17. See Fung Yu-lan, *A History of Chinese Philosophy*, II, 55.

tradition is evidenced by the fact that many of the rites mentioned above have continued to be observed throughout Japan's history. We can trace the rite of repentance and cosmic renewal in the tradition of Mt. Kōya, the headquarters of the Shingon School, which has faithfully preserved many ancient rituals. During the last four days of the year, December 28–31, Shingon Buddhist monks perform the rite of *Gohei hasami*. *Gohei* 御幣 is a Shinto symbol of the presence of kami and also an instrument for purification.[18] While reciting the *Hannya shin-gyō* 般若心經,[19] the monks make *gohei*, which are consecrated and enshrined in the temple until New Year's Eve. At midnight they are carried to the shrine and burned. Their embers are distributed to the congregation to make a new fire on New Year's Day.[20]

Buddhism served to internalize ancient Japanese rituals such as purification rites and ancestor rites. Traditional rituals and symbols persisted because of their significance for human life, although they were given new meanings.[21] Dharma was interpreted by Kyōkai as the universal law in the sense of *tao* 道. He included the way of kami, *yin-yang tao*, and all other ways in dharma itself, for dharma is universal and comprehensive, and there is common ground for them in the idea of cosmic interrelation of all existences. The cosmos can be renewed and restructured according to traditional patterns and rhythms of life, which Buddhism incorporated in its cosmology.

b. *Symbolism of the Visit to the Other World*

In Japanese literature prior to the *Nihon ryōiki*, there are legends in which heroes such as Urashima no ko 浦島子[22] and Tajimamori 田道間守[23] visit the other world beyond the sea. The *Yu-hsien-k'u* 遊仙窟,[24]

18. Also called *mitegura*; it consists of a twig or a stick with some strips of folded paper attached and is often held by a mediator; hence, it serves as an offering to *kami*.

19. *Hannya haramitsu shin-gyō* 般若波羅蜜心經 (*Taishō*, VIII, Nos. 250–255, 257). See Max Müller, trans., *The Larger and Smaller Prajñāpāramitāhṛdayasūtra, Buddhist Mahāyāna Text* (*SBE*, XLIX).

20. J. M. Kitagawa, "Gohei hasami—A Rite of Purification of Time at Mt. Kōya," *Proceedings of the XIth International Congress of IAHR*, II, 173–174.

21. See Eliade, "Methodological Remarks on the Study of Religious Symbolism," *The History of Religions: Essays in Methodology*, 86–107, for a general discussion of the function of symbols.

22. *Nihon shoki*, XIV (Yūryaku 22:7): "Mizunoe no Urashimako of Tsutsukawa, Yoza district, Tanba province, went fishing on a boat. Eventually he caught a big tortoise, which turned into a woman. Thereupon, he felt desire and made love with her. Then they went into sea together and visited the land of immortality (常世國) to see a saint." See Aston, "Nihongi," I, 368. Also see other versions in the *Manyōshū* (*NKBT*, 5, No. 383); *Tango Fudoki, Fudoki* 風土記 (*NKBT*, 2, 470–477).

23. *Nihon shoki*, VI (Suinin 90:2:1); *Kojiki*, II (*NKBT*, 1, 202–203). See Aston, "Nihongi," I, 186; Philippi, *Kojiki*, 226.

24. Chinese novelette ascribed to Chang Chou 張鷟 (?660–732). See *The Dwelling of Playful Goddess*, trans. by Howard S. Levy. For its influence on Japanese literature, see Kojima, *Jōdai Nihon bungaku*, II, 1013–1071; III, 1443–1456.

a Chinese novelette which enjoyed great popularity among educated people during the Nara and Heian periods, is a tale of a visit to the ideal land of immortals in the mountains.[25] The popularity of these tales suggests that the Taoist idea of the eternal land was accepted in Japan at an early date and spread widely from the seventh century.

"The other world" as a creation of popular imagination does not present a uniform image. However, several ideas of the other world found in the *Kojiki*, *Nihon shoki*, and *Fudoki* may be classified as follows: a heavenly land known as Takamagahara 高天原, an underground land known as Yomi no kuni, which is a Japanese reading of the Chinese Huang-ch'üan-kuo or "Land of the Yellow Springs" 黄泉國, and a distant land beyond the sea known as Tokoyo no kuni 常世國. Although these categories are diverse in origin and nature, they are not necessarily exclusive of each other and together they suggest a common symbolic understanding of the other world.[26] For the ancient Japanese, the other world meant the land of the dead or the abode of kami or immortals which lies somewhere above, below, or beyond this world, where the living might visit under certain conditions.

Buddhist ideas of the other world fascinated those who lacked a well-delineated cosmology in China as well as in Japan. Just as the doctrines of karma and samsara were novel and appealing, so, too, were the ideas of paradise and hell, which offered a differentiated view of the other world, and the notion of judgment after death with a judge presiding. In the Indian tradition inherited by Buddhism, five or six levels of existence characterize the cosmos.[27] Although different peoples at different periods of their history had their own particular beliefs, there were also some basic similarities: the hells were located at the bottom; the heavens which housed the deities were on top; men and animals existed in between. One of the earliest Buddhist scriptures presents such a cosmic image:

> The four lands [that is, Jambudvīpa in the south, Pūrvavidehadvīpa in the east, Avaragodānīyadvīpa in the west, and Uttarakurudvīpa in the north] are surrounded by eight thousand lands, which are again enclosed by the great ocean. There is a great mountain, Mt. Diamond, encircled by the waters and again by an outer mountain, a second Mt. Diamond. Between them there

25. According to Stith Thompson's *Motif-Index*, "visit to the other world" is indexed as F. 111.
26. See Matsumura Takeo, *Nihon shinwa no kenkyū*, IV, chap. 5. For a good English summary of various theories on the other world, see C. Ouwehand, *Namazue and their Themes*, 85–96.
27. See Chap. I(2)a, n. 127.

is an abyss so deep that no light of the solar or lunar deities, although effective in the heavens, could penetrate it.[28]
This abyss is hell (naraka).

When this conception of hell was introduced into China, it was transliterated as 奈落迦, or translated as 地獄, ti-yü or underground prison, and often combined with the name of T'ai shan 泰 (太) 山 or Mt. T'ai in early translations.[29] This was a device for presenting a new idea in old clothing to facilitate understanding and acceptance. In many regions of pre-Buddhist China, people venerated mountains as an abode of deities, and emperors and nobles made offerings on the mountains to pray for the prosperity of the land. T'ai shan in Shantung province gained national preeminence as the residence of the lord who was believed to control life and death, and as a gathering place for the spirits of the dead.[30] Taoist and Buddhist ascetics chose mountains for their retreats, seeking a better understanding of the mystery of the universe; they believed that deities, spirits, or Buddhas would appear and help them attain mystical knowledge.[31] Mountains were identified with the other world, including both the land of the dead and the land of immortals. However, before the introduction of Buddhist ideas, hell and paradise were not clearly differentiated.

The Nihon ryōiki does not present a uniform image of the other world. We can recognize a difference between the earlier and later tales: the former are more varied and reflect some pre-Buddhist but not necessarily indigenous ideas, while the latter tend to be stereotyped and patterned on the Buddhist tradition. Fourteen of the one hundred and sixteen stories that share the same motif of a visit to the other world, are distributed as follows:

| Vol. | Tale | Reign | Year |
|------|------|-------|------|
| I. | 5 | Empress Suiko | 593–628 |
| | 30 | Emperor Monmu | 697–707 |
| II. | 5, 7, 16, 19, 25 | Emperor Shōmu | 724–748 |
| III. | 9 | Empress Shōtoku | 764–770 |
| | 22, 23, 26, 37 | Emperor Kōnin | 771–780 |
| | 35, 36 | Emperor Kanmu | 781–796 |

28. Jōagon-gyō 長阿含經, I (Taishō, I, 121bc). Cf. Vasubandhu, Abhidharmakośaśāstra 阿毘達磨倶舍論 (Taishō, XXIX, 57c–58a).
29. See Sawada Mizuho, Jigoku-hen, 43ff., for references to the Rokudo jik-kyō·六度集經 (trans. 251–280), Hokku hiyu-gyō 法句比喩經 (trans. 290–306), Shutchō-gyō 出曜經 (trans. 350–417), etc.
30. Cf. Edouard Chavannes, Le T'ai chan.
31. Cf. Ko Hung 葛洪, Pao-p'u-tzu 抱朴子, XVII. See James R. Ware, trans., Alchemy, Medicine, Religion in the China of A.D. 320, 279.

The first two stories date from the seventh century; the remainder, from the eighth. The earliest one is of a journey to the golden mountain in the Prince Shōtoku legend mentioned above.[32] In the second story the other world lies beyond a river and is called "the land in the southern direction" 圖南國, or "a strange wonder land" (I.30). It owes its origin to the *Chuang-tzu* 莊子, a Taoist classic, in which the Southern Ocean or "the Pool of Heaven" 天池, a Chinese mythological resort of deities, is known as the destination of the flight of the mythical bird, *p'eng* 鵬.[33]

Therefore, we may conclude that early stories give the idea of the other world as a distant land, whether in the mountains or beyond the waters, although hell and Yama, the lord of the dead, are also included in the second story.

The Buddhist tradition combined the southern paradise, Kannon's land, with an oceanic image of the other world. In India it is called Mt. Potalaka (Ch. Po-t'o-lo shan; Jap. Fudarakusan 補陀落山), a legendary mountain on the southern coast of India or an island in the southern ocean, where Avalokiteśvara resides and protects navigators.[34] Although the *Nihon ryōiki* does not refer to this land, which became a focus for devotion during the Heian period, the second story discussed above shows a possible link with such a development. The ancient Japanese idea of the other world beyond the sea is filled with Taoist and Buddhist images and symbols.

In the later stories in which hell is a major feature of the other world, the image of a distant land is stronger than that of an underground land. Water often separates the land of the living from that of the dead. One can reach the other world only by crossing a bridge (I.30) or fording a river, guided by messengers from the lord of the dead.[35]

> Ahead of us there was a deep river; the water being as black as ink, did not run but stood still. A good-sized young branch was placed in the middle of the stream, but it was not long enough to reach both sides of the river. The messenger said to me, "Follow me into the stream and ford it by following in my footsteps." Thus he guided me across [III.9].

32. See Chap. I(2)c.

33. *Chuang-tzu*, I(1)l. See James Legge, trans., *The Text of Taoism* (SBE, XXXIX, 164).

34. This belief originated with the chapter on Kannon of the *Hoke-kyō* (*Myōhōrenge-kyō*, XXV) (*Taishō*, IX, 56c); Kern, trans., *Saddharma* (XXIV, 406–407); Katō, trans., *Myōhōrenge-kyō* (XXV, 404); and *Kegon-gyō* (*Taishō*, X, 366c).

35. These stories suggest a possible relation to the symbols in the Iranian tradition, that is, Cinvat Bridge, Bridge of Requiter, which leads to heaven or hell, and which the dead have to cross. However, in the *Nihon ryōiki* the other world is not differentiated into two parts. See R. C. Zaehner, *The Dawn and Twilight of Zoroastrianism*, 302–308.

This crossing may symbolize a rite of passage from one world to the other. Purification by ablution was known to the Japanese from early times. A good illustration is found in the story of the primordial kami couple: Izanagi 伊邪那伎 followed his deceased consort Izanami 伊邪那美 to Yomi no kuni, the dark land of defilement; on his return from the land of the dead, he purified himself in the river and gave birth to several kami, including Amaterasu Ōmikami.[36] The river of death became the river of life.

Izanagi, as we see, could freely visit the other world, although there were certain prohibitions and rites to which he had to subscribe. Similarly, one story of the *Nihon ryōiki* tells of a prohibition against eating food cooked in the land of the dead, violation of which prevents one's return to the world of the living (II.7).[37] After the age of kami, only folk heroes, ascetics, or shamans, who practiced austerities, could attain such power, which is symbolized by a jewel or treasure obtained through a visit to the other world.[38] They came back to the world to help people by means of the power which they had gained.[39] Various experiences through which one discovered the mystery of the world were symbolically expressed as visits to the other worlds, whereby the hero might encounter the divine, the Buddha, or spirits.

A similar form is found in stories which tell how a bodhisattva, instead of entering nirvana, returns to this world to work for the universal salvation of all sentient beings. Mahayana Buddhism shifted the the emphasis from the goal of personal liberation to the process of bringing liberation for all. The bodhisattva ideal, expressed in such a form, was actualized by Buddhist monks and ascetics, who entered the mountains in pursuit of mystical experiences and then returned to their villages and temples to guide their fellow beings. In other words, the traditional cosmology provided a frame of reference for the bodhisattva ideal which had been actualized in the traditional practice of entering the mountains for retreats.

The *Hoke-kyō* gives a scriptural basis for such practices carried out in remote areas and in the mountains. The following is from Maitreya's discourse with Mañjuśrī, explaining Buddha's miraculous signs:

36. Kojiki, I (*NKBT*, I, 68–73). See Philippi, trans., *Kojiki*, 61–70.

37. For a detailed analysis, see Matsumura, *Nihon shinwa*, II, 427–439.

38. Skt. *maṇi*, which has the power to protect man from disaster and misfortune; Buddhist tradition says that Śākyamuni's relics were transformed into jewels. In China jade corresponds to *maṇi*. (See Berthold Laufer, *Jade*.) Jade symbolizes sovereign power, immortality, cosmic deities, etc.

39. See Maeda Egaku, "Ryokō no tochū tasekai ni sōgū suru monogatari kō," *IBK*, VI (No. 1, January 1958), 196–200; expanded in "Indo Bukkyō ni arawareta tasekai hōmontan no seikaku," *Bungaku ni okeru higan hyōshō no kenkyū*, ed. by Ueda Yoshifumi and others.

"I see also many monks in the mountains and woods leading rigorous lives as if they are protecting a bright jewel."[40] The *Nihon ryōiki* contains two stories of monks who entered the mountains, recited the *Hoke-kyō* and eventually died there. The fact that even after death their tongues never ceased the recitation suggests the significance of this scripture for such ascetic monks and lay brothers (III.1).[41]

Throughout Japan there are mountains which have become centers for such religious activities. In Kinai, the central region of Japan in its early history, the Yoshino 吉野 area was a great center for ascetic practices, and Mt. Golden Peak, Kane no take 金峯, was particularly well known (I.28, 31; II.26; III.1, 6). The legend of E no Ozunu says that he disciplined himself in this region and, as a result, gained control of the local spirits and deities. He was later involved in a power struggle with Hitokotonushi no Kami of Mt. Kazuraki 葛城 (木).[42] After he was exiled as a result of Hitokotonushi no Kami's complaints about him to the emperor, he went to Mt. Fuji 富岷 (土) to practice austerities (I.28). This legend suggests that the practice of austerities in the mountains was known at an early date, and the following story is another example:

> In Kamino district in Iyo province there was a mountain called Iwazuchi-yama 石槌山. The name was derived from that of the Kami of Iwazuchi who lived on the mountain. It was so high that ordinary persons could not reach the summit. Only men pure in mind and deed could climb up and live there [III.39].

Buddhist ascetics climbed the mountains to make their retreats, and the kami of the mountains were believed to help them. Only special persons could carry out austerities and receive the blessing of the kami.

Encounters between men and the Buddha, local spirits, or other manifestations of divinity in the mountains is a recurrent theme in many religious traditions. As we have seen, Emperor Yūryaku met Hitokotonushi no Kami in the mountains and received a blessing in exchange for his offerings. However, the same kami was bound by E no Ozunu's spell. The legend of Mañjuśrī's descent on Mt. Wu-t'ai played an important role in legitimizing Buddhism in Tibet, China, Korea, and Japan. In these countries, legends were ascribed to some members of the royal family, identifying them as incarnations of bodhisattvas. In each tradition people looked for a mountain in their

40. *Myōhōrenge-kyō*, I (*Taishō*, IX, 4c). 或有諸比丘在於山林中精神持戒猶護明珠.

41. The possible prototype of these stories is the biography of Kumārajīva in the *Kao-seng chuan*, II (*Taishō*, L. 333a), by Hui-ch'iao. When he died and was cremated, only his tongue remained unburned. 即於逍遙園依外國法以火焚屍薪滅形碎唯舌不灰.

42. See Chap. I(1)d, n. 119.

own land to claim as the center of the cosmos, or the point where the sacred jutted into the world of men.

The *Nihon ryōiki* mentions several mountains famous as retreats for ascetics and suggests that they became centers for religious practices in their particular localities: for example, Mts. Yoshino and Kumano in Kinai 畿内; Mt. Iwazuchi in Shikoku 四國; and Mt. Fuji in Kantō 關東. Each mountain was the symbolic center of the cosmos for those who accepted it as the place where revelations might take place.

> *There*, in *that* place, the hierophany repeats itself. In this way the place becomes an inexhaustible source of power and sacredness and enables man, simply by entering it, to have a share in the power, to hold communion with the sacredness.[43]

In the Heian period many pilgrims and ascetics were attracted to Mt. Yoshino. Originally it was believed to be the prospective site for Maitreya's descent at the end of the world, and later to be the site for the appearnace of Amida and Kannon. There is a list of Buddhist monks who entered the sea and were drowned in their attempt to cross over to Kannon's pure land from the foot of Mt. Nachi 那智山 at Kumano, which was identified as the gate to that pure land.[44]

The Prince Shōtoku legend is a good illustration of the fusion of Taoist and Buddhist symbols. He stands on the peak of the golden mountain and is given a jewel by a monk, Mañjuśrī's incarnation. In ancient China, jade and gold were prominent symbols of power and immortality. The symbolic structure remains unchanged, although the jade may now take the form of a bead in a Buddhist rosary and immortality be interpreted to mean rebirth as a bodhisattva who will save all sentient beings.

The Buddhist cosmology had a great influence on the vague, undifferentiated world view of the Japanese, although new symbols tended to be accepted in the traditional frame of reference. In Japan the fantastic scale of the Hindu–Buddhist cosmos was restricted frequently to the physical boundaries of the Japanese islands. As cosmology is the fundamental and essential ground for Buddhist doctrines in Mahayana Buddhism, these cosmic symbols played a crucial role in the understanding of Buddhism in Japan.

## c. *Paradise and Hell*

For the Chinese and the Japanese, the most novel ideas in the Buddhist cosmology were those of paradise and hell and of judgment

43. Eliade, *Patterns in Comparative Religion*, 368.
44. Hori, *Wagakuni minkan shinkōshi no kenkyū*, II, 231–236.

after death.[45] In the *Nihon ryōiki* a prominent feature of the other world is the golden pavilion which stands at its entrance. This is the palace of King Yama (I.30), where men of good karma are welcomed (II.7, 16). Yama is a deity in early Vedic literature and the first dead person to rule the land of the dead.[46] As life and death meet in him and his palace, he has become a symbol of the beginning and the end of life. In these tales of visits to the other world, King Yama appears to inform the dead person which of the five or six paths of destiny he is to take, depending on the records of the dead person's past karma.[47]

Judgment after death is postulated in many religious traditions. For the Hindu-Buddhist tradition it has the following significance: Yama could never exist apart from karmic retribution, and the sentence given by him is not of his own making. He is not a judge in the common legal sense but simply an administrator of the law of causation.

As one story of the *Nihon ryōiki* depicts him, Yama himself is one of these sentient beings who aspire to enlightenment through faith in the Three Treasures. Yama is said to have sent for a devout lay sister who was famous for reciting the *Hannya shin-gyō*.

> Seeing her, the king stood up, made a seat, and spread a mat [for her], saying, "I have heard that you are very good at reciting the *Shin-gyō*. I am longing to hear you, and this is why I have invited you here for a short visit. Will you please recite the scripture? I am listening" [II.19].

Delighted with her recitation, he paid his respects and sent her back to the world. This aspiration of Yama finds a parallel in the story of the Great Kami of Taga, who longed to hear the dharma. Although he was the enshrined guardian of a particular locality, he was also a sentient being seeking his own enlightenment (III.24).[48] This is not a peculiarly Japanese interpretation since we find the following passage in an early Buddhist scripture:

> Once upon a time, monks, it occurred to King Yama: "Those that do evil deeds in the world are subjected to a variety of punishments like these. O that I might acquire human status and that a Tathāgata might arise in the world, a perfected one, a fully Self-Awakened One, and that I might wait on that Lord, and that

45. See S.G.F. Brandon, *The Judgement of the Dead: A Historical and Comparative Study*, for a global treatment of this subject.

46. See Alex Wayman, "Studies in Yama and Māra," *Indo-Iranian Journal*, III (No. 1, 1959), 44–73, for a diverse image of Yama presented in his various titles.

47. See Chap. I(2)a.

48. See Alicia Matsunaga, *The Buddhist Philosophy of Assimilation*, for a general discussion of such phenomena.

that Lord might teach me *dhamma*, and that I might understand that Lord's *dhamma.*"[49]

It was necessary for Yama or this kami to be born as a human being to work for enlightenment.

The Buddhist tradition says that a man's activity is composed of three aspects, that is, the physical, the verbal, and the mental. Scriptures emphasize that the mind is the basis for all deeds: "All that we are is the result of what we have thought; it is founded on our thoughts, and it is made up of our thought."[50] Kyōkai quotes the following line of the *Nehan-gyō* to the same effect: "All evil deeds originate in wicked minds" (I.29).[51] A passage from the *Daijōbu-ron* 大丈夫論 further expounds the same teaching: "If you offer alms with compassion, the merit will be as great as the earth; but if you offer alms to everyone and it is for your own sake, the reward will be as tiny as a mustard seed" (I.29).[52] There is a constant admonition against good works becoming a mere formality.

A story, probably written as an exposition of a passage of the *Hoke-kyō*, tells how an ignorant man suffered violent death because he deliberately broke a statue made by a child while playing. The pure devotion of the child stands in contrast to the wicked man's intentional violation of dharma (III.29).[53] Faith in the Three Treasures is essential for leading a good life, while particular forms of its expression are subordinate. In the *Nihon ryōiki* the notion that a good life is equal to a long, happy, healthy life, is held by both clergy and laity. Those who had visited the other world lived past the age of ninety (I.5; II.5); eminent monks of virtue lived past the age of seventy or eighty (I.7, 22; II.7; III.30); devout women lived long lives (II.2, 8, 34). Those who confessed their past deeds and accumulated merits were healed of their diseases (I.8; III.11, 12, 34).

On the other hand, people suffer in hell or in the form of an animal because of their evil deeds. Such offenses were those against the

---

49. *Majjhimanikāya*, 130:186; I. B. Horner, trans., *The Middle Length Sayings*, III, 229–230.
50. *Dhammapada*, I (*SBE*, X, 3).
51. *Daihatsu nehan-gyō*, XXXV, 12 (*Taishō*, 573c).
52. *Daijōbu-ron* (*Taishō*, XXX, 257b).
53. *Myōhōrenge-kyō*, II (*Taishō*, IX, 8c–9a). See Katō, trans., *Myōhō-renge-kyō*, 57.
 Even boys, in their play,
 Who, either with reed, wood or pen,
 Or with finger-nail,
 Have drawn buddhas' images,
 All such ones as these,
 Gradually accumulating merit,
 And perfecting hearts of great pity,
 Have all attained the Buddha-way; . . .

Buddha, dharma, and samgha, and killing, which included not only matricide (I.23, 24; II.3) and patricide (III.4), but the killing of animals (I.16; II.40) and the taking of birds' eggs (II.10). The persecutors of monks and usurpers of the samgha properties are pictured as being most severely punished, which may reflect the longings of monks who lived in the decadent age of dharma.

In spite of some preoccupation with man's rebirth in the realm of hell and in the form of animals, the world view of the *Nihon ryōiki* reflects the optimistic attitude of the ancient Japanese. There is little indication of an existential sense of crisis, but rather lamentation for the decadence of the times. The idea of a sinful self is absent, and, instead, emphasis is placed on efforts to improve. The idea of a pure land was still novel and lacked popular appeal; only eminent monks such as Dōshō (I.22), Shingon (II.2), and Kanki (III.30) are known to have been born in such a land. On the other hand, in the *Ōjōden* series compiled between the tenth and the twelfth centuries, there are biographies of those from all social strata—high and low, clerical and lay—who attained rebirth in the pure land.[54]

Hell in Buddhist tradition has something of the quality of purgatory and is not a place of eternal damnation since Buddha-nature inheres in all living beings. In order to pursue the bodhisattva ideal, rebirth as a human being was preferred to rebirth in the pure land or heavens. Jizō 地藏, the Bodhisattva Ksitigarbha, out of his compassion for those who suffer, descends to hell to save them. A story, dated in 768, of Fujiwara no asomi Hirotari 藤原朝臣廣足 identifies Jizō with Yama, a tradition which probably originated with the *Daihōkō jūrin-gyō* 大方廣十輪經.[55] Although Jizō was known in Japan as early as the eighth century, the cult centering on him did not become popular until the late Heian period.[56] With the advent of eschatological ideas, he came to be looked upon as a savior who had vowed not to seek his own salvation until all sentient beings had been saved from the world of samsara.

If the autonomy of the law of karmic retribution is emphasized, there is little need for the intervention of a judge or savior. Since the *Nihon ryōiki* represents various stages of transition, it includes con-

54. See Chap. I(2)d, n. 186.
55. *Taishō*, XIII, No. 410. Translated for the first time in the period 397–439. The new translation done by Hsüan-tsang in 651 is *Daijō daijū Jizō jūrin-gyō* 大乘大集地藏十輪經 (*Ibid.*, No. 411, 684c–685a). 是地藏菩薩作沙門像 現神通力之所變化 或作閻羅王身 或作地獄卒身 或作地獄身.
56. See Takase Shigeo, *Kodai sangaku shinkō no shiteki kōsatsu*, 364–368; Manabe Kōsai, *Jizō-bosatsu no kenkyū*, 16–17.

flicting views. For instance, stories dated in 773 and 774 discuss the three paths: the first path is flat and wide; the second is covered with weeds; the third is narrow and hard to pass through because of thick bushes (III.22, 23). Each seems to lead to hell, and Yama tells the dead person which path to follow based on his past karma. The wide and flat path is reserved for devotees of the *Hoke-kyō* or those who have accumulated merits. The narrow and hard path is for the most wicked. However, in the Buddhist scriptures these three paths are interpreted as leading to rebirth in hell, as an animal or as a hungry ghost. In contrast, the stories in the *Nihon ryōiki* do not provide such an exegesis. "The three paths" was a universally popular motif, which was probably adapted to Buddhist tradition. In hero tales a man who chooses the hardest path will be victorious,[57] but in the Buddhist tradition the order of the paths has been reversed as a consequence of the law of karma. In other words, a doer of good deeds will pass along an easy path, while a doer of evil deeds will travel painfully along a difficult one. There is a striking resemblance with the Zoroastrian image of the paths to the nether world.

> (79) And when the soul of the saved passes over that bridge, the breadth of the bridge appears to be one parasang broad. (80) And the soul of the saved passes on accompanied by the blessed Srōsh. (81) And his own good deeds come to meet him in the form of a young girl, . . .[58]

This is the "Bridge of the Requiter" which every man must cross for three days and nights.

In contrast to the well-delineated Iranian or Chinese versions of the other world, the Japanese version in the *Nihon ryōiki* is vague, fragmented, and inconsistent. The Chinese tradition established a bureaucratic system in hell, while the Japanese tradition located hell in a volcano, emphasizing concrete visual imagery.[59] The other world remained essentially homogeneous with this world in spite of its mythical aspects. Another example of this vagueness is found in the notion of time. Indian cosmological thought is full of astronomical units of time duration and numbers. One day and night in hell is said to correspond to a hundred years (III.35); and one day in paradise, to a single year in this world (I.5). Only the Maeda manuscript specifies a "hundred days" in place of the "hundred years" of the other manu-

---

57. See G. Dumézil, "The Three Last Voyages of Il'Ja of Murom," *Myths and Symbols: Studies in Honor of Mircea Eliade*, ed. by Kitagawa and Long, 153–162, for a general discussion of this motif. It is indexed as N. 122 in Stith Thompson, *Motif Index*.

58. *Mēnōk i Khrat*, trans. and quoted by Zaehner, in *The Teachings of the Magi*, 133–134.

59. Cf. Takase, *Kodai sangaku shinkō*.

scripts, and there is an obvious tendency for this manuscript to mini-
mize the use of such astronomical units (III.35).[60] We may conclude
that the Japanese popular imagination incorporated foreign ideas to
agree with traditional ones. Although novel ideas had considerable
appeal, they were not determinative, and the center of attention remained in the life of this world.

In the *Nihon ryōiki*, however, there is an interpretation of the other
world that transcends time and space. One such instance is the story
about a wicked man who used to eat birds' eggs. One day a messenger
from Yama came to lead him into hell. Villagers saw the man running
around in the field as if he were crazy until eventually he died from
burns. Kyōkai's note says: "Now we are sure of the existence of hell
in this world. We should believe in the law of karmic retribution"
(II.10). The passage gives a popular understanding of hell as a mode
of existence. Although Kyōkai quotes from the *Zen'aku inga-kyō*
"The one who roasts and boils chickens in this life will fall into the
Hell of the River of Ashes after death,"[61] he insists on the idea of
"hell here and now." Hell exists in this world in this life and not in
the other world after death. This interpretation is parallel to the
popular understanding that Buddhahood was attainable in the life of
this world. Accordingly, the world view of the *Nihon ryōiki* is said to
be "this-world centered," and stands in sharp contrast to that of a
later period when men longed for rebirth in the pure land because of
their conviction that they were living in the degenerate age of dharma.

(2) MAN AND POWER

a. *What Makes Man Human*

In the Buddhist world view not only human beings but all living
beings are destined to die and to suffer as a result of their desires. Each
being forms a psychic entity intricately connected with all other
beings. As shown by Kyōkai, the doctrines of karma and samsara are
understood in the following way: "Beasts in the present life might
have been our parents in a past life" (I.21). Therefore, every act,
whether good or bad, will leave its effect on the community of all
beings as well as on the actor. For this reason many Buddhist treatises
have the same ending as the three prefaces in the *Nihon ryōiki*.

60. See Koizumi Michi, "*Ryōiki no shohon o megutte*," *Kuntengo to kunten shiryō*, No. 34
(December 1966), 18–38. Another case is found in the size of Kṣitigarbha's finger (III.9).
Although the other manuscripts have "about ten yards around," the Maeda manuscript specifies
"about five feet around."
61. *Zen'aku inga-kyō* (*Taishō*, LXXXV, 1381).

The deep significance of the three karmas as taught by Buddha,
I have thus completed elucidating in accord with the Dharma
and logic:
By dint of this merit I pray to deliver all sentient beings
And to make them soon attain perfect enlightenment.[62]

This passage expresses the author's sincere wish to offer his merit for the deliverance of his fellow beings. "Merit" (Skt. *puṇya*) is the motive force toward enlightenment, but the realization of interdependent relationships among all existences is a positive restraint against the accumulation of merit for oneself alone.

Kyōkai reveals his view of man in a section of his autobiographical material (III.38). Although man is driven by desire, he also possesses potential for enlightenment. Kyōkai believed that some people totally lacked such potential, for in interpreting his first dream, he says: "'He does not have any ways to support them' means that those who lack potential are not oriented for enlightenment" (III.38). In the note to a story on a wicked robber who broke a Buddhist statue, he quotes from the *Nehan-gyō*, and adds his comment:

"Those of the *ichisendai* 一闡提 shall perish forever. If you kill even an ant, you will be accused of the sin of killing; you will not, however, be accused of the sin of killing if you kill the *ichisendai*." (Because the *ichisendai* slanders the Three Treasures, fails to preach to all beings, and lacks a sense of gratitude, killing him is not a sin.) [II.22].

*Ichisendai* is a transliteration of a Sanskrit term *icchantika*, which is translated as "culmination of desires" 極欲, "one lacking faith" 信不具足, "one lacking good stock" 斷善根. It designates a man who is driven continuously by his desires and lacks any potential for enlightenment,[63] who commits sins and never repents.

*Ichisendai* was a controversial concept in both Chinese and Japanese Buddhism, for it conflicts with the idea of universal Buddha-nature expounded in the same *Nehan-gyō*.[64] Since the goal of Buddhists is

62. Vasubandhu, *Karmasiddhiprakaraṇa*, trans. and quoted by D. T. Suzuki, *Outlines of Mahāyāna Buddhism*, 194. See Yamaguchi Susumu, *Seshin no Jōgō-ron*, 254–256.

63. Skt. *gotra* translated as *shushō* (*shujō*) 種性 (姓): potential for enlightenment which leads men to any of the three *yāna*. Buddhist schools differ on the concept of *gotra*; some consider it a priori 本性住種性, while the others a posteriori 習所成種性. See Tokiwa Daijō, *Busshō no kenkyū*, for the whole doctrinal development of the Buddha-nature in human beings.

64. See Mizutani Kōshō, "Ichisendai kō," *Bukkyō daigaku kenkyū kiyō*, XL (December 1961), 63–107.

enlightenment, the doctrine of Buddha-nature or *Tathāgatagarbha* is fundamental. The *Hoke-kyō* and *Nehan-gyō*, which influenced Kyōkai more than any other scriptures, are known for the doctrine that Buddha-nature exists in all sentient beings, while both denounce those who slander Mahayana teachings. However, Kyōkai never stressed the central message of the *Nehan-gyō*, that all sentient beings have Buddha-nature; instead, he repeatedly warned against those who committed offenses against the Three Treasures, such as persecutors of monks, usurpers of temple properties, and slanderers of dharma. Kyōkai explicitly says that a man who commits such acts is inferior to an ant. He also says:

> Without compassion man is just like a crow. The *Nehan-gyō* says: "Though there is a distinction in respectability between man and animal, they share the fact that they cherish life and take death seriously." [II.10][65]

Man shares a common destiny of mortality with other living beings, and knowledge of mortality makes him cherish both his own life and that of others. However, he differs from them in that he is able to attain enlightenment. Buddhists often say that it is difficult to obtain birth as a human being and hear dharma.[66] This statement can be understood only in the context of the Buddhist cosmology which presupposes an infinite expanse of time and various modes of existence. If a man fails to make good use of this rare opportunity with gratitude, he is no better than an animal.

Kyōkai expounds this further in a group of tales on the theme of repaying kindness, in which animals and ghosts, having been saved, rescue their benefactors (I.7, 12; II.5, 8, 12, 16; III.27). His note says: "Even an animal does not forget gratitude, and repays an act of kindness. How, then, could a righteous man fail to have a sense of gratitude? (I.7) The passage echoes a story about a wild fox in which Śākyamuni says that even a wild fox knows gratitude and pays back an act of kindness; how much more, then, should a man feel grateful for having been born as a man and been given an opportunity to hear the preaching of the dharma. In the Buddhist cosmology the notion of *on* 恩 based on the realization that there is interdependent relationship among all living beings. *On* became a central principle for guiding

---

65. *Daihatsu nehan-gyō* (*Taishō*, XII, 484b). 雖復人畜 尊卑差別 寶命畏死 二俱無異.

66. See *Dhammapada*, 182: "Difficult (to obtain) is the conception of men, difficult is the life of mortals, difficult is the hearing of the true Law, difficult is the birth of the Awakened (the attainment of Buddhahood)." Translated by Max Müller (*SBE*, X, 50).

67. *Zōagon-gyō* 雜阿含經, XLVII (*Taishō*, II, No. 99, 346ab).

conduct in a hierarchical society.[68] The concept of the four kinds of *on* (*shion* 四恩) originated about the sixth century; the *Shōbō nenjo-kyō* 正法念處經 identifies them as indebtedness to mother, father, Tath-āgata (Ja. Nyorai),[69] and monks, while the *Shinji kan-gyō* 心地觀經 gives another list, namely, indebtedness to parents, all fellow beings, king, and the Three Treasures.[70] In China, Confucian ethical teaching was combined with the Buddhist notion of *on* (Ch. *en*), and under-stood as the path of bodhisattvas.[71]

The motif of "the grateful dead" is universal (I.12; III.27), and that of animals, fish, and other creatures repaying indebtedness often occurs in Buddhist scriptures.[72] The *Nihon ryōiki* contains tales of "the grateful crabs (II.8, 12), a tortoise (I.7), fish (II.5), and oysters (II.16)." The tales on crabs became the prototype of the Kaniman-ji 蟹滿寺 cycle, legends concerning the foundation of temples or the origin of local names,[73] and gave rise to many versions of folktales about the crab. On the other hand, a crow is used as a symbol of evil, as we have seen in Kyōkai's note quoted above (II.10), and in the story of Shingon (II.2). The popular belief in the crow as an unlucky bird may go back to the earliest period of history.

Śākyamuni taught that misery arises from desire and attachment and concluded that their eradication would lead to enlightenment. Thus, the mind is the focus of discipline in the Buddhist tradition, and enlightenment means a state free from any desire. The Chinese and Japanese interpreted this as an affirmation of life, the goal of which is an orderly restructuring of desire rather than an attempt at its total annihilation. Desire is not only the cause of misery, but also the cause for positive action. Therefore, lay life is valued as much as monastic life in Japan, and the *Nihon ryōiki* tales illustrate this wide humanism.

Kyōkai's positive attitude is evident in the way he deals with stories about human passion. He quotes a scriptural passage in the story of a

68. For *on* in the later social context in Japan, see Robert N. Bellah, *Tokugawa Religion*, 20–21, 70–73, 77–78, and elsewhere, and Ruth Benedict, *The Chrysanthemum and the Sword*, 99–116, although these authors ignored the Buddhist cosmological significance and limited *on* to the social ethical context.

69. *Shōbō nenjo-kyō*, LXI (*Taishō*, XVII, No. 721, 359b). 有四種恩甚其難報何等爲四 一者母二者父三者如來 四者說法法師若有供養此四種人得無量福.

70. *Daijō honjō shinji kan-gyō* 大乘本生心地觀經, II (*Taishō*, III, No. 159, 297a). 出世恩有其四種 一父母恩二衆生恩三國王恩四三寶恩如是四恩.

71. See Mibu Taishun, "On the Thought 'kṛtajña' or '知恩' in Buddhism," *IBK*, XIV (No. 2, March 1966), 951–961; Sasaki Kentoku, "Bukkyō no onshisō o kiwamete Jōdomon no soreni oyobu," *Umehara Kangaku koki kinen ronbunshū*, 19–47.

72. The *Shokyō yōshū* which influenced Kyōkai contains one chapter on repaying kindness (*Taishō*, LIV, 67c–70c). See Chap. I(2)c, n. 154.

73. See Kurosawa Kōzō, "Kaniman-ji engi no genryū to sono seiritsu," *Kokugo to kokubun-gaku*, No. 535 (September 1968), 14–24.

scripture copier who, driven by lust, had intercourse with a girl while he was at work in a temple and was punished by death. "If you know what the five kinds of desire are, you will not find any pleasure in them. Nor will you remain a slave to them . . . even momentarily"[74] (III.18). Kyōkai does not necessarily negate desire per se; he negates the desire that drives man to oppose the Three Treasures. In other words, he is against any desire which prevents man from accepting dharma. One story tells of a lay brother who lusted after the statue of a female deity[75] until the deity responded to him because of his single-mindedness (II.13). Kyōkai does not condemn him for his lust, but simply remarks, "Indeed we know that profound faith never fails in gaining a response." He does reject another kind of lust, however. A wicked husband violated his wife while she was observing a period of strict discipline for a day and night, and he was punished by death as a consequence of his wicked lust (II.11). In another story a licentious woman who had affairs with many men and deserted her children died suffering from swollen breasts, but after death she asked her children to forgive her (III.16). These acts are called wicked by the author, and those who committed such acts are all punished by death. These offenses are religious rather than moralistic since the fundamental cause lies in the ignorance of dharma.

It is clear that the *Nehan-gyō* influenced Kyōkai's view of man. In spite of his denunciation of *ichisendai*, Kyōkai basically agreed with Saichō in not recognizing any distinction between clergy and laity.[76] In an attempt to unify the conflicting doctrines, the *Nehan-gyō* says that if the *ichisendai* confesses his sin, he will attain the way of Buddha.[77] What makes possible this fundamental change is faith in dharma, which is a turning of the heart to the Three Treasures. More than half of the legends in the *Nihon ryōiki* are about poor helpless people who were saved by Buddha in answer to their single-hearted faith. Even men driven by desire are accepted by Buddha for their great devotion. Notes by the author which explicitly stress the significance of faith are found in twelve stories: one from the first volume (I.17), four from the second (II.6, 13, 15, 28), and seven from the third (III.3, 7, 8, 11, 12, 25, 34). Since the *Nihon ryōiki* is arranged chronologically, this distribution shows that profound faith and utmost devotion (至心) were increasingly emphasized. Katayose says that "utmost

74. *Daihatsu nehan-gyō*, XXII (*Taishō*, XII, 496); *Bonmō-kyō koshakki* (*Taishō*, XL, 705).
75. Kichijō-ten; see Chap. II(1)a, n. 6.
76. Saichō, "Kenkai-ron," *Dengyō Daishi zenshū*, I, 112. See Nakao Toshihiro, "Dengyō Daishi Saichō no ningenkan," *Bukkyō no ningenkan*, ed. by Nihon Bukkyō gakkai, 188–203.
77. *Daihatsu nehan-gyō* (*Taishō*, XII, 425c–426a).

devotion" is a central theme in the Buddhist legends of the *Konjaku monogatarishū*, compiled in the twelfth century, and that it is the forerunner of the rise of the pure land faith which swept Japan during the Kamakura period (1192–1333).[78] As we have seen, however, the *Nihon ryōiki* has already insisted that faith is the basis for salvation, which is available to all beings.

A story is told of two ignorant fishermen who, on a stormy night, were told to collect driftwood by their master. While doing so, they drifted out of port on their broken raft. After repeatedly crying out: "Śākyamuni Buddha, please deliver us from this calamity!" they were eventually saved by the Buddha's compassion, repented of their past occupation, and became monks. The author comments as follows:

> The sea being full of danger, it was owing to the power of Shaka-nyorai and the deep faith of those who drifted on the sea that they could survive the peril [III.25].

This story illustrates a typical pattern of conversion in the *Nihon ryōiki*: men come to repent of their past karma in their experience of peril, illness, misery, or rescue, and thereafter they become devout followers of Buddha. As soon as faith arises in their hearts, they are saved. Repentance of past karma leads to the confession of sins in the present as well as to the making of a vow for the future. The seeds of faith are sown in man, but because of ignorance some men fail to discover and cultivate them.

Kyōkai's view of man is also substantiated in the way he treats people of noble birth. As we have seen, he accepted the traditions of the court histories, such as the *Nihon shoki* and *Shoku Nihongi*, but he tried to interpret history from the Buddhist view of the law of karmic causality. A high status at birth indicated, for him, merit accumulated in previous lives. There is a story of two virtuous monks who were born as princes as a consequence of their past karma (III.39). This does not mean that highborn men were infallible or free from evil; rather, there were emperors and princes who erred because they were too proud, inconsiderate, or passionate. For instance, Prince Nagaya 長屋王 perished because he insulted some monks (II.1); Prince Uji 宇遅王 was punished by death because he persecuted a Buddhist mendicant (II.35); Empress Jitō was admonished by her loyal minister for being inconsiderate of her subjects (I.25). Above all, Kyōkai describes the love affair between Empress Shōtoku (Kōken) and the Buddhist monk Dōkyō more frankly than any court chronicle ever dared to do (III.38). Kyōkai does not state his opinion directly, but records the popular

78. Katayose, *Konjaku monogatarishū-ron*, Part I, Chap. 2.

satirical songs about the empress and the monk that were sung on the streets at that time. Although the empress was noted in other writings as a great patron of Buddhism, this fact is never mentioned in the *Nihon ryōiki*, and little restraint is shown in describing the sexual indiscretion of the empress. It is important to remember that Kyōkai compiled the *Nihon ryōiki* in the early Heian period when the government was trying to break its close ties with Buddhist institutions in Nara, for which the empress was partially responsible. However, this realism may also be the natural outcome of the Buddhist emphasis upon seeing the world as it really is.

In Indian history, the Brahmans held the highest place in the caste structure, and the ruler had to seek their sanction and support. The idea of *cakravartin* (*tenrin jōō* 轉輪聖王), a universal king who turns the wheel of the land, developed among the Buddhists as a result of the universality of their teachings.[79] The *cakravartin* is an ideal king who protects all sentient beings by ruling the world on the sole basis of the dharma as revealed by Śākyamuni. Early Buddhist scriptures present him as the best of all men; later ones mythologize and emphasize his superhuman character. This idea of *cakravartin* was readily accepted outside of India, where rulers were viewed as cosmic figures or mediators between the divine and human realms. Since Buddhism was introduced to those lands mainly on the initiative of the rulers, they were receptive to the idea of *cakravartin* and identified themselves with the ideal universal king.

In Japanese history, actual political power has customarily been exercised by influential court nobles and later by a growing warrior class, rather than by the emperor. The Japanese emperor traditionally was more a symbol of the unity of the people than an active political ruler. The Confucian image of the sage emperor and probably the Buddhist idea of *cakravartin* were adopted when the court started compiling the earliest histories, and this gave Kyōkai an impressive precedent. In his preface he looks back at Japanese history and says:

> There are many examples of piety in the imperial line. For instance, it is said that there was an emperor who climbed a hill to survey his domain, had compassion for the people, and thereafter contented himself with a palace that had a leaky roof. Again, there was a prince who was innately prudent and foresighted, able to listen to ten men addressing him at the same time without

79. See Fujita Kōtatsu, "Tenrin jōō ni tsuite," in *Indogaku Bukkyōgaku ronshū*, 145–156. For a general treatment of Indian kingship see J. Gonda, *Ancient Indian Kingship from the Religious Point of View* (reprint from *Numen*, III, IV).

missing a single word. . . . Another emperor made great vows and, as an act of devotion, built a statue of Buddha. Heaven aided his vows, and the earth opened its treasure house to offer gold [I.Preface].

This passage is based on the accounts in the *Nihon shoki* concerning Emperor Nintoku, Prince Shōtoku, and Emperor Shōmu. These men are venerated not because of their hereditary status but because of their deeds of compassion and faith as illustrated in their legends.

Prince Shōtoku and Emperor Shōmu are regarded as incarnations of the Bodhisattva Mañjuśrī (I.5), who came to Japan to propagate the Buddhist teachings. Kyōkai shows great veneration for Emperor Saga in whose reign he probably concluded the writing of the *Nihon ryōiki*. Emperor Saga was a great patron of learning and of the new Buddhist schools of Tendai and Shingon. In the *Nihon ryōiki* Emperor Saga is described as an incarnation of Dhyāna Master Jakusen 寂仙, and, therefore, a sage emperor. Kyōkai argues for the merits of Emperor Saga as a sage emperor. Those who favored Emperor Saga said that he was a sage emperor because he had abolished capital punishment and had ruled the state with benevolence. Those who were against him said that he was not compassionate because he enjoyed hunting, and he was not virtuous enough to maintain the harmony of the universe and prevent natural calamities from descending on the people. Kyōkai says in reply to the latter:

Their charge, however, is not right. Everything in the country he reigns over belongs to him, and we cannot claim as our own even a piece of earth the size of a needle point. All are at the will of the emperor. How could we accuse him of such things? Even in the reign of the sage emperors Yao and Shun, there were also droughts and plagues. So we should refrain from such abuse [III.39].

In Kyōkai's defense of Emperor Saga we hear the echoes of the ideology of universal sovereignty found in the Chinese classics. Some Buddhist scriptures reveal similar ideas; the *Shinji kan-gyō* states:

Mountain, river, earth of the land,
Reaching all the way to the ocean,
Belong to the Lord;
For in fortune and virtue he excels all others.[80]

80. *Shinji kan-gyō*, II (*Taishō*, III, 297c). 於其國界山河大地 盡大海際屬千國王 一人福德勝過 一切衆生福故. Cf. Matsunaga Yūkei, "Gokoku shisō no kigen," *IBK*, XV (No. 1, December 1966), 69–78; Kanaoka Shūyū, "Konkōmyō-kyō no teiō-kan to sono Shina-Nihon-teki juyō," *Bukkyō shigaku*, VI (No. 4, October 1957), 21–32.

The monarchy being a divine institution, passive obedience on the part of the people is enjoined. Buddhist rulers govern the state with the altruistic love of bodhisattvas, and the people should respond with obedience and loyalty. The Buddhist idea of dependent origination is applied to the social hierarchy in this case, and the sense of gratitude, particularly toward a ruler, is emphasized.

The significance of the emperor in the Japanese tradition rests on the notions that there is temporal continuity of an unbroken line of imperial rule from ancestors in the remote past to descendants in the future and that there is a cosmic unity of heaven, earth, and man. Kyōkai's attempts to reconcile such fundamental notions about his own tradition with Buddhist universalistic ideas met with only limited success. One difficulty in delineating his view of man is due to conflicting materials present in the Buddhist scriptures, which had been written at different times and places. The primary difficulty, however, is that his participation in a social order based on such deeply rooted hierarchical principles limited his claims for the universal dharma.

b. *Woman as a Cosmic Symbol*

During the one hundred and seventy-seven years of the Asuka and Nara periods, roughly the years covered by the *Nihon ryōiki*, six empresses reigned for a total of seventy-two years.[81] They were all members of the imperial family, and one reason for their selection was the difficulty of deciding on a male ruler. Female rulers in the sixth and seventh centuries were empress dowagers. In the eighth century, after the establishment of the Chinese legal system, women became empresses as a result of the principle of parent–child succession that replaced the traditional principle of succession from brother to brother. Several theories have been advanced for the large number of women rulers. Orikuchi Shinobu, a contemporary Japanese classicist, stresses the shamanistic role of the empress on the presupposition that the ancient tribal rule was carried out through the collaboration of the male chieftain and a female shaman.[82] His theory does not hold

81.

| Empress | Reign | Empress | Reign |
|---------|-------|---------|-------|
| Suiko | 593–628 | Genmyō | 708–714 |
| Kōgyoku | 642–644 | Genshō | 715–723 |
| Saimei (Kōgyoku) | 655–661 | Kōken | 749–757 |
| Jitō | 687–696 | Shōtoku (Kōken) | 764–770 |

Parentheses indicate rule for a second period.

82. Orikuchi, "Nyotei-kō," *Orikuchi Shinobu zenshū*, XX, 1–23.

up in the case of an empress dowager succeeding her deceased husband because a female shaman such as Amaterasu Ōmikami[83] and Himiko 卑彌呼[84] was a virgin of the tribe and not a chieftain's wife with children.

Inoue Mitsusada makes a clear distinction between female rulers of the sixth and seventh centuries and those of the eighth century and rejects Orikuchi's theory as an excessively mythological interpretation. However, he does not deny the influence of a mythical, shamanistic female ruler even as late as the Nara period. According to Inoue, the frequent appearance of female rulers in that age is not an isolated phenomenon at court but an indication of the persistence of a matrilineal tradition that had existed before the Taika Reform (645) and was patterned on the Chinese patrilineal tradition. Although family registries dating from 702 show that the heads of families were usually males, it is assumed that the early tradition was still alive in the practice of using the mother's surname in naming the child during the Nara period and even in the Heian period.[85]

The stories of the *Nihon ryōiki* describe a rich diversity of women, both high and low, rich and poor, lay and clerical. Thirty tales out of one hundred and sixteen feature heroines, and women appear in in another ten. Nuns appear in six stories (I.35; II.2, 17, 19; III.19, 34), and the remainder are devoted to lay women. As mentioned above, the legal system of the society was patrilineal, but social convention betrayed the persistence of the matrilineal tradition. A typical family of a freeman consisted of a dozen members: husband and wife, children, close relatives, and servants. After marriage a wife usually lived in her husband's family (I.2; II.27; III.4). On the other hand, going to the wife's home for courtship and marriage was also in practice (I.31; II.33, 34). Supporting parents was an established practice, and failure to do so brought ethical condemnation (I.23, 24). In spite of such a patrilineal society, stories about parent-child relationships stress the maternal ties in all but three instances (I.9, 10, 15).

83. The sun goddess and mythological ancestor of the imperial family whose name literally means Heaven-shining-great-deity. According to Naoki Kōjirō, Amaterasu was probably a local deity of Ise or a priestess of the sun-god enshrined at Ise. The Grand Shrine of Ise originated in the latter part of the fifth century, and the close tie with the imperial family was established probably in the reign of Emperor Kinmei in the early sixth century. See his *Nihon kodai no shizoku to tennō*, 241–268.

84. The *Wei chih* 魏志 compiled about 297 A.D. gives passages on Wa 倭 (Japan), and refers to Himiko (or Pimiko) as its ruler. "She occupied herself with magic and sorcery bewitching the people. Though mature in age, she remained unmarried. She had a younger brother who assisted her in ruling the country . . . ." See R. Tsunoda and L. C. Goodrich, *Japan in Chinese Dynastic Histories*, 8–16.

85. Inoue Mitsusada, *Nihon Kodai*, 223–253. See III.16, 39. Cf. *Kojiki*, II (*NKBT*, 1, 145).

Buddhism introduced in its world view the notion of the equality of all beings before dharma. Śākyamuni's teachings which challenged social discrimination and the caste-oriented society, appealed to women as well as to lower-caste people in India. Equality was realized within the samgha in which discussions and decisions were made in the council of all members. However, some qualifications were made on the status of woman in the samgha. In spite of the fact that early Pāli scriptures include biographies of eminent nuns, as well as monks who attained enlightenment,[86] other scriptures disparage women and stress their inferior ability to practice the disciplines that lead to enlightenment. A tradition has it that Śākyamuni consented to the admission of women to the samgha as long as the regulations pertaining to them were stricter than those for monks.[87] He is credited with saying that the admission of woman to the samgha would shorten the thousand years of Buddhism's golden age by five hundred years.[88] Although there are many reasons to doubt the historicity of these words ascribed to Śākyamuni, the existence of such a tradition indicates that there was a conflict between Śākyamuni's teachings and the traditional Hindu world view.

In Vedic India, women had not only the right of offering sacrifiees in their own names but also that of composing hymns.[89] Later, in the Brahmanical period, women lost freedom in religious practices as well as in other social activities. Women were expected to live in complete subservience to their parents in childhood, to their husbands after marriage, and to their sons after the death of their spouses.[90] Such discrimination may be explained in various ways: women's suffering in childbirth was interpreted as a result of evil deeds in past lives; the path to the enlightenment which Śākyamuni had preached was thought to be more suitable for men; women were considered to be more emotional than men, and, therefore, to have more difficulty in reaching enlightenment. No matter what the reasons, the traditional low view of woman gained prominence in later Buddhist literature.

In the Mahayana tradition, the *Hoke-kyō, Nehan-gyō,* and *Muryōju-kyō* 無量壽經 are famous for their message of salvation for women. However, in these scriptures women gain enlightenment only after

---

86. *Therigāthā.* See *Psalms of the Early Buddhists: 1. Psalms of the Sisters,* trans. by Mrs. Rhys Davids.

87. See Hirakawa Akira, *Ritsuzō no kenkyū,* 493. A certain Vinaya text gives two hundred and fifty precepts for a full-fledged monk and three hundred and forty-eight precepts for a full-fledged nun.

88. *Cullavagga,* X, 1 (*SBE,* XX, 320–326).

89. Clarisse Bader, *Women in Ancient India,* trans. by Mary E. R. Martin, 9.

90. See *The Laws of Manu,* V, 148 (*SBE,* XXV, 195).

they have changed sex and become men. The *Hoke-kyō* contains a story about an eight-year old daughter of King Nāga who was enlightened. She was so intelligent that she could acquire in one moment a thousand meditations and proofs of the essence of dharma. Śāriputra, Śākyamuni's disciple, told her that there was no example of a woman having reached Buddhahood because a woman cannot attain any of the five ranks: Brahmā, Indra, the Guardians of the Four Quarters, *cakravartin* (universal Buddhist king), or bodhisattva. She miraculously transformed herself from female to male, thereupon manifesting herself as a bodhisattva, and went to the pure land.[91] In the same manner, the *Nehan-gyō* narrates that two thousand billion women and female deities transformed their female bodies into male bodies and attained arhatship.[92] The same view is expressed in the scriptures of the pure land school, in which the pure land is depicted as a land without any women. Amida vowed that he would not attain enlightenment if women should fail to turn their thoughts toward attaining enlightenment and to despise their female nature, and [they should] be born again as women after having heard his name.[93] There is even a scripture written specifically on the transformation of women into men.[94] Change of sex is accomplished by meditation, Amida's vow, or recitation of dharani.

Kyōkai learned the Buddhist teachings through these scriptures, but he did not accept the view of woman contained in them. The women in the *Nihon ryōiki* convey a quite different impression. Generally Kyōkai not only depicts women as devout and compassionate, even capable of attaining enlightenment, but he also alters the meaning of the scriptural passages to fit his own purposes. For instance, in a story of a poor mother with nine children, a bodhisattva comes to their rescue in response to the mother's faith (II.42). In the note, Kyōkai gives a quotation from the *Nehan-gyō*: "By loving the child the mother is reborn into Brahmā's heaven." This quotation is a modified version of the following passage: "Although women are innately inferior and worse [than men], they may be born in heaven as a consequence of their motherly love."[95] Obviously this scriptural

91. *Myōhōrenge-kyō*, XI (*Taishō*, IX, 35bc). 當時集會 皆見龍女忽然之間變成男子 具菩薩行. See Katō, trans., *Myōhō-renge-kyō*, 258–260.

92. *Daihatsu nehan-gyō*, XL (*Taishō*, XII, 603c). 人女天女二萬億人現轉女身得男子身 須跋陀羅 得阿羅漢果.

93. *Muryōju-kyō*, I (*Taishō*, XII, 268c). Cf. Max Müller, trans., *The Larger Sukhāvatīvyūha*, 19.

94. For example, *Tennyoshin-kyō* 轉女身經 (*Taishō*, XIV, No. 564).

95. *Daihatsu nehan-gyō*, X (*Taishō*, XII, 425c). See *The Laws of Manu*, V, 147–166 (*SBE*, XXV, 195–196). Women are promised birth in heaven by means of their loyalty to their husbands and motherly care and love.

passage makes a distinction between male and female concerning the capacity for enlightenment, although there is concern for the salvation of women devotees.

However, such a view of women's nature was unacceptable to the compiler and his contemporaries and it was eliminated. The *Nihon ryōiki*, instead of making negative statements about women, maintains the equality of men and women before dharma. A more explicit statement of such equality is found in the story of a nun of miraculous birth.[96] Though a dwarf and deformed, she was innately intelligent. When two monks bullied her, a divine man came down to punish them. Once a local magistrate invited a provincial preceptor to act as lecturer on a Buddhist scripture, and this nun was seated in the audience.[97]

> Seeing her, the lecturer said accusingly, "Who is that nun unscrupulously seated among the monks?" In reply she said, "Buddha promulgated the right teaching out of his great compassion for all sentient beings. Why do you restrain me in particular?" Then she asked a question by quoting a verse from the scripture, and the lecturer could not interpret it. In amazement, all the famous wise men questioned and examined her, but she never failed [III.19].

This story reveals influences of the Indian tradition: in her birth from a ball of hard flesh, in her title of Sari-bosatsu (bodhisattva) 舍利菩薩,[98] and in her lack of female sexual organs. In the *Nihon ryōiki* she is the only woman that is given the title of bodhisattva. Accordingly we interpret her physical lack of gender as the persistence of the Indian tradition in the process of being feminized in Japan and as a stage in the process of transition from male to female. This story serves as a bridge between an early Mahayana trend and a later Tantric trend in which woman plays a central role as a cosmic symbol. There must have been some hesitancy about conferring the title of bodhisattva on a nun. On the other hand, there is nothing new or striking about the nun's statement on the equality of women before

96. She was born out of a ball of hard flesh, a popular Indian theme which is found in a few Buddhist scriptures as well as in the *Mahābhārata*. In the Indian tradition sons are born of such a ball in contrast to the birth of a girl in the *Nihon ryōiki*. See S. C. Nott, ed. *The Mahābhārata*, 54–55.

97. The *Sōni-ryō*, Article 12, says, "A monk may not enter a nunnery and a nun may not enter a monastery, except to be received by an elder, or for a visit on account of death or sickness or for the purpose of religious ceremony, observance, or instruction." See Sansom, "Early Japanese Laws," Part Two, 130.

98. *Sari*, a transliteration of Skt. *śarira*, means Śākyamuni's relics, which were popularly believed to be the source of miraculous power. Cf. Jean Przyluski, "Le Partage des Reliques du Buddha," *Mélanges chinois et bouddhiques*, IV (1935–36), 341–367.

dharma. One Pāli scripture says: "How should the woman's nature hinder us? Whose hearts are firmly set, who ever move with growing knowledge onward in the Path?"[99] The scene closely resembles that of the daughter of King Nāga who showed a miraculous change of sex in the congregation of monks and attained Buddhahood. Kyōkai apparently adapted a portion of the story in the *Hoke-kyō* to put forward the early Japanese view of woman, which is shown in other tales in the *Nihon ryōiki*.

The *Nihon ryōiki* includes several legends which make us hesitate to call it simply a collection of Buddhist legends. They are "non-Buddhist" legends in the sense that they neither express Buddhist ideas nor use Buddhist terms. Among them there is a cycle of legends on the Venerable Dōjō 道場 which drew the attention of Yanagita Kunio, the founder of Japanese folklore studies. The Venerable Dōjō was a monk of Gangō-ji, a state temple in Nara, who was famous for his great physical strength. Since he was a monk, the story about his life might be classified as a Buddhist legend (I.3). However, it seems proper to classify this and several other legends as "non-Buddhist" because they are thematically and structurally related to each other and distinguishable from the main group of stories. They include:

I.2 On Taking a Fox as a Wife and Bringing Forth a Child
   3 On a Boy of Great Physical Strength Whose Birth Was Given by the Thunder's Blessing
II.4 On a Contest between Women of Extraordinary Strength
   27 On a Woman of Great Strength

These stories are based on the local tradition of Mino and Owari provinces, where they originated and were transmitted. The two heroes and heroines possess great strength, which has been granted them by the thunder. Another story (I.1) may be added to this group; it shares the element of thunder with the legends about the Venerable Dōjō. Yanagita states that these are legends which show a transfer of power from a heavenly deity.[100]

In addition, there are more "non-Buddhist" legends of this type to which Yanagita never refers. They are as follows:

I.25 On a Loyal and Selfless Minister Who Gained Heaven's Sympathy and Was Rewarded by a Miraculous Event
II.33 On a Woman Devoured by an Evil Fiend
   41 On a Woman Who Survived the Violation of a Big Snake Owing to the Power of Drugs

99. *Therīgāthā*, 61–62. See *Psalms of the Early Buddhists: 1. Psalms of the Sisters,* trans. by Mrs. Rhys Davids, 45–46, 181–182.
100. Yanagita Kunio, *Imōto no chikara (Teihon Yanagita Kunio shū*, IX), 64.

III.31 On a Woman Who Gave Birth to Stones and Enshrined Them
   as Kami

As examination of these eight "non-Buddhist" stories shows that
five heroines and three heroes are concerned with thunder (I.1, 3, 25).
Most of the stories belong to a category in which a transfer of power
from a heavenly deity takes place. All of the heroine-centered stories
are somehow related to sexual matters; two of them are about inexplicable events (II.33, 41); the remainder are based on the belief in the
power given through an extraordinary birth.

One example is the story of a girl in a village in Mino province.

   She was over twenty but unmarried, and she became pregnant
   without any sexual intercourse. At the end of the second month
   in the spring of the tenth year of the boar . . . she gave birth to
   two stones after a three-year pregnancy. They measured five
   inches in diameter. One was blue and white mixed together,
   while the other was pure blue. They grew year after year [III.31].

Then one local kami possessed a diviner, who announced that the two
stones were the children of the kami. Therefore, they were enshrined
in the residence of the maiden who had given birth to the stones, and
she served them as a priestess. The stones had special significance: they
were born of a virgin, they grew as if they were alive, and they were
identified as descendants of the kami. It is assumed that the kami who
uttered the oracle was the ancestor of the girl's family, that is, their
*ujigami*. Invested with miraculous power as a result of their origin,
they were venerated as symbols of the identity of the ancestral kami,
as his descendants, and as protectors and enrichers of life in the universe. The transfer of power through birth is based on the importance
of the blood tie between kami and man. The symbolism of woman
as a mediator of such power helps explain the Japanese phenomenon
of female shamans and priestesses. Procreation was viewed as a mysterious process in which, as a result of the union of male and female,
woman became the source of life.

Divine marriage is a recurrent theme in Japanese myths. The pattern
is for a woman or a man to be betrothed to a deity who comes to
them in a disguised form. Such a marriage often ends with the permanent separation of the couple after the birth of a child because
of the curiosity of the human spouse.[101] One of the legends about the
Venerable Dōjō illustrates this point: A man married a girl whom he

101. *Kojiki*, I (*NKBT*, I, 136–147) Hoori no mikoto 火遠理命 and Toyotama hime no
mikoto 豐玉毘賣命, a daughter of the marine kami going back home in the form of a crocodile;
*ibid.* (*NKBT*, I, 180–183) Kami of Mt. Miwa 三輪山 and Ikutamayori-hime 活玉依毘賣. See
Philippi, trans., *Kojiki*, 150–155, 203–204. Cf. Yanagita, *Imōto no chikara*, 41–62.

dharma. One Pāli scripture says: "How should the woman's nature hinder us? Whose hearts are firmly set, who ever move with growing knowledge onward in the Path?"[99] The scene closely resembles that of the daughter of King Nāga who showed a miraculous change of sex in the congregation of monks and attained Buddhahood. Kyōkai apparently adapted a portion of the story in the *Hoke-kyō* to put forward the early Japanese view of woman, which is shown in other tales in the *Nihon ryōiki*.

The *Nihon ryōiki* includes several legends which make us hesitate to call it simply a collection of Buddhist legends. They are "non-Buddhist" legends in the sense that they neither express Buddhist ideas nor use Buddhist terms. Among them there is a cycle of legends on the Venerable Dōjō 道場 which drew the attention of Yanagita Kunio, the founder of Japanese folklore studies. The Venerable Dōjō was a monk of Gangō-ji, a state temple in Nara, who was famous for his great physical strength. Since he was a monk, the story about his life might be classified as a Buddhist legend (I.3). However, it seems proper to classify this and several other legends as "non-Buddhist" because they are thematically and structurally related to each other and distinguishable from the main group of stories. They include:

I.2 On Taking a Fox as a Wife and Bringing Forth a Child

3 On a Boy of Great Physical Strength Whose Birth Was Given by the Thunder's Blessing

II.4 On a Contest between Women of Extraordinary Strength

27 On a Woman of Great Strength

These stories are based on the local tradition of Mino and Owari provinces, where they originated and were transmitted. The two heroes and heroines possess great strength, which has been granted them by the thunder. Another story (I.1) may be added to this group; it shares the element of thunder with the legends about the Venerable Dōjō. Yanagita states that these are legends which show a transfer of power from a heavenly deity.[100]

In addition, there are more "non-Buddhist" legends of this type to which Yanagita never refers. They are as follows:

I.25 On a Loyal and Selfless Minister Who Gained Heaven's Sympathy and Was Rewarded by a Miraculous Event

II.33 On a Woman Devoured by an Evil Fiend

41 On a Woman Who Survived the Violation of a Big Snake Owing to the Power of Drugs

99. *Therīgāthā*, 61–62. See *Psalms of the Early Buddhists: 1. Psalms of the Sisters,* trans. by Mrs. Rhys Davids, 45–46, 181–182.

100. Yanagita Kunio, *Imōto no chikara* (*Teihon Yanagita Kunio shū*, IX), 64.

### III.31 On a Woman Who Gave Birth to Stones and Enshrined Them as Kami

As examination of these eight "non-Buddhist" stories shows that five heroines and three heroes are concerned with thunder (I.1, 3, 25). Most of the stories belong to a category in which a transfer of power from a heavenly deity takes place. All of the heroine-centered stories are somehow related to sexual matters; two of them are about inexplicable events (II.33, 41); the remainder are based on the belief in the power given through an extraordinary birth.

One example is the story of a girl in a village in Mino province.

> She was over twenty but unmarried, and she became pregnant without any sexual intercourse. At the end of the second month in the spring of the tenth year of the boar . . . she gave birth to two stones after a three-year pregnancy. They measured five inches in diameter. One was blue and white mixed together, while the other was pure blue. They grew year after year [III.31].

Then one local kami possessed a diviner, who announced that the two stones were the children of the kami. Therefore, they were enshrined in the residence of the maiden who had given birth to the stones, and she served them as a priestess. The stones had special significance: they were born of a virgin, they grew as if they were alive, and they were identified as descendants of the kami. It is assumed that the kami who uttered the oracle was the ancestor of the girl's family, that is, their *ujigami*. Invested with miraculous power as a result of their origin, they were venerated as symbols of the identity of the ancestral kami, as his descendants, and as protectors and enrichers of life in the universe. The transfer of power through birth is based on the importance of the blood tie between kami and man. The symbolism of woman as a mediator of such power helps explain the Japanese phenomenon of female shamans and priestesses. Procreation was viewed as a mysterious process in which, as a result of the union of male and female, woman became the source of life.

Divine marriage is a recurrent theme in Japanese myths. The pattern is for a woman or a man to be betrothed to a deity who comes to them in a disguised form. Such a marriage often ends with the permanent separation of the couple after the birth of a child because of the curiosity of the human spouse.[101] One of the legends about the Venerable Dōjō illustrates this point: A man married a girl whom he

---

101. *Kojiki*, I (*NKBT*, 1, 136–147) Hoori no mikoto 火遠理命 and Toyotama hime no mikoto 豐玉毘賣命, a daughter of the marine kami going back home in the form of a crocodile; *ibid.* (*NKBT*, I, 180–183) Kami of Mt. Miwa 三輪山 and Ikutamayori-hime 活玉依毘賣. See Philippi, trans., *Kojiki*, 150–155, 203–204. Cf. Yanagita, *Imōto no chikara*, 41–62.

had met in the fields, and she bore a son. When she was discovered to be a fox, she was forced to leave her husband's home. Her son was named after her and possessed the gift of great strength (I.2). All his descendants inherited this extraordinary strength.

Gradually changes in the symbolism of woman took place. After the arrival of Buddhism, women became symbols of Buddha's boundless compassion, and motherly love was idealized. For instance, there is a story of a man who was sent to the frontier to serve his term of duty in the defense force. He took his mother to the frontier, leaving his wife in charge of the household (II.3). This was contrary to the common practice, exemplified in other stories, of government officials going to the frontier accompanied by their wives and leaving their parents behind (II.20; III.4). Overcome with love for his wife, he tried to kill his mother to obtain permission for a period of mourning so that he could go home to his wife.

> When the wicked son stepped forward to cut off his mother's head, the earth opened to swallow him. At that moment his mother grabbed her falling son by the hair and appealed to Heaven, wailing, "My child is possessed by some spirit and driven to such an evil deed. He is out of his mind. I beseech you to forgive his sin." In spite of all her efforts to pull him up by the hair, he fell down [II.3].

The author says in the note: "How great the mother's compassion was! She was so compassionate that she loved an evil son and practiced good on his behalf."[102]

Motherhood was the major reason for deferring to women, whose status was low in society. Buddhism often teaches the practice of altruistic love in terms of a mother's love for her child:

> As a mother at the risk of her life watches over her own child, her only child, so also let everyone cultivate a boundless (friendly) mind toward all beings.[103]

Unlimited motherly love is embodied in the bodhisattva, who was believed to possess the power to save children destined to die (II.2, 20). A mother's milk symbolizes her love.

> When her dear son contracted a fatal disease and was dying, he said to her, "It will prolong my life if I drink my mother's milk." The mother gave her breast to her son as he had asked. Sucking

---

102. Boundless motherly love is a universally popular theme. A medieval Neapolitan poem on a mother killed by her son sounds a similar note: ". . . she said: 'Son, did you hurt yourself?' and looking at his finger, sighing, she died. . . ." Salvatore de Giacomo, *Poesie*, 112 (trans. by Louis F. Salano).

103. *Suttanipāta*, 148 (*SBE*, X, 25).

her breast, he lamented, saying, "I am abandoning the sweet milk of my mother and dying!" and breathed his last [II.2].

Even if man is confronted with the reality of life and death, and knows the inescapable destiny out of which Śākyamuni's teachings originate, there still remains some hope and longing for life sustained by love.

However, motherly love needed to be extended and transformed into the universal Buddhist principle which seeks salvation for all living beings. The *Nihon ryōiki* gives several stories on the theme of saving life, two of which are particularly relevant here (II.8, 12). The heroine of each story is a devout maiden who meets a snake about to swallow a toad. Each maiden risks her chastity in exchange for the toad's life, and eventually is saved owing to her faith. It is evident that these tales are Buddhist adaptations of the divine marriage theme. She is an embodiment of the altruistic love of a bodhisattva, which is compassion based on the Buddhist cosmological idea of the interdependence of all sentient beings.

In ancient Japanese tradition, woman had particular importance as a symbol of cosmic power, a role which is exemplified in her procreative function. Buddhism added the ethical significance of motherly love to the symbolism of woman. In China and Japan, Kannon acquired feminine features as the embodiment of great compassion in spite of a reluctance to see the bodhisattva in female form. Women as well as men are potential bodhisattvas in the *Nihon ryōiki*. Kyōkai does not accept the view of women's inferior nature, but insists on the equality of all before dharma.

c. *Ideal Image of Man*

As dharma never exists apart from the cosmos, so dharma never exists apart from men, in particular Śākyamuni and his followers. In a third of the legends in the *Nihon ryōiki*, there appear monks of widely varying character: virtuous and corrupt, scholarly and ignorant, officially ordained and self-ordained. The most noteworthy and highly venerated is Gyōgi, who appears in seven legends (I.5; II.2, 7, 8, 12, 29, 30). One legend is particularly informative because it compares Gyōgi with Chikō, who was one of the most learned monks of the Nara period. When we compare the epithets given to the two eminent monks, there are similarities. Of Chiko, it is said: "He was innately intelligent, and no one excelled him in knowledge." On the other hand, it says of Gyōgi: "He was innately intelligent, endowed with inborn wisdom." (II.7). What makes a real difference between the two is the fact that Chikō was interested in doctrinal studies and scholarly activities while the compassionate Gyōgi was concerned with missionary activities. Therefore, his contemporaries called him a bodhisattva and regarded him as an incarnation of Mañjuśrī (I.5).

The title of bodhisattva is given to four other eminent religious persons: Konsu, the Ascetic 金鷲行者 (II.21); Dhyāna Master Eigō 永興 (III.1); Saru-hijiri 猴聖 (III.19); and Dhyāna Master Jakusen 寂仙 (III.39). These persons were free from attachments to the world, led a disciplined life, engaged in missionary works, and, except for Saru-hijiri, were venerated by the emperors. Their relationship with the emperors reflects the development of the imperial practice of granting the title of bodhisattva (bosatsu) to eminent monks, the first record of which is found in 749.[104] The exceptional case of Saru-hijiri leads to a consideration of what hijiri means in the Nihon ryōiki.

Hijiri may be defined as a charismatic leader of lay Buddhist movements in medieval Japan, particularly in the pure land school. Originally the concept of hijiri developed not only under Buddhist but also Taoist and Confucian influences.[105] In China, where legendary emperors such as the Yellow Emperor, Yao and Shun, or Lao-tzu and Confucius were venerated as sages, Śākyamuni was accepted as another great sage and added to the list. Kyōkai, in compiling the Nihon ryōiki, may be seeking to portray Japanese sages under the influence of Chinese hagiography.[106]

The Nihon ryōiki identifies only two persons as hijiri: one is Saru-hijiri, and the other is Prince Shōtoku. If we compare these two figures with the other monks, it is evident that they are more legendary than historical. As has been pointed out, Saru-hijiri, an extraordinary nun with a deformed body, shows strong influences of the Indian tradition. On the other hand, Prince Shōtoku's legend reveals a Taoist influence in the concept of a "hidden sage." Although a distinction between clergy and laity is not stressed very much in Japan, Prince Shōtoku was a lay Buddhist, and Saru-hijiri was a nun. Obviously the Buddhist and Taoist ideal images of man overlap in the Nihon ryōiki, with the Taoist being particularly prominent in the earlier legends. This syncretic tendency took place in China and was transmitted to Japan. According to the Taoist tradition, there are three kinds of hsien 仙: heavenly immortals 天仙, earthly immortals 地仙, and disembodied immortals 尸解仙.[107] The beggar and Gangaku (I.4) seem to be

104. Shoku Nihongi (Tenpyō shōhō 1:2:2). The title was conferred on Gyōgi.
105. See Hori, "On the Concept of Hijiri (Holy-man)," Numen, V (1958), 128–160, 199–232.
106. The influence of Hui-chiao's Kao-seng chuan is documented in the Nihon ryōiki (see Chap. I(2)b, n. 137), but that of the biographies of Taoist sages probably came indirectly through Chinese Buddhist literature.
107. Ko Hung, Pao-p'u tzu, II, 9a. See Ware, Alchemy, Medicine, Religion, 47–48.

disembodied immortals, while E no Ozunu (I.28) and a mother of seven children (I.13) seem to be heavenly immortals, for they ascend to heaven. The anecdote of Prince Shōtoku's meeting with a beggar is the most famous, and it is found in several different versions.[108] The difference between the *Nihon shoki* and *Nihon ryōiki* is that the former emphasizes Prince Shōtoku as a saint admired by his contemporaries and the latter depicts the beggar as a saint. In the *Nihon ryōiki*, Prince Shōtoku is admired indirectly because of his ability to recognize saintliness in a beggar.

A sage is said to differ from an ordinary person in this way:

> We learn that a sage recognizes a sage, whereas an ordinary man cannot recognize a sage. The ordinary man sees nothing but the outer form of a beggar, while the sage has a penetrating eye able to recognize the hidden essence. It is a miraculous event [I.4].

In the Buddhist tradition the penetrating eye[109] is the faculty that distinguishes the Buddha and bodhisattva from ordinary men. With such an eye, a person can see into the past and the future, as well as the present; they can also see into other people's minds. It is a sign of the ascetic's passage from conditioned existence to a state of deliverance, or from samsara to nirvana. Prince Shōtoku and Gyōgi are prominent instances. On the other hand, there are stories of men who reveal other sorts of miraculous powers. Gigaku 義覺, a Korean monk, used to recite the *Shin-gyō*,[110] and, as a result, he could become visible or invisible at will and move around without any restrictions (I.15).[111] Knowledge of previous existences is one such power, and there is a story of a devotee of the *Hoke-kyō* who was rewarded with such knowledge of his past life (I.18).[112] As a consequence of the penetrating eye, or clairvoyance, many eminent monks knew when they were

108. *Nihon shoki* (Suiko 21:12:1); *Jōgū Shōtoku hōō teisetsu, Jōgū Shōtoku taishi-den hoketsuki* (46:11:15); *Shōtoku taishi-den ryaku* (*DBZ*, 112); *Manyōshū* (III, 415).

109. *Tengen* 天眼 (Skt. *divyacakṣus*). See Vasubandhu, *Abhidharmakośaśāstra*, IX (*Buddhist Scriptures*, trans. by Conze, 121–133). According to Eliade, these "miraculous powers" are for the most part stereotyped, and occur in all the ascetic and mystical literatures of India. See his *Yoga*, 177–180.

110. *Prjñāpāramitāhṛdayasūtra, Buddhist Mahāyāna Texts* (*SBE*, XLIX).

111. The description of various modes of miraculous power occurs in all the *nikāyas*. For example, *Dighanikāya* (III, 112–113) divides them into two categories, that is, ignoble supernormal power which is concomitant with mental intoxicants and with worldly aims, and the noble supernormal power which is attained only by Buddhist monks. In the former, from being one a man becomes multiform; from being multiform he becomes one; from being visible he becomes invisible; he passes without hindrance to the further side of a wall, or a battlement, or a mountain, as if through air; he travels cross-legged through the sky, like a bird on the wing. In the latter, he is free from desire and attains self-mastery. See *Dialogues of the Buddha*, trans. by T. W. and C. A. F. Rhys Davids, Part III, 106–107.

112. See *Dialogues of the Buddha*, trans. by Rhys Davids, Part Three, 104–106. Cf. Eliade, *Yoga*, 180–185.

to die and what their future life would be (I.22; III.20, 39).[113] In spite of the popularity of stories concerning such miraculous powers, possession of them or particularly exhibition of them was regarded in early Buddhism as dangerous for a monk whose goal was nirvana.

In the Japanese religious tradition, no clear-cut distinction can be made between sacred and secular. What is closest to "sacred" is 聖 (sei, shō, or hijiri), but its antonym is 凡, "ordinary," as understood by Kyōkai. "Sacred" means "supreme, preeminent, extraordinary." No discontinuity exists. This is the basis for the doctrine of universal salvation. Each person has the potential to be a bodhisattva, although there are differences in the degrees of achievement, which is by no means predestined. The ideal image of man is not a scholarly and virtuous monk, but one who lives an ordinary life yet reveals an extraordinary quality through such a life. In other words, he is in society and at the same time rises above society. Generally speaking, bodhisattvas are monks noted for their virtuous lives, while hijiri is a term applied to those who possess charismatic or miraculous qualities. The person who combined these two is Gyōgi, the most admired figure throughout the Nihon ryōiki. He is the embodiment of compassionate love, wherein the two aspects are incorporated.

There is an anecdote of Gyōgi's love for his disciple, Shingon. Out of his love for Gyōgi, Shingon used to say that he would die and go to the pure land with his master, but he died young. Gyōgi, grieving over the death of his disciple who had made such a vow, composed a poem:

Did you not promise me we would die together?
But, alas! You are gone,
Leaving me behind.
Are you a crow, to be such a great liar? [II.2].

This is simply an expression of human love. Gyōgi's grief over his favorite disciple's death shows the depth of his human feeling.

Other legends of Gyōgi, however, stress his extraordinary ability to penetrate into other people's minds and to see things as an extended series of cause and effect from the past into the future. When Chikō came to see Gyōgi after he had abused Gyōgi and had been punished for his inordinate pride, Gyōgi welcomed him with open arms, knowing what had taken place (II.7). In another story "the penetrating eye" is used as a motif whereby Gyōgi accuses a woman in his audience of having smeared her hair with animal oil, for he saw in the oil the act of killing life (II.29). In another story he told a mother with a crying

---

113. *Buddhist Scriptures*, trans. by Conze, 133.

child to throw it into the river. Naturally the mother's affection prevented her from abandoning the child, and she came back to listen to Gyōgi again, bringing the child with her. He rebuked her and repeated the same words. Finally, when she obeyed Gyōgi and threw the child into the water, she learned that she had not settled all her debts in a previous life and that her former creditor had been born as her child to make her suffer and pay her debts. The telling of this story is a skillful means for preaching karmic retribution. This woman came to hear dharma, but had difficulties in putting her trust in Gyōgi and obeying him; she was pressed to choose between not hearing dharma and making a total commitment. After she chose the latter, she learned how her karma was being worked out in the past, present, and future.

Wisdom and compassion are means for fulfilling the bodhisattva's vow. Wisdom is cultivated by looking at reality, by seeing things as they are. No discontinuity exists between the great mercy of Buddha and human love. What distinguishes them is the degree to which right knowledge sustains love. Ordinary men are conscious only of physical, carnal love as in the case of the mother with the crying child. But a sage's love is based on right knowledge with which he may see events on a macrocosmic scale. Human love is never rejected, but it must be elevated and expanded on the basis of the right understanding of existence.

### (3) MIRACULOUS WORLD

a. *Belief in the Spirits of the Dead*

We find two types of miraculous tale in the *Nihon ryōiki*. In one type, a man or his spirit reveals his extraordinary power through miraculous signs; in the other type, the *dharmakāya*, essential body of Buddha,[114] or the Buddha's spirit (*shōryō* 聖靈) works as an agent through such things as Buddha images and scriptural scrolls to cause miraculous signs which bring people lacking in faith to the realization of the eternal presence of *dharmakāya*. According to Kyōkai, these two are not separate, but united in one dharma transcendent and immanent. Let us begin with a discussion of stories of the miraculous power of the spirits of the dead and that of extraordinary men.

114. Dharma-body of Buddha: one aspect of the threefold body of Buddha, namely, *dharmakāya; sambhogakāya*, functional aspect of Buddha which appears in Buddhas and bodhisattvas, such as Amida or Kannon; and *nirmāṇakāya*, historical manifestation in Śākyamuni. Cf. Louis de la Vallée Pousin, "The Three Bodies of a Buddha," *JRAS* (October 1906), 943–977; Chizen Akanuma, "On the Triple Body of the Buddha," *The Eastern Buddhist*, IV (No. 1, 1922), 1–29.

In the account of the funeral rites we find a great concern with spirits of the dead. There is evidence of the practice of *mogari* 殯, the ancient custom of preserving the corpse for a short period before burial. During this period some spirits of the dead visit the land of the dead and come back to report on what has happened to them. The dead come back to life in three days (I.5, 30; II.19; III.9), five days (III.23), seven days (II.16; III.22, 26), or nine days (II.5, 7). A three-day period[115] seems to have been most common, while longer periods were exceptional and resulted from an imperial decree (I.5) or the dead man's last wish (II.5, 7, 16; III.26). The *Myōhōki*, a collection of Chinese Buddhist legends which influenced the *Nihon ryōiki*, also tells of the dead being revived: four times on the seventh day, two each on the first and third days, and one each on the second, fourth, and fortieth days. The frequency of revivals on the seventh day may reflect the influence of the Chinese custom of holding the service for the dead on the seventh day (II.33), and repeating it thereafter at the end of each seven-day interval until the forty-ninth day (III.37). Buddhism assimilated this practice of the ancestral cult and incorporated it into Buddhist rites.[116]

Buddhists brought the Indian custom of cremation to China, Korea, and Japan. The Chinese resisted this strange custom, and it was largely adopted by Buddhist monks,[117] while in Japan it was adopted by people of high court rank as well as monks. The first Japanese recorded case is that of the Venerable Dōshō (I.22), who died and was cremated in 700. Empress Jitō, cremated in 703, is the first case among members of the imperial household.[118] However, people seemed to be afraid of losing the body through cremation in case the spirit should return to this world. This might happen in the event that death took place prematurely as a result of some error of Yama or his messenger, or if the merit accumulated by the dead man or his family was judged by Yama to be great enough to allow him to return to life again. Some people stipulated in their wills that their bodies not be cremated, providing for the possibility of coming back to life (II.5, 7, 16). There

115. Temporary burial preceding final burial is a universal practice, although the length of the period varies. According to the Zoroastrian tradition, the soul of the dead hovers around the body for three days and nights. See Zaehner, *The Teachings of the Magi*, 133.

116. See Takeda Chōshū, *Sosen sūhai*, 214–244.

117. See J. J. M. de Groot, *The Religious System of China*, III, 1391–1417. Since very ancient times, cremation has been odious to the Chinese, for elaborate funeral and burial was esteemed as the highest duty prescribed by filial piety. In spite of the development of Buddhism in China, we find little positive reference to cremation in Chinese documents for nearly a millennium.

118. *Shoku Nihongi*, I (Monmu 4:3:10), *Dōshō* was cremated; III (Daihō 3:12:17), ex-Empress Jitō was cremated; III (Keiun 4:11:12) Emperor Monmu was cremated.

is a story of a girl who was sent to the land of the dead by the intentional error of Yama's messengers, who had been bribed by another girl destined to die to substitute the former girl for herself. Yama, after discovering the error, told her to go home, but her body had already been cremated (II.22). The same thing happened to a former minister of the state who could not be revived because his body had been cremated (III.36). The taboo that a man born in the year of fire[119] cannot be cremated is recorded in one story (III.20). These cases reveal a belief that, when a man dies, his spirit leaves the body and goes to the land of the dead. A duality of spirit and body is found in such thought.

In contrast, a monistic view is found in the legends of the beggar met by Prince Shōtoku (I.4), Monk Gangaku (I.4), E no Ozunu (I.28), and the mother of seven children (I.13). These four are clearly depicted in terms of the imagery of Taoist saints who attained immortality. In the first story (I.4) the beggar died and was buried while Gangaku died and was cremated, but both were revived and seen alive. These three legends, in spite of their Buddhist coloring, are primarily Taoist. However, this monistic view of man does not appear prominently in the legends of the *Nihon ryōiki*. The Japanese attitude to the Taoist ideal of immortality, similar to the way in which the Japanese accepted the Buddhist teaching of the transience of life, was largely one of sentimental appreciation.[120]

In the Heian period the belief in spirits of the dead grew into a morbid fear of evil and vindictive spirits,[121] but the *Nihon ryōiki* already exhibits such a tendency. It was believed that, after a violent death, often as a result of political intrigue, the spirit would not leave the body but would linger in this world to haunt the living. For example, Emperor Shōmu had the rebellious Prince Nagaya killed and ordered that he be cremated and his ashes thrown into a river. However, his cremated bones were buried in a distant province. The local people ascribed an outbreak of disease to the vindictive spirit of the prince and appealed to the court. Thereupon, the bones were reburied on an island off the coast of Kii, closer to the capital, in order to appease the spirit. According to Kyōkai, the prince incurred his

119. *Hinoe* (*ping* 丙), the third of the Ten Stems, referring to the south and fire in the Chinese *yin-yang wu-hsing* cosmology, and there are many taboos for a person born in this year. See Fung Yu-lan, *A History of Chinese Philosophy*, II, 11–16, for the Ten Stems.

120. Cf. Kobayashi Tomoaki, *Mujōkan no bungaku* 無常感の文學. In order to emphasize the Japanese sentimental appreciation of the Buddhist idea of transiency 無常觀, the author replaces *kan* 觀 (aspect, idea, view) with another *kan* 感 (feeling, sentiment, emotion).

121. Hori, *Folk Religion*, 111–117. *Goryō* 御靈 is an angry spirit. Cf. Thompson, *Folklore*, 257. In his *Motif-Index*, it is classified as E. 413.

violent death as a result of his insulting treatment of a mendicant monk. Although the *Shoku Nihongi* gives a different version of the story,[122] it seems clear that even a rebel's spirit deserved a proper burial in a grave (II.1).

There was a belief that the spirit would not leave the bones even after the flesh decayed, or the body was cremated. Therefore, after cremation, bones were collected and buried properly in a grave. The spirit of the dead person existed somewhere in the universe, and, in the case of a violent death, the spirit haunted the living by hovering around the bones, the only remaining portion of the body. Several stories in the *Nihon ryōiki* reveal this belief. The skull, which was regarded as the essential part of the human body, was the place where the spirit resided (I.12; III.27). The complete Buddhist version of this belief is found in the stories in which the strong faith of a dead ascetic remained in the tongue of the skull and made it recite the *Hoke-kyō* (III.1). Belief in the miraculous power of Śākyamuni's relics may be classified in the same group (II.31, 36). That flesh decays but bone does not is an ancient belief which may be traced back as far as the Paleolithic age. In the tradition of hunting peoples, bone represents the core of life; in death man and animals are reduced to bone and reborn from it according to the perpetual cycle of life and death.[123]

A mediator between the dead and the living was the diviner, *kamnagi* 卜者.[124] When a person died, the bereaved family sent for a diviner to ask him to instruct them of the dead person's last wish or of any message from him (II.16; III.39). This is an ancient rite to call back the dead. The diviner also had the role of healer. When "neither doctor nor medicine could cure the disease," diviners were summoned to purify and pray for the sick person (III.5). Doctors were professional physicians who made use of drugs to cure the sick (II.5, 41). They were concentrated in the vicinity of the capital, and the first to be summoned on occasions of illness.[125] However, since sickness was believed to be the result of past evil karma, confession and prayer was a fundamental means of treating the patient's soul and body, particularly if he was seriously ill.

122. *Shoku Nihongi*, X (Tempyō 1:2:13). It says that Prince Nagaya and his spouse were buried at Ikomayama 生駒山, which is situated in the same province as the capital.

123. See Eliade, *Myths, Dreams, and Mysteries*, 83–84, 169, and *Shamanism*, 162–163, 323–326.

124. Female shamans (巫) who are the mouthpieces of spirits; *kamnagi* probably derived from *kamu* (kami) and *nagi* (pacify). *Shoku Nihongi*, XVIII (Tempyō shōhō 4:8:17) says that seventeen diviners in the capital were arrested and exiled to distant provinces such as Izu, Oki, Tosa.

125. Suzuki Shūji, "Konjaku monogatarishū ni okeru byōsha to chiryōsha," *Nihon rekishi*, No. 243 (August 1968), 92–105.

These two functions of a diviner were gradually taken over by Buddhist monks who, through ascetic practices, gained the power of "the penetrating eye." Dharani was considered the most effective medium for such purposes. Tajō 多常, (or Tarajō 多羅常), a Korean monk, won the empress' respect for his compassionate acts of healing.

He lived a life of strict discipline in Hōki-yamadera in Takechi district and made it his chief concern to cure diseases. The dying were restored to health by his miraculous works. Whenever he recited formulas for the sick, there was a miraculous event. . . . This is the fruit of his disciplined life. His fame and compassionate virtue will be praised forever [I.26].

The Sōni-ryō prohibited monks and nuns from healing by exorcism or magic, but the healing of the sick by the recitation of Buddhist formulas was permitted.[126] Although the Sōni-ryō tried to differentiate between Buddhist healing practices and those of the Onmyōdō[127] and of pre-Buddhist origin, on the practical level they fused.[128] Buddhism tended to internalize ancient healing practices and emphasized self-introspection and repentence as a necessary part of the healing process. On the other hand, there were ascetics (gyōja) whose only contact with Buddhist discipline was the practice of recitation of the name of a Buddha, mantra, or dharani, and who became religious leaders in villages. Most of them were lay brothers (ubasoku 優婆塞) who lived in a village temple or mountain retreat. Some of them were promoted to the status of ordained monk, while others remained as gyōja, performing a role similar to that of kamnagi, although the former were predominantly male and the latter female.[129]

b. *Wonder of the Three Treasures*

Let us turn now from the stories about the miraculous power of holy men to the stories of the miraculous power displayed by such objects as scriptures and Buddha images. Among the miraculous tales of the Nihon ryōiki, the most prominent are the stories about Kannon and the Hoke-kyō. Although devotion to Kannon is based on a chapter of the Hoke-kyō,[130] we will discuss separately the Kannon legends and the Hoke-kyō legends, partly because the chapter on Kannon was often

126. Ryō no gige, "Sōni-ryō," Article 2. See Sansom, "Early Japanese Law," TASJ, Second Series, XI, 128.

127. Japanese reading of yin-yang tao; it became popular in Japan through divination and astrology. See Murayama Shūichi, "Jōdai no onmyōdō," in Kokumin seikatsushi kenkyū, ed. by Itō Tasaburō, IV, 121–156.

128. Divination and healing by kamnagi were prohibited by the authorities. See Ruijū sandai-kyaku, XII (Hōki 11:12:14) and (Daidō 2:9:28).

129. Cf. Nakayama Tarō, Nihon fujo-shi.

130. Myōhōrenge-kyō, XXV (Taishō, IX, 56c–58b); Katō, trans., Myōhō-renge-kyō, XXV, 404–415; Kern, trans., Saddharma, XXIV, 406–418.

taken as an independent scripture, and partly because there is a distinction between the two groups of legends in the *Nihon ryōiki.*

Among the Buddhas and bodhisattvas found in the *Nihon ryōiki,* Kannon is the most popular and remains a center for devotion by all classes of people. There are seventeen stories on Kannon, six on Miroku 彌勒,[131] three each on Amida,[132] Śākyamuni, and Myōken 妙見;[133] and two each on Kichijōten,[134] and Yakushi 藥師.[135] Their distribution is as follows:[136]

| Buddhas and bodhisattvas | Number of tales | Volume | Tale |
|---|---|---|---|
| Kannon | 17 | I | 6, 17, 18, 20, 31 |
| | | II | 11, 17, 26, 34, 36, 42 |
| | | III | 3, 7, 12, 13, 14, 30 |
| Miroku | 6 | II | 23, 26 |
| | | III | 8, 12, 13, 30 |
| Amida | 3 | I | 5, 33 |
| | | II | 26 |
| Śākyamuni | 3 | II | 28 |
| | | III | 25, 30 |
| Myōken | 3 | I | 34 |
| | | III | 5, 32 |
| Kichijōten | 2 | II | 13, 14 |
| Yakushi | 2 | II | 39 |
| | | III | 11 |

131. Maitreya, whose future coming is prophesied in Pāli, Sanskrit, Chinese scriptures such as the *Dīghanikāya* (iii, 76), *Mahāvastu* (iii, 240), *Hoke-kyō, Maitreyavyākaraṇa, Miroku geshō-kyō* 彌勒下生經, *Miroku-bosatsu jōshō Tosotsuten-kyō* 彌勒菩薩上生兜率天經, and others. Maitreya resides in the Tuṣita heaven (Tosotsuten) and will descend to earth to teach dharma at the end of the world. The Maitreya cult shows similarities to the Amida cult, but the latter outnumbers the former in China and Japan in terms of those who aspired to birth in the western paradise. See Ienaga Saburō, *Jōdai Bukkyō shisōshi kenkyū,* 28–37.

132. Amitābha (Infinite Light) or Amitāyus (Infinite Life) rose in popularity toward the end end of the Heian period in Japan. The *Hoke-kyō* mentions Amitāyus as one of the sixteen Buddhas and the lord of the western paradise. For the western paradise, see Chap. I(1)a, n. 16. The *Nihon ryōiki* does not refer to any scriptures of the pure land school, although there are indications of the belief in the western paradise.

133. A bodhisattva who originated with the Chinese folk worship of the North Pole Star, which was believed to control the life of people as well as their fortunes; Buddhist tradition regards the North Pole as the apex of Mt. Meru, a cosmic mountain. In Japan the cult, centering on the figure of Myōken, was celebrated not only at Buddhist temples but also at Shintō shrines. The first evidence of the cult at court is recorded as 785, and the enshrined images resemble those of Kichijōten. See Murayama, "Jōdai no onmyōdō," in *Kokumin seikatsushi,* ed. by Itō, IV, 131–133; Nomura Yōshō, "Kindai ni okeru Myōken shinkō," *Kindai Nihon no Hokke Bukkyō,* ed. by Mochizuki Kankō, 201–246.

134. See Chap. II(1)a, n. 6.

135. Bhaiṣajyaguru, Buddha of Healing, who resides in the land of pure emerald in the east. See *Yakushi nyorai hongan-kyō* 藥師如來本願經, *Myōhōrenge-kyō,* XXIII (*Taishō,* IX, 53a–55a).

136. Buddhas and bodhisattvas referred to only once are omitted.

The great popularity of Kannon rests on the message of the *Kannon-gyō* (the chapter on Kannon of the *Hoke-kyō*), which affirms life in this world, human nature, and the doctrine of universal salvation. It teaches the saving power of Kannon over the seven calamities of fire, water, storm, sword, evil spirits, enemies, and inner evils such as lust, anger, and ignorance.

The stories about the *Hoke-kyō* are distributed as follows:

I. 11, 18, 19, 28

II. 3, 6, 15, 18

III. 1, 6, 9, 10, 13, 18, 19, 20, 22, 24, 29, 34, 35, 37, 38.

Only two stories appear in both lists (I.18; III.13). This is due to the fact that the Kannon cult was centered more around images than scriptures, and devotees simply meditated on Kannon, invoked Kannon by calling the name, or made offerings of lights, flowers, and incense to Kannon. In response to their devotion, Kannon never failed to answer their requests. On the other hand, in the *Hoke-kyō* cult devotees recited or copied the scripture, which required some degree of learning. The concentration of the *Hoke-kyō* stories in the third volume shows their rising popularity toward the end of the Nara and early Heian periods, for the common people did not have access to the scriptures in the early years of Japanese Buddhism, when a limited number of scriptures were available only in Chinese.

Kannon was known to the Japanese not only through the *Hoke-kyō* but also through the scriptures of the pure land school such as the *Muryōju-kyō* and Tantric scriptures such as the *Jūichimen kanzeon shinju-kyō* 十一面觀世音神呪經,[137] and *Senju sengen darani-kyō* 千手千眼陀羅尼經.[138] Over one hundred and thirty Tantric scriptures were transmitted to Japan by eminent monks such as Dōji (d. 700) and Genbō (d. 746) and spread quickly.[139] The Eleven-headed Kannon (Ekādaśamukha Avalokiteśvara 十一面觀音) and the Thousand-armed Kannon (Sahasrabhujasahasrākṣa Avalokiteśvara 千手 [千眼] 觀音), which became popular with the practice of reciting the relevant dharani, are the embodiment of the cosmic nature of Kannon. Avalokiteśvara was originally a mythological creation of Indian Buddhists; the being was seldom represented as a human, but was invested with supernatural forms. Avalokiteśvara absorbed so many attributes

137. *Jūichimen kanzeon shinju-kyō* (*Taishō*, XX, No. 1070). *Jūichimen kanzeon shinju shin-gyō* (*Ibid.*, No. 1071).

138. *Senju sengen kanzeon bosatsu kōdai enman muge daihishin darani-kyō* 千手千眼觀世音菩薩廣大圓滿無礙大悲心陀羅尼經 (*Ibid.*, No. 1060).

139. See Inaya Yūsen, "Nara jidai mikkyō kyōten to Kūkai," *Mikkyō bunka*, No. 73 (June 1965), 52–59. Genbō of the Hossō School who had studied in China (716–734) made a vow to make a thousand copies of the *Senju sengen darani-kyō*, and achieved it in 743.

of Buddhas and bodhisattvas that it became almost an independent cosmic figure in the northern Buddhist countries.[140] Kannon incarnated in thirty-three forms is a mediator of this world and the other world, life and death, and Buddhas and all living beings. Ganjin, a famous blind preceptor who came from China to establish the ordination platform at Emperor Shōmu's invitation, was a great devotee of the Thousand-armed Kannon, probably because that Kannon was believed to cure blindness (III.12).[141]

In boundless compassion Kannon is eternally at work to protect and save all sentient beings in this world and an infinite number of other worlds. One tradition explains how the Eleven-headed Kannon came into being by a story: Avalokiteśvara once looked down on the suffering of the world and was so distressed by the sight that his head split into eleven pieces.[142] Female features which characterize Kannon in Japan and Kuan-yin in China may have originated with Kannon's role of savior, and the fusion of these features with the folk belief in mother divinities. In medieval China, many legends about a girl who is identified as an incarnation of the Thousand-armed Kuan-yin illustrate the process of acceptance of Kuan-yin as a young woman.[143] Obviously Tantric Kuan-yins preceded beautiful female Kuan-yins in China. In the Nihon ryōiki, three stories are on the Eleven-headed Kannon (II.11; III.3, 30) and Thousand-armed Kannon (II.42; III.12, 14), while one is on the Kannon based on the Hoke-kyō (I.18).

The same miraculous qualities are attributed to the Hoke-kyō. Its scrolls were believed to be repositories of miraculous power, which worked against those who slandered the scripture or its devotees (III.6, 20, etc.). Copying the Hoke-kyō was considered to be an act of great merit, a fact well illustrated in the story of a high official who was sent to hell. Yama tried to offset his offenses with the merit of the 69,384 characters of the Hoke-kyō he had copied during his lifetime, but found that the merit was insufficient (III.37). The biographies of the Ōjōden series record the accounts of those born in the pure land by reciting or copying the Hoke-kyō. The Hokke kenki[144] shows that the devotees of the Hoke-kyō were born in Maitreya's heaven or

140. See Paul Mus, "Thousand-armed Kannon: A Mystery or a Problem?" IBK, XII (No. 1, January 1964), 438–470.
141. See Kobayashi Taichirō, "Naracho no Senju Kannon," Bukkyō geijutsu, XXV (1955), 55–80.
142. L. A. Waddell, "The Indian Buddhist Cult of Avalokita and His Consort Tārā 'the Savioress,' Illustrated from the Remains in Magadha," JRAS (1894), 59–60.
143. Tsukamoto Zenryū, "Kinsei Shina taishū no nyoshin Kannon shinkō," Yamaguchi hakushi kanreki kinen Indogaku Bukkyōgaku ronsō, 262–280; Kobayashi Taichirō, "Tōdai no Daihi Kannon," Bukkyō geijutsu, XX (1953), 3–27; XXI (1954), 89–109; XXII (1954), 3–28.
144. See Chap. I(2)d, n. 181.

Kannon's pure land. Mahayana scriptures state it to be a bodhisattva practice to uphold and propagate dharma. Since the scriptures contain dharma, upholding, reading, expounding, and copying them are effective means for spreading dharma, and, therefore, a bodhisattva practice. The Buddha is said to be present in the scriptures.

The *Hoke-kyō* was influential in the Japanese understanding of Śākyamuni, for it was one of the earliest scriptures in Japan and it had gained great popularity among the people. Prince Shōtoku's commentary on the *Hoke-kyō*, *Hokke gisho* 法華義疏[145] is a good illustration of the appeal which it exercised as early as the sixth century (I.Preface). It emphasizes that faith in the Śākyamuni's teaching is favored above all else, and with faith even karma is destroyed by dharani, although good works are neither excluded nor rejected. Bodhisattvas are ready to help devotees reach Buddhahood. In China as well as Japan, the *Hoke-kyō* cult was gradually overshadowed by the Amida cult, but they share a common emphasis on devotion, although the stress shifted from this world to the hereafter. In the *Hoke-kyō*, Kannon is the counterpart of Amida, the Savior.

Speculation on the nature of Buddha led to the formulation of the doctrine of *trikāya*, the three bodies of Buddha, namely, the dharma-body, enjoyment body, and apparitional body. The *Hoke-kyō* says that Śākyamuni attained enlightenment many ages ago, and he will exist for countless more in the future. Thus his transcendental quality is greatly enhanced, and he is identified with dharma. On the other hand, the *Nehan-gyō* developed the idea of the immanent Buddha-nature within all beings. As stated above, these two scriptures were those most familiar to Kyōkai. Kyōkai interprets many miraculous signs of Buddha images by saying:

> The dharma-body Buddha of the ultimate reality has neither flesh nor blood. Why then did it suffer from pain? This took place only to show that dharma exists changeless. It is another miraculous event [II.23].

Why does the dharma-body Buddha reveal miraculous signs? Dharma was understood as the ultimate reality underlying every phenomenon. The dharma-body is not one since it pervades and supports everything; nor is it multiple since it remains identical with itself.[146]

145. *Hokke gisho* (*DBZ*, 14, 1–130). See Hanayama Shinshō, *Hokke gisho no kenkyū* (*Tōyō bunko ronsō*, XVIII, 1). Hanayama, an exponent of the traditional theory on its authorship, ascribes it to Prince Shōtoku, while Tsuda Sōkichi challenges this and would shift the date of compilation to the Nara period (*Nihon koten no kenkyū*, II; *Tsuda Sōkichi zenshū*, II, 129–138).
146. Poussin, "The Three Bodies of Buddha," *JRAS* (1907), 956.

Indeed we know that the dharma-body of wisdom exists. This is a miraculous sign to bring the faithless to a realization of this [II.36].

In some stories he explains such miraculous signs as the work of the Buddha's spirit 聖靈 (II.22, 26) or the Buddha's mind 聖心[147] (III.26), which resided in Buddha statues.

It is said that the Buddha statue is not alive, so how could it suffer and be sick? Indeed, we learn that this was the manifestation of the Buddha's mind. Even after the death of Buddha, the dharma-body always exists, eternal and unchangeable [III.28].[148]

All beings exist in the dharma and reveal it. Buddha is a major cosmic symbol of the dharma, and Buddha's spirit or mind functions in the cosmos.

When we compare miraculous stories about the spirits of the dead with those about the Buddha's spirit or mind and dharma-body Buddha, we find structural similarities that lead us to think that Kyōkai may have understood the latter as analogous to the former. The dharma-body Buddha is present in scriptures and statues, just as the spirits of the dead reside in bones and elsewhere. In the *Nihon ryōiki* there is no reference to the historical Buddha, and Śākyamuni Buddha is depicted as a savior similar to Amida or Kannon (II.28; III.25). The dharma-body Buddha, transcendent and immanent, became the source of faith for the Japanese who lived far away from India and accepted Buddhism a millennium after Śākyamuni's lifetime.

In the Buddhist tradition, *triratna*, the Three Treasures, is the foundation of salvation, and the Buddhist profession of faith is formulated into the vow of faith in the Three Treasures. As to the understanding of the Three Treasures in Japan, Ienaga has discussed the second article of Prince Shōtoku's Seventeen-Article Constitution, which reads: "Venerate highly the Three Treasures. The Three Treasures are Buddha, Dharma, and Samgha."[149] He points out that the Japanese understanding of the Three Treasures centered around the dharma-body Buddha, which became the basis of Japanese Buddhism as early as the time of Prince Shōtoku.[150] He infers that the second sentence was

---

147. See W. Liebenthal, "One-mind-dharma 一心法," *Tsukamoto hakushi shōju kinen Bukkyō shigaku ronshū*, 41–47. According to Seng Chao 僧肇 (374–414), the mind of the Sage, that is, Buddha's mind, is life靈, which is identified with *prajñā*, and permeates the universe: the Sage is the universal soul, which participates in individual lives, latent and manifest, one and divided. Liebenthal suggests its possible derivation from *dharmakāya*.

148. 雖佛滅後法身常住 may be a modified version of 明雖滅盡燈爐猶存 如來亦爾煩惱雖滅 法身常存 in the *Daihatsu nehan-gyō*, V (*Taishō*, XII, No. 374, 390a).

149. *Nihon shoki*, XXII (Suiko 12:4:3).

150. Ienaga, *Jōdai Bukkyō shisōshi kenkyū*, 26–27.

originally a note of a later commentator, included in the main text by mistake, and that the three components of the Three Treasures were not considered of equal significance.

The *Nihon ryōiki* gives more than a dozen citations of "the Three Treasures" (*sanbō* 三寶), and two of "Buddha, Dharma, Samgha" (*buppōsō* 佛法僧), the latter two being apparently Kyōkai's words since one is found in his comment on the term *ichisendai*[151] and the other in his preface to the third volume. The term "Three Treasures" means the Buddhist teachings as often as it means the embodiment of Buddha, Dharma, and Samgha in Buddha images, scrolls, and monks. Therefore we agree with Ienaga that the Japanese Buddhists had faith in the dharma-body Buddha, and we may add that they have also shown a strong tendency to embody the Three Treasures in specific objects that became symbols of the dharma-body Buddha. This explains why there are miraculous tales concerning holy men, statues, and scrolls in the *Nihon ryōiki*. Through devotion to a particular symbol, devotees have experienced the eternal presence of the dharma-body Buddha revealed in miraculous signs.

From early scriptures we learn that primitive Buddhists did not reject the miraculous, but they held it in low esteem. There are three categories of the miraculous: the mystical wonder, the wonder of manifestation, and the wonder of education.[152] The real wonder is that of education, that is, the wonder of transforming the self, or self-mastery. Monks were not allowed to display miraculous power before the laity.[153] On the other hand, there was a strong tendency to ascribe power to Śākyamuni and his famous disciples out of veneration for them. In the Mahayana tradition in which the power of Śākyamuni and other Buddhas and bodhisattvas is revealed through their compassion in the saving of all sentient beings, such power is manifested in all times and places as a skillful means for guiding men to faith, to the path of enlightenment. Biographies of Buddhist monks have a special chapter on those who were famous for miraculous powers.[154] Signs of miraculous power serve as stimuli for the faithful, as the observance of precepts is considered an aid to the realization of enlightenment.

151. See Chap. II(3)a, n. 114.

152. *Dighanikāya*, I, III, and elsewhere. See *Dialogues of the Buddha*, trans. by Rhys Davids, Part I, 272–284, III, 95–110, and elsewhere. See Chap. II(2)c, n. 111.

153. See *The Vinaya Texts*, trans. by T. W. Rhys Davids and H. Oldenberg, III (*SBE*, XX, 81), *Cullavagga*, V, 8, 2: "You are not, O Bhikkus, to display before the laity the superhuman power of *Iddhi*. Whosoever does so shall be guilty of a *dukkaṭa* (a wrong act)."

154. Hui-chiao's *Kao-seng chuan* has a chapter on *shen-i* 神異 (IX–X), while Tao-hsüan's *Kao-seng chuan* (道宣, 高僧傳) and Pao-ch'ang's *Ming-seng chuan* (寶唱, 名僧傳) have a chapter on *kan-t'ung* 感通.

If miracles are narrowly defined as the intervention of the divine which is designed to suspend or change the law of nature, then wondrous occurences in the Buddhist tradition are not miracles, but the work of karma (I.26). As a consequence of past karma, man becomes a sage, holy man, bodhisattva, or buddha, and attains self-mastery. To the popular imagination, however, wonders held such appeal that they served as signs to invite men through the gate along the path toward enlightenment.

PART TWO

# Annotated Translation of the *Nihon ryōiki*

# NIHONKOKU GENPŌ ZEN'AKU RYŌIKI

## VOLUME I

by Kyōkai

Monk of Yakushi-ji
on the West Side of Nara

## CONTENTS

Thirty-five Stories on the Karmic Retribution of Good and Evil

Preface     99

1. On Catching Thunder     102
2. On Taking a Fox as a Wife and Bringing Forth a Child     104
3. On a Boy of Great Physical Strength Whose Birth Was Given by the Thunder's Blessing     105
4. On Prince Regent Shōtoku's Showing Extraordinary Signs     108
5. On Gaining an Immediate Reward for Faith in the Three Treasures     111
6. On Gaining an Immediate Reward for Faith in Bodhisattva Kannon     115
7. On Paying for and Freeing Turtles and Being Rewarded Immediately and Saved by Them     116
8. On a Deaf Man Whose Hearing was Restored Immediately Owing to his Faith in a Mahayana Scripture     118
9. On the Reunion in a Foreign Land of a Father with his Child Who was Carried Away by an Eagle     119
10. On a Man's Rebirth as an Ox for Labor and Showing an Extraordinary Sign Because of Stealing from His Son     120
11. On Gaining an Immediate Penalty for a Lifetime of Catching Fish in a Net     122
12. On a Skull, Which Was Saved from Being Stepped on by Men and Beasts, Showing an Extraordinary Sign and Repaying the Benefactor Immediately     123
13. On a Woman Who Performed Work in an Extraordinary Way, Ate Sacred Herbs, and Flew up to Heaven Alive     124
14. On a Monk Who Got an Immediate Reward for Recollecting and Reciting the *Shin-gyō* and Showed an Extraordinary Sign     125

15. On a Wicked Man Who Persecuted a Begging Monk and
Gained an Immediate Penalty    126

16. On Gaining an Immediate Penalty for Skinning a
Live Rabbit without Mercy    127

17. On Suffering War Damage and Gaining an Immediate
Reward for Faith in an Image of Bodhisattva Kannon    128

18. On Recollecting and Reciting the *Hoke-kyō* and Gaining
an Immediate Reward to Show an Extraordinary Sign    129

19. On Ridiculing a Reciter of the *Hoke-kyō* and Getting a
Twisted Mouth as an Immediate Penalty    130

20. On a Monk Who Gave away the Firewood Provided to
Heat the Bath and Was Reborn as an Ox for Labor,
Showing an Extraordinary Sign    131

21. On Gaining an Immediate Penalty for Driving a Heavily
Burdened Horse Without Mercy    132

22. On Showing an Extraordinary Sign at the Moment of
Death Owing to Devotion to Buddhist Studies and
Spreading the Teaching for the Benefit of All Beings    133

23. On an Evil Man Who Was Negligent in Filial Piety to
His Mother and Gained an Immediate Penalty of
Violent Death    135

24. On an Evil Daughter Who Was Negligent in Filial Piety
to Her Mother and Gained an Immediate Penalty of
Violent Death    136

25. On a Loyal and Selfless Minister Who Gained Heaven's
Sympathy and Was Rewarded by a Miraculous Event    137

26. On a Full-fledged Monk Who kept Precepts, Practiced
Austerities, and Attained a Miraculous Power in this Life    138

27. On an Evil Anonymous Novice Who Tore Down a Pillar
of the Pagoda and Gained a Penalty    139

28. On Practicing the Formula of the Peacock King, and
Thereby Gaining an Extraordinary Power to Become a
Saint and Fly to Heaven in This Life    140

29. On Breaking Wickedly the Bowl of a Begging Novice
and Gaining an Immediate Penalty of Violent Death    142

30. On Taking Others' Possessions Unrighteously, Causing
Evil, and Gaining a Penalty Showing an Extraordinary
Event    143

31. On Attaining a Great Fortune Immediately Owing to
Devotion to Kannon and Praying for a Share of Benefits    146

32. On Gaining an Immediate Reward for Faith in the Three
Treasures, Reverence to Monks, and Having Scriptures
Recited    147

33. On the Miraculous Survival of a Buddha's Picture Offered
by a Widow Who Made a Vow to Have It Painted for
Her Deceased Husband    148

34. On Taking Back Silk Robes Once Stolen Owing to the
Petition to Bodhisattva Myōken    149

35. On a Nun Who Painted a Buddha Image out of Gratitude
    for the Four Kinds of Blessings and Gained a Power to
    Show an Extraordinary Sign    150

# Preface to Volume I

The Inner Scriptures[1] and Outer Writings[2] initially came to Japan by way of Paekche[3] in two waves: the latter arrived during the reign of Emperor Homuda 譽田,[4] who resided at the Palace of Toyoakira in Karushima 輕嶋豐明宮;[5] the former, during the reign of Emperor Kinmei 欽明,[6] who resided at the palace of Kanazashi in Shikishima 磯城嶋金刺宮.[7] Nowadays, it is fashionable for scholars who study the Outer Writings to slander Buddhist teachings, and for those who read the Inner Scriptures to neglect the Outer Writings. They are foolish and deceive themselves, ignoring the consequences of good and evil deeds.[8] But the wise, who are well versed in both the Inner and Outer traditions, stand in awe and believe in the law of karmic causation.[9]

There are many examples of piety in the imperial line. For instance, it is said that there was an emperor who climbed a hill to survey his domain, had compassion for the people, and thereafter contented himself with a palace that had a leaky roof.[10] Again, there was a prince who was innately prudent and foresighted, able to listen to ten men addressing him at the same time without missing a single word.[11] At the emperor's bidding he lectured on a Mahayana scripture when he was twenty-five years old, and his commentaries on Buddhist scriptures have been handed down for posterity. Another emperor made

1. 內經 naikyō; Buddhist scriptures.
2. 外書 gesho; non-Buddhist writings, that is, Chinese classics.
3. 百濟 Kudara (traditionally 18 B.C.–663 A.D.); one of the Korean Kingdoms which unified the southwestern part of the Korean peninsula in the beginning of the fourth century and served as the chief route for the introduction of continental culture to Japan.
4. (traditional reign, 270–310) posthumous name Ōjin 應神. Homuda might be a local name. About 400 the King of Paekche, whose country had been aided by the Japanese expedition against Koguryŏ 高句麗 in 291, sent scholars (阿直岐, 王仁) and Chinese classics to the Japanese court. See *Nihon shoki* (Ōjin 15:8:6; 16:2); Aston, "Nihongi," I, 262–263.
5. Located at present Ōkaru, Kashihara-shi, Nara-ken 奈良縣橿原市大輕.
6. (traditional reign, 539–571) According to the *Nihon shoki*, the introduction of Buddhism took place in 552, when King Syŏng-myŏng 聖明王 of Paekche presented to Emperor Kinmei a bronze statue of Śākyamuni Buddha, several flags and canopies, and a number of scriptures. See Chap. I(1)b, n. 37; see also I.5.
7. Located at present Kanaya, Sakurai-shi, Nara-ken 奈良縣櫻井市金屋.
8. 罪福 zaifuku; evil deeds which lead to penalties and good deeds which lead to rewards.
9. 因果 inga; cause and effect, that is, the law of karmic causation. It is juxtaposed with *zaifuku* in the preceding sentence.
10. Refers to Emperor Nintoku 仁德 (traditionally, 290–399); depicted in the Confucian image of an ideal king in the *Kojiki* (III.110) and *Nihon shoki* (XI, Nintoku 4:2:6; 7:4:1).
11. Refers to Prince Shōtoku. See I.4, 5.
12. The *Sangyō gisho* 三經義疏; commentaries on three Buddhist scriptures, that is, *Hoke-kyō* (*Saddharmapuṇḍarīkasūtra*), *Yuima-kyō* (*Vimalakīrtinirdeśasūtra*), *Shōman-gyō* (*Śrīmālādevīsiṃhanādasūtra*), which are traditionally ascribed to Prince Shōtoku (*Taishō*, LXI, Nos. 2185–2187). See Chap. II(3)b, n. 145.

great vows[13] and, as an act of devotion, built a statue of Buddha. Heaven aided his vows, and the earth opened its treasure house to offer gold.[14]

There were also eminent monks whose virtues equaled those in the ten stages[15] and whose path went beyond the two vehicles.[16] They brought the light of wisdom to dark corners, rescued the drowning with the boat of compassion, practiced religious austerities, and were known even in distant lands. As to those of our own age who are enlightened, we cannot yet know how great their merits are.

Now I, Kyōkai, monk[17] of Yakushi-ji[18] in Nara, see the world closely. There are men who are able, but they are selfishly motivated. Their desire for gain is stronger than a magnet that can pull a mountain of iron; their lust for the possessions of others and their tightfisted hold

13. 弘誓願 guzeigan; four great vows of bodhisattvas, formulated in reference to the Four Noble Truths in Śākyamuni's teaching. The contents of the vows differ according to various traditions, and the following is widely accepted in the Tendai School: 1. However innumerable sentient beings are, I vow to save them; 2. However inexhaustible cravings are, I vow to extinguish them; 3. However limitless dharma is, I vow to study it; 4. However endless the quest for enlightenment is, I vow to attain it. For the significance of a vow, see M. Anesaki, "Prayer (Buddhist)," ERE, X, 166–170.

14. Refers to Emperor Shōmu 聖武, who made a vow in 743 to build a statue of Lochana Buddha in gold and copper but had difficulty in accomplishing it, because the statue was more than fifty feet high. In 749 gold was discovered in Japan for the first time, and eventually the statue was completed with popular support organized by Gyōgi. See Sansom, trans., "The Imperial Edicts in the Shoku Nihongi," TASJ, Second Series, I (1923–24), 26.

15. 十地 jūji (Skt. daśabhūmi); the ten stages in the disciplinary process of the bodhisattva; according to the Kegon-gyō, they are as follows:

1. paramuditā: stage of joy at benefiting oneself and others;
2. vimalā: stage of freedom from all possible defilement;
3. prabhākarī: stage of emission of the light of wisdom;
   發光地
4. arcismatī: stage of glowing wisdom;
   焰慧地
5. sudurjayā: stage of overcoming utmost difficulties;
   難勝地
6. abhimukhī: stage of realization of wisdom;
   現前地
7. dūramgamā: stage of proceeding far;
   遠行地
8. acalā: stage of attainment of immobility;
   不動地
9. sādhumatī: stage of attainment of expedient wisdom;
   善意地
10. dharmameghā: stage of attainment of ability to spread the teaching.
    法雲地

16. 二乘 nijō; śrāvakayāna, the path of listeners, and pratyekabuddhayāna, the path of solitary Buddha; Mahayana Buddhists place bodhisattvayāna beyond these two paths, saying that the goal of these two paths is self-enlightenment while that of the bodhisattvayāna is enlightenment for all beings. See III.38, n. 42.

17. 沙門; see Chap. I(1)a, n. 4.

18. See Chap. I(1)c.

on their own goods are greater than that of a grinder[19] which relent-lessly squeezes even the husk of a single millet seed. Some men defraud temples and are reborn as calves to toil and repay the debts of their former lives;[20] some speak ill of Buddhist teachings and monks and meet with calamity in this present life;[21] some seek the path [of Bud-dha] by leading a disciplined life of practice and are rewarded in this life;[22] some practice good with a profound faith and are blissful.[23]

Good and evil deeds cause karmic retribution as a figure causes its shadow, and suffering and pleasure follow such deeds as an echo follows a sound in the valley.[24] Those who witness such experiences marvel at them and forget they are real happenings in the world. The penitent withdraws to hide himself, for he burns with shame at once. Were the fact of karmic retribution not known, how could we rec-tify wickedness and establish righteousness? And how would it be possible to make men mend their wicked minds and practice the path of virtue without demonstrating the law of karmic causation?

In China,[25] the *Myōhōki* (Record of Invisible Work of Karmic Retribution)[26] was compiled, and, during the great T'ang dynasty, the *Hannya kenki* (A Collection of Miraculous Stories Concerning the *Kongō hannya-kyō*)[27] was written. Since we respect the documents of foreign lands, should we not also believe and stand in awe of the mi-raculous events in our own land? Having witnessed these events my-self, I cannot remain idle. After long meditation on this, I now break my silence. I have recorded the limited information that has come to me in these three volumes called the *Nihonkoku genpō zen'aku ryōiki*,[28] for future generations.

However, I am not gifted with either wisdom or lucidity. Learning acquired in a narrow well loses its way when out in the open. My work resembles that of a poor craftsman working on the carving of a master. I am afraid that I will cut my hand and suffer from the injury

19. 流頭 may be a mis-copying of 臼頭, which is a grinder. Itabashi holds that the script is a combination of water and grinder 磑. In T'ang China, Buddhist monasteries were engaged in milling with grinders 碾磑 for profit. See Michihata, *Tōdai Bukkyōshi no kenkyū*, 450–452.
20. See I.20; II.9, 32, etc.
21. See I.19; II.7, 11, etc.
22. See I.14, 26, 38; II.21; III.1, 6, etc.
23. See I.31; II.14, 28, 42; III.21, etc.
24. 善惡之報如影隨形．苦樂之響如谷應音. See Chap. I(2)a, n. 139.
25. 漢地 literally means "the land of the Han," that is, China.
26. See Chap. I(1)b, n. 34; Chap. I(2)b.
27. See Chap. I(2)b. 般若驗記, a shortened title of *Kongō hannya-kyō jikkenki*, 3 vols., com-piled by Meng Hsien-chung 孟獻忠 in 718 in the reign of Hsüan-tsung of the T'ang dynasty (*Dainihon zokuzō-kyō*, Part II. 乙, case 22:1).
28. See n. 1, above.

long afterward. My work is comparable to a rough pebble beside the K'un-lun Mountains.[29] Its source in the oral tradition is so indistinct that I am afraid of omitting much. Only the desire to do good has moved me to try, in spite of the fear that this might turn out to be a presumptuous work by an incompetent author. I hope that learned men in future generations will not laugh at my efforts, and I pray that those who happen upon this collection of miraculous stories will put aside evil, live in righteousness, and, without causing evil, practice good.[30]

# I

## On Catching Thunder[1]

Chīsakobe no Sugaru 小子部栖輕[2] was a favorite of Emperor Yū-ryaku 雄略天皇 (called Ōhatsuse-wakatake no sumeramikoto 大泊瀬稚武天皇) who reigned for twenty-three years at the Palace of Asakura in Hatsuse 泊瀬朝倉宮.[3]

Once the emperor stayed at the Palace of Iware 磐余,[4] and it happened that Sugaru stepped into the Ōyasumidono 大安殿[5] without

29. 崑崙山 a mountain range in Sinkiang province which is famous for jade.

30. 諸惡莫作諸善奉行, a popular maxim found in most Buddhist scriptures.

1. Another version of the same story is found in the *Nihon shoki*, XIV (Yūryaku 7:7:3); Aston, "Nihongi," I, 347. The emperor commanded Sugaru to go and seize the kami of Mt. Mimoro. Sugaru climbed the hill and caught a great snake. When he showed it to the emperor, thunder rolled, and its eyeballs flamed. The emperor was frightened and sent it back to Mt. Mimoro, renaming it Ikazuchi, thunder. For a discussion of snake (dragon)-thunder themes, see De Visser, *The Dragon in China and Japan*.

2. Chīsakobe is a surname, and Sugaru a given name. The *Nihon Shoki*, XIV (Yūryaku 6:3:7) gives a story on the origin of Chīsakobe; Aston, "Nihongi." Once Emperor Yūryaku (traditionally, 456–479) told Sugaru to collect silkworms (Ja. *kaiko*) in order to encourage court ladies to work for the silk industry. Sugaru collected babies (*kaiko*) instead of silkworms. The emperor was amused and gave him the title of Chīsakobe, literally meaning "little children cooperation." Shida, on the basis of these stories, holds that Sugaru was in charge of preventive magic against thunder and was related to the Hata 秦 family which had immigrated from Silla early in the fifth century and probably taught the Japanese the process for making silk. See his "Chīsakobe no seikaku ni tsuite," *Nihon rekishi*, No. 214 (March 1966), 66–79. Naoki says that Sugaru was a royal guard in his "Chīsakobe no seishitsu ni tsuite," *Shoku Nihongi kenkyū*, VII (No. 9, September 1960), 225–228.

3. Located in the eastern part of present Sakurai-shi, Nara-ken 奈良縣櫻井市.

4. It may be a detached palace somewhere in present Shiki-gun, Nara-ken; neither the *Kojiki* nor *Nihon shoki* refers to this palace.

5. The main building in the imperial palace during the Asuka and Nara periods; identified by some scholars with the later Daigyokuden 大極殿.

knowing that the emperor lay with the empress there. The emperor, ashamed of his conduct, stopped making love, and it thundered in the heavens. The emperor then said to Sugaru, "Won't you invite the rolling thunder to come here?" "Certainly," answered Sugaru, whereat the emperor commanded him, "Go, invite it here."

Leaving the palace, Sugaru hurried away on horseback, wearing a red headband[6] on his forehead and carrying a halberd with a red banner.[7] He passed the heights of Yamada in the village of Abe[8] and Toyura-dera 豊浦寺,[9] finally arriving at the crossroads of Karu no morokoshi.[10] He cried out: "The emperor has invited the rolling thunder of heaven to his palace." While galloping back to the palace, he asked himself why, even if it were a thunder kami, would it not accept the emperor's invitation.

As he returned, it happened that the lightning struck between Toyura-dera and Ioka 飯岡.[11] On seeing it, Sugaru sent for priests to place the thunder on the portable carriage,[12] and he escorted it to the imperial palace, saying to the emperor, "I have brought the thunder kami." The thunder gave off such a dazzling light that the emperor was terrified. He made many offerings[13] and then had it sent back to the original site, which is called "Hill of Thunder" 雷岡.[14] (It is situated to the north of the Palace of Owarida 小治田 in the old capital.)[15]

After a while Sugaru died. The emperor let the corpse stay, in its coffin for seven days and nights.[16] Then, recalling Sugaru's loyalty, the emperor had a tomb built at the place which had been struck by lightning and had a pillar inscribed: "The tomb of Sugaru who caught the thunder." The thunder was not pleased. It struck the pillar and was caught between the splintered pieces. When emperor heard this,

6. 緋蘰 a piece of red cloth tied around the head; also worn by a guard of the land of the dead (II.7). According to Shida, wearing it was a protective measure against thunder ("Chisa-kobe," 74).

7. 赤幡桙 a sign of a royal messenger; see n. 6, above.

8. 阿部山田, a village to the south of Mt. Kagu 香具, the eastern part of the present Takechi-gun 高市郡, Nara-ken.

9. Also known as Mukuhara-dera 向原寺 or Kōken-ji 興建寺; a nunnery originally built by Soga no Iname 蘇我稲目 (d. 570) at his residence, which is located at present Asuka-mura, Takechi-gun, Nara-ken.

10. 諸越 morokoshi may be a place name which derived from the intercourse between China and Japan, hence meaning Chinese or trading center.

11. Unidentified local name.

12. 轝籠 koshiko; a palanquin made of bamboo.

13. 幣帛 mitegura; see Chap. II(1)a, n. 18.

14. A low hill located in the present Asuka-mura on the bank of the Asuka River.

15. Since Kyōkai lived in the late Nara and early Heian periods, "the old capital" refers to the capitals before the Nara period, that is, during the Asuka and Fujiwara periods.

16. See Chap. II(3)a, n. 115.

he freed the thunder loose, narrowly rescuing it from death. The experience left the thunder in a confused state of mind which lasted for seven days and nights. The emperor's officer, in rebuilding the pillar, inscribed it with the following epitaph: "Here lies Sugaru who caught the thunder both in his lifetime and after his death."

This is the origin of the name, "Hill of Thunder," given in the time of the old capital.

# 2

## On Taking a Fox as a Wife and Bringing Forth a Child[1]

In the reign of Emperor Kinmei (that is, Amekuni-oshihiraki-hironiwa no mikoto 天國押開廣庭命, the emperor who resided at the Palace of Kanazashi in Shikishima),[2] a man from Ōno district of Mino province 三野國大野郡[3] set out on horseback in search of a good wife. In a field he came across a pretty and responsive girl. He winked at her and asked, "Where are you going, Miss?" "I am looking for a good husband," she answered. So he asked, "Will you be my wife?" and, when she agreed, he took her to his house and married her.

Before long she became pregnant and gave birth to a boy. At the same time their dog also gave birth to a puppy, it being the fifteenth of the twelfth month. This puppy constantly barked at the mistress[4] and seemed fierce and ready to bite. She became so frightened that she asked her husband[5] to beat the dog to death. But he felt sorry for the dog and could not bear to kill it.

In the second or third month, when the annual quota of rice[6] was hulled, she went to the place where the female servants were pounding rice in a mortar to give them some refreshments. The dog, seeing her, ran after her barking and almost bit her. Startled and terrified, she

1. The prototype of Japanese folktales concerning a fox; one tale of the Venerable Dōjō cycle; see Chap. II(2)b. Cf. M. W. de Visser, "The Fox and the Badger in Japanese Folklore," *TASJ*, XXXVI, Part Three (1908), 20–21. Cf. *Fusō ryakki* (III, Kinmei), *Mizukagami* (I, Kinmei).
2. See Preface, n. 7, above.
3. The eastern part of present Ibi-gun, Gifu-ken 岐阜縣揖斐郡. The country was divided into provinces (*kuni* 國), and provinces were divided into districts (*kōri* 郡). In the beginning of the eighth century, there were sixty-six provinces comprising 592 districts.
4. 家室 *ietoji*, housewife.
5. 家長 *iegimi*, master of the family.
6. The rice harvested in the preceding autumn had to be delivered to the capital before the end of the eighth month.

suddenly changed into a wild fox and jumped up on top of the hedge.

Having seen this, the man said, "Since a child was born between us, I cannot forget you. Please come always and sleep with me." She acted in accordance with her husband's words and came and slept with him. For this reason she was named "Kitsune" meaning "come and sleep."[7]

Slender and beautiful in her red skirt (it is called pink), she would rustle away from her husband, whereupon he sang of his love for his wife:

Love fills me completely
After a moment of reunion.
Alas! She is gone.[8]

The man named his child Kitsune, which became the child's surname—Kitsune no atae.[9] The child, famous for his enormous strength, could run as fast as a bird flies. He is the ancestor of the Kitsune-no-atae family in Mino province.[10]

# 3

## On a Boy of Great Physical Strength Whose Birth Was Given by the Thunder's Blessing[1]

In the reign of Emperor Bitatsu 敏達 (that is, Nunakura-futotama-shiki no mikoto 渟名倉太玉敷命, who resided at the Palace of Osada in Iware 磐余譯語田宮),[2] there was a farmer in the village of Katawa in Ayuchi district of Owari province 尾張國阿育知郡片蘕里.[3] While he was working to irrigate the rice fields, it began to rain. He took shelter under a tree and stood there holding a metal rod[4] in his hands. When it thundered, he raised the rod in fear. At that moment the thunder struck in front of him in the form of a child, who made a

---

7. Folk etymology of kitsune, fox; kitsu-ne 來寝 means "Come and sleep," while ki-tsune 來每 means "come always."

8. In the form of a thirty-one syllable poem (5-7-5-7-7).

9. 狐直; although Kitsune no atae is not listed in the Shinsen shōjiroku 新撰姓氏錄, atae is a hereditary title conferred on the family of a local governor who was of the local gentry class.

10. For his descendant, see II.4.

1. One tale of the Venerable Dōjō cycle; see II.4, 27; quoted in the Fusō ryakki (III, Bitatsu), Mizukagami (II, Bitatsu), etc.

2. Emperor Bitatsu's palace is located in the western part of present Sakurai-shi, Nara-ken.

3. Present Furuwatari-chō, Naka-ku, Nagoya-shi 名古屋市中區古渡町.

4. 金杖 metal rod or plow (the Fusō ryakki gives "plow").

deep bow. The farmer was about to strike it with the metal rod when the child said, "Please don't hit me. I will repay your kindness." The farmer asked, "What will you do for me, then?" The thunder answered, "I will send you a baby to repay your kindness.[5] Make me a boat of camphor, fill it with water, and give it to me with a bamboo leaf on the water."[6] When the farmer did this, the thunder said, "Keep away from me," and it ascended to heaven in a rising mist.

Some time later a baby was born to the farmer; the baby had a snake coiled twice around his head, and the snake's head and tail hung down his back. When the child reached his teens, he heard of a man of great strength at the court, and he went to the capital, for he thought of challenging the man in a contest of strength. An unusually strong prince lived in a detached house on the northeast corner of the imperial palace grounds, where a stone eight feet square also stood. Once, the powerful prince came out, picked up the huge stone, and threw it. Then he went back into his house and closed the door to prevent people from entering. The boy[7] saw this, and he knew that the prince was the very man he sought.

That night the boy crept into the place and threw the stone one foot farther than the prince had. When the mighty prince discovered this, he clapped his hands to warm up, tried to throw it farther, but failed. A second time the boy threw it two feet farther, and again the prince failed. Then the boy, making footprints three inches deep, threw it three feet farther. The prince wanted to catch the boy, who was easily identified by his small footprints, but the boy ran away quickly. The prince tried to catch the boy as he was creeping out through the hedge, but he found that the boy was inside the hedge. When the prince jumped over the hedge to reach the boy, the boy was already on the other side, and the mighty prince was unable to catch him. The prince, realizing that the boy was indeed the stronger, gave up chasing him.

Some time later the boy became an acolyte[8] at Gangō-ji 元興寺.[9] At that time no night passed without some of the acolytes in service

---

5. 我報汝之恩; see Chap. II(2)a, for the idea of *on*.

6. In ancient Japan camphorwood was used to make boats.

7. 少子 a child between three and sixteen according to the *Ryō no gige*, "Ko-ryō," Article 6; see Sansom, "Early Japanese Law," Part Two, 135.

8. 童子 *dōji* or *warawa*, Skt. *kumāra*; an unordained boy under the age of twenty who works at the temple as an apprentice.

9. Originally called Asuka-dera 飛鳥寺 or Hōkō-ji 法興寺, founded by Soga no Umako 蘇我馬子 in 588 and completed in 596; it was the first temple to have a pagoda and halls and showed Korean influence, and it was moved to the capital of Nara in 716. The present Angoin 安居院 stands at the site of the original temple at Asuka-mura.

at the bell hall being murdered. The new acolyte said to the monks at the temple, "I will put an end to these tragedies by killing the evil fiend,"[10] and the monks approved of his proposal. He proceeded to set four lamps and four men at the four corners of the bell hall and said to them, "When I get hold of the fiend, take the covers off the lamps." Then he hid himself at the base of the door.

At midnight the huge fiend appeared, but departed at the sight of the boy, returning again before dawn.[11] The boy seized it by the hair and pulled hard. The fiend struggled to extricate itself, but the acolyte pulled it into the hall. The four men at the four corners, frightened, were unable to remove the lamp covers so the boy had to light the lamps, one by one, while dragging the fiend around the hall. About dawn,[12] the fiend, its hair having been torn completely out, escaped. In the morning people traced the blood stains as far as the crossroads, where a wicked former slave[13] of the temple was buried,[14] and they discovered that it was the ghost of that dead man. The hair is still preserved in Gangō-ji as a treasure.[15]

Meanwhile the acolyte became a lay brother[16] and lived on at Gangō-ji. The temple owned some irrigated rice fields. When some princes stopped the flow of water and the fields became parched, the lay brother said, "I will irrigate the fields." The monks agreed to his plan. First, he made a plow so heavy that it took ten men to carry it. He took the plow in his hand like a cane and went to the fields, where he put it at the sluice gate to prop it open. But the princes took it away and closed the sluice gate that controlled the irrigation of the fields of the temple. Whereupon the lay brother placed at the sluice a stone so heavy that it would have required more than a hundred men to move it and proceeded to work in the fields. The princes, terrified by his great strength, did not dare to cause any more trouble. After that the fields were never dry, and they yielded good crops. The monks of the

---

10. 鬼 *oni*; hungry ghost, one of five or six modes of existence in Buddhist cosmology. See Chap. I(2)a, n. 127.

11. 後夜 *goya*, from three to five a.m.

12. 晨朝 *jinchō*, from five to seven a.m.

13. 奴 *yakko* (*nuhi*); see Chap. I(1)a, n. 24.

14. There was a belief that the spirits of the dead, particularly of those who died violently, would linger in this world and cause harm to the living. In order to prevent the activities of the evil spirits, wicked people were buried at a crossroads or the end of the bridge in the hope that the pressure of heavy traffic would keep them in their graves.

15. This passage reflects a belief that anything extraordinary or strange had power and thus should be properly cared for.

16. See Chap. I(1)d, n. 92.

temple allowed the lay brother to be ordained and to renounce the world, naming him Dharma Master Dōjō 道場法師.

This is the story of the mighty hero of Gangō-ji, renowned in later legends, whose extraordinary strength originated in the merits accumulated in his former lives. This miraculous event was witnessed in Japan.

# 4

*On Prince Regent Shōtoku's Showing Extraordinary Signs*[1]

Prince Regent Shōtoku 聖德皇太子 was the son of Emperor Tachibana-no-toyohi 橘豐日,[2] who reigned at the Palace of Ikebe-no-namitsuki in Iware 磐余池邊雙襕宮.[3] He became Prince Regent in the reign of Empress Suiko 推古,[4] who resided at the Palace of Owarida 小墾田. He had three names: Umayado no toyotomimi 厩戸豐聰耳; Shōtoku; and Kamitsu-miya 上宮. Since he was born in front of the stables, he was called "Umayado" [meaning "stable door"]. "Toyotomimi" [which means "intelligent ear"] originated because he was by nature so wise that he could attend to the legal claims of ten men at a time and decide them without missing a single word. He was also called "Shōtoku" [which means "sacred virtue"] because he not only behaved like a monk but was so well versed in Buddhist teachings that he could write commentaries on the *Shōman-gyō*, *Hoke-kyō*, etc.,[5] and so well versed in Chinese classics as to institute the system of court

1. This tale consists of two independent stories; the first is an anecdote of Prince Regent Shōtoku; the second concerns Ensei and Gangaku, two Buddhist monks. A common structure is found in these two stories: the beggar in the first and Gangaku in the second are sages in disguise, whom Prince Shōtoku and Ensei recognized with their penetrating eyes, thereby demonstrating their own sagacity. The former is similar to a popular legend found in works such as the *Nihon shoki*, *Jōgū Shōtoku hōō teisetsu*, *Jōgū taishiden hokejsuki* 上宮太子傳補闕記, *Sanbō ekotoba* (II,2), *Nihon ōjō gokurakuki*, *Konjaku monogatarishū* (XI, 1), etc. Also see Herman Bohner, "Shōtoku taishi," *Mitteilungen der Deutschen Gesellschaft für Natur- und Völkerkunde Ostasiens*, XXVIII (1936).

2. Emperor Yōmei 用明 (585–587).

3. Situated in present Ikejiri 池尻 and Ikeuchi 池內, Sakurai-shi, Nara-ken.

4. (592–628), Emperor Bitatsu's consort and the aunt of Prince Shōtoku, who appointed him Prince Regent in 593.

5. See Preface, n. 12, above.

ranks and honors.[6] He was called Kamitsu-miya no kimi [which literally means "Prince of the Upper Palace"] because his residence was located above the imperial palace.

Once, when the Prince Regent lived at the Palace of Okamoto in Ikaruga 鵤岡本宮,[7] he happened to go to Kataoka 片岡[8] and, on the way, he found a sick beggar lying by the side of the road.[9] Alighting from his palanquin, the prince talked with the beggar, took off his cloak to cover him, and went on his way. On his return he did not see the beggar, but only his cloak hanging on the branch of a tree. The prince put it on again. One of his ministers said to him, "Are you so poor that you must wear the soiled garment once worn by a beggar?" "It's all right, you wouldn't understand," was his reply. Meanwhile the beggar died in another place. The prince sent a messenger to have him buried temporarily[10] while a tomb which was named Hitoki no haka 人木墓 (Man-tree-tomb)[11] was built for him at Moribeyama 守部山 in the northeast corner of Hōrin-ji 法林寺[12] in the village of Okamoto. A messenger sent to visit the tomb found it too tightly closed to allow anybody to enter. Only a poem was found at the door, and it read:

> The name of my Lord
> Would be forgotten,
> Should the stream of Tomi of Ikaruga
> Cease to flow.[13]

6. The *Nihon shoki*, XXII (Suiko 11:12:5), gives an account of the initiation of the twelve-grade ranking system (603); see Aston, "Nihongi," II, 128. Cf. Inoue Mitsusada, *Nihon kodai kokka no kenkyū*, for the significance of this system in Japanese history.

7. Situated in the present site of Hokki-ji 法起寺 at Okamoto, Ikaruga-machi, Ikoma-gun, Nara-ken 奈良縣生駒郡斑鳩町岡本. Cf. *Nihon shoki*, XXII (Suiko 9:2); Aston, "Nihongi," II, 125.

8. In the vicinity of present Kamimaki-mura, Kita-kazuraki-gun, Nara-ken 奈良縣北葛城郡上牧村·

9. The *Nihon shoki*, XXII (Suiko 21:12:1, 2); Aston, "Nihongi," II, 144–145. The difference between the *Nihon ryōiki* and the *Nihon shoki* is as follows: in the former the sage is a sick beggar while in the latter he is a starving man; in the former the poem expresses admiration for Prince Shōtoku, while in the latter it expresses grief for a dying man; in the former people do not understand what really happened, while in the latter they understand and increase their veneration of Prince Shōtoku. See Tamura Enchō, *Asuka Bukkyōshi kenkyū*, 262–278.

10. 殯 *mogari*; see Chap. II(3)a.

11. The name may have originated in the preceding passage: "he could not see the beggar, but only his garment hanging on the branch of a tree," implying that the beggar had been replaced by a tree.

12. Founded in 622 by Prince Yamashiro no Ōe 山背大兄王 for his late father, Prince Regent Shōtoku, who died in 621.

13. It is one of the three funeral songs composed by Kose no Sanjō daifu 巨勢三杖大夫, according to the *Jōgū Shōtoku hōō teisetsu* (*DBZ*, 112, 46b).

The messenger, on his return, reported this to the prince, who was silent.

We learn that a sage 聖 recognizes a sage, whereas an ordinary man cannot recognize a sage. The ordinary man sees nothing but the outer form of a beggar, while the sage has a penetrating eye able to recognize the hidden essence.[14] It is a miraculous event.

The Venerable Ensei 圓勢師, a disciple of Dharma Master Shaku 藉 法師, was a national preceptor of Paekche.[15] He lived in the Takamiya-dera 高宮寺 at Kazuraki in Yamato province 大倭國葛木 in Japan.[16] In the north chamber of that temple, there once lived a monk whose name was Gangaku 願覺, who used to go out to the village at dawn and come back at dusk. When a lay brother, a disciple of the Venerable Ensei, told his master about Gangaku, the master said "Don't say a word about him." The lay brother secretly bored a hole in the wall of Gangaku's chamber to spy on him and found the chamber full of light. Again he reported to his master, who answered, "This is why I told you to keep quiet about him." Before long it happened that Gangaku suddenly passed away. Ensei told the lay brother to cremate him and bury the ashes, and this was done. Later the lay brother came to live in Ōmi 近江.[17] Once he heard someone say, "Here lives the Venerable Gangaku." At once he paid a visit, finding Gangaku exactly as he had been. Gangaku said to the lay brother, "It is a long time since I last saw you, but I have been thinking of you all the time. How have you been getting along?"

We learn that he was incarnated as a sage.[18] Eating five kinds of strong herbs[19] is forbidden in Buddhist precepts, but, if a sage eats them, he will not incur any sin.[20]

14. See Chap. II(2)c.

15. In the Maeda manuscript this story is found in III.39. The three monks are otherwise unknown; a similar story is found in Hui-chiao's *Kao-seng chuan* (X, 2, 邵碩). 百濟國之師 may be interpreted in two ways: "national preceptor of Paekche," or "monk from the land of Paekche."

16. A mountain temple in present Minami-kazuraki-gun, Nara-ken.

17. Present Shiga-ken 滋賀縣. .

18. 聖反化 *hijiri no henge;* the alternate reading is *shōhenge*, meaning "sacred incarnation, Buddha incarnated."

19. 五辛 *goshin;* garlic, scallion, onion, ginger, leek; see *Ryō no gige,* "Sōni-ryō," Article 7; Sansom, "Early Japanese Laws," Part Two, 128–129.

20. This note does not fit the story, but it may have been added to emphasize the idea that a sage is free from all precepts and conventions.

# 5

## On Gaining an Immediate Reward for Faith in
## the Three Treasures[1]

Lord Ōtomo no Yasunoko no muraji 大部屋栖野古連[2] of the Great Flower Rank[3] was an ancestor of the Ōtomo no muraji in Uji, Nagusa district, Kii province 紀伊國名草郡宇治.[4] He was endowed with a lucid mind and highly revered the Three Treasures.[5]

According to a record,[6] in the reign of Emperor Bitatsu,[7] sounds of musical instruments were heard off the coast of Izumi 和泉 province.[8] They sounded like pipes and strings or rolling thunder. They were heard in the daytime and at night a light spread eastward. Lord Ōtomo no Yasunoko no muraji heard this tale and reported it to the emperor, who did not believe it and remained silent. When he reported it to the empress, however, she ordered him to investigate. He went to the seaside to witness the scene himself and found it exactly as reported. While there, he came upon a camphor log which had been struck by thunder.[9] On his return, he said to the empress, "I have found a camphor log on the beach of Takaashi 高脚濱.[10] I humbly request permission to make Buddha images out of it." The empress gave permission saying, "Your wish is granted."

Yasunoko was very happy and announced the imperial decree to Shima no ōomi 嶋大臣,[11] who, in great joy, commissioned Ikebe no

1. Cf. *Nihon shoki* (Kinmei, Bitatsu, Suiko), *Konjaku monogatarishū* (XI, 23), *Fusō ryakki* (III, IV), etc.
2. The Ōtomo family is one of the influential families mainly in charge of the imperial guards, whose ancestry can be traced to the age of kami. See *Nihon shoki*, II, III, XVI, etc.; Aston, "Nihongi," I, 86, 116, 133, 403, etc. *Muraji* is a hereditary title for high ranking administrators from the end of the fifth century to the first half of the seventh century at the Yamato court.
3. 大花位 *daikei*; the seventh of the nineteen ranks instituted in 649 by Emperor Kōtoku 孝德 (645–654). See the *Nihon shoki*, XXV (Taika 5:2); Aston, "Nihongi," II, 231–232.
4. Present Uji, Kimiidera, Wakayama-shi 和歌山市紀三井寺宇治.
5. See Chap. II(3)b.
6. 本記 *honki*; this story must have been quoted from a source which no longer exists.
7. According to the *Nihon shoki*, this event took place in 553 in the reign of Emperor Kinmei, not that of Emperor Bitatsu (XIX Kinmei 14:5:1); Aston, "Nihongi," II, 68. In the *Nihon shoki*, it was Ikebe no atae 溝邊直 who was sent to make an investigation by the emperor.
8. The *Nihon shoki* gives "Chinu no umi, Izumi," 和泉茅淳海 (present Izumi-nada, south of the Gulf of Ōsaka).
9. See I.3.
10. Present Hamadera beach in Sakai-shi, Ōsaka-fu 大阪府堺市濱寺.
11. Meaning Minister of the Island, a popular name for Soga no Umako; in the courtyard of his mansion he had a pond dug with a small island in the middle. See *Nihon shoki*, XXII (Suiko 34:5:20); Aston, "Nihongi," II, 154. *Ōmi* is a hereditary title for high-ranking administrators.

atae Hita 池邊直氷田[12] to carve three bodhisattvas.[13] They were consecrated in a hall at Toyura[14] to inspire awe and reverence in the people. However, Lord Mononobe no yuge no Moriya no ōmuraji 物部弓削守屋大連[15] addressed the empress, saying, "No Buddha images should be kept in this country. They must be thrown away." Hearing this, the empress called Lord Yasunoko no muraji, saying, "Hide these Buddha images without delay." Thereupon he had Hita no atae hide them among rice sheaves. Lord Yuge no ōmuraji eventually burned the hall and threw the remaining images into the canal at Naniwa 難破.[16] He rebuked Yasunoko, saying, "The cause of our present disaster lies in keeping pagan images sent from a neighboring country. Give them up and throw them into the current which flows toward Korea." ("Pagan images" means "Buddha images.") Yasunoko firmly refused. Yuge no ōmuraji, deranged and rebellious, looked for an opportunity for treason, but heaven disliked him and earth hated him. He was at last overthrown in the reign of Emperor Yōmei,[17] and the Buddhist images were brought into the open to be kept for posterity. The image of Amida 阿彌陀[18] is now enshrined at Hiso-dera 比蘇寺[19] at Yoshino.

In the first month in the spring of the tenth year of the ox,[20] the empress was enthroned at the Palace of Owarida, and reigned for thirty-six years. On the tenth of the fourth month, in the summer of the first year of her reign, Prince Umayado was appointed Prince Regent,[21] and Yasunoko no muraji was made his personal attendant. On the fifth of the fifth month in the thirteenth year of the reign, the empress gave him the Great Faith Rank,[22] saying, "Your distinguished service shall be remembered forever." In the second month

12. The *Nihon shoki*, XX (Bitatsu 13:9), says that Soga no Umako asked for the two Buddha images imported from Paekche and sent Ikebe no atae Hita and others to find practitioners. See Aston, "Nihongi," II, 101.

13. This differs from the passage quoted above, and the three images are unidentified.

14. See above, I.1, n. 9.

15. A central figure of the anti-Buddhist group at court; the Mononobe family, whose ancestry can be traced to the age of kami, was in charge of military affairs. See *Nihon shoki*, III, VI, XX, XXI; Aston, "Nihongi," I, 128, 184; II, 90, 102–112.

16. Or 難波, present Ōsaka-shi 大阪市.

17. Mononobe no Moriya and his family were defeated by the Soga family in 587 after the death of Emperor Yōmei.

18. See Chap. II(3)b, n. 132.

19. Also known as Hōkō-ji 放光寺, which exists at Hiso, Ōaza, Ōyodo-chō, Yoshino-gun, Nara-ken 奈良縣吉野郡大淀町大字比曽.

20. For the traditional Chinese usage of the Ten Stems and Twelve Branches for the Calendar, see *Mathew's Chinese English Dictionary*, Appendix A, 1176–1177.

21. See *Nihon shoki*, XXII (Suiko 1:4:10); Aston, "Nihongi," II, 122.

22. 大信位 *daishin'i*, the seventh of the twelve ranks instituted by Prince Shōtoku; see I.4, n. 6.

of the seventeenth year, the Prince Regent entrusted him with six hundred and seventy acres of rice fields at Iho district in Harima province 播磨國揖保郡.[23] When the Prince Regent died at the Palace of Ikaruga in the second month of the twenty-ninth year,[24] Yasunoko no muraji revealed his desire to renounce the world, but the empress did not permit this.

In the fourth month of the thirty-second year, a Buddhist monk took an axe and smote his father with it.[25] Yasunoko no muraji immediately petitioned the throne, saying, "All monks and nuns should be examined and a presiding officer[26] appointed in order to guide them and establish righteousness." The empress agreed and granted him the right to carry out the task. It turned out that there were eight hundred and thirty-seven monks and five hundred and seventy-nine nuns.[27] The monk Kanroku 觀勒 was appointed daisōjō,[28] and Yasunoko no muraji and Kuratsukuri no Tokosaka 鞍部徳積[29] were appointed sōzu.[30]

On the eighth of the tenth month of the thirty-third year, Yasunoko died suddenly at Naniwa. His corpse was unusually fragrant, and the empress declared seven days' mourning in honor of his loyalty. He returned to life in three days, however, and told his family the following tale:

"There were five-colored clouds like a rainbow stretching to the north.[31] I was walking along that roadway of clouds, and it smelled fragrant, as if valuable incense was being mixed. At the end of the way

23. Situated in the western suburbs of present Himeji-shi, Hyōgo-ken 兵庫縣姫路市. When the Prince Regent lectured on the *Hoke-kyō*, the empress was so pleased that she granted him the rice fields in Harima, which may have been administered by Yasunoko. See *Nihon shoki*, XXII (Suiko 14); Aston, "Nihongi," II,135.

24. *Nihon shoki*, XXII (Suiko 29:2:5); Aston, "Nihongi," II, 148.

25. See Chap. I(1)d, for the initiation of the *Sōgō-sei*, a supervisory system for monks and nuns. The *Nihon ryōiki* gives "father"; the *Nihon shoki*, "grandfather."

26. 上座 *jōza*, the highest official of the monastic community in a temple; see Chap. I(1)d, n. 84.

27. The *Nihon shoki*, XXII (Suiko 32:9:3) states that there were 816 monks and 569 nuns.

28. Kwal-leuk came from Paekche in 602. The *Nihon shoki*, XXII (Suiko 10:10) says that he presented many books on calendar making, astrology, geography, and magical arts. He lived at Gangō-ji. He was appointed *sōjō*, and not *daisōjō*, a title later conferred on Gyōgi. See Chap. I (1)d, n. 74.

29. The Kuratsukuri family were craftsmen who immigrated from Paekche and were related to the Shiba family who played an important role in the introduction of Buddhism to Japan. See *Fusō ryakki* (Kinmei 13) for Shiba no Tachito 司馬達等.

30. The *Nihon shoki* gives Azumi no muraji instead of Yasunoko. See Chap. I(1)d, n. 74.

31. The rainbow bridge to the land of the dead is a motif (Thompson, *Motif-Index*, F 152.1.1) traced in many traditions of the world. And the North Pole Star is the point of cosmic breakthrough in the Chinese tradition and is the place where the deity in charge of life and death presides. See Chap. II(3)b, n. 129. For the symbolic meaning of this story, see Chap. II(1)b.

there appeared a golden mountain which dazzled my eyes as I approached it. There the late Prince Regent Shōtoku was waiting for me and we climbed to the summit together. A full-fledged monk[32] was standing on the top of the golden mountain. Bowing to the prince, he said, 'I have come from the Palace of the East. In eight days you will fall into danger. I beseech you to take this elixir of life.'[33] Then he gave one bead of his bracelet to be swallowed, and, with the penetrating eye,[34] he had the prince recite three times, 'Homage to the Bodhisattva of Miraculous Power'[35] and retired. The prince said to me, 'Go back home without any delay and prepare a place to make a Buddha statue. When I finish performing the rite of repentance,[36] I will return to the court to make it.' I came back along the way I had taken before, and all of a sudden I was brought back to life."

Accordingly, people called him the "Revived Muraji." In the ninth month in the autumn of the seventh year of the dog, the sixth year of the reign of Emperor Kōtoku, he was decorated with the Great Flower Rank, Upper Grade, and when he died he was over ninety.

A note says: How praiseworthy the member of the Ōtomo family is for his devotion to Buddha, for his commitment to dharma with purity of heart and loyalty, and for his longevity and fortune! He was known for his courage, and for the sense of filial piety he handed down to his descendants. Indeed we know it is a testimony to the Three Treasures, and it is due to protection by good deities.[37] On reflection we discover that a danger in eight days corresponds to the revolt of Soga no Iruka,[38] for "eight days" corresponds to eight years; "Bodhisattva of Miraculous Power" corresponds to Bodhisattva Monjushiri 文珠師利菩薩;[39] the "one bead" which was swallowed is a pill to escape danger. "The golden mountain" is identified with Wu-t'ai shan 五臺山 in China,[40] while the "Palace of the East" means Japan. The "going

32. 比丘 *biku*, a transliteration of *bhikṣu*, a monk who has been ordained and has accepted the full list of more than two hundred precepts. For the ordination system, see Chap. I(1)d.

33. Itabashi gives a different interpretation of this passage: The prince, bowing to the full-fledged monk, said, "This is a man from the Palace of the East. He will fall into danger in eight days. Please let him have the elixir of life" (*Nihon ryōiki*, 31).

34. 天眼 *tengen*; see Chap. II(2)c, n. 109.

35. 南无妙徳菩薩 *Namu myōtoku-bosatsu*; *namu* is a transliteration of Skt. *namas*; Myōtoku-bosatsu does not refer to any specific bodhisattva, for *myōtoku* means "miraculous power."

36. 悔過 *keka*; see Chap. II(1)a.

37. 善神 *zenjin*; also known as *gohō* 護法, guardians of dharma; numerous deities in the Mahayana assembly of Buddhas and bodhisattvas who protect dharma, particularly during the age of degenerate dharma.

38. *Nihon shoki*, XXIV (Kōgyoku 2:11:1) Prince Yamashiro no Ōe was killed by Soga no Iruka; *ibid.* (Kōgyoku 4:6:12) Iruka was killed at the court. But "eight years" does not fit the historical record. See Aston, "Nihongi," II, 181–194.

39. Transliteration of Mañjuśrī; see Lamotte, "Mañjuśrī."

40. See Chap. I(2)b, n. 164.

back to the court to make an image" was realized in the birth of ex-Emperor Shōhō-ōjin-shōmu 勝寶應眞聖武太上天皇,[41] who built a temple and Buddha statue.[42] The Most Venerable Gyōgi,[43] a contemporary of Emperor Shōmu, is an incarnation[44] of Bodhisattva Monjushiri. This is a miraculous story.

# 6

## On Gaining an Immediate Reward for Faith in
## Bodhisattva Kannon[1]

Elder Master Gyōzen 行善 came from the Katashibe 堅部 family[2] and was sent to Koryō 高麗 for Buddhist studies during the reign of the empress who resided at the Palace of Owarida.[3] When that country was invaded, he wandered from place to place. When he came to a river, he was at a loss how to cross it, for there was neither bridge nor boat. Sitting on a broken-down bridge, he was meditating on Kannon 觀音[4] when an old man came by in a boat to take him to the other side. Upon landing, he could see neither the old man nor the boat. Thus he learned that the old man was an incarnation[5] of Kannon, and on the spot he made a vow[6] that he would make an image to be venerated.

41. *Shoku Nihongi* (Tenpyō hōji 2:8:1, 9). Posthumous names were given to the former emperor (Shōhō-kanjin-shōmu 勝寶感神聖武) and the former empress (Chūdai-tenpyō-ōjin-ninshō 中臺天平應眞仁正). Kyōkai apparently confused these two names.

42. See Preface, n. 14, above.

43. For Gyōgi, see Chap. I(1)d. *Daitoku* 大德 is a transliteration of Skt. *bhadanta*, which means one who has great virtues, and is used as an honorific title for Buddhas, bodhisattvas, elder monks, etc.; in China and Japan the usage as an honorific title for eminent monks was added.

44. 反化 *henge*; see I.4, n. 18.

1. Cf. *Fusō ryakki* (VI, Yōrō 2:9), *Konjaku monogatarishū* (XVI, 1), etc.

2. An immigrant family from Paekche. *Shoku Nihongi*, VIII (Yōrō 5:6:23) gives a decree: Monk Gyōzen studied abroad and, after ascetic practices, learned the miraculous art and eventually returned home. If he visits a temple to pay homage to the Buddha, entertain him as a samgha official.

3. Or Kogrö (traditionally 37 B.C.–668 A.D.); it was the most northern of the three Korean Kingdoms. Gyōzen went to Korea, probably in the reign of Empress Suiko (592–628). However, the *Fusō ryakki* and *Shoku Nihongi* date this story in the reign of Empress Genshō (715–724), even though Koryö was subjugated by the T'ang army in 668.

4. See Chap. I(1)a, n. 11, and Chap. II(3)b.

5. 應化 *ōge* (Skt. *nirmāṇa*), meaning transformation, incarnation; Kannon is known to appear in thirty-three forms.

6. 誓願 *seigan*, a translation of Skt. *Praṇidhāna*; in this case the vow is addressed to Kannon as an expression of faith and to himself as a confirmation of commitment to disciplinary practice. Also see Preface, n. 13, above.

Eventually he reached Great T'ang China where he made an image to worship day and night. He was called Dharma Master Riverside 河邊法師. No one exceeded him in fortitude,[7] and he was respected by the emperor of the T'ang dynasty.[8] He returned home with the Japanese envoys to China in the second year of the Yōrō era.[9] He lived at Kōfuku-ji 興福寺[10] and never ceased performing services before that image until he died.

Surely we learn that the power of Kannon is beyond understanding. The note says: An eminent monk went to study abroad, fell into danger, and was unable to cross at the ferry. On a bridge he meditated on Kannon[11] and trusted holy power. Kannon, in the form of an old man, came to his rescue and disappeared after they had parted. The monk made an image of Kannon and worshiped it continuously until his last day.

# 7

*On Paying for and Freeing Turtles and Being*
*Rewarded Immediately and Saved by Them*[1]

Dhyāna Master[2] Gusai 弘濟[3] came from Paekche. When that country was invaded, an ancestor of the governor[4] of Mitani district in Bingo province 備後國三谷郡[5] was put in charge of reinforcements and

7. 忍辱 *nin'niku* (Skt. *kṣānti*), one of the six practices of bodhisattvas for attaining Buddhahood. The *Hoke-kyō*, XIII (*Taishō*, IX, 36c), advocates it as the most suitable for working among ignorant people in the age of the degenerate dharma. See Katō, trans., *Myōhō-renge-kyō*, 266–268.
8. Probably Hsüan-tsung 玄宗 (713–755) of the T'ang dynasty (618–906).
9. *Shoku Nihongi*, VIII (Yōrō 2:10:20). An envoy to China, Tajihi no Mahito agatamori 多治比眞人縣守, returned to Japan.
10. Originally founded in 669 at Yamashina and called Yamashina-dera 山階寺; next moved to Asuka, and then to Nara in 710.
11. 聖 Buddha or bodhisattva; in this case, Kannon.

1. The same motif of repaying kindness is found in tales II.5, 8, 12, 16, etc. See Chap. II(2)a. Cf. *Myōhoki* (I, On Yen-kung 嚴恭), *Konjaku monogatarishū* (XIX, 30), etc.
2. 禪師 *zenji* is a title often used honorifically for monks in general.
3. Unknown.
4. 大領 *dairyō* is the first among the four high officials in the district, generally a man of influence from the local gentry.
5. Present Futami-gun, Hiroshima-ken 廣島縣双三郡.

sent to Paekche.[6] At that time the present governor's ancestor vowed that he would build a temple[7] to dedicate to the deities[8] of heaven and earth if he came home safely. Eventually, he escaped harm. Thereupon, he invited Dhyāna Master Gusai to return to Japan with him. Mitani-dera 三谷寺[9] is the temple that was founded by this master, and both monks and laymen felt awe and reverence at its sight.

Once, in going to the capital to exchange his belongings for gold and paints,[10] the master reached the port of Naniwa.[11] He happened to see a seaman selling four big turtles, and he advised people to buy them and set them free.[12] After that he rented a boat and boarded it with two acolytes[13] to cross the sea. Late at night, the sailors, filled with greed, threw the acolytes into the sea near of Kabanejima 骨嶋, in Bizen 備前,[14] and turned to him, saying, "Quick, into the sea with you!" The monk tried to reason with them, but they would not listen. Finally, after making a vow,[15] he sank into the water. When the water came up to his waist, he felt a stone supporting his legs. In the morning light he found that he was being carried by the turtles. They left him on the beach of Bitchū 備中[16] after nodding to him three times. It seems that the turtles which had been set free came back to repay his kindness.[17]

Eventually the thieving sailors, six in all, happened to visit his temple to sell the gold and paints they had stolen from him. The patron[18] of

6. *Nihon shoki*, XXVI (Saimei 6–7), XXVII (Tenchi 1–2); Aston, "Nihongi," II, 263–270, 274–280. Paekche and Koryŏ joined forces to fight against Silla in 641. Silla sought help from T'ang China, which sent troops in 658 and 659, but had no success in conquering Koryŏ. In 660 T'ang China joined by Silla conquered Paekche, but in 661 Paekche rose and fought back, receiving help from the Japanese expeditionary forces in 662. In the next year, however, Silla and T'ang joined forces again to invade Paekche where they destroyed the Japanese base, putting an end to Japanese influence in Korea.

7. 伽藍 *garan*, also written 僧伽藍 *sōgaran*; see Chap. I(1)d, n. 116.

8. 諸神祇 *kamigami*; deities of heaven and earth in which all the Buddhas and Bodhisattvas are included.

9. Unidentified; there are temples built by local officials and given local names such as Iwata-dera (II.31), Miki-dera (III.36), etc.

10. Probably for the use of painting Buddha images and temple buildings.

11. The port of present Ōsaka-shi.

12. 放生 *hōjō*, the practice of buying captive fish, birds, or animals and releasing them is highly recommended for promoting the Buddhist doctrine of *ahiṃsā*, nonkilling, particularly among fishermen. The first reference to *hōjō* in the *Nihon shoki* is found in the reign of Emperor Tenmu (676), who promulgated a decree to release all living beings in captivity. See *Nihon shoki*, XXIX (Tenmu 5:8:17); Aston, "Nihongi," II, 334.

13. See I.3, n. 8.

14. Unidentified, but situated off the coast of present Okayama-ken 岡山縣.

15. 願 *gan*; this has a meaning closer to prayer as a confession of faith. Compare with *seigan* (See I.6, n. 6).

16. Present Okayama-ken.

17. 報恩 *hōon*; see Chap. II(2)a.

18. 檀越 *taniochi* or *dan'otsu*, a translation of Skt. *dānapati*, meaning one who makes offerings; in Japan, a patron, often an influential member of the local gentry who makes donations to the temple and, hence, controls financial matters of the temple.

the temple first came out to make an estimate, and then the master appeared to see them. The thieves were petrified with terror. Out of mercy he did not punish them, but rather made a Buddha image to be consecrated in the pagoda and performed rites of dedication. Later he lived by the seaside, and preached to passersby. He passed away when he was over eighty.

Even an animal does not forget gratitude, and repays an act of kindness. How, then, could a righteous man[19] fail to have a sense of gratitude?

# 8

## On a Deaf Man Whose Hearing Was Restored Immediately Owing to His Faith in a Mahayana Scripture[1]

In the reign of the empress residing at the Palace of Owarida[2] there was a man whose name was Kinunui no tomonomiyatsuko Gitsū 衣縫伴造義通[3] who suddenly became seriously ill. He was deaf in both ears and suffered a chronic skin disease which never healed. He said to himself, "My past deeds[4] influence my life not only in the present but also in the future. It is better to do good and die soon than to live long and be hated by others." Therefore he swept the ground, cleaned the hall, summoned a *dhyāna* master[5] with all due reverence, and, after purifying himself with holy water,[6] devoted himself to reading a Mahayana scripture 方廣經.[7]

Meanwhile, he experienced an extraordinary sensation and said to the master, "I am hearing the name of a bodhisattva in my ear, so I beg you, Most Venerable Master,[8] to continue the service." During

19. 義人 *ginin*.

1. Cf. *Sanbō ekotoba* (II, 5), *Fusō ryakki* (IV, Suiko), *Konjaku monogatarishū* (XIV, 36), etc.
2. Refers to Empress Suiko; see I.6, n. 3.
3. According to the *Shinsen shōjiroku*, Kinunui is the name of an immigrant family.
4. 宿業 *sukugō* or *shukugō*; the term is ethically neutral, including both good and evil deeds, but it usually refers to evil deeds.
5. 義禪師 Gi-zenji may be a combination of a personal name Gi and *zenji*, an honorific title, or a monk who is well-read in scriptures.
6. 香水 *kōzui*, ritually purified water.
7. *Hōkō-kyō*; 方廣 *hōkō* is a shortened compound of 方正 *hōsei*, "square, upright," and 廣大 *kōdai*, "large, great"; hence, in the Buddhist tradition it designates Mahayana. Therefore, *Hōkō-kyō* means Mahayana scripture; for another possible meaning, however, see Chap. II(1)a, n. 8.
8. 大德 *daitoku*; see I.5, n. 43.

the master's performance, one ear was completely healed. With great
joy, Gitsū repeated his request to go on, and, as the master went on
with the service, both ears were healed. People far and near marveled
at the news. We learn that there really exists a mysterious correspondence.[9]

# 9

## On the Reunion in a Foreign Land of a Father with
## His Child Who Was Carried Away by an Eagle

In the third month, in the spring of the tenth year of the hare, in the
reign of the empress who resided in the Palace of Itabuki, Asuka
Kawara 飛鳥川原板葺宮,[2] there was a baby girl in a certain home in a
remote village in Shizumi district of Tajima province 但馬國七美郡.[3]
While she was crawling in the courtyard, an eagle seized her and
carried her high into the sky toward the east. Her parents, lamenting,
grieving, and wailing, ran in the direction the eagle had gone, but
could not find it. Therefore, they held a memorial service for her.[4]

Eight years passed. At the end of the eighth month, in the autumn
of the seventh year of the dog, in the reign of the emperor who resided
at the Palace of Nagara-no-Toyosaki in Naniwa 難破長柄豊前宮,[5] her
father happened to lodge for the night in Kasa district, Tanba province
丹波國加佐郡.[6] Wishing to wash his feet, he accompanied his host's
daughter who had been sent to the village well to get water. Around
the well there were some village girls who snatched away the daughter's pail and would not allow her to draw water. They joined together to bully her, saying, "You, who were not eaten by the eagle,
why don't you have any manners!" They shouted all kinds of abusive
remarks and hit her, so that she came home crying. The host[7] asked,
"Why are you crying?" Whereupon the traveller told him what he

9. 感應 *kannō* means a mysterious correspondence between Buddhas and all sentient beings.
Every prayer or vow addressed to Buddha elicits a response owing to the unity of existence.
See Chap. II(3)b, n. 147.

1. Cf. *Fusō ryakki* (IV, Kōgyoku), *Konjaku monogatarishū* (XXVI, 1), *Mizukagami* (II, Kōgyoku), etc. A similar plot is found in the legend on Rōben 良辨 (689–773), the charismatic
founder of Tōdai-ji. See II.21; Yanagita, "Densetsu," *Teihon Yanagita Kunio shū*, V, 88–90.
2. Empress Kōgyoku (642–645), whose palace was situated in present Asuka-mura, Takechi-
gun, Nara-ken. This event took place in 643.
3. Present Mikata-gun, Hyōgo-ken 兵庫縣美方郡.
4. 修福 *shūfuku*; holding a Buddhist service on a person's behalf to store up merit for his
well-being in the other world.
5. Emperor Kōtoku (645–654), whose palace was situated at present Ōsaka-shi.
6. The coastal area of the Maizuru Bay

had seen in detail, and asked why it was. The host replied, "At such and such a date, I was up in a tree to catch doves, when an eagle carrying a baby flew from the west and dropped it in the nest to be eaten by the young eagles. The baby screamed in fear, and the young eagles hesitated to peck at it. This is the girl whom I brought back from the nest and reared." The date of the accident and this story identified the girl as the lost child of the traveler. Crying bitterly, the traveler told the host the entire story of how an eagle had flown away with his baby daughter. When the host understood all the circumstances, he agreed to return the girl to her real parents.

Ah! This father happened to stay with the lost child's foster parents and finally regained his child. We surely know what sympathy Heaven[8] had for them, and how deep the parent-child relation is. It is a miraculous event.

# IO

## *On a Man's Rebirth as an Ox for Labor and Showing an Extraordinary Sign Because of Stealing from His Son*[1]

In the central village of Yamamura in Sou upper district, Yamato province 大和國添上郡山村,[2] there was once a man who was called Lord Kura no iegimi 椋家長.[3] In the twelfth month he wanted to atone for his past sins by having a Mahayana scripture recited.[4] Therefore he ordered his servant, "Go and call a monk."[5] The servant asked,

---

7. 家主 *iegimi*; see I.2, n. 5.
8. 天 *ten*; although the Buddhist influence is not so strong in this story, it does show how intricately karma is interwoven and points out that, with the intervention of Heaven, miraculous interrelationships exist.

1. Cf. *Myōhōki* (III, On Wang 王, Yü 瑜, etc.), *Fusō ryakki* (IV, Saimei), *Konjaku mono-gatarishū* (XIV, 37). See II.15.
2. Present Obitoke, Nara-shi 奈良市帯解. According to the *Ryō no gige*, "Ko-ryō," Articles 1 and 2, a village, *sato* 里, consists of fifty households, but less in mountainous or remote areas; a great district 大郡 consists of from 16 to 20 villages; an upper district 上郡, from 12 to 15; a middle district 中郡, from 8 to 11; a lower district 下郡, from 4 to 7; a small district 小郡, from 2 to 3. An alternative reading is Sou no kami district. 村 *mura* is not legally defined, but consists of twenty houses or less.
3. Although *iegimi* 家長 is a common noun meaning "the head of the family," it is used here as a popular name; *kura* means "storehouse." See n. 10, below.
4. *Hōkō-kyō*; see Chap. II(1)a, n. 8.
5. *Zenji*; obviously it means "monk" in general.

"To which temple shall I go to find a monk?" The master answered, "I have no preference; you may invite any monk you happen to meet." Thereupon the servant brought home a monk whom he had met on the way, as he had been told. The master put faith[6] in this monk and made offerings.[7]

In the evening when the monk was retiring after the service,[8] the host[9] made him a bed with quilts, and the monk was tempted to take the quilts rather than wait to receive offerings the next morning. Then he heard a voice saying, "Don't steal the quilts." Startled, the monk looked around and found only an ox standing under the eaves of the storehouse.[10] When the monk approached the ox, it began to speak: "I am the father of Iegimi, the master of this house. In my previous life I stole ten sheaves[11] of rice belonging to my son in order to give them to others. Because of that, I was reborn in the form of an ox to make up for my evil deed. How dare you, who have entered the priesthood, steal the quilts? If you want to know whether or not my story is true, make a seat for me. I will come to lie on it so that you may know that I am the father of your host." The monk passed the night stricken with shame.

The next morning, after the service, he said to his host, "Have the other people withdraw." Then he summoned the host's family and told them the story he had heard the night before. The host went to the ox in grief and made a seat of straw, saying, "If you are my real father, will you take this seat?" And the ox knelt down and lay on the seat. All the relatives cried bitterly, and the host said that the ox was really his father. The host stood up and, with a bow, said to the ox, "I will cancel the accounts in your former life." At this the ox sighed and shed tears. The ox died at four o'clock that afternoon, whereupon the host presented the quilts and offerings to the monk and accumulated merits[12] for his deceased father.

We cannot but believe in the law of karmic causality.

6. 信心 shinjin, the mind to believe in the Three Treasures. See I.15, n. 7.
7. 供養 kuyō, a translation of Skt. pūjā, which means making offerings of food, clothes, incense, flowers, candles, etc., to the Three Treasures.
8. 禮經 raikyō, rai means worship and kyō means scripture recitation.
9. 檀越 taniochi, sponsor of the service, one who makes offerings.
10. 倉下 kura no moto, which means literally "under the storehouse"; if it is a storehouse on stilts, the floor is several feet elevated from the ground, and it is possible for a man to take shelter under it. See Naoki Kōjirō, "Kura no moto no gogi ni tsuite," Shoku Nihongi kenkyū, VII (No. 7, July 1955), 178–181.
11. One sheaf yields about a quarter bushel of rice, according to the Ryō no gige, "Den-ryō," Article 1.
12. 功德 kudoku; see Chap. I(1)b, n. 50.

# I I

*On Gaining an Immediate Penalty for a Lifetime*
*of Catching Fish in a Net*[1]

The Most Venerable Jiō 慈應,[2] monk[3] of Gangō-ji[4] in the capital,[5] went on a summer retreat[6] to lecture on the *Hoke-kyō*[7] at Noo-dera 濃於寺[8] in Shikama district, Harima province 播磨國餝磨郡, on the invitation of the patron of the temple. In the neighborhood, there was a fisherman who had been netting fish since his childhood. One day he began to crawl in the mulberry bushes on his property, crying aloud, "Fire is devouring me!" His family tried to help him, but he only repeated, "Don't come close to me. I shall be in flames soon." In the meantime, his parents rushed to the temple to ask the ascetic[9] to save their son. The ascetic came and recited formulas[10] for a while, and the fisherman was released from the devouring flames. His breeches had already been burnt. Stricken with terror, the fisherman paid a visit to Noo-dera, confessed his sins in the congregation,[11] and repented, offering clothes and having a scripture recited. Thereafter he never did any evil.

The *Ganshi kakun* 顔氏家訓[12] gives an analogous passage: "Once there was a man who belonged to the Liu family in Chiang-ling,[13]

1. Cf. *Sanbō ekotoba* (II, 6), *Honchō kōsōden* (75).
2. Otherwise unknown.
3. *Shamon;* see Chap. I(1)a, n. 4.
4. See I.3, n. 9.
5. Since no date is given, it is not clear whether this is the new Gangō-ji in Nara or the former one (Asuka-dera or Hōkō-ji) in Asuka.
6. 夏安居 *geango* (also [*u*]*ango* (雨) 安居, *gegyō* 夏行, etc), a translation of Skt. *varṣavārṣika*, which is "summer retreat"; during the rainy season monks in India held a ninety day retreat for study and disciplinary practice.
7. See Chap. II(3)b.
8. Uncertain; it may be a provincial temple in present Gochaku, Himeji-shi, Hyōgo-ken 兵庫縣姫路市御着.
9. 行者 *gyōja;* in this passage refers to Jiō. It means "one who practices the path."
10. 咒 *ju;* see Chap. I(1)b, n. 47.
11. 大衆 *daishū;* the congregation consisting of the participants of the retreat.
12. Yen Chih-t'ui, *Yen-shih chia-hsün* (*SPTK*, No. 169). See Teng ssu-yü, trans., *Family Instructions for the Yen Clan.* Yen Chih-t'ui (531–591) presents a synthesis of Buddhist and Confucian teachings, and in Chapter XVI (On Faith 歸心篇) in particular, he emphasizes the law of karmic retribution. His work was popular during the Nara period, and its influence may be detected in Fujiwara no Kamatari's *Kaden* (see Chap. I(1)c, nn. 67, 68) and other biographical and moralistic writings. That particular chapter is included in the *Kuang hung-ming chi* 廣弘明集, XI (*Taishō*, LII, 107b–108c).
13. Present Hupei province 湖北省.

who made a living by selling stewed eel. Later he had a child with the head of an eel and a human body,"[14] which demonstrates the same moral.

# 12

## On a Skull, Which Was Saved from Being Stepped on by Men and Beasts, Showing an Extraordinary Sign and Repaying the Benefactor Immediately[1]

Dōtō 道登,[2] a Buddhist scholar[3] of Koryö, was a monk of Gangō-ji.[4] He came from the Ema 惠滿 family[5] in Yamashiro 山背 province.[6] In the second year of the horse, the second year of the Taika era,[7] he built the Uji Bridge 宇治椅.[8] Once, when he was passing through the valley in the Nara hills 奈良山,[9] he saw a skull that had been trampled by men and animals. In sorrow, he had his attendant Maro 萬侶 place it on a tree.

On New Year's Eve[10] of the same year, a man came to the temple gate, saying, "I would like to see the Venerable Dōtō's attendant Maro." When Maro came out to see him, he said, "Thanks to the mercy of your master, I have been happy and at peace. And I can repay your kindness only on this evening." Then he took Maro home with him. Through the closed gate they entered the back quarters of the house, where they found abundant food and drink already prepared. The man divided his fare with Maro, and they ate together.

14. This passage is omitted in the *Kuang hung-ming chi*. See *Family Instructions*, 149. 江陵劉氏以賣鱧爲業後生一兒頭是鱧自頸以下爲人耳.

1. Cf. *Fusō ryakki* (IV, Kōtoku), *Konjaku monogatarishū* (XIX, 31). There is another version of the same story (III.27). For the significance of the story, see Chap. II(1)a, and (3)a.
2. Dōtō's name is found among the ten great masters (*jusshi* 十師) appointed by Emperor Kōtoku in 645. See *Nihon shoki*, XXV (Taika 1:8:8); Aston, "Nihongi," II, 203.
3. 學生 *gakushō* is one who studied Buddhist teachings, or Chinese classics at a state college. See Chap. I(1)d, n. 91.
4. See I.3, n. 9.
5. It is unclear whether Ema is his family name, or that of a friend he visited.
6. After 794 it was written as 山城, present Kyoto-fu.
7. 646.
8. See *Shoku Nihongi* (I (Monmu 4:3:10). There it gives Dōshō, not Dōtō, as the builder of the Uji Bridge, but other documents agree with the *Nihon ryōiki* in making Dōtō its builder.
9. The hills between Kyoto and Nara. See II.40, n. 6.
10. It was believed that deceased family members visited their former homes at the end of the year, and a cosmic renewal rite was held then. See Chap. II(1)a.

Shortly after midnight they heard a male voice, and the man said to Maro, "Go away quickly, for here comes my brother who killed me!" In wonder, Maro asked him about this, and he answered, "Once my brother and I were traveling on business, and I acquired about fifty pounds[11] of silver in my trade. Out of envy and hate my brother killed me to take the silver. For many years my skull was trampled by passing men and beasts, till your master mercifully rescued me from that suffering, which is why I have given you a banquet this evening."

It was at this point that the man's mother and elder brother entered the room to worship all spirits.[12] Being surprised at the sight of Maro, they asked why he was there, and Maro told them what he had just heard. The mother thereby accused her elder son, saying, "Ah! You killed my dear son. It was not a robber, but you!" Then she thanked Maro and gave him a feast. On his return, Maro reported this to his master.

Even a spirit of the dead or a skeleton repays an act of kindness;[13] how can a living man forget?

# 13

## On a Woman Who Performed Work in an Extraordinary Way, Ate Sacred Herbs, and Flew up to Heaven Alive[1]

In a village of Nuribe, Uda district, Yamato province 大倭國宇太郡漆部里,[2] there lived an extraordinary woman,[3] who was married to Nuribe no miyatsuko Maro 漆部造麿.[4] Innately pure and straightforward in upholding what was right, she gave birth to seven children, but she was too poor to feed them since she had no one to depend on. Since the children had no clothes, she wove vines into clothes for them. Every day she purified herself in a bath and clothed herself in rags. She would gather edible herbs in the fields, and devoted herself to staying at home and cleaning the house. When she cooked the herbs, she called her children, sat up straight, and ate the food, all the

11. 斤 gon; as 1 gon is 1.323 lbs., so 40 gon makes 53 lbs.
12. 諸靈 shoryō.
13. For the motif of "the grateful dead," see Chap. II(1)a, n. 10.

1. Cf. Konjaku monogatarishū (XX, 42).
2. Present Soni-mura or Mitsue-mura, Uda-gun, Nara-ken 奈良縣宇陀郡曾爾村，御杖村.
3. 風流 misao.
4. 妾 not the legal wife, but a concubine.

while smiling, talking cheerfully, and being grateful. This constant discipline in mind and body made her spirit resemble that of a guest from heaven.[5]

In the fifth year of the Hakuchi era[6] of the emperor who resided at the Palace of Nagara no Toyosaki in Naniwa,[7] heavenly beings[8] communicated with her,[9] and she ate special herbs[10] gathered in the field in springtime and flew about in the heavens.

Indeed, we know that her extraordinary qualities and her diet of special herbs are well recognized, even though she has not studied Buddhist teachings. The *Shōjin nyomon-kyō* 精進女問經[11] gives this relevant passage: "You will be able to achieve five kinds of merit[12] by leading a lay life and sweeping the garden with an upright mind."[13]

# 14

*On a Monk Who Got an Immediate Reward for Recollecting and Reciting the* Shin-gyō *and Showed an Extraordinary Sign*[1]

Saka Gigaku 釋義覺[2] was originally from Paekche.[3] When it was destroyed[4] in the reign of the empress who resided at the later Palace of Okamoto,[5] he immigrated to this country and lived in Kudara-dera

5. 天上客 *tenjō no kyaku*, literally, a guest from heaven, that is, a *hsien* or Chinese Taoist saint. See I.28, n. 10.
6. Hakuchi era (650–654) during the reign of Emperor Kōtoku.
7. See I.9, n. 5.
8. 神仙 *shinsen*; Taoist saints.
9. 感應 *kan'nō*; see I.8, n. 9.
10. 仙草 *sensō*; diet for Taoist saints.
11. *Muku ubaimon-kyō* 無垢優婆夷問經 (*Taishō*, XIV, 950c).
12. 五功德 *go-kudoku*, five kinds of merit attained after rebirth in the pure land.
13. The quotation differs from the original, which reads: "Buddha taught a pure lay sister, saying, 'sweep the precinct of the pagoda, and you will be rewarded with five kinds of merit." The original text stresses the merit of sweeping the precinct of the pagoda, while Kyōkai's altered quotation shifted the emphasis to everyday household work by replacing the "precinct of the pagoda" with the "garden" and adding, "leading a lay life . . . ." See Chap. II(2)b.

1. Cf. *Sanbō ekotoba* (II, 7), *Fusō ryakki* (IV, Saimei), *Konjaku monogatarishū* (XIV, 32), *Mizu-kagami* (II, Saimei), *Genkō shakusho* (IX), etc.
2. *Saka* is a shortened form of Śākyamuni; those who renounced the world are regarded as descendants of Śākyamuni, and given the surname Saka.
3. See Preface, n. 3, above.
4. See I.7, n. 6.
5. Empress Saimei (655–661), whose palace was called the later Palace of Asuka no Okamoto because it was built on the site of Emperor Jomei's Palace of Okamoto, presently Asuka-mura, Takechi-gun, Nara-ken. See *Nihon shoki*, XXIII (Jomei 2:10:12), XXVI (Saimei, 2:9); Aston, "Nihongi," II, 165, 250.

百濟寺,[6] in Naniwa. He was seven feet tall, studied Buddhist teachings extensively, and recited the *Shin hannya-gyō* 心般若經.[7] Egi 慧義,[8] a fellow monk in the same temple, happened to go out at midnight and found Gigaku's room brightly illuminated. Wondering why, Egi made a hole in the paper window, peeped secretly into the room, and saw Gigaku sitting and reciting the scripture, the light coming out of his mouth. Struck with awe and surprise, Egi confessed his offense[9] the next morning, in the congregation of his fellowmen.

Once Dharma Master Gigaku said to his disciple, "One evening I had recited the *Shin-gyō* 心經 about one hundred times and had then opened my eyes when I found I could see right through the four walls of the room and into the middle of the garden. Then I had an extraordinary experience. I went out, walked about in the temple grounds, and came back to my room, but all the walls and doors had remained closed. When I recited the *Shin-gyō* outside, they opened and became passable as before. This is the wonder of the *Shin hannya-gyō*."[10]

The note says: How great is this child of Śākyamuni! He listens to and advocates Buddhist teachings, devotes himself to reciting the scripture, and attains a mind that penetrates everything. It manifests itself in extreme quietness without agitation, but, once in motion, it pierces walls and generates light of its own accord.

# I5

## On a Wicked Man Who Persecuted a Begging Monk and Gained an Immediate Penalty[1]

In the days of an old capital,[2] there was a foolish man who did not believe in the law of karmic causality. Once, when he saw a monk begging food, he grew angry and wanted to restrain the monk. The

6. Founded in 639 by Emperor Jomei (See *Nihon shoki*, XXIII, 11:7) on the bank of the Kudara River, presently Sumiyoshi-ku. Ōsaka-shi 大阪市住吉區. Kudara-dera and Hōkō-ji were considered great (state) temples (*ibid.*, XXIX, Tenmu 9:4). In the reign of Emperor Tenmu its status and function were taken over by Takechi-no-ōtera 高市大寺 or Ōtsukasa-no-ōtera 大官大寺 (see Chap. I(1)c).
7. Also called *Hannya shin-gyō* or *Shin-gyō*; see Chap. II(1)a, n. 17.
8. Otherwise unknown.
9. 悔過 *keka*; see Chap. II(1)a.
10. See Chap. II(3)b.

1. Cf. *Konjaku monogatarishū* (XX, 25). Similar stories are found in II.1, 11, 35; III.15, etc.
2. See I.1, n. 15.

monk ran into the water of a rice field, but the man chased him and caught him. When the monk could stand this no longer, he cast a spell[3] on the man, who rolled on the ground and ran about[4] hysterically. Then the monk disappeared from the scene.

The man had two sons. In order to break the spell binding their father, they went to the temple and asked a *dhyāna* master to come and see their father. When the master learned what had happened, he at first refused to make a visit. Again and again the two sons begged him earnestly to save their father, and at last the monk came. Hardly had he finished reciting the first passage of the Chapter on the Kannon 觀音品[5] when the man was released from the spell.[6] Thereafter his faith[7] was awakened, and he turned wickedness into good.

# 16

## *On Gaining an Immediate Penalty for Skinning a Live Rabbit without Mercy*[1]

In Yamato province 大和國[2] there was a man whose name and native place are not identified. He was not benevolent[3] and liked to kill living beings. He caught a rabbit and set it free in the fields after skinning it alive. Before long he contracted a fatal disease; his whole body was covered with scabs that broke out in extremely painful sores. He was never cured and died groaning loudly.

Ah! How soon wicked deeds incur a penalty in this life! We should be considerate[4] and benevolent. Above all, we should show mercy.[5]

3. 咒縛 *jubaku*.

4. 東西 literally means "east and west," that is, in all directions.

5. *Kannon-bon;* Chap. XXV of the *Hoke-kyō*, often used as an independent scripture. See Chap. II(3)b; also, Katō, trans., *Myōhō-renge-kyō*, 405–415.

6. 解脱 *gedatsu*; a translation of Skt. *mokṣa*, meaning liberation, freedom from the bonds of illusion and suffering. In this passage, however, it means release from the spell.

7. 信心 *shinjin*; a pure heart, free from doubt, which believes in the Three Treasures and the law of karmic causation, the first requisite for following the Buddha's path.

1. Cf. *Konjaku monogatarishū* (XX, 28). A famous story on skinning a live rabbit is found in the *Kojiki* (I, On Ōkuninushi no kami); see Philippi, trans., *Kojiki*, I, 21, 93–95.

2. Present Nara-ken.

3. 仁 *jin*; the most important Confucian virtue which is the basis for the ideal image of man. See Arthur Waley, *The Analects of Confucius*, 27–29.

4. 恕 *shu* or *ju*; 夫子之道 忠恕而已矣. See *ibid.*, 105, n. 1.

5. 慈悲 *jihi*; a compound originally formed of two Skt. words, that is, *maitrī* (friendship, love 慈) and *karuṇā* (sympathy, mercy 悲). For a general discussion, see Nakamura Hajime, *Jihi*.

# 17

## On Suffering War Damage and Gaining an Immediate Reward
## for Faith in an Image of Bodhisattva Kannon[1]

Ochi no atae 越智直,[2] ancestor of the governor[3] of Ochi district in Iyo province 伊豫國越知郡,[4] was sent to Paekche in the Japanese expeditionary force[5] and taken prisoner by Chinese soldiers and brought to T'ang China.

In China, he and some other Japanese, eight in all, came to live on an island. They acquired an image of Bodhisattva Kannon,[6] worshiping it together with great devotion. They worked together cutting down a pine tree to make a boat, enshrined the Kannon image in the boat, and, meditating on the image, made their individual vows.[7] Fortunately the boat drifted straight to Tsukushi 筑紫[8] with the help of the west wind.

At this news the court summoned them for an investigation. When the emperor[9] heard them, he was so moved that he granted them a wish. Ochi no atae said, "I would like to serve you by establishing an estate,"[10] and it was granted. Thereupon he established the estate and built a temple in which to consecrate the Kannon image. After that, his descendants followed his example in worshiping the Kannon.

This is nothing but the work of Kannon, and the total maturation of faith. It is said that even a wooden image of Ting-lan's 丁蘭 mother[11] appeared to be alive, and the woman in a picture loved by a monk[12] responded with sympathy. How, then, can it be possible for the Bodhisattva not to respond?

---

1. Cf. *Konjaku monogatarishū* (XV, 2); *Kannon riyaku-shū* (*Kanazawa bunko*, 43).

2. According to the *Shinsen shōjiroku*, the Ochi family descended from kami.

3. 大領 *dairyō*; see I.7, n. 4.

4. Present Ochi-gun, Ehime-ken 愛媛縣越智郡.

5. There seem to be two possible dates for this: one is a war in 660, the sixth year of Empress Saimei; the other is a war in 663, the second year of Emperor Tenchi. See I.7, n. 6.

6. See Chap. I(1)a, n. 12; Chap. II(3)b. Kannon is known for protecting devotees from calamities, and particularly for guarding navigators (See *Hoke-kyō*, XXV).

7. 誓願 *seigan*; see I.6, n. 6.

8. Present Kyūshū 九州.

9. Empress Saimei or Emperor Tenchi; see n. 5, above.

10. 郡 *kōri*; an administrative unit which was instituted at the time of the Taika Reform. District governors often came from the local gentry class. See I.10, n. 2.

11. Refers to a story in the *Hsiao-tzu chuan* 孝子傳 (Biographies of Filial Sons), compiled by Liu Hsiang 劉向. When Ting-lan was fifteen years old, he lost his mother. He made a wooden image of her and cared for it as if it were alive. Out of jealousy, his wife burnt its face; after her hair fell out as if it had been cut, she repented her offense. (*Taishō*, LIV, 74).

12. See II.13, n. 7.

# 18

## On Recollecting and Reciting the Hoke-kyō and Gaining an Immediate Reward to Show an Extraordinary Sign[1]

In Kazuraki upper district, Yamato province 大和國葛木上郡,[2] there was once a devotee of the *Hoke-kyō*.[3] He came from the Tajihi 丹治比 family,[4] and, even before he was eight years old, he could recite the *Hoke-kyō* with the exception of one character which always escaped his memory and continued to escape it even when he was in his twenties.

Once he prayed to Kannon, confessing his offenses,[5] and had a dream.[6] A man said to him, "In your previous existence you were the child of Kusakabe no Saru 日下部猴[7] in Wake district, Iyo province 伊豫國別郡.[8] At that time while reciting the scripture you burned one character with a lamp so that you could no longer read it. Now, go and see."

When he awoke, he was filled with wonder, and he said to his parents, "I want to go to Iyo on urgent business." They consented.

Setting forth on his quest, he reached Saru's home at last and knocked at the door. A woman came and reported back to her mistress with a smile, saying, "There is a guest at the door who looks exactly like your deceased son." On hearing this, the mistress went to the door to see the guest, finding him the very image of her deceased son. In wonder, the master asked the guest, "Who are you?" And the latter answered by announcing the name of his home district and province. In turn, the

---

1. Cf. *Myōhōki* (II, On Ch'an (Yen)-wu 産(彦) 武), *Hokke kenki* (I, 31), *Konjaku monogatari-shū* (VII, 20; XIV, 6, 12), etc. The Prince Shōtoku cycle gives one legend on the *Hoke-kyō* which was said to have been brought from China by Ono no Imoko 小野妹子 and used by the prince, Dhyāna Master Hui-ssu 慧思, in his former life. See "*Shichidaiki*" 七代記 in *Nara ibun*, II, 890–895; *Jōgū Shōtoku taishi-den hoketsuki* (DBZ, 112). In the late Nara and early Heian periods this legend was formed and became popular. See Iida Mizuho, "Ono no Imoko *Hoke-kyō* shōrai setsuwa," *Nihon kodaishi ronshū*, II, 435–478.

2. Present Minami-kazuraki-gun, Nara-ken.

3. 持經人 *jikyō no hito*; a translation of Skt. *sūtrāntadhāraka*; one who upholds, recollects, reads, recites, and expounds the scriptures.

4. According to the *Shinsen shōjiroku*, the Tajihi family descended from kami.

5. He repented of his past karma, for he thought he could not remember the character because of his evil deeds in the past.

6. Dreams are often occasions for revelation in which the spirit is said to leave the body and travel to the abodes of deities or the land of the dead. See Alex Waymann, "Significance of Dreams in India and Tibet," *History of Religions*, VII (No. 1, August 1967), 1–12.

7. Kusakabe is the name of a large group in the service of the emperor who were descendants of kami; they were probably first organized in Kawachi 河内 and later posted throughout the country. Saru means "monkey"; the name might be given because he was born in the year of the monkey according to the traditional Chinese calendar.

8. Present Onsen-gun, Ehime-ken 愛媛縣溫泉郡.

guest asked the same question, and he was given a detailed answer. It became evident to him that they were his parents in his former life. He knelt down to pay respect to them. Saru affectionately invited him into the house, and, staring at him as he sat in the seat of honor, said, "Aren't you the spirit of my deceased son?" Their guest told them in detail about his dream and announced that the old couple were his parents. Saru, after some reminiscing, motioned to him, saying, "My late son, so and so, lived in this hall, read this scripture, and used this pitcher." The son entered the hall, opened the scripture, and found that the character which he could never remember was missing, for it had been burned with a lamp. When the young man repented of his offense and repaired the text, he could recite it correctly. Parents and son were amazed and delighted, and the son never lost the parent-child relationship and his sense of filial piety.[9]

The note says: How happy is this member of the Kusakabe family who, in pursuit of the path through Buddhist scriptures, recited the Hoke-kyō in two lives, present and past, and served two fathers to be renowned in posterity.[10] It is an extraordinary phenomenon, and not commonplace. Indeed, we are sure it is due to the divine influence of the Hoke-kyō and the miraculous power of Kannon. In the same spirit, the Zen'aku inga-kyō 善惡因果經[11] says, "Look at present effects if you want to know past causes. Look at present deeds if you want to know future effects."[12]

# 19

## On Ridiculing a Reciter of the Hoke-kyō and Getting a Twisted Mouth as an Immediate Penalty[1]

In Yamashiro 山背 province[2] there was once a self-ordained novice[3]

9. 孝養 kōyō; cf. Michihata, Tōdai Bukkyōshi, 271–380.

10. He who remembers his previous births succeeds in freeing himself from the world of samsara, according to Buddhist tradition. See Chap. II(2)c.

11. Taishō, LXXXV, No. 2881. The quotation is not found in this scripture.

12. Quoted from the Shokyō yōshū, XI (Taishō, LIX, 53c). 欲知過去因 見其現在果 欲知未來報 見其現在業.

1. Cf. Sanbō ekotoba (II, 9), Hokke kenki (III, 96), Konjaku monogatarishū (XIV, 28).

2. Southern part of present Kyoto-fu.

3. 自度 jido or 私度 shido; a novice or monk without an official permit 度牒. Although the Sōni-ryō prescribes punishments for lay people who pretend to be monks and nuns (Article 22), a number of people left home and attempted to obtain immunity from taxation. See Chap. I(1)d; Tsumoto Ryōgaku, "Nihon ryōiki ni mieru shido no shami ni tsuite," Ryūkoku daigaku ronshū, No. 348 (December 1954), 37–46.

whose name is unknown. He used to play *go* 碁[4] all the time. One day when he was playing *go* with a layman,[5] a mendicant came to recite the *Hoke-kyō*[6] and beg for alms. The novice laughed at him, mimicking his accent with a twisted mouth. The layman was greatly shocked at this and exclaimed, "How awful!" at each turn in the game. The layman won the game every time, and the novice lost. Meanwhile the novice's mouth became twisted, and no medicine could cure it.

The gist of this story is stated in the *Hoke-kyō* as follows: "Those who laugh at and slight this scripture will lose many teeth and get a twisted mouth, a flattened nose, crippled limbs and squint eyes."[7] It is better to be possessed by evil spirits and talk in a daze than to abuse the devotees of the *Hoke-kyō*. Remember that evil comes from one's mouth.[8]

# 20

### *On a Monk Who Gave away the Firewood Provided to Heat the Bath and Was Reborn as an Ox for Labor, Showing an Extraordinary Sign*[1]

Saka Eshō 釋惠勝[2] was a monk[3] of Engō-ji 延興寺.[4] Once he gave away a bundle of firewood to be used for boiling water for the bath,[5] and then he died.

At that time the temple kept a cow which gave birth to a calf. When the calf grew into an ox, it was continually made to draw a cart filled with firewood. One day, as it entered the temple precincts

4. The *Sōni-ryō* (Article 9) prohibits monks and nuns from performing music or games of chance, but they are allowed to play the *koto* 琴 (a string instrument) and the game of *go*. See Sansom, "Early Japanese Laws," Part Two, 129.

5. 白衣 *byakue*, meaning literally "white robe," in contrast to the saffron or black robes of monks.

6. *Hoke-kyō-bon*.

7. *Hoke-kyō*, XXVIII (*Taishō*, IX, 62a). 若有輕笑之者 當世世牙齒踈缺 醜唇平鼻 手脚繚戾 眼目角睞. See Katō, trans., *Myōhō-renge-kyō*, 438.

8. 惡鬼 *akuki*; when one is possessed by an evil spirit, one's mouth becomes the channel for its message. There was a belief that illness or madness was caused by evil spirits.

1. Cf. *Konjaku monogatarishū* (XX, 20).

2. For Saka, see I.14, n. 2. Eshō is unknown.

3. 沙門 *shamon*; see Chap. I(1)a, n. 4.

4. Unidentified.

5. The practice of taking a steam bath was introduced to Japan by Buddhist monks during the Nara period, and a special room for taking a hot bath, which was almost a luxury, was built in many temples. Cf. *Onjitsu senyoku shūsō-gyō* 溫室洗浴衆僧經 (*Taishō*, XVI, No. 701).

pulling the cart, a strange monk at the gate was heard to say, "Though Dharma Master Eshō could read the *Nehan-gyō* 涅槃經[6] very well, he could not draw a cart." Hearing this, the ox shed tears, sighed, and passed away instantly. The driver of the ox accused the monk, saying, "You killed the ox with a curse," and reported him to the officials. The official who heard the driver's charge turned to question the monk and was surprised at his extraordinarily noble look and radiant body. In secret he invited the monk to a purified room and told painters to paint the monk exactly as he appeared. Presently they brought the portraits of the monk, all of which turned out to be pictures of Bodhisattva Kannon.[7] Meanwhile, the monk suddenly disappeared.

We are sure that the monk was none other than an incarnation of Kannon. No matter how hungry you are, it is better to eat dust rather than what belongs to the samgha,[8] which is always present. This is what the *Daihōdō-kyō* 大方等經[9] tells us in the following passage: "I would save those who have committed the four grave sins[10] and the five deadly sins,[11] but not those who have stolen from the samgha."[12]

# 21

## *On Gaining an Immediate Penalty for Driving a Heavily Burdened Horse without Mercy*[1]

In Kawachi 河內 province[2] there was once a man named Isowake 石別 who used to sell melons. He would saddle a horse[3] with an over-

6. *Daihatsu nehan-gyō* (*Taishō*, XII, No. 375).

7. See I.6, n. 4.

8. 常住僧 *jōjū no sō*, which is a manifestation of one of the Three Treasures for the purpose of maintaining and transmitting Buddha's teachings. See Chap. II(3)b.

9. Probably a shortened title of the *Daihōdō daijik-kyō* 大方等大集經 (*Taishō*, XIII, No. 397).

10. 四重 *shijū*; the four grave sins are killing, stealing, licentious acts, and telling lies; monks and nuns who commit any one of them will be expelled from the samgha.

11. 五逆 *gogyaku*; the five deadly sins are killing one's father, killing one's mother, killing an arhat, injuring the body of Buddha, and causing disunity in the samgha. It is said that those who commit any one of them will fall into hell.

12. 四重五逆我亦能救 盗僧物者我所不救 *Bonmō-kyō koshakki* 梵網經古迹記 (III, 2) gives this passage as a quotation from *Hōdō-kyō* 方等經, but it cannot be located in that text (*Taishō*, XL, No. 1815).

1. Cf. *Konjaku monogatarishū* (XX, 29).

2. Present Ōsaka-fu.

3. Although this story does not give any date, the use of a horse may indicate a date later than the seventh century, when horses began to be used widely. See Naoki, *Nihon kodai heiseishi no kenkyū*, 200.

whelming burden and, if it failed to move, would whip it angrily and drive it forward. The horse staggered along with its eyes full of tears. When Isowake had sold all of the melons, he would then kill the horse. After he had killed a number of horses in this way, Isowake happened to look into a kettle of boiling water, whereupon his two eyes fell into the kettle and were boiled.

Swift is the penalty for evil deeds. How can we not believe in the law of karmic causality? Beasts in the present life might have been our parents in a past life. We pass through the six modes of existence[4] and four manners of birth.[5] Reflection shows us that we cannot be without mercy.[6]

# 22

## On Showing an Extraordinary Sign at the Moment of Death Owing to Devotion to Buddhist Studies and Spreading the Teaching for the Benefit of All Beings[1]

The late Dharma Master Dōshō 道照[2] belonged to the Fune 船 family[3] in Kawachi province.[4] Under the emperor's auspices[5] he went abroad for Buddhist studies to T'ang China, where he met and studied with Hsüan-tsang san-tsang 玄弉三藏.[6] This master said to his

4. 六道 rokudō; heaven, man, asura, animal, hungry ghosts, and hell (being). See Chap. I(2)a, n. 126.

5. 四生 shishō; 胎生 (jarāyuja) birth from the womb (man, animal), 卵生 (aṇḍaja) birth from the egg (bird), 濕生 (saṃsvedaja) birth from moisture (insect), and 化生 (upapāduka) emanation by the force of karma (heavenly being, hell being).

6. 慈悲 jihi; see I.10, n. 5.

1. Cf. Shoku Nihongi (I, Monmu 4:3:10), Fusō ryakki (IV, V), Genkō shakusho (I, 1, i), Sanbō ekotoba (II, 2), Konjaku monogatarishū (XI, 4), etc. See Chap. I(1)d.

2. He went to T'ang China in 653, returned in 661, and founded the Hossō School in Japan. See Chap. I(1)a, n. 6, and d, n. 105. His was the first recorded cremation in Japan, in 700.

3. The Fune family is descended from Ō Shin-ni 王辰爾 of Paekche. (See Nihon shoki, XIX, Kinmei 14:7; XXIV, Kōgyoku 4:4:12.) In the early history of Japanese Buddhism, immigrants' descendants played a significant role, and many became eminent monks. See Chap. I(1)c, n. 61.

4. The Shoku Nihongi says he is of Tajihi district in Kawachi province, that is, present Fujii-dera-shi, Ōsaka-fu 大阪府藤井寺市.

5. Emperor Kōtoku sent envoys to China accompanied by student monks, among whom Dōshō's name is found. See Nihon shoki (XXV, Hakuchi 4:5:12); Aston, "Nihongi," II, 242–244.

6. (d. 664) An eminent monk and the most famous T'ang pilgrim to India. He went to China in 629 and came back in 645 with many Buddhist scriptures. He dedicated himself to the task of translating as many as seventy-three items. He is also known as the author of the Ta-T'ang hsi-yü chi 大唐西域記 (Records of the Western Regions). 三藏 san-tsang means the Three Baskets of the Buddhist Canon, tripiṭaka. In China it is also used as an honorific title for those well-read in the Buddhist scriptures or those who translate them. See Thomas Watters, On Yuan Chuang's Travels in India, 2 vols.

other disciples, "This man will teach many on his return home. You should not slight him but guide him well."

After completing his studies, he came home to establish a meditation hall, called Zen'in-ji 禪院寺,[7] and he lived there. His virtue in keeping the precepts[8] attained perfection, while his wisdom was a constant source of light as clear as a mirror. He traveled far and wide, proclaiming Buddhist teaching to all beings. When he grew older, he remained at the meditation hall and lectured on the essentials of the scriptures he had brought back from China.

At the time of his death, he purified himself in the bath,[9] changed his clothes, and seated himself facing west.[10] Light filled the room, and he opened his eyes and asked his disciple Chichō 知調,[11] "Did you see the light?" Chichō replied, "Yes, I did." Then Master Dōshō asked him not to tell others of it. Very early the next morning [12] a light emanated from the hall and moved round to illuminate the pine trees in the garden. Presently it flew away to the west. All of his disciples were struck with wonder, and it was at that very moment that the Most Venerable Master passed away seated calmly, facing west.

We are sure of his rebirth in the pure land of bliss.[13] The note says: This member of the Fune family is extraordinary and not common, for he exemplified virtue, traveled far to seek for Buddhist scriptures,[14] and ended his life in radiant light.

7. A temple which was built at the southeastern corner of Gangō-ji at Asuka in 662 and later moved to Nara in 711. See Fujino Michio, "Zen'in-ji kō," *Shigaku zasshi*, LXVI (No. 9, September 1957), 1–43.

8. 戒珠 *kaishu*; perfection of virtue is symbolized in a gem.

9. Purification with water is an important rite in the Japanese native tradition as well as in the Buddhist tradition.

10. "The west" indicates the western pure land of Amida. Accordingly, this passage is taken as an indication that Dōshō had faith in rebirth in the pure land, though this fact cannot be proved. Traditionally, the Hossō School was known for its connections with the Maitreya cult, but, among the Buddhist scriptures Dōshō brought back from China, there is one belonging to the Pure Land School, *Ōjō raisan* 往生禮讚 (see Ishida, *Shakyō yori mitaru Narachō Bukkyō no kenkyū*, 24–30). In Kyōkai's lifetime, a tradition developed, even within the circle of the Hossō School, which held that Dōshō and Gyōgi attained rebirth in Amida's pure land. See Inoue Mitsusada, *Nihon Jōdokyō seritsushi no kenkyū*, 74–81. For *Ōjō raisan*, see II. 20, n. 1.

11. Unknown.

12. 後夜 *goya*; about 3–5 a.m.

13. 極樂淨土 *gokuraku jōdo*; see Chap. I(1)a, n. 16.

14. Kariya's text gives 求法性 instead of 求法藏. In that case it means "seek for the Hossō School teaching." Based on the fact that the usage of 法性 is limited to the period 749–790, Fujino infers that this biography was written independently of the *Shoku Nihongi* during the Nara period. (See his "Zen'in-ji kō.")

# 23

## On an Evil Man Who Was Negligent in Filial Piety to His Mother and Gained an Immediate Penalty of Violent Death[1]

In Sou upper district, Yamato province 大和國添上郡,[2] there once lived a wicked man whose identity is lost except for his nickname, Miyasu 瞻保. In the reign of the emperor residing at the Palace of Naniwa,[3] he became a student of the Confucian classics,[4] but he attained merely book knowledge and did not support his mother.

His mother had borrowed rice from him and could not return it. Miyasu angrily pressed his mother for payment. His friends, who could no longer endure the sight of the mother seated on the ground while the son sat on a mat, asked him, "Good man,[5] why are you not respectful? Some people build pagodas, make Buddha images, copy scriptures, and invite monks to a retreat[6] for their parents' sake. You are rich and fortunate enough to lend much rice.[7] Why do you neglect your dear mother and contradict what you have studied?" Miyasu ignored them, saying, "That's none of your business." Whereupon they paid the debt on her behalf and hurried away.

His mother, for her part, bared her breasts and, in tears, said to her son, "When I reared you, I never rested day or night. I have seen people repaying their parents for their affection,[8] but, when I thought I could rely on my son, I incurred only disgrace. I was wrong in relying upon you. Since you have pressed me for repayment of the rice, I will now demand repayment of my milk. The mother-child tie is from this day broken. Heaven and earth will take cognizance of this. How sad, how pitiful!"

Without a word Miyasu stood up, went into the back room, and,

1. Cf. *Konjaku monogatarishū* (XX, 21).
2. See I.10, n. 2.
3. See I.9, n. 5.
4. 學生 *gakushō* is in this case a student of a state college (*daigaku*) who prepares for a career as a government official by studying the Chinese classics. See I.12, n. 3.
5. A respectful address which his friends must have used to ridicule him.
6. 安居 *ango*; see I.11, n. 6.
7. 貸稻 *irashi no ine*; see below, n. 9.
8. 恩 *on*; see Chap. II(2)a.

returning with the bonds,[9] burnt them all in the yard. Then he went into the mountains where he wandered about not knowing what to do, ran wildly this way and that with disheveled hair and a bleeding body, and could not stay in his home. Three days later a fire broke out suddenly, and all of his houses and storehouses in and out of the premises burned. Eventually Miyasu turned his family into the streets, and he himself died of hunger and cold without any shelter.

Now we cannot help believing that a penalty will be imposed, not in the distant future, but in this life.[10] Accordingly, a scripture says, "The unfilial are destined to hell; the filial, to the pure land."[11] This is what Nyorai 如來[12] preaches, the true teaching of Mahayana tradition.[13]

# 24

*On an Evil Daughter Who Was Negligent in Filial Piety to Her Mother and Gained an Immediate Penalty of Violent Death*[1]

In an old capital[2] there lived a wicked woman whose name is unknown. She had no sense of filial piety and never loved her mother. On one fasting day[3] her mother did not cook rice and visited her

9. 出擧 *suiko*; a system whereby the public granary lent rice to farmers in spring and allowed them to repay it after harvest with an interest of 1/16 per month within a limited period of one and a half years. In addition to the public system, various private arrangements for lending rice, rice wine, cloth, money, etc., with interest are documented for the period covered by the *Nihon ryōiki*, as well as several government orders against high interest rates. This story indicates that a bond was in use even in the family. See Sonoda Kōyū, "Suiko," *Ritsuryō kokka no kiso kōzō*, ed. by Ōsaka rekishi gakkai, 397–466; Yoshida Akira, "8, 9 seiki ni okeru shisuiko ni tsuite," *ibid.*, 467–514.

10. 現報 *genpō*, immediate karmic retribution. See Chap. I(2)a.

11. 不孝衆生必墮地獄 孝養父母往生淨土. This quotation cannot be located in the scripture, but one possible source is the *Kan muryōju-kyō* (*Taishō*, XII, 341c). 欲生彼國者當修三福 一者孝養 父母 奉事師長 慈心不殺 修十善業.

12. A translation of Skt. Tathāgata.

13. 大乘, Mahayana Buddhism. The virtue of filial piety is particularly emphasized in scriptures forged in China. See I.18, n. 9.

1. Cf. *Konjaku monogatarishū* (XX, 32).

2. See I.1, n. 15.

3. 齋日 *sainichi*; particular days are set aside for the laity to observe the eight precepts instead of the usual five and to participate in ceremonies at temples. See above, Chap. I(1)d, n. 88, for the ten precepts, the first eight of which were observed on these days. Since the eight precepts include a prohibition against eating after mid-day, *saijiki* 齋食 means the meal taken during designated hours, and hence, the vegetarian meal offered in Buddhist ceremonies.

daughter for the ceremonial meal. Her daughter said, "My husband and I are going to have our meal. We have nothing else to offer you."

Carrying her young child with her, the mother went home and lay down. Looking outside, she saw a package of boiled rice left by the roadside. She filled her empty stomach with that and fell asleep exhausted. Late that night someone knocked at the door, saying, "Your daughter is screaming that she has a nail stuck in her chest. She is about to die. You must go and see her!" The mother, however, was sleeping so soundly from exhaustion that she could not go and help bring her daughter back to life. The daughter finally died without seeing her mother.

It is better for us to give our portion to our mother and starve to death than to die without serving her.

# 25

## On a Loyal and Selfless Minister Who Gained Heaven's Sympathy and Was Rewarded by a Miraculous Event[1]

The late Middle Councillor 中納言,[2] Lord Ōmiwa no Takechimaro 大神高市萬侶,[3] of the Junior Third Rank[4] awarded posthumously, was a loyal minister of Empress Jitō 持統.[5] According to a record[6] in the second month of the ninth year of the dragon, the seventh year of the Akamidori era,[7] an imperial order was given to the officials, telling them to prepare for the empress' visit to Ise 伊勢 on the third of the third month. The Middle Councillor, fearing that the proposed visit would interfere with agricultural work, presented a memorial to dissuade the empress. She did not yield to his remonstrance and demanded to have her own way. Thereupon he took off his official cap[8] and returned it to the empress, saying, "When farmers are most busy in the fields, you should not make a trip," reiterating his remonstrance.

1. Cf. *Nihon shoki* (XXX, Jitō 6:2:11), *Konjaku monogatarishū* (XX, 41).
2. *Chūnagon*, one of the high ranking officials under the prime minister.
3. Or 大三輪高市麻呂 (*Nihon shoki*).
4. When he died in 706, his rank was the Upper Junior Fourth Rank.
5. (686–697) Emperor Tenmu's consort.
6. A possible source of the *Nihon shoki*, but not clearly identified. According to the *Nihon shoki*, he resigned his position as the empress eventually proceeded to Ise on a two-week trip.
7. As the era of Akamidori (or Akemidori) ended in one year, its seventh year falls on the sixth year of the reign of Empress Jitō, 692.
8. The cap signifies his court rank, and removing it is a gesture of resignation.

Another time during a drought he had the ditch of his fields closed in order to irrigate the fields of other people.[9] When the water in his fields dried up, the dragon kami[10] sent down rain showing the empathy of all the heavens.[11] It rained only on his fields. Yao 堯 sent clouds and Shun 舜 poured down rain[12] to reward his extreme loyalty and great virtue.

The note says: How praiseworthy is this member of the Ōmiwa family who since infancy has favored studies and been both loyal and benevolent![13] His mind never became unclear, and he conferred benefits on people, irrigating their fields at the expense of his own till he moved the heavens to send the seasonal rains. His fame will last forever.

# 26

### On a Full-fledged Monk Who Kept Precepts,
### Practiced Austerities, and Attained a Miraculous
### Power in This Life[1]

In the reign of Empress Jitō, there was a *dhyāna* master of Paekche whose name was Tajō 多常.[2] He lived a life of strict discipline in Hōki-yamadera 法器山寺[3] in Takechi district and made it his chief

9. 百姓 *ōmitakara*; as *ōmi* is an honorific prefix and *takara* is treasure, it means "emperor's treasure." Under the *ritsuryō* government all except slaves were given *kabane* 姓, and, therefore, one hundred *kabane* means people on all social levels and in all occupations.

10. 龍神; see De Visser, *The Dragon in China and Japan*.

11. 諸天感應.

12. 堯雲更靄 舜雨遍需. The above expression is a metaphor describing how the Chinese ideal sage emperors, Yao and Shun, bestowed benevolence on their subjects.

13. Both the *Nihon ryōiki* and *Nihon shoki* depict him as an ideal Confucian minister and Empress Jitō as a stubborn lady. However, contemporary historians assess her as a shrewd ruler and maintain that she made a trip to Ise, Iga, and Shima in order to appease the local gentry after she had begun to construct the capital of Fujiwara. See Kitayama Shigeo, "Jitō tennō," *Nihon kodai seijishi no kenkyū*, 119–233; Naoki, *Jitō tennō*.

1. The motif of a stick growing into a tree or a Buddhist monk causing water to spring out of the ground by striking it with a stick is found throughout Japan. The Buddhist tradition gives an anecdote of Śākyamuni: After Buddha chewed on a stick, he stuck it in the ground, and it grew into a tree seven feet high. See *Fa-hsien chuan* 法顯傳 (*Taishō*, LI, No. 2085, 860b); James Legge, trans., *A Record of Buddhist Kingdoms*, 54–55, text 17; Hsüan-tsang 玄弉, *Ta-t'ang hsi-yü-chi* 大唐西域記, IV (*Taishō*, LI, No. 2087); Watters, trans., *On Yuan Chuang's Travels in India*, I, 129.

2. Or Tarajō 多羅常; unknown.

3. Identified with Hokonoki-dera 桙削寺 (later Kojima-dera 子島寺), or Minami-hokke-ji 南法華寺 in Takechi district. See Fukuyama, *Narachō jiin*, 230–234.

concern to cure diseases.[4] The dying were restored to health by his miraculous works. Whenever he recited formulas for the sick, there was a miraculous event. Once he climbed a tree to get a willow twig,[5] using a monk's stick[6] with another on top of it as a ladder. The two sticks did not fall, but stood as if they had been grafted together. The empress respected him and made offerings to him, and the people put faith in him and revered him. This is the fruit of his disciplined life.[7] His fame and compassionate virtue will be praised forever.

# 27

## On an Evil Anonymous Novice Who Tore Down a Pillar of the Pagoda and Gained a Penalty[1]

The novice[2] of Ishikawa was a self-ordained[3] monk without a clerical name, and his secular name is unknown. The only fact known about his origin is that his wife came from Ishikawa district, Kawachi province 河内國石川郡,[4] which is why he is called the novice Shami of Ishikawa. He had the appearance of a novice monk but the mind of a thief. Once he swindled people out of donations under the pretext of building a pagoda and spent the money for various foods. Or again, when he lived in the Tsukiyone-dera 舂米寺[5] in Shimashimo district, Settsu province 攝津國嶋下郡,[6] he tore down a pillar of the pagoda to burn, and thus he failed to honor dharma. No one could be as wicked as he.

Eventually, he reached the village of Ajiki 味木里 in Shimashimo district,[7] and came down with a fever. He cried aloud, "I am on

4. 看病第一.
5. 楊枝 *yōshi*; Indian monks chewed a piece of a banyan tree to clean their teeth every morning (Skt. *dantakāṣṭha*). The Chinese, not having a banyan tree, substituted a twig from a willow tree to protect them from evil.
6. 錫杖 *shakujō*, the stick with a metal ring on the top used by ascetics and monks.
7. 修行 *shugyō*, self-discipline oriented toward enlightenment, cultivation of the mind by means of disciplining the body. Cf. *Bukkyō ni okeru gyō no mondai,* ed. by Nihon Bukkyō gakkai.

1. Cf. *Konjaku monogatarishū* (XX, 38).
2. 沙彌 *shami*; see Chap. I(1)a, n. 10.
3. 自度 *jido*; see I.19, n. 3.
4. Present Minami-kawachi-gun, Ōsaka-fu.
5. Unidentified; its name suggests that there was a mill in the temple precincts. See Preface, n. 19, above.
6. Present Mishima-gun, Ōsaka-fu 大阪府三島郡.
7. Unidentified.

fire!'' and jumped one or two feet off the ground. People gathered around to look and asked, "Why are you screaming like that?" He answered, "Because hell fire has come to devour me, and I am suffering. Why are you asking me such questions?" He breathed his last on that day.

What a pity it is! We should reflect on ourselves since we know that retribution[8] is no idle fancy. This is what the *Nehan-gyō*[9] means when it says: "If a man does good deeds, his name will be noticed among heavenly beings;[10] while, if he does evil deeds, his name will be recorded in hell.[11] For retribution is a real fact."

# 28

*On Practicing the Formula of the Peacock King,*
*and Thereby Gaining an Extraordinary Power to Become*
*a Saint and Fly to Heaven in This Life*[1]

E no ubasoku 役優婆塞[2] was of the Kamo-no-enokimi 賀茂役君 family,[3] presently the Takakamo-no-asomi 高賀茂朝臣 family.[4] He came from the village of Chihara, Upper Kazuraki district, Yamato province 大和國葛木上郡茅原村.[5] By nature he was endowed with wisdom; he excelled in learning and attained ultimate knowledge.[6]

8. 罪報 *zaihō*.
9. *Daihatsu nehan-gyō*, XI (*Taishō*, XII, 524b). 若見有人修行善者名見天人修行惡者名見地獄定受報故.
10. 天人 *tenjin*, interpreted as heavenly beings or "heavens and this world."
11. 地獄 *jigoku*. See Chap. I(2)a, n. 127.

1. Cf. *Shoku Nihongi* (I, Monmu 5:5:24), *Fusō ryakki* (V, Monmu), *Sanbō ekotoba* (II), *Genkō shakusho* (XV), *Konjaku monogatarishū* (XI, 3), etc. See H. Byron Earhart, "Shugendō, the Traditions of En no Gyōja, and Mikkyō Influence," *Studies of Esoteric Buddhism and Tantrism*, 297–317.
2. For *E*, his family name, see Chap. I(1)d, n. 118. For *ubasoku*, see Chap. I(1)d, n. 92.
3. *Shoku Nihongi* (VIII, Yōrō 3:7:13). 從六位上賀茂役首石穂 賜賀茂役君姓. A title, Kamo no enokimi, was given to the family in 719.
4. *Ibid.* (XXIX, Jingo keiun 3:5:13). 正六位上賀茂朝臣清濱賜姓高賀茂朝臣; a *title*, Takamo no asomi, was given in 769.
5. Present Chihara, Ōaza, Ekinoe-mura, Minami-katsuragi-gun, Nara-ken 奈良縣南葛城郡被上村大字茅原.
6. 生知博學得一 Kariya Ekisai says 得 may be an error of the compiler or copyist, and later editors interpret this sentence: ". . . with wisdom, and excelled all in learning." However, as 一 is the beginning of the numbers and end *of all* phenomena, 得一 or 守一 refers to the mystical unity of man with the ultimate cosmic principle, tao or dharma. In the early Chinese translation of Buddhist scriptures, 守一 *means dhyāna* (meditation). See Yoshioka Gihō, "Shoki Dōkyō no shuitsu shisō to Bukkyō," *Taishō daigaku kenkyū kiyō*, No. 53 (1968), 61–84.

ShipVia: lib rate

NeedBy: 3/2/02

**Return To:**

Scribner Library
Skidmore College
815 No. Broadway
Saratoga Springs, NY 12866

**Ship To:**

univ.lib.rm 110
suny albany
1400 washington ave.
albany, ny 12222

**BOUND PRINTED MATTER**

ILL.: **4230173**    Borrower: NAM

Req Date: **1/31/02**    OCLC #: 740808

Patron: **Blum, Mark**

Author: **Keikai, 8th/9th cent.**

Title: **Miraculous stories from the Japanese Bud**

Article:

Vol.:    No.:

Date:    Pages:

Verified: <TN:10169>OCLC

Maxcost: 15IFM    Due Date:

Lending Notes:

Bor Notes: ariel if possible 169.226.11.129

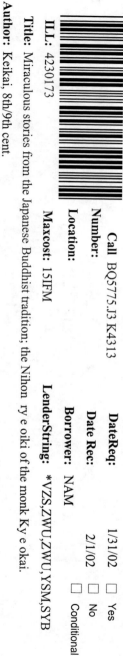

He lived with reverence and faith in the Three Treasures. His greatest desire was to fly on a five-colored cloud[7] beyond the sky[8] and play in the garden of eternity[9] with the guests of the heavenly palace,[10] lying in the flowering garden and sucking vital force out of the haze to nourish his nature.[11]

Accordingly, in his late forties he went to live in a cave, wore clothing made of vines, drank the dewdrops on pine needles, bathed in pure spring water to rinse away the filth of the world of desire,[12] and learned the formula of the Peacock[13] to attain extraordinary power. Thus he could employ spirits and kami[14] at his command.

Once he summoned them all and ordered them, "Make a bridge between Kane-no-take 金峯[15] and Kazuraki-no-take 葛木峯."[16] They were not happy about this, and in the reign of the emperor residing at Fujiwara Palace 藤原宮,[17] Hitokotonushi no Ōkami 一語主大神[18] of Kazuraki-no-take was possessed and slandered him, saying, "E no ubasoku plans to usurp the throne." The emperor dispatched messengers to capture him, but they found it hard to take him due to his mysterious magical power, so they captured his mother instead. In order that his mother might be freed, he gave himself up.

He was exiled to the island of Izu 伊圖嶋.[19] One time his body went floating on the sea as if he were walking on land. Again, his body perched on a mountain ten thousand feet high and looked like a huge phoenix[20] in flight. In the daytime he stayed on the island in accord with the emperor's command, but at night he went to Fuji-no-take in Suruga 駿河富岷嶺[21] to practice austerities. As he prayed for

7. 五色雲, on the rainbow; see I.5.
8. 飛仲虛之外; see II.Preface, n. 14.
9. 億載庭, meaning the garden which does not change for 100 million years.
10. 仙宮賓. See I.13, n. 5.
11. 養性 *yōjō*; 性 nature means body and spirit.
12. 欲界 *yokukai*; see II.2, n. 6.
13. 孔雀王 Skt. *Mahāmayūrividyārājñī*; several scriptures are related to the Peacock (-hen) King. Śrīmitra 帛尸梨密多羅 of fourth-century China translated *K'ung-ch'üeh-wang shen-chou-ching* 孔雀王神咒經 and *K'ung-ch'üeh-wang tsa-shen-chou* 孔雀王雜神咒, which are no longer extant. Kumārajīva translated the *K'ung ch'üeh-wang chou-ching* (*Taishō*, XIX, No. 988), and in T'ang China expanded works appeared. Although it is impossible to identify the formulas E no ubasoku learned, some of them might have been transmitted to Japan quite early.
14. 鬼神.
15. Or Kinpu-san 金峯山 located at present Yoshino-gun, Nara-ken.
16. Or Kazuraki-san 葛木山 on the boundary between Nara-ken and Ōsaka-fu: *Shoku Nihongi* says that E no Ozunu lived on Mt. Kazuraki in the beginning.
17. Emperor Monmu 文武 (r. 697–700).
18. Meaning Lord of One Word. See Chap. I(1)d, n. 119.
19. See Chap. I(1)d, n. 120.
20. 鳳 ōtori; a male Chinese phoenix.
21. Or 富士山; Mt. Fuji, the highest mountain in Japan, located in present Shizuoka-ken 靜岡縣.

pardon from his severe punishment and for permission to return to the capital, he lay down on the blade of an assassin's sword and ascended to Mt. Fuji. Three years passed in ascetic practice after he was exiled to the island. At the turn of the eighth year of the ox, the first year of the Taihō era,[22] he was pardoned and approached the capital, finally becoming a saint[23] and flying to heaven.

Dharma Master Dōshō 道照[24] of our country received an imperial order to go to Great T'ang China in order to search out Buddhist teachings. On the request of five hundred tigers he went to Silla 新羅[25] to lecture in the mountains on the *Hoke-kyō*.[26] At that time there was a man among the tigers who raised a question in Japanese. The monk asked, "Who are you?" and the man answered, "E no ubasoku." The monk thought that the man was a Japanese sage[27] and came down from his high seat to inquire about him, but he was gone.

Hitokotonushi no Ōkami was bound with a spell by E no gyōja 役行者, and he has not escaped[28] even to this day. E no ubasoku did so many miraculous deeds that we cannot enumerate them all. Indeed we learn that Buddhist miraculous arts are comprehensive. Those who have faith will attain them without fail.

# 29

*On Breaking Wickedly the Bowl of a Begging Novice and*
*Gaining an Immediate Penalty of Violent Death*[1]

Shiragabe no Imaro白髮部猪麿[2] was a man from Oda district, Bitchū province 備中國少田郡.[3] He was evil[4] by nature and did not believe in the Three Treasures.[5]

22. 701.
23. 仙; Taoist saint.
24. See above, I.22. Since Dōshō died in 700, his encounter with E no ubasoku lacks historical evidence.
25. Silla unified Korea in 668 and flourished for the following century.
26. See Chap. I(1)d, n. 93; Chap. II(3)b.
27. 我國聖人.
28. 解脱; see I.15, n. 6.

1. Cf. *Konjaku monogatarishū* (XX, 26).
2. The Shiragabe family is well known from early times. The *Shinsen shōjiroku* cites it as an indigenous family (both 神別 and 皇別).
3. Present Oda-gun, Okayama-ken 岡山縣小田郡.
4. 邪見 *jaken*.
5. 三寶 *sanbō*; see Chap. II(3)b.

One day a monk came to him begging for food. Imaro offered him not food but abuse, broke his begging bowl, and chased him away. Then Imaro went on a trip to a strange land. On the way he was caught in a storm and crushed to death when the storehouse in which he had taken shelter collapsed.[6]

Truly we learn that retribution is close at hand in the present life. Why do we not behave ourselves prudently? The *Nehan-gyō* is referring to this when it says: "All evil deeds originate in wicked minds."[7] The *Daijōbu-ron* says: "If you offer alms with compassion, the merit will be as great as earth; if you do so to all for your own sake, the reward will be as tiny as a mustard seed. It is better to save a person in danger than to make all kinds of offerings . . . ."[8]

# 30

## *On Taking Others' Possessions Unrighteously, Causing Evil, and Gaining a Penalty Showing an Extraordinary Event*[1]

Kashiwade no omi Hirokuni 膳臣廣國[2] was an assistant governor[3] of Miyako district, Buzen province 豐前國宮子郡.[4] In the reign of the emperor at Fujiwara Palace, on the fifteenth of the ninth month in the autumn of the second year of the snake, the second year of the Keiun era,[5] Hirokuni passed away suddenly. On the fourth day after his death, about four o'clock in the afternoon, he was brought back to life and told the following tale:

"There came two messengers, one with an adult's hair style, the other with a child's. I accompanied them for the distance of about two stages,[6] and on our way there was a river with a golden bridge.

6. See I.10, n. 10.
7. *Daihatsu nehan-gyō*, XXXV (*Taishō*, XII, 573c). 如我所說 一切惡行 邪見爲因.
8. *Daijōbu-ron* (*Taishō*, XXX, 257b).

1. Cf. *Fusō ryakki* (V, Monmu), *Konjaku monogatarishū* (XX, 16). The motif is the visit to the other world; see Chap. II(1)b.
2. Kashiwade is a family name; *omi*, a title; Hirokuni, a given name.
3. 少領 *shōryō*, an official who assists a district governor, *dairyō* 大領.
4. Present Miyako-gun, Fukuoka-ken 福岡縣京都郡.
5. 705, in the reign of Emperor Monmu.
6. One stage (*umaya* 驛) is about twelve miles, the distance between stages which were established to facilitate the transportation of taxed goods and messengers along main roads.

Crossing the bridge, I found myself in a strange land. I asked the messengers, 'What country is this?' They answered, 'It is the land in the southern direction.'[7]

"As we reached the capital, we saw eight armed officials following us. We found ourselves in front of a golden palace. When we entered the palace, a king was seated on the golden throne, and he told me, 'I have summoned you on a complaint by your wife.' Then the king called a woman whom I recognized as my deceased wife. Eight men carried her in: iron nails pierced her from top to bottom and from her forehead to the nape of her neck, while an iron chain tied her limbs. The king asked me, 'Do you know her?' I answered, 'Indeed, she is my wife.' Again the king asked, 'Do you know the sin of which you are accused?' I answered 'No.' When my wife was asked the same question, she answered, 'Yes, indeed. Because he drove me from home, I still bear a grudge and feel envious and hateful.' The king said to me, 'You are really innocent. You may go home. I warn you, however, not to talk thoughtlessly about the land of the dead.[8] If you want to see your father, go to the south.'

"I went south to find my father standing and holding a hot copper pillar. He had thirty-seven nails in his body and was beaten with an iron stick, three hundred times in the morning, three hundred times in the afternoon, three hundred times in the evening, or, altogether, nine hundred times a day. I grieved at this and said, 'I never dreamed that you were suffering such punishment!' Then he spoke to me, saying: 'My son, probably you do not know why I am suffering. In order to support my family I killed living beings, pressed men to repay ten *ryō* on a loan of eight *ryō*[9] of cotton, or lent rice and collected three times the amount.[10] Also, I robbed others of their possessions, committed adultery with the wives of others, neglected filial piety and reverence to my elders, and used foul language to abuse those who were not slaves.[11] Because of such offenses I have thirty-seven iron nails in my small body and receive nine hundred beatings daily with an iron stick. What pain! What suffering! When shall I be excused from my sin? When shall my body find rest? Please hurry to atone for

---

7. 圖南國 Tonan no kuni; see Chap. II(1)b, n. 33.
8. 黄泉國 Yomi no kuni; see Chap. II(1)b, n. 26.
9. 兩 a *ryō* is a unit of measurement; sixteen *ryō* equal one *gon* 斤.
10. There are two kinds of *gon, daigon* 大斤 and *shōgon* 小斤. The former is three times as much as the latter. See I.12, n. 11. An interest rate higher than 100 percent was prohibited (see *Shoku Nihongi*, XXXL, Hōki 10:9:28). In the decree of 797 the practice of 50 percent interest was banned. See I.23, n. 9.
11. 奴婢 *nuhi*; see Chap. I(1)a, n. 24. Those who could not pay back their debts often fell into the status of slaves. Therefore, he may have treated his debtors in the same manner as slaves.

my sins by making a Buddha-image and copying scriptures. Never forget this. When I visited you in hunger in the form of a big snake on the seventh[12] of the seventh month and was about to enter the house, you picked up the snake and threw it away. Again, when I went to your home in the form of a small red dog on the fifth[13] of the fifth month, you called a big dog to chase me, and I left hungry and exhausted. However, when I entered your house in the form of a cat on New Year's Day,[14] I filled my stomach with the various offerings and was able to make up for three years' lack of food. Then, I lost my sense of social order and reason and became a dog eating and watering. I am sure to become a small red dog again.'

"If you make an offering of one quart[15] of rice, you will gain a reward of thirty days' food; if you make an offering of one set of clothes, you will gain a reward of one year's clothing. Those who have Buddhist scriptures recited will live in the eastern golden palace[16] and be born in the heaven according to their wish; those who have Buddha-images made will be born in the Western Pure Land of Unlimited Life;[17] those who set living beings free will be born in the Northern Pure Land of Unlimited Life.[18] Or, those who fast for a day[19] will gain a reward of ten years' food.

"Shocked at the sight of so many instances of retribution, I came back to the big bridge. The guards watching the gate checked me and said, 'We cannot let you go out, since you have been in.' I was wandering around when the child appeared. The gatekeepers knelt to greet him. Then the child called me, led me to a side gate, and opened the door. When I was leaving, he said, 'Go quickly.' I asked him, 'Whose child are you?' He answered, 'If you want to know who I am, I am the *Kanzeon-gyō*[20] which you copied in your childhood.' He was gone, whereupon I looked around to find myself in this world again."

As Hirokuni visited the land of the dead and saw the karmic retribution of good and evil, he recorded it for circulation.[21] Who can fail

12. Tanabata 七夕 festival; one of the five popular festivals which originated in China. After transmission to Japan, they were celebrated at court as well as in private homes. This festival is associated with the legend of the cowherd (牽牛 Altair) and the spinning maid (織女 Vega).
13. Tango 端午; one of the five festivals mentioned above, at which prayers for protection from evil were offered.
14. See Chap. II(1)a, for the New Year renewal rite.
15. 升 *shō*.
16. 東方金宮; unidentified. Yakushi-Nyorai's pure land lies in the eastern quarter, but from the following sentence it seems to be a heaven rather than the pure land. Cf. I.5.
17. 西方无量淨土; see above, Chap. I(1)a, n. 16.
18. 北方无量淨土; the abode of the Bodhisattva Samantabhadra 普賢菩薩. See *Hika-kyō*, IV (*Taishō*, III, No. 57b).
19. 齋食 *saijiki*; see I.24, n. 3.
20. *Myōhōrenge-kyō*, XXV; Katō, trans., *Myōhō-renge-kyō*, XXV.
21. See Chap. I(2)c.

to believe in the law of karmic retribution, as expounded widely in the Mahayana scriptures? This is what the scripture means when it says: "Honeydew in the present will be an iron ball in the future."[22] Hirokuni made Buddha images, copied scriptures, and made offerings to the Three Treasures to repay his father's love[23] and atone for his sin, thereafter turning evil into righteousness.

# 3 I

## On Attaining a Great Fortune Immediately Owing to Devotion to Kannon and Praying for a Share of Benefits[1]

In the reign of ex-Emperor Shōhō-ōjin-shōmu[2] residing at Nara Palace 諾樂宮,[3] Miteshiro no Azumabito 御手代東人[4] went to Mt. Yoshino 吉野山[5] to practice Buddhist teachings and seek his fortune. Three years passed during which he worshiped Kannon 觀音, reciting the name,[6] and saying, "Homage to Kannon.[7] Please give me ten thousand kan[8] of copper coins, ten thousand koku[9] of white rice and many beautiful girls."

At that time, Awata no asomi 粟田朝臣 of the Junior Third Rank[10] had a daughter who was both unmarried and a virgin. She suddenly fell ill in her home in Hirose 廣瀬.[11] Her suffering was so great that there seemed no prospect of a cure. Her father sent messengers in all directions to call Buddhist monks[12] and lay brothers.[13] Azumabito was called and begged to save her by chanting formulas.[14] The power of

22. 現在甘露未來鐵丸. This given as a scriptural passage in this story, but as an ancient proverb in II.9. 甘露 and 鐵丸 are familiar metaphors in scriptures.
23. Gratitude to one's father is one of the four essential kinds of on. See Chap. II(2)a, nn. 69, 70.

1. Cf. Konjaku monogatarishū (XVI, 14).
2. See I.5, n. 41.
3. Also written 奈良, 平城.
4. The Miteshiro family descended from kami, according to the Shinsen shōjiroku.
5. Including mountains located in present Yoshino-gun, Nara-ken. See I.28, n. 15.
6. 稱禮 devotional rite of reciting Kannon's name while prostrated before the image.
7. 南無, a transliteration of Skt. namas.
8. 貫; one kan consists of one thousand pieces, mon.
9. 石; one koku equals about five bushels.
10. Unidentified; Awata no asomi Mahito of the Senior Third Rank may be the person referred to, but he died in 719, before the reign of Emperor Shōmu (724–749).
11. Present Kita-kazuraki-gun, Nara-ken 奈良縣北葛城郡.
12. 禪師 zenji; dhyāna master.
13. 優婆塞 ubasoku.
14. 咒 ju; see Chap. I(1)d, n. 97.

the formulas cured the illness, and she fell in love with him, eventually giving herself to him. Her family seized him and kept him confined in a room. Out of her affection, she cried and would not leave the place of his confinement. After a conference, her family decided to free Azumabito and let him marry her and inherit the fortune. He was given the Fifth Rank owing to the report to the Throne.[15]

After several years, when she was dying, she called her sister, and said, "I am dying now. I have but one wish; will you listen?" Her sister said, "I will do as you like." Whereupon Azumabito's wife said, "I can never forget my gratitude to Azumabito. I would like to make your daughter his wife and let her be in charge of the household."[16] Faithful to her wish, the sister gave her daughter to Azumabito and put her in charge of the fortune.

Azumabito was richly blessed in this life because of the mysterious power he gained from his devotional practices and the great virtue of Kannon. How can anyone not believe that?

# 32

*On Gaining an Immediate Reward for Faith in the*
*Three Treasures, Reverence to Monks, and Having*
*Scriptures Recited*[1]

In the ninth month of the fourth year of the hare, the fourth year of the Jinki era,[2] Emperor Shōmu went hunting with his officers in the mountain at Yamamura in Sou upper district 添上郡山村.[3] A deer ran into a farmer's house in the village of Hosome 納見里,[4] and the family killed and ate it without knowing whose it was. Later, when the emperor heard this, he sent messengers to take them prisoner. More than ten men and women met with this misfortune, and they shuddered in fear without any recourse. Their only thought was that nothing but the divine power[5] of the Three Treasures would save

15. As he became the son-in-law of Awata no asomi, he was given the rank.
16. This story demonstrates the practice of handing down authority for the ancestral cult and the family fortune from the aunt to the niece, which is still common in a priestess' family. See Sakurai Mitsuru, "Mei no chikara: Naka no sumeramikoto o megutte," *Kokugo to koku-bungaku*, XLII (No. 12, December 1965), 23–33.

1. Cf. *Konjaku monogatarishū* (XII, 16).
2. 727.
3. See I.10, n. 2.
4. Present Tenri-shi 天理市, south of Yamamura.
5. 神力.

them from their sad plight. As they heard that the Sixteen-foot Buddha of Daian-ji 大安寺丈六[6] would respond to the people's prayers, they sent a man to visit the temple and have scriptures recited. They made an appeal to the monks, saying, "When we are led to court, please open the southern gate of the temple so that we may pay homage to the Buddha. Also we beg you to ring the bell when we are taken to court so that the sound of the bell may follow us."

According to their wishes, the monks rang the bell, recited scriptures,[7] and opened the gate so that the people might worship. The latter were sent to court by the messengers and confined in a guard-room.[8] Just then a prince was born,[9] and the emperor granted a general amnesty to criminals and did not punish them. Instead, he gave alms to the people, and their happiness and joy could not be measured.

We learn that this is due to the influence of the Sixteen-foot Buddha and the merit of reciting scriptures.

# 33

*On the Miraculous Survival of a Buddha's Picture*
*Offered by a Widow Who Made a Vow to Have It*
*Painted for Her Deceased Husband*[1]

There is a painted image of Amida阿彌陀[2] in the Hata-dera八多寺[3] in Ishikawa district, Kawachi province 河内國石川郡.[4] Villagers say that a wise woman once lived in this neighborhood, but her name is

---

6. Daian-ji was located at theWest Side of Nara, on the way to the court from the southern district. *Jō-roku* means one *jō* 一丈 and six *shaku* 六尺, which is about sixteen feet. One *jō* is ten *shaku* and one *shaku* is about one foot.

7. 轉讀 *tendoku;* a ritual reading of scriptures or portions of lengthy scriptures. Since the *Dai hannya-kyō* is a voluminous scripture, some portions of it are read in a service. When we think of the probable relation between Daian-ji and the study of this scripture (see Chap. II(1)c, n. 65), this passage also may be translated ". . . read portions of the *Dai hannya-kyō,* . . ."

8. 授刀寮; an office for the imperial guards which was instituted in 707. Only those who had committed some crime against the emperor were imprisoned there. See *Shoku Nihongi,* IV (Keiun 4:7:21): "The Office of Tachihaki no Toneri was created."

9. See *ibid.,* X (Jinki 4:9:29, 4:10:5).

1. Cf. *Konjaku monogatarishū* (XII, 18).

2. See Chap. II(3)b, n. 132.

3. Unidentified; it may be a temple of the Hata family, originally immigrated from China by way of Korea.

4. Present Minami-kawachi-gun, Ōsaka-fu

unknown. On the day her husband was dying, she vowed to make an image of Amida, but many years passed and the vow was not fulfilled because of her poverty.

One autumn she gleaned in the rice fields, commissioned a painter, and made offerings to the dead for the first time, weeping in her sorrow. In sympathy, the painter joined in her devotion and completed a beautiful painting. After a ceremonial feast[5] it was consecrated in the golden hall of the temple, and she paid constant homage to it.

A thief later set fire to the hall, and it was destroyed. Only the Buddha image survived the fire, suffering no damage.

Wasn't it a miraculous work of Buddha to help the woman? The note says: How good a wife she was in holding a memorial rite for her husband![6] Eventually she held it in the autumn. We know indeed how devoted she was. Even blazing flames cannot consume the holy image. Heaven's help is beyond our comprehension.

# 34

## On Taking Back Silk Robes Once Stolen Owing to the Petition to Bodhisattva Myōken[1]

Once there was a house in front of the Kisakibe-dera私部寺[2] in Ate district, Kii province 紀伊國安諦郡.[3] As ten silk robes were stolen from the owners, they prayed devotedly through Bodhisattva Myō-ken 妙見菩薩[4] in the temple. The stolen silk robes were sold to a merchant in Kii. Hardly a week passed before a gale hit, and the robes were whisked south on the back of a deer to the original owners' garden; the deer then disappeared in the heavens. The merchant who had bought them, hearing that they were stolen goods, did not ask for them back but kept quiet.

5. 齋會 saie; a (dedication) ceremony in which a vegetarian feast is offered. See I.24, n. 3.
6. 追遠報恩 tsuion hōon; tsuion means "perform proper rites to pray for the dead," and hōon means "repay for the kindness, love given." It is customary during the first year after a person's death to perform various religious acts in the hopes that the merits accumulated by such acts may benefit the deceased.

1. Cf. Konjaku monogatarishū (XVII, 4).
2. Unidentified.
3. Present Arita-gun, Wakayama-ken 和歌山縣有田郡.
4. See Chap. II(3)b, n. 133.

# 35

## On a Nun Who Painted a Buddha Image out of Gratitude for the Four Kinds of Blessings and Gained a Power to Show an Extraordinary Sign[1]

In a village of Yuge, Wakae district, Kawachi province 河內國若江郡遊宜村,[2] there lived a highly disciplined novice nun 練行沙彌尼.[3] Her name is unknown. She lived in a mountain temple at Heguri 平群,[4] and, organizing a devotees' association,[5] painted a Buddha image with a picture of the six existences[6] in order to give thanks for the four kinds of blessings.[7] When completed, it was enshrined in the temple after the dedication ceremony.

Meanwhile she left the temple, going from place to place on errands. During that time the picture was stolen, and she looked for it in vain, crying pitifully. Still leading the devotees' organization, she wanted to free living beings,[8] and the members went to Naniwa 難破 to visit the market. When they saw a basket in a tree, they heard various animals crying in the basket. They waited for the owner to return, for they thought there must be animals in the basket and they wanted to buy them and set them free. Meanwhile, the owner returned. When they said to him, "We heard some animals in your basket, and we have been waiting to buy them from you," the owner said, "No, there is nothing alive in it." The nun did not give up, however. She continued begging till the merchants around them said to the owner, "You should open the basket." The owner was frightened, and he ran away, leaving the basket. When they opened it, they discovered the stolen image. In joy and tears the devotees cried, "Since we lost this image, we have been longing for it day and night. Now, by chance, we have found it. How happy we are!" When the merchants heard this, they gathered around and praised the nun's perseverance.

1. Cf. *Konjaku monogatarishū* (XII, 17).
2. The southern part of present Hachio-shi, Ōsaka-fu.
3. 沙彌尼 *shamini*, a transliteration of Skt. *śrāmaṇerikā*, originally a nun under the age of twenty who keeps the ten precepts, but in this case the same as a nun. Cf. Chap. I(1)a, n. 10.
4. Present Heguri-mura, Ikoma-gun, Nara-ken.
5. 知識 *chishiki*; see Chap. I(1)d, nn. 110, 111.
6. 六道 *rokudō*; see Chap. I(2)a, n. 126.
7. 四恩 *shion*, that is, the blessing of the parents, lords, all sentient beings, and the Three Treasures; or mother, father, Tathāgata, and monks. See Chap. II(2)a, nn. 69, 70.
8. 放生 *hōjō*; see I.7, n. 12.

Joyfully the nun and the others set living beings free, held memorial services, and reconsecrated the image in the original temple, where it remained an object of devotion for both clergy and laity. This is indeed a miraculous event.

# NIHONKOKU GENPŌ ZEN'AKU RYŌIKI

## VOLUME II

by Kyōkai

Monk of Yakushi-ji
on the West Side of Nara

## CONTENTS

Forty-two Stories on the Karmic Retribution of Good and Evil

Preface     157
1. On the Death Penalty in This Life for Taking Pride in One's Own Virtue and Hitting a Humble-looking Novice     158
2. On Renouncing the World to Practice Good at the Sight of the Adultery of Crows     160
3. On the Death Penalty in This Life of an Evil Son Who Tried to Kill His Mother out of Love for His Wife     161
4. On a Contest between Women of Extraordinary Strength     163
5. On Gaining an Immediate Penalty for Sacrificing Oxen to a Pagan Deity and the Merit of Good Deeds of Freeing Living Beings     164
6. On Copying the *Hoke-kyō* with Utmost Devotion and Witnessing an Extraordinary Event     166
7. On a Wise Man Who Abused an Incarnated Sage out of Envy, Visited the Palace of King Yama, and Experienced Suffering in Hell     167
8. On the Immediate Reward of Salvaging the Lives of a Crab and a Frog and Setting Them Free     171
9. On Being Born in the Form of an Ox and Made to Work for Usurping the Properties of the Temple of One's Own Dedication     173
10. On the Death Penalty for Constantly Boiling and Eating Birds' Eggs     174
11. On the Penalty of a Fatal Disease for Abusing a Monk and Committing a Lustful Deed     175
12. On the Immediate Reward of Being Saved by Crabs for Saving the Lives of Crabs and a Frog     176
13. On Lustful Love for the Image of Kichijō-tennyo Which Responded with an Extraordinary Sign     178

14. On the Immediate Reward of the Destitute Princess'
Devotion to the Image of Kichijō-tennyo   179
15. On the Reward of Copying the *Hoke-kyō* and Holding a
Service for a Mother in Revealing the Cause of Her
Rebirth as a Cow   180
16. On the Immediate Retribution of Good and Evil because
of Giving No Alms and Freeing Living Beings   182
17. On Bronze Kannon Images Which Showed an
Extraordinary Sign in Their Transformation into the Form
of a Heron   184
18. On the Immediate Penalty of Being Given a Twisted
Mouth and Death for Speaking Ill of the Monk, Devotee of
the *Hoke-kyō*   185
19. On the Visit to the Palace of King Yama by a Woman
Devotee of the *Shin-gyō*, and the Following
Extraordinary Event   186
20. On the Mother Who Had a Bad Dream, with the Utmost
Faith Had a Scripture Recited, and Saved Her Daughter by
an Extraordinary Sign   187
21. On the Clay Divine Image Which Showed an
Extraordinary Sign by Emanating Light From Its Legs and
Incurred an Immediate Reward   188
22. On the Stolen Bronze Buddha Which Gave an
Extraordinary Sign and Identified a Thief   190
23. On the Bronze Bodhisattva Miroku Which was Stolen by
a Thief and Revealed His Identity by a Miraculous Sign   191
24. On the Fiends, Messengers of King Yama, Who Canceled
Death in Exchange for a Bribe   192
25. On the Fiend, Messenger of King Yama, Who Accepted
the Hospitality of the One for Whom He Had Been Sent
and Repaid It   194
26. On the Miraculous Sign of the Unfinished Log Which Was
Cut Out for Buddha Images but Abandoned   196
27. On a Woman of Great Strength   197
28. On the Destitute Woman Who Prayed to the Sixteen-foot
Śākyamuni Buddha for a Share of Benefits and Immediately
Attained a Great Fortune Brought by a Miraculous Event   199
29. On the Most Venerable Gyōgi, Who Accused a Woman of
Having Smeared Her Hair with Animal Oil Recognized
with His Penetrating Eye   201
30. On the Extraordinary Sign of the Most Venerable Gyōgi
Who Perceived a Woman with a Child Loaded with Past
Enmity and Made Her Throw the Child into the Stream   201
31. On the Birth of a Girl with *Sari* in Her Hand Owing to
Her Parents' Vow to Build a Pagoda   203
32. On Rebirth as an Ox to Make up for the Unpaid Debt of
Rice Wine for the Temple Fund   203
33. On a Woman Devoured by an Evil Fiend   205

34. On an Orphaned Girl Whose Devotion to the Bronze
Kannon Brought Her an Immediate Reward in a
Miraculous Event    206
35. On the Penalty of Immediate Death from a Bad Disease for
Hitting a Monk    208
36. On the Wooden Image of Kannon Revealing Divine Power    210
37. On the Wooden Image of Kannon Which Revealed
Divine Power, and Survived Fire    210
38. On Rebirth as a Snake because of Avarice    211
39. On the Wooden Image of Yakushi Buddha Which Showed
an Extraordinary Sign, Washed away in the Water and
Buried in the Sand    211
40. On the Evil-loving Man Who Was Killed with Swords
and Thus Got an Immediate Death Penalty    212
41. On a Woman Who Survived Violation of a Big Snake
Owing to the Power of Drugs    213
42. On the Destitute Woman Whose Devotion to the Image
of the Thousand-armed Kannon Brought a Great Fortune
in Response to Her Wish for a Share of Benefits    215

# Preface to Volume II[1]

After some loyal subjects burned the temple and threw away Buddha images[2] and some built temples to spread the Buddhist teaching,[3]
ex-Emperor Shōhō-ōjin-shōmu made a huge image of the Buddha
for the first time.[4] He established the eternal Buddhist tradition in
this country, shaved his head, and wore a surplice. He was ordained
and practiced good, ruling the people with justice. His compassion
was extended to animals and plants, while his virtue was incompa-
rable in history. On the throne he attained unity,[5] had excellent fortune, and appeased all spirits, taking his stand on the three components of the universe.[6] Owing to this fortune and virtue, even insects
flying in the sky brought grasses to thatch a temple, while ants running on the ground gathered golden sands to build a pagoda. Buddhist banners[7] were raised high with their fringes flying in all directions. The boat of Buddhism floated lightly on the water, and the
shadow of the sails seemed to send wind into the sky. Flowers of good
omen opened in rivalry here and there, and karmic retribution of
good and evil was revealed in lights and shadows. This is why he was
named ex-Emperor Shōhō-ōjin-shōmu, meaning Excellent-treas-
ure-truth-corresponding-sacred-power.

. . . incurred much suffering.[8] Evil deeds bring us to lands of suffering, one after another, while good deeds lead us to a safe place.
Great compassion can tame and train tigers to sit on our knees;[9] natural affection can make birds live on our head.[10] The same lesson will
be found in the episode of the seven virtues of Meng-ch'ang 孟嘗[11] or
the three wonders of Prince Kung of Lu 魯恭.[12]

1. The first part of this preface is missing in the existing manuscripts. The opening paragraph
in the *Nihon ryōiki* (*NKBT*) is taken from the *Tōdai-ji yōroku* 東大寺要録 (II, 2), which gives a
quotation probably from this preface (see Nagai Yoshinori, *Nihon Bukkyō bungaku kenkyū*, 139–
141).
2. Refers to opponents of Buddhism such as the Monobe family; see I.5.
3. Refers to Buddhists such as the Soga family, Ōtomo no Yasunoko; see I.5.
4. Refers to the Great Buddha of Tōdai-ji; see I.Preface, n. 14. Also see I.5, n. 41.
5. 得一; see I.28, n. 6. Most commentators interpret 一 as the imperial throne.
6. The three are Heaven, man, and earth.
7. 法幢 *hōdō* or *hatahoko*; see I.1, n. 7.
8. The first part of the sentence is lost: . . . 愛萬苦.
9. See *Shokyō yōshū*, X (*Taishō*, LIV, 100 ab):所以曇光釋子 降孟虎於膝前 螺髻仙人 宿禽於頂上.
10. See *ibid*.
11. Minister of Ch'i during the age of the warring states (403–221 B.C.); "seven virtues"
七善, source unknown.
12. See *Hou-Han shu*, XV Biographies. The three wonders 三異 are that even insects do not
transgress the border, that even birds and animals can be taught, and that even children have
the benevolent mind.

Kyōkai, however, is neither wise nor eloquent. His mind is as slow and dull as a lead sword, and his writings do not seem beautiful. He is as foolish as the man who marked on the boat,[13] and, in writing, he cannot get his phrases into order. However, I cannot suppress my passion to do good, so I dare to write down oral traditions [at the risk of] soiling clean paper with mistakes. On reflection, I cannot help feeling ashamed of myself, blushing in the face and ears. Therefore I beseech you, the reader of my poor work, to confess, forget worldly matters, and keep your mind lofty, making a master of your mind and never the mind your master. By the help of my humble work I hope we shall fly beyond the firmament on the right wing of fortune and virtue and the left wing of wisdom, climb to the top of the Buddha-nature, and attain the path of Buddha, giving alms to all beings.[14]

# I

*On the Death Penalty in This Life for Taking Pride in One's Own Virtue and Hitting a Humble-looking Novice*[1]

On the eighth of the second month in the spring of the sixth year of the snake, the first year of the Tenpyō era,[2] ex-Emperor Shōhō-ōjin-shōmu, who reigned over Ōyashima 大八嶋[3] at Nara Palace, made a great vow and held an impressive service to make offerings to the Three Treasures at Gangō-ji 元興寺 on the East Side of the capital.[4] Prince Nagaya 長屋親王, Chancellor of the Senior Second Rank,[5]

13. See *Lü-shih ch'un ch'iu* 呂氏春秋 (Ch'a chin 察今): A man of Ch'u dropped a sword when he was crossing a river. He marked the spot on the edge of the boat where it had fallen overboard for later identification, never thinking that the boat itself was moving.

14. A bodhisattva is often compared to a bird in Mahayana Buddhist scriptures; see *Daichido-ron*, XXXVII (*Taishō*, XXV, 332a). 復次雖有慈悲 般若波羅密 無五神通者 如鳥無兩翼不能高翔; Ibid., XXXVII (*Taishō*, XXV, 566b). 鳥身是菩薩 . . . 無兩翅者是無般若波羅密無方便; *Maka hannya haramitsu-kyō* 摩訶般若波羅密經, XXVI (*Taishō*, XIII, 410c). 譬如鳥無翅不能高翔 菩薩無神通 不能隨意敎化衆生.

1. Cf. *Shoku Nihongi*, X (Tenpyō 1:2:10), *Fusō ryakki* (VI, Shōmu), *Konjaku monogatarishū* (XX, 27).

2. 729.

3. According to the *Kojiki* (*NKBT*, 54–56), Izanagi and Izanami created the eight islands, namely, Awaji Island 淡路島, Iyo Island 伊豫島 (Shikoku 四國), Oki Island 隱岐島, Tsukushi Island 筑紫島 (Kyūshū 九州), Iki Island 壹岐島, Tsushima Island 津島, Sado Island 佐渡島, and Ōyamato-toyoakitsu Island 大倭豐秋津島 (Honshū 本州).

4. See I.3, n. 9.

5. Although the text gives 太政大臣正二位長屋親王, the right title is 正二位左大臣長屋王 (see *Shoku Nihongi*, IX, Jinki 1:2:22), since 親王 is used only for the emperor's sons.

was appointed by edict to be in charge of serving food to the monks.

At the banquet there was a novice unscrupulous enough to go to the serving place and hold up a bowl for food. The prince, when he saw this, struck the novice on the head with an ivory scepter, and blood came from the wound on the head. Wailing bitterly, the novice rubbed his head, wiped away the blood, and disappeared at once. No one knew where he had gone, but both the clergy and laity present at the service whispered in secret, "An ill omen, it is not good."

In two days an envious man went to the throne to slander the prince, saying, "Prince Nagaya is rising in revolt against the state to usurp the throne."[6] The emperor grew angry and sent an army against the prince. Prince Nagaya thought to himself, "I am falsely charged and surely will be killed. It is better to kill myself than to be killed by others." After making his children take poison and strangling them, the prince took the same poison and killed himself.[7] The emperor ordered their corpses thrown out of the castle, burned to ashes, and cast into the waters.[8] Only the prince's bones were exiled to Tosa province 土佐國,[9] where many people died. In fear the people petitioned the officials, saying, "All of us in this province will die because of the prince's spirit!" At this the emperor moved the bones to an island off the coast of Hajikami, Ama district, Kii province 紀伊國海部郡椒抄[10] so that they might lie closer to the capital.

What a pity! However widely known when his fortune was at its height, the prince perished suddenly when an evil fate befell him. Indeed, we learn that, taking pride in his virtue, he struck a novice, and, because of this, divine guardians of dharma frowned on him and good deities hated him.[11] We should respect those who wear a surplice, even if they look humble, for there is a sage hidden among them. Therefore, the *Kyōman-gyō* 憍慢經[12] speaks of ". . . the sin of those

6. Nuribe no miyatsuko Kimitari 漆部造君足 and Nakatomi no miyatokoro muraji Azumabito 中臣宮處連東人, slandered Prince Nagaya, saying he had secretly studied evil arts and wanted to overthrow the government. See *ibid.*, X (Tenpyō 1:2:10).

7. See *ibid.*, X (Tenpyō 1:2:12).

8. The following passage including this sentence differs from the passage in the *Shoku Nihongi*, which says that Prince Nagaya and Princess Kibi were buried at Ikoma-yama, for she was innocent and he was the grandson of Emperor Tenmu. See *ibid.*, X (Tenpyō 1:2:13).

9. Present Kōchi-ken, Shikoku 四國高知縣.

10. 奧嶋 may be the name of an island, Oki no shima, off the coast of present Kaisō-gun, Wakayama-ken 和歌山縣海草郡, or 沖島 *oki no shima* as translated above.

11. 護法善神 *gohō zenjin* means "beneficial deities protecting dharma" but Kyōkai often uses *gohō* without *zenjin*. The *Zenjin* are Brahma, Indra, the Guardians of the Four Quarters, the Twelve Divine Generals, and the Twenty-eight Deities, who vowed to protect dharma after they had heard of it.

12. Unknown source.

who held high social status and of those who stepped on the head of Śākyamuni Buddha . . . ." Needless to say, the sin of those who despise one who wears a surplice is very grave.


# 2

## On Renouncing the World to Practice Good at the Sight of the Adultery of Crows[1]

Dhyāna Master Shingon 信嚴 was Chinu no agatanushi Yamatomaro 血沼縣主倭麻呂,[2] governor of Izumi district, Izumi province 和泉國泉郡,[3] in the reign of Emperor Shōmu. By the gate of his house there stood a big tree in which two crows built a nest, hatched eggs, and sheltered their chicks under their wings. The male crow flew here and there to bring food for his mate who sheltered the chicks. Once when he left the nest for food, another crow flew into the nest and began to flirt. Attracted by the newcomer, the female crow flew high up into the sky toward the north, abandoning her chicks in the nest. When the male crow came back with food in his mouth and could not find his wife, he watched over the chicks affectionately and did not look for food for many days.

The governor noticed this and had someone climb the tree in order to see the nest. The crow and the chicks were dead. Realizing the female crow's adultery, the governor was overcome with pity and his mind was filled with mercy. He renounced the world, leaving his home, family, and rank, and followed the Most Venerable Gyōgi 行基[4] to practice good and seek the path. He was named Shingon.

His wife was also of the Chinu no agatanushi. After her husband left her, she remained faithful to him without bitterness. When her dear son contracted a fatal disease and was dying, he said to her, "It will prolong my life if I drink my mother's milk." The mother gave her breast to her son as he had asked. Sucking the breast, he lamented, saying, "I am abandoning the sweet milk of my mother and dying!" and breathed his last. Sorrowing for her deceased son, she renounced

1. Cf. *Shūchū-shō* (VIII).
2. The Chinu family was of the local gentry, native to Japan, according to the *Shinsen shōji-roku*.
3. Present Sennan- and Senboku-gun, Ōsaka-fu 大阪府泉南, 泉北郡.
4. See Chap. I(1)d, II(2)c, etc.

the world as her husband had done and devoted herself to learning and practicing good dharma.[5]

Dhyāna Master Shingon, however, had little luck and, after short association with the Most Venerable Gyōgi, preceded Gyōgi to the grave. Wailing, the master composed the following poem:

Did you not promise me we would die together?
But, alas! You are gone,
Leaving me behind.
Are you a crow, to be such a great liar?

When man makes a fire, he must gather firewood of pine. When it rains, the slate has been moistened beforehand.[6] The governor renounced the world after seeing the crow's wicked deed. It is the Buddha's work to lead man to enlightenment by showing him the reality of suffering, which is the reality of living beings in the world of desire.[7] Those who do not like this reality renounce such a world, while those who are foolish indulge in it. The note says how praiseworthy it was for Mr. Chinu no agatanushi, who saw the wickedness of a crow, to avoid worldly filth and the transience of fleeting flowers; to purify himself, devote himself to practicing good, and pray for wisdom; and to look forward to birth in the pure land, liberated from this world. He excelled particularly in his wish for liberation from this world.

# 3

## On the Death Penalty in This Life of an Evil Son
## Who Tried to Kill His Mother out of Love
## for His Wife[1]

Kishi no Ōmaro 吉志大麻呂[2] came from the village of Kamo, Tama district, Musashi province 武藏國多麻郡鴨里.[3] Ōmaro's mother was

5. For the significance of this episode, see Chap. II(2)b.
6. In some localities in Japan there is a proverb: When the surface of the rock gets moist with dew, it will rain without fail. This may well refer to the rain-making ceremony in which water is poured on the sacred stone to induce a rainfall.
7. 欲界 yakukai (Skt. kāmadhātu); the sphere of desire, one of the three spheres of the world, which includes the six lowest heavens and five other ways of existence, that is, man, asura, animal, hungry fiend, and hell.

1. Cf. Konjaku monogatarishū (XX, 33), Zōhōzō-kyō, IX (Taishō, IV, 492), Hōon jurin, XXII (Taishō, LIII, 448).
2. Or Kishi no Homaro 吉志火麿; life unknown, but the Shōsōin monjo 正倉院文書 gives his name.
3. The village is unidentified. Tama is in Greater Tokyo.

Kusakabe no Matoji 日下部眞�.[4] In the reign of Emperor Shōmu he was appointed a frontier soldier[5] at Tsukushi 筑紫 by Ōtomo 大伴[6] (his name is unknown)[7] and had to spend three years there. His mother accompanied him and lived with him, while his wife stayed behind to take care of the house.

Ōmaro, out of love for his wife who had been left behind, thought up the wicked idea of killing his mother and returning home to his wife, claiming exemption from duty on the pretext of mourning.[8] As his mother's mind was set on doing good, he said to her, "There will be a great meeting for a week's lecture on the *Hoke-kyō* 法華經 in the eastern mountain. Shall we go to hear the teaching?"

His mother, deceived, was eager to go, and, devoutly purifying herself in a hot bath, accompanied her son to the mountain. Then he looked at her fiercely, as though with the eyes of a bull, and said, "You, kneel down on the ground!" Gazing at his face, she said, "Why are you talking like that? Are you possessed by a fiend?" The son, however, drew a sword to kill her. Kneeling down in front of her son, she said to him, "We plant a tree in order to get its fruit and to take shelter in its shade.[9] We bring up children in order to get their help and to depend on them. What on earth has driven you so crazy! I feel as though the tree I have been depending on has suddenly ceased to protect me from the rain." He would not listen to her, so she sorrowfully took off her clothes, put them in three piles, knelt down, and told him her last wish: "Will you wrap up these clothes for me? One pile goes to you, my eldest son, one to my second son, and one to my third son."

When the wicked son stepped forward to cut off his mother's head, the earth opened to swallow him. At that moment his mother grabbed her falling son by the hair and appealed to Heaven, wailing, "My child is possessed by some spirit and driven to such an evil deed. He is out of his mind. I beseech you to forgive his sin." In spite of all her

4. Kusakabe is a family name (see I.18, n. 7), and Matoji is a given name which originated in the common noun, meaning "legal wife."

5. 前守 (崎守, 防人) *sakimori*; soldiers sent to Tsukushi (present-day Kyūshū) to defend the country from a possible invasion by foreign troops from Korea or China. They had three years' duty there and were not allowed to bring any family member. See *Ryō no gige*, "Gunbō-ryō," Articles 8, 27.

6. The Ōtomos were traditionally in charge of military matters and served the emperors as imperial guards. Cf. *Nihon shoki*, *Kojiki*, etc.

7. The compiler's note.

8. The mourning period for parents was one year, during which people were exempted from any labor duties. (See *Ryō no gige*, "Fueki-ryō," Article 21). However, "Gunbō-ryō," Article 28, prescribes that the mourning period should be observed after soldiers have fulfilled their tour of duty.

9. *Daihatsu nehan-gyō*, XXI (*Taishō*, XII, 493). 如人種樹 爲得蔭涼 爲得花果 及以材木.

efforts to pull him up by the hair, he fell down. The merciful mother brought his hair back home to hold funeral rites and put it in a box in front of a Buddha image, asking monks to chant scriptures.[10]

How great was the mother's compassion! So much that she loved an evil son and practiced good on his behalf. Indeed, we know that an unfilial sin is punished immediately and that an evil deed never goes without a penalty.

# 4

## On a Contest Between Women of Extraordinary Strength[1]

In the reign of Emperor Shōmu there was a woman of extraordinary strength in Ogawa Market, Katakata district, Mino province 三野國片縣郡小川市.[2] She was large, and her name was Mino no kitsune 三野狐[3] (the fourth generation of the one whose mother was Mino no kitsune). Her strength equaled that of one hundred men. Living within the marketplace of Ogawa and taking pride in her strength, she used to rob passing merchants of their goods by force.

At that time there was another woman of great strength in the village of Katawa, Aichi district, Owari province 尾張國愛智郡片輪里.[4] She was small (a granddaughter of the Venerable Dōjō who once lived at Gangō-ji).[5] As she heard that Mino no kitsune robbed passersby of their goods, she sought to challenge her by loading two hundred and fifty bushels[6] of clams on a boat, and anchoring next to the market. In addition, she prepared and loaded on a boat twenty pliable vine whips.

Kitsune came to the boat, seized all the clams, and had them sold. "Where did you come from?" she asked the owner of the clams, but she got no reply. She repeated the question, but again got no answer. After Kitsune had repeated the same question four times, the owner answered, "I don't know where I came from." Kitsune, insulted, rose

10. See Chap. II(2)b, for the significance of this story.

1. Cf. *Konjaku monogatarishū* (XXIII, 17). This is a part of the Venerable Dōjō cycle (see I.2, 3; II.27). See above, Chap. II(2)b, for the significance of women who inherited extraordinary strength.
2. According to Takeda, it is the market located at present Gifu-shi 岐阜市.
3. See I.2.
4. See I.2, n. 9.
5. See I.3, n. 3.
6. In Japanese measurement, fifty *koku* 斛(石). One *koku* is ten *to* 斗, and one hundred *shō* 升.

to hit her. Thereupon the other woman seized Kitsune's two hands and whipped her once. The whip cut the flesh. Then she used another whip which also cut the flesh. Presently ten whips had cut the flesh.

Kitsune said, "I give up! I am sorry for what I have done." The other woman, whose strength was obviously greater than Kitsune's, insisted, "From now on you shall not live in this market. If you dare do so, I will beat you to death." Completely subdued, Kitsune did not live in the market or steal again, and people in the market rejoiced over the restoration of peace.

There has always been someone in the world with great physical power. Indeed, we know such power is attained as a result of causes in past lives.[7]

# 5

### On Gaining an Immediate Penalty for Sacrificing Oxen to a Pagan Deity and the Merit of Good Deeds of Freeing Living Beings[1]

In the village of Nadekubo, Higashinari district, Settsu province 攝津國東生郡撫凹村,[2] there was a wealthy householder, whose name is unknown. In the reign of ex-Emperor Shōmu, the householder, fearful of the evil influence of a Chinese deity,[3] held services for seven years, sacrificing an ox each year until he had killed seven.[4] At the end of seven years he contracted a serious disease, and, during the following seven years, neither doctor nor medicine could cure him. He called diviners[5] to purify and pray for him, but his disease became worse. Then it occurred to him that his serious disease must have been caused by his past deeds of killing; after that he never failed in keeping the precepts and freeing living beings on the six holy days of each month.[6] When he saw someone killing living beings, he would buy

7. The compiler's attempt to make native legends put on Buddhist clothing is obvious in the victory of the Venerable Dōjō's descendants over the descendants of the fox, and in the ascribing of strength to the ancestor's merit.

1. Cf. *Konjaku monogatarishū* (XX, 15).
2. Present Higashinari-ku, Ōsaka-shi 大阪市東成區.
3. 漢神.
4. Animal sacrifice was foreign to Japan. See *Shoku Nihongi*, XL (Enryaku 10:9:5).
5. 卜者 *kamnagi*; see Chap. II(3)a, n. 124.
6. 六節 *rokusetsu* probably means 六齋日 *rokukusainichi*, six holy days: 8, 14, 15, 23, 29, and 30 of each month, when lay Buddhists keep the first eight of the ten precepts and devote themselves to doing good.

them without asking their price, and he would send for living beings to buy and set them free.

When he was dying at the end of the seven years, he said to his family, "Don't cremate my corpse after I die, but keep it for nine days."[7] After his death they did as he had told them, waiting for the promised day. When nine days had passed, he came back to life and told this story:

"There were seven subhumans,[8] each with the head of an ox and a human body. They bound me by the hair and led me along under guard. In front of us there appeared a towering palace. I asked, 'What palace is this?' but they only gave me a terrifying look and said, 'Go on quickly!'

"When we entered the palace gate, they said, 'We have brought him.' I realized that they were addressing King Yama.[9] He asked them, 'Is this man the enemy who killed you?' In reply, they said, 'Yes, he is the one.' Presently they brought a chopping board and knife and said, 'Hurry and pass sentence on him! We are going to chop him up and eat him the way he did us!'

"At that moment ten million men suddenly appeared to unbind me, saying, 'This man is not accountable for that accusation, for he killed them to make offerings to the evil deity which had haunted him.' Thereupon the seven subhumans and ten million men fought over me every day like water and fire. The king refrained from judging me. The subhumans continued to argue, saying, 'It is evident that this person was the host who cut off our limbs, held the service at the shrine[10] for his own benefit, and chopped us up to eat.' The ten million men, on the other hand, appealed to the king, saying, 'We know very well that the deity is to blame, and not this man. Remember, Your Majesty, that truth has more witnesses.'[11]

"Eight days passed in this way, and on the evening of the eighth day I was told to appear at court the following day. On the ninth day I went to the court as I had been told. Presently the king said to me, 'As most of our judgments are formed by what witnesses say, we side

7. Common people were buried within a day after their death. See Chap. II(3)a. Cf. *Nihon shoki* (Taika 2:3:22); Aston, "Nihongi," II, 219.

8. 非人 *hinin*.

9. 閻羅王 Enraō; see Chap. II(1)c.

10. 廟 *byō* (Ch. *miao*), Chinese temple or shrine.

11. The other possible interpretation is: "We know very well that the deity is to blame, and not this man." The king thought that the truth was on the side of the majority of witnesses. 我等委曲知非此人咎 識鬼神咎 王自思惟 理就多證.

with the majority,' The sentence was thus given. When the seven oxen heard this, they licked their lips and swallowed, pretending to chop up and eat my flesh. Indignantly, they raised their swords, saying severally, 'How can we forget our vengeance? We will have revenge some day.' The ten million men surrounded me and left the palace, carrying me on a palanquin and leading the way with upheld banners; they saw me off with praise, and knelt to salute me. All of them looked alike. I asked them, saying, 'Who are you?' They answered, 'We are the creatures you set free. Because we can never forget your kindness, we have merely come to repay you.'"

After his return from the palace of King Yama, he made more and more vows. After that he never worshiped any deities, but had faith in the Three Treasures, turned his house into a temple by raising a banner[12] and enshrining a Buddha-image, and practiced the teaching and freeing of living beings. The temple was called the Nade-dō 那天堂.[13] Being spared from illness, the man finally died past the age of ninety.

One *Vinaya-kyō*[14] says as follows: "As Kāludāyi[15] was once a priest and sacrificed a sheep, he was killed, revenged by a Brahman wife, even after he had attained arhatship . . . ."[16] The *Saishōō-kyō*[17] gives the following passage to the same effect: "Rusui-chōza 流水長者 set free ten thousand fish, which were reborn in heaven and repaid his kindness by presenting him with forty thousand jewels."

# 6

*On Copying the* Hoke-kyō *with Utmost Devotion and Witnessing an Extraordinary Event*[1]

In the reign of Emperor Shōmu, there was a man who made a vow in Sagaraka district, Yamashiro province 山背國相樂郡.[2] His name is

---

12. 幢 *hatahoko*, a symbol of dharma, hence, a temple; see I.1, n. 7; Preface, n. 7, above.

13. It was named after the village Nade-kubo. Private temples were often named after the village; see Chap. I(1)d.

14. *Vinaya-kyō* 毘奈耶經, IX (*Taishō*, XXIV, 893); quoted in the *Shokyō yōshū*, XIV (*Taishō*, LIV, 129).

15. A disciple of Śākyamuni; a Brahman who performed a sacrificial rite.

16. 羅漢 *rakan*, a shortened form of 阿羅漢, transliterated from Skt. *arhat*, which means "one who is free from craving and rebirth."

17. *Konkōmyō saishōō-kyō*, XVI (*Taishō*, XVI, 352b–353c).

1. Cf. *Sanbō ekotoba* (II, 10), *Hokke kenki* (III, 105), *Konjaku monogatarishū* (XII, 26).

2. Present Sōraku-gun, Kyoto-fu 京都府相樂郡.

unknown. He copied the *Hoke-kyō* in order to repay the four kinds of blessing[3] and sent his messengers to the four quarters in search of sandalwood[4] to make a container for the scrolls of the scripture.[5] Eventually he bought it in the capital of Nara for one hundred *kan*[6] and asked a craftsman to measure and make a container. When he tried to put the scrolls in it, he found he could not do so because the chest was too short. He was terribly disappointed, for he did not see how he could acquire such materials again. Therefore he made a vow, held a service as directed in the scripture, invited monks to confess offenses for three weeks, and wailing, he pleaded, "Please let me find such wood again."

After two weeks he tried to put the scrolls in the chest and found that it had stretched a little of its own accord though it was still a little shorter than the scrolls. The man tried harder to discipline himself[7] and to repent, and, at the end of the third week, he could put the scrolls in the chest. Wondering whether the scrolls had become shorter or the chest larger, he compared them with the original and found they were the same length. Indeed, we know that this was a test of the vower's supreme faith and a sign of the miraculous power of the Mahayana scripture. There can be no doubt about it.

# 7

## On a Wise Man Who Abused an Incarnated Sage out of Envy, Visited the Palace of King Yama, and Experienced Suffering in Hell[1]

Saka Chikō[2] was a monk of Sukita-dera 鋤田寺[3] in Asukabe dis-

3. 四恩; see Chap. II(2)a, nn. 69, 70.
4. 白檀紫檀, literally, white sandalwood and purple sandalwood which is solid, lustrous, and fragrant. Brought to Japan by Buddhist monks, it was highly valued and used to make chests for scriptures, Buddhist images, altars, etc. It was rare and very expensive since it had to be imported.
5. 大乗 *daijō*; a Mahayana scripture, in this case the *Hoke-kyō*.
6. 貫; monetary unit consisting of 1,000 *mon* 文, coins.
7. 精進 *shōjin*, a translation of Skt. *virya;* the mind and deed to make the utmost effort to attain the path. In the popular understanding it means purifying oneself and abstaining from eating meat and drinking rice wine.

1. Cf. *Sanbō ekotoba* (II, 3), *Hokke kenki* (I, 2), *Fusō ryakki* (II, Shōmu), *Konjaku monogatarishū* (XI, 2), *Nihon ōjō gokurakuki*, etc. See Chap. II(2)c.
2. For Saka (or Shaku) 釋, see I.14, n. 2. Chikō (b. 709), an eminent monk of Gangō-ji and the Sanron School 三論宗 in Chi-tsang's tradition (see Chap. I(1)c, n. 66), is also known for his faith in the pure land. See Inoue Mitsusada, *Nihon Jōdokyō seiritsushi no kenkyū*, 48–58.
3. Unidentified.

trict, Kawachi province 河內國安宿郡,[4] his native land. His secular
name was Sukita no muraji,[5] later changed to Kami no suguri 上村主.[6]
(His mother was of the Asukabe-no-miyatsuko 飛鳥部造[7] family.) He
was innately intelligent, and no one excelled him in knowledge. He
wrote commentaries on the *Urabon-kyō* 盂蘭盆經,[8] *Dai hannya-kyō*
大般若經,[9] *Shin hannya-gyō* 心般若經,[10] and other works and lectured
on Buddhist teachings[11] to many students.

There was a monk whose name was Gyōgi.[12] His secular name had
been Koshi no fuhito 越史,[13] and he came from Kubiki district, Echigo
province 越後國頸城郡.[14] His mother was of the Hachita no kusushi
蜂田藥師[15] in Ōtori district, Izumi province 和泉國大鳥郡.[16] He renounced lay life, attained freedom from desire, and spread dharma to
guide the deluded masses. He was innately intelligent, endowed with
inborn wisdom. On the outside he had the form of a monk,[17] but
within were hidden the deeds of a bodhisattva. Emperor Shōmu was
so impressed with his virtue that he had great respect for and belief
in Gyōgi. In reverence and praise his contemporaries called him
Bodhisattva. In the eleventh month, in the winter of the first year of
the monkey, the sixteenth year of the Tenpyō era, Gyōgi was appointed great chief executive.[18] At this, Dharma Master Chikō became envious and abused him, saying, "I am a wise man, and Gyōgi
is a mere novice. Why does the emperor admire and use him without
any regard for my wisdom?" Being dissatisfied with this situation,

4. Present Minami-kawachi-gun, Ōsaka-fu 大阪府南河內郡.
5. 鋤田連; see *Nihon shoki*, XXIX (Tenmu 10:4:12). Aston, "Nihongi," II, 351. The title
of *muraji* was conferred on Sukita no Kurahito 次田倉人 in 681.
6. According to the *Shinsen shōjiroku*, the Kami-no-suguri family immigrated from Korea.
*Suguri* 村主 is a title given to an immigrant family.
7. The *Shinsen shōjiroku* says that the family was descended from a king of Paekche.
8. *Urabon-kyō sho* (or *jitsugi*) 盂蘭盆經疏 (述義), no longer extant.
9. *Dai hannya-kyō sho* 大般若經疏 (recorded in the *Tōiki dentō mokuroku* 東域傳燈目錄, but
extinct).
10. *Hannya shin-gyō jitsugi* 般若心經述義 (*Taishō*, LVII, No. 2202).
11. 佛教 *Bukkyō*.
12. Or Gyōki (668–749); see Chap. I(1)d, nn. 100, 101, 102, 103.
13. 高志; see *Shoku Nihongi* (Wadō 1:3:13; Yōrō 7:1:10; Tenpyō jingo 2:12:4, 4:30). This
is a branch of the Fumi family 書(文)氏 who descended from Wani 王仁 (see I.Preface, n. 4).
越 is never found in other documents about Gyōgi.
14. Present Nishi-kubiki-gun, Nīgata-ken 新潟縣西頸城郡. The *Shoku Nihongi* gives Kawachi as his native place. According to Inoue Kaoru, Kyōkai made a mistake by writing his family
name 越 instead of 高志, inferring that Gyōgi had come from Echigo 越後. (See his *Gyōki*, 12).
15. According to the *Shinsen shōjiroku*, his mother's family descended from immigrants from
Paekche who may have specialized in medicine.
16. Present Senboku-gun, Ōsaka-fu 大阪府泉北郡 and Sakai-shi 堺市.
17. 聲聞 *shōmon*, a translation of Skt. *śrāvaka*, which means "one who is enlightened by hearing Buddha's teachings." See I. Preface, n. 16. This sentence is adapted from the *Myōhōrenge-kyō*
(*Taishō*, IX, 28a): 內秘菩薩行 外現是聲聞. See Katō, *Myōhō-renge-kyō*, 205.
18. 大僧正 *daisōjō*, the highest clerical rank (see Chap. I(1)d). This date is incorrect, for Gyōgi
was made great chief executive in 745, not 744. See *Shoku Nihongi*, XVI (Tenpyō 17:1:21).

he retired to Sukita-dera. Before long, he developed a stomach disease. After a month, when he was dying, he said to his disciples, "When I pass away, do not cremate my corpse, but let it remain for nine days.[19] If a student comes to see me, tell him I have some errands to do here and there, and offer him meals. Do not let others know of my death." Faithful to their master's words, the disciples closed the door of their master's room so as not to let others discover what had happened and, grieving secretly, they stood guard at the door day and night, waiting only for the promised day. If a student came to see the master, they answered as they had been told, asked him to stay, and provided him with food and shelter.

As for the Venerable Chikō, two messengers came from King Yama to take him to his land. They headed west, and Chikō saw a golden pavilion in front of them. He asked them, "What palace is that?" In reply, they said, "You are a famous wise man in the land of Ashihara 葦原國,[20] how is it you do not know? You should know that that is the palace where Bodhisattva Gyōgi will be born."

On both sides of the gate there were two divine men[21] in armor with red headbands.[22] The messengers knelt and said to them, "Here he is." They asked, "Are you the Venerable Chikō in the land of Toyoashihara no mizuho 豐葦原瑞穗國?"[23] Chikō replied, "Yes, I am." Then they pointed north, saying, "Go along this way." So he went, accompanied by the messengers, and his body and face were scorched with a terrible heat though he saw neither fire nor sun. In spite of his suffering from the heat, he had a desire to move forward. When he asked, "Why is it so hot?" they answered, "The heat of hell is broiling you."

In front of them stood an extremely hot iron pillar. The messengers told him to embrace it. When Chikō did so, all his flesh broke out in sores until only his bones were left. After three days the messengers brushed the pillar with a worn broom, saying, "Let him live, let him live," and he regained the same body as before.

Again they started northward, and there was a copper pillar hotter than the former one. Although he knew it was extremely hot, again led by evil, he wanted to embrace it, and he was told to do so. When he did, his body broke out in sores. After three days, when the mes-

19. The text has 九日一日, but 一日 makes no sense in this context.
20. Or Toyoashihara no mizuho no kuni, a complimentary name for Japan, which means the "Land of the Plentiful Reed Plain and of the Fresh Rice-ears." Cf. Philippi, *Kojiki*, 137–138.
21. 神人 *shinjin*, those who look like kami, or who serve kami.
22. See I.1, n. 6.
23. *Ibid.*, n. 20.

sengers said, "Let him live, let him live," and brushed the pillar as before; he regained his former body.

Then they went further to the north. There was such a hazy scorching heat that birds fell from the air. He asked "Where am I?" and the answer was, "This is the Hell of Abi 阿鼻地獄[24] where you will be broiled." On arrival he was caught and broiled. Only when he heard temple bells ringing did the heat cool and allow him a rest. After three days, when the messengers knocked at the gate of hell saying, "Let him live, let him live," he became alive again.

They led him to the gate of the golden pavilion, and said as before, "Here he is." The two men at the gate said to him, "The reason you were called here is that you abused Bodhisattva Gyōgi in the land of Ashihara. You were called here to atone for your sin. The Bodhisattva will be born in this palace after he finishes his life in that land. We are waiting for him, for his arrival is close at hand. Be sure not to eat anything at this place. Go back as quickly as possible." He returned eastward with the messengers and realized that nine days had passed since his death.

When he awoke, he called his disciples. Hearing their master calling, they came to see him, delighted to the point of tears. Chikō, however, was greatly grieved and told his disciples about hell. In great awe he looked for a chance to confess that he had been envious of the Most Venerable Gyōgi.

In the meantime Bodhisattva Gyōgi had bridges made, canals dug, and wharfs built in Naniwa. Hardly had Chikō recovered from exhaustion when he went to see Bodhisattva Gyōgi. At first sight the latter perceived by divine omniscience what the former had in his mind, and out of mercy Gyōgi said to him, "I wonder why we could not see each other before." Chikō confessed his sin, saying, "I was once so envious of you that I remarked, 'I am not only a great monk of a long virtuous life, but I am also endowed with natural wisdom while Gyōgi is a man of superficial knowledge and not ordained. Why does the emperor admire Gyōgi and ignore me?' Because of this sin of my mouth I was called to King Yama to embrace the iron and copper pillars. For nine days I stayed in his land to atone for my sin of abuse. I am confessing this to you, for I am afraid other sins will affect

24. Or 無間地獄. In the Buddhist cosmology hell is divided into eight divisions, that is, Hell of Repetition 等活地獄, Hell of the Black Rope 黑繩地獄, Hell of Assembly (All Living Beings) 衆合地獄, Hell of Lamentations 叫喚地獄, Hell of Great Lamentations 大叫喚地獄, Hell of Scorching Heat 焦熱地獄, Hell of Great Scorching Heat 大焦熱地獄, and Hell of No-interval 無間地獄. For a detailed description of this hell, see A. K. Reischauer, "Genshin's Ojo Yoshu," 40–46.

my future life. I beseech you to help me become free from sins." The Most Venerable Gyōgi, looking compassionate, kept silent. Then Chikō said to him, "I saw a palace built of gold where you will be born." On hearing this, Gyōgi said, "What a delight! What an honor!"

Indeed we learn that the mouth is a gate to invite calamities which hurt us, and the tongue is a sharp axe to chop up the good. Thus the *Fushigikō bosatsu-kyō* 不思議光菩薩經[25] has a passage which refers to this: "Bodhisattva Nyūzai 饒財菩薩 is destined for ninety-one *kalpa*[26] to fall into the wombs of lewd women, to be deserted after birth, and to be eaten by foxes and wolves because he talked about the faults of Bodhisattva Kenten 賢天菩薩."

After that time the Venerable Chikō had faith in Bodhisattva Gyōgi, knowing that the latter was really a sage.[27] On the second day of the second month in the spring of the sixth year of the ox, the twenty-first year of the Tenpyō era, Bodhisattva Gyōgi realized that his life here was completed and left his clerical form on Mt. Ikoma 生馬山,[28] while his compassionate spirit moved on to the golden palace. The Most Venerable Chikō, on the other hand, proclaimed Buddhist teachings and guided the people from illusion to righteousness. In the reign of Emperor Shirakabe 白壁天皇,[29] this storehouse of wisdom left the land of Japan, and nobody knows where his extraordinary spirit has gone.

# 8

*On the Immediate Reward of Salvaging the Lives of a
Crab and a Frog and Setting Them Free*[1]

Okisome no omi Taime 置染臣鯛女 was the daughter of a nun named Hōni 法邇,[2] the presiding officer[3] of the nunnery of Tomi 富尼寺[4] in the capital of Nara. She was so devoted in her pursuit of the path

25. Quoted in the *Bonmō-kyō koshakki* (*Taishō*, XL, 706b).
26. 劫 *kō*, a Hindu Buddhist cosmological unit of time.
27. 聖人 *shōnin*; see Chap II(2)c.
28. Gyōgi was cremated on the eastern side of Mt. Ikoma on the border of Yamato and Kawachi, according to his wishes.
29. Emperor Kōnin 光仁 (709–781).

1. One of the "grateful animal" tales, similar to II.12. Cf. *Sanbō ekotoba* (II, 13).
2. Unknown.
3. 上座 : see Chap. I(1)d, n. 84.
4. Or 隆福尼院; it was located at present Nara-shi 奈良市. Although Ekisai identifies it with Ryūfuku-ji 隆福寺, Fukuyama maintains that they are different temples founded by Gyōgi, See Fukuyama, *Narachō jiin*, 266–267.

of Buddha that she preserved her chastity. She used to collect herbs every day and serve them to the Most Venerable Gyōgi.

One day she went to the mountain to collect herbs and saw a large snake swallowing a big frog. She entreated the snake, "Please set the frog free for my sake." But the snake would not. She entreated again, saying, "I will become your wife if you do me the favor of letting the frog go." On hearing that, the large snake raised its head high to see her face and disgorged the frog. Whereupon she said to the snake, "Come to me in seven days."

On the appointed day, she hid herself in the house with all the openings closed. The snake came as expected and knocked on the wall with its tail. The next morning, terrified, she went to her master, who lived at the mountain temple of Ikoma.[5] He said to her, "You cannot break your promise. Only be strict in observing the precepts." Therefore, she reaffirmed her faith in the Three Treasures and her acceptance of the five precepts,[6] and returned home.

On the way she met a strange old man with a big crab. She said, "Who are you, old man? Will you please set the crab free for me?" He answered, "I am Edoi no Nimaro 畫問邇麻呂 from Uhara district, Settsu province 攝津國兎原郡.[7] At the age of seventy-eight I had neither sons to depend upon nor the means of making a living. In Naniwa I happened to find this crab. I cannot give it to you, for I have promised it to someone." She took off her robe, begging him to sell her the crab in exchange for her robe, but he would not listen. She then took off her skirt to add to its price, and he finally agreed to her offer. Thereupon, she brought the crab back home[8] and invited the Most Venerable Gyōgi to hold a service for it, setting it free with a prayer.[9] Impressed with her deed, the master exclaimed, "How noble! How good!"

That evening the snake came back again, climbed to the roof, and dropped into the house by pulling off part of the thatched roof. The terrified girl heard something jumping and flapping around in her

---

5. Ikoma-yamadera 生馬山寺 or Chikurin-ji 竹林寺, at present Arisato in Ikoma-chō, Ikoma-gun, Nara-ken 奈良縣生駒郡生駒町有里, the site of Gyōgi's tomb.

6. When a man becomes a Buddhist, he professes his faith in the Three Treasures and observes the five precepts, namely, no killing, no stealing, no adultery, no lying, and no drinking. See Chap. I(1)d, n. 88.

7. Present Muko-gun, Hyōgo-ken 兵庫縣武庫郡.

8. The *Sanbō ekotoba* gives a different reading: ". . . she went back to the temple with the crab . . . ," which makes more sense than going back home and inviting Gyōgi to her home.

9. When a devotee buys and frees captive fish or birds, he usually invites a Buddhist monk to perform proper rites (放生會 *hōjō-e*). This practice was regarded as a deed of great merit and observed in Buddhist temples and Shinto shrines in Japan. See I.7, n. 12. For 咒願 prayer, see III.38, n. 35.

bed, and the next morning she found a big crab and a large snake that had been chopped into pieces. Then she realized that the crab she had liberated had come to her rescue out of gratitude. This was also due to the virtue gained by keeping the precepts. Although she wanted to unravel the mystery and tried to identify the old man, she could not find him. It was evident he was an incarnation of Buddha. This is a miraculous event.

# 9

## On Being Born in the Form of an Ox and Made to Work for Usurping the Properties of the Temple of One's Own Dedication[1]

Ōtomo no Akamaro 大伴赤麻呂[2] was the governor of Tama district, Musashi province 武藏國多磨郡.[3] He died on the nineteenth of the tenth month, in the first year of the Tenpyō shōhō era,[4] and was reborn as a black-spotted calf on the seventh of the fifth month in the second year of the same era, with an inscription on its skin.[5] It could be made out as follows:

"Akamaro dedicated the temple he had built, took liberties with the properties of the temple, and died without paying for them. He was born as an ox to atone for this."

Both his family and friends were led to reflect on themselves and were extremely horrified. They realized how terrible it was to commit such a sin which was bound to be accompanied by retribution. On the first of the sixth month in the same year, this fact was made public for they thought that such an event should be recorded as an example for posterity.[6]

I hope that even those who have nothing of which to repent will read this story, set right their minds, and practice good. Even if you suffer from hunger and drink hot molten copper, never touch the properties of a temple. There is an old saying, "Honeydew in the

1. Cf. *Konjaku monogatarishū* (XX, 21).
2. Unknown, but there were a number of Ōtomo families in Musashi.
3. See II.3, n. 3.
4. 749.
5. Probably black spots that looked like an inscription.
6. According to Torao Toshiya, the date falls on the day when Akamaro's family and friends offered the account of this event to the temple. See *Nihon ryōiki* (NBKT, 70), 205.

present is an iron ball in the future."[7] Indeed, we learn that the law of karmic causation never fails. We should be ever mindful of that and behave ourselves. Thus the *Daijik-kyō*[8] says: "Those who steal from the samgha commit a sin graver than the five sins . . . ."[9]

# IO

## On the Death Penalty for Constantly Boiling and Eating Birds' Eggs[1]

In the village of Shimoanashi, Izumi district, Izumi province 和泉國 和泉郡下痛脚村,[2] there was a youth[3] whose name is unknown. Innately evil, he did not believe in the law of karmic causation and used to hunt birds' eggs to boil and eat.

In the third month in the spring of the first year of the horse, the sixth year of the Tenpyō shōhō era, a strange soldier came to him and said, "I was sent to get you by a provincial official."[4] He had a plate four feet long[5] fastened to his waist. So they went off together, and, when they came to the village of Yamatae in Hitada district 纐郡 山直里,[6] they made their way into a field covered with several acres of wheat two feet tall. The youth saw the field all aflame and it was too full of embers for him to put his feet down. Running about in the field, he wailed, "It's hot, it's hot."

It happened that a villager was collecting firewood on the hill. As he saw the boy running and falling down and heard his wailing, he came down from the hill and tried to stop him, but the boy resisted. Nonetheless, the villager tried hard to catch the boy until he was able to pull him out of the enclosure. The boy fell to the ground without a word.

---

7. See I.30, n. 22.
8. *Daihōdō daijik-kyō* (*Taishō*, XIII, No. 397).
9. This quotation is the preceding line of the quotation in I.20, n. 12.

1. Cf. *Myōhōki* (III, On Emperor Wu of the Chou dynasty 周武帝, and on a boy), *Konjaku monogatarishū* (IX, 24; XX, 30). This story is based on the folk etymology of the local name Anashi 痛脚, which literally means "sore legs," dressed in the Buddhist clothing of karmic retribution.
2. Present Izumi-ōtsu-shi, Ōsaka-fu 大阪府和泉大津市.
3. 中男 *chūnan*, a boy between the ages of seventeen and twenty (*Yōrō-ryō*, "Ko-ryō," Article 6); after 757, between ages eighteen and twenty-one (*Shoku Nihongi*, Tenpyō hōji 1:4:4).
4. 國司 *kuni no tsukasa*.
5. 札 *funda*, a writ of summons on a wooden plate.
6. In present Kishiwada-shi, Ōsaka-fu 大阪府岸和田市.

After a while he woke up and groaned in pain, saying, "Oh, my sore feet!" The villager asked him, "Why did you behave like that?" He replied, "A soldier came to take me and forced me to step on embers so hot that I felt as if my feet had been boiled. Looking around, I found myself surrounded by mountains of fire without any way out and so I was crying and running about." Hearing this, the villager rolled up the boy's pants and looked at his legs. The flesh was all gone and nothing was left but the bones. He died the next day.

Now we are sure of the existence of hell in this world. We should believe in the law of karmic retribution. We should not behave like a crow which loves its own chicks and eats others. Without compassion man is just like a crow. The *Nehan-gyō* 涅槃經[7] says: "Though there is a distinction in respectability between man and animal, they share the fact that they cherish life and take death gravely . . . ." The *Zen'aku inga-kyō* 善惡因果經[8] contains a passage which gets right to the point: "The one who roasts and boils chickens in this life will fall into the Hell of the River of Ashes[9] after death."

# I I

## *On the Penalty of a Fatal Disease for Abusing a Monk and Committing a Lustful Deed*[1]

In the reign of Emperor Shōmu, nuns of Saya-dera 狹屋寺[2] in Kuwahara, Ito district, Kii province 紀伊國伊刀郡桑原, vowed to hold a service and invited a monk of Yakushi-ji[3] on the West Side of Nara, Dharma Master Daie 題惠 (popularly called Dharma Master Yosami 依網, for his secular name was Yosami no muraji),[4] to perform the rite of repentance[5] devoted to the Eleven-headed Kannon 十一面觀音.[6]

It happened that a wicked man lived in that village. His surname

7. *Daihatsu nehan-gyō*, XX (*Taishō*, XII, 484b); see Chap. II(2)a, n. 65.
8. *Zen'aku inga-kyō* (*Taishō*, LXXXV, 1381). See Chap. II(1)c, n. 61.
9. 灰河地獄Kega-jigoku, one of the sixteen subhells that belong to the eight Hells of Heat (see II.7, n. 24), in which scorching ashes flow.

1. Cf. *Konjaku monogatarishū* (XVI, 38).
2. A nunnery which once existed at present Saya, Katsuragi-chō, Ito-gun, Wakayama-ken 和歌山縣伊都郡葛城町佐野.
3. See Editor's Preface, n. 4; also Chap. I(1)c.
4. The parenthesis is inserted by Kyōkai. Although nothing is known of Daie, the *Shinsen shōjiroku* cites Yosami as a family descended from kami in the capital or an immigrant family in Kawachi.
5. See Chap. II(1)a, nn. 5, 6.
6. See Chap. II(3)b.

was Fumi no imiki 文忌寸[7] (his popular name was Ueda no Saburō 上田三郎).[8] He was evil by nature and had no faith in the Three Treasures. The wife of this wicked man was a daughter of Kamitsuke no kimi Ōhashi 上毛野公大椅.[9] She observed the eight precepts for one day and one night,[10] and went to the temple to participate in the rite of repentance in the congregation. When her husband came home, he could not find her. Having asked where she was, he heard his servant[11] say, "She has gone for the rite of repentance." At this he became angry and immediately went to the temple to bring his wife back. The officiating monk[12] saw him and tried to enlighten him, preaching the Buddhist doctrine. However, he would not listen to the monk, saying, "None of your nonsense! You vulgar monk, you seduced my wife! Watch out or you'll get your head smashed!" His vile speech cannot be described in detail. He called his wife to go home with him, and on their return he violated her. Suddenly an ant bit his penis, and he died in acute pain.

He brought on his own death, immediate retribution, since he was so evil minded as to insult the monk unreservedly and not to refrain from wicked lust.

Even if you have a hundred tongues in your mouth and utter a thousand words, never speak ill of monks. Otherwise you will incur immediate penalties.

# 12

## On the Immediate Reward of Being Saved by Crabs for Saving the Lives of Crabs and a Frog[1]

In Kii district, Yamashiro province 山背國紀伊郡,[2] there lived a woman whose name is unknown. She was born with a compassionate

---

7. For the Fumi family, see II.7, n. 13. The title of *imiki* was conferred on the Fumi family in 685. See *Nihon shoki*, XXIX (Tenmu 14:6:20); Aston, "Nihongi," II, 369–370.
8. The parenthesis by Kyōkai.
9. The *Shinsen shōjiroku* cites this family as being native Japanese.
10. 八齋戒 *hachi-saikai*; see I.24, n. 3.
11. 家人 *kenin*, domestic servants whose status was hereditary and who were allowed their own dwellings. They differ from slaves who could be bought and sold. *Ryō no gige*, "Ko-ryō," Articles 35, 40; Sansom, "Early Japanese Laws," Part Two, 145-147.
12. 導師 *dōshi*, Dharma Master Daie in this case.

1. See II.8, which shows the same plot of "the grateful animal" repaying a kindness. Cf. D. L. Philippi, "Ancient Tales of Supernatural Marriage," *Today's Japan*, V (No. 3, March-April, 1960), 19–23. Cf. *Hokke kenki* (III, 123), *Genkō shakusho* (XXVIII, 2), *Konjaku monogatarishū* (XVI, 16), *Kokon chomonshū* (XX), etc.
2. Present Kyoto-fu.

heart, and she believed in the law of karmic causation so she never took life, observing the five precepts[3] and the ten virtues.[4]

In the reign of Emperor Shōmu, young cowherds in her village caught eight crabs in a mountain brook and were about to roast and eat them. She saw this and begged them, "Will you please be good enough to give them to me?" They would not listen to her, but said, "We will roast and eat them." Repeating her wholehearted entreaty, she removed her robe to pay for the crabs. Eventually they gave the crabs to her. She invited a *dhyāna* master[5] to give a blessing in releasing them.

Afterward she was in the mountain and saw a large snake swallowing a big toad. She implored the large snake, "Please set this frog free for my sake, and I will give you many offerings."[6] The snake did not respond. Then, she collected more offerings and prayed, saying, "I will consecrate you as a kami. Please give it to me." Still without answering, the snake continued to swallow the toad. Again she pleaded, "I will become your wife in exchange for this toad. I implore you to release it to me." Raising its head high, the snake listened and stared at her face, then disgorged the toad. The woman made a promise to the snake, saying, "Come to me in seven days."

She told her parents of the whole affair in detail. They lamented, saying, "Why on earth did you, our only child, make such a promise you cannot fulfill?"

At that time the Most Venerable Gyōgi was staying at Fukaosa-dera 深長寺[7] in Kii district. She went and told him what had happened. When he heard her story, he said, "What an unfathomable story! Just keep a steadfast faith in the Three Treasures." With these instructions she went home, and, on the evening of the appointed day, she tightly closed the house, prepared herself for the ordeal, and made various vows with renewed faith in the Three Treasures. The snake came, crawled round and round the house, knocked on the walls with its tail, climbed onto the top of the roof, tore a hole in the thatch of the roof with its fangs, and dropped in front of her. She merely heard the noise of scuffling, as if there was jumping and biting. The next morning she found the eight crabs assembled and the snake cut to

3. 五戒 *gokai*; see II.8, n. 6.
4. 十善 *jūzen* (Skt. *daśakuśala*); they are: not to kill, not to steal, not to commit adultery, not to lie, not to use immoral language, not to slander, not to equivocate, not to covet, not to give way to anger, and not to hold false views. Tradition says that the reward for observing these precepts is rebirth in one of the heavens or among men, depending on the degree of observance.
5. 義禪師 Gi-zenji; see I.8, n. 5.
6. 幣帛 *mitegura*; see Chap. II(1)a, n. 18.
7. Or 深草寺, unidentified.

shreds by them. She then learned that the released crabs had come to repay her kindness to them.

Even an insect which has no means of attaining enlightenment returns a favor. How can a man ever forget kindness he has received? From this time on, people in Yamashiro province have honored big crabs in the mountain streams and, if they were caught, set them free in order to do good.[8]

# I 3

## On Lustful Love for the Image of Kichijō-tennyo Which Responded with an Extraordinary Sign[1]

In a mountain temple of Chinu, Izumi district, Izumi province 和泉國泉郡血渟,[2] there was a clay image of Kichijō-tennyo 吉祥天女.[3] In the reign of Emperor Shōmu, a lay brother[4] of Shinano province 信濃國[5] came to live in the temple. Attracted to the female image, he felt desire, fell in love with it, and prayed six times a day,[6] saying, "Please give me a beautiful woman like you."

Once he dreamed of lying with the female deity and the next morning discovered a stain on the skirt of the image. Seeing this, he repented, saying, "I prayed to you to give me a woman like yourself, but what a sacrifice you made to give yourself to me." He was too ashamed to tell others of the event. One disciple, however, heard about it in secret. When he was scolded and expelled from the temple because of disrespect for his teacher, he spoke ill of his teacher and revealed the whole affair. Villagers went to the temple to verify the rumor, and they discovered the stain on the statue. The lay brother could not deceive them and described in detail what had happened.

Indeed, we know that deep faith never fails to gain response. To this effect the Nehan-gyō 涅槃經[7] says: "A lewd man feels desire even for a woman in a picture."

8. See Chap. II(2)a, n. 73, for the Kaniman-ji cycle and the grateful crabs.

1. Cf. Konjaku monogatarishū (XVII, 45).
2. See II.2, n. 3.
3. Or Kichijō-(Kisshō-)ten, a Hindu female deity adopted into the assembly of Buddhas and bodhisattvas. See Chap. II(1)a, n. 6.
4. 優婆塞; see Chap. I(1)d, n. 91.
5. Present Nagano-ken 長野縣.
6. The twenty-four hours are divided into six units, four hours each, and a service is held in each unit; therefore, six times a day.
7. 多淫之人畫女生欲, unlocated in the Daihatsu nehan-gyō.

# 14

## On the Immediate Reward of the Destitute Princess' Devotion to the Image of Kichijō-tennyo[1]

In the reign of Emperor Shōmu, twenty-three members of the imperial family[2] agreed to give banquets and provide entertainment by turn. There was a poor princess[3] among them. She had no means to give a banquet when the rest of the group had already done so. Being ashamed of her poverty, the effect of her past deeds, she went to Hatori-dō on the East Side of Nara 諾樂左京服部堂[4] to worship the image of Kichijō-tennyo.[5] In tears she said, "As I planted the seed of poverty in my former existence, I reap the fruit now. I went to the banquets, and, after consuming the food of others, I have no means to invite them in return. I implore you to bring me a fortune."

At that moment her child ran to her in haste and said, "A great amount of food has been sent from the former capital."[6] She ran out and found her former wet nurse saying, "I heard you had received guests and brought you food." The food and drinks were incredibly delicious and fragrant. Nothing was missing. The metal tableware[7] was carried by thirty men.

All the princes invited to the banquet came and were delighted. There was twice as much food as for the preceding banquets, and she was praised as a rich princess. Each one said, "If she were poor, how could she prepare such an extravagant banquet? It is better than the one I made before." The songs and dances were as extraordinary as the heavenly music.[8] Some gave away their robes, some their skirts, and others coins, silk, cloth, cotton, etc. The princess, in her joy, gave the robes to her wet nurse to wear, but later, when she went to the temple to worship the sacred image, she found the statue wearing

1. Cf. *Konjaku monogatarishū* (XVII, 46). A similar story is found in II.34.
2. 王宗 or 王衆.
3. 女王 *nyoō* or *ōkimi*.
4. Kichijō-tennyo-dō was in Kichijōji-machi, Nara 奈良吉祥寺町. See Fukuyama, *Narachō jiin*, 304–307.
5. See Chap. II(1)d, n. 91.
6. 故京; see I.1, n. 15.
7. Rare and expensive in those days.
8. 釣天樂 *Kinten no gaku*; the music played at the palace of Shang-ti 上帝, Supreme Lord, located in the center of heaven.

them. Filled with doubt, she went to inquire of her former wet nurse who answered, "I do not know anything about your banquet."

Now it was evident that the bodhisattva[9] had helped the princess out of sympathy. She acquired a fortune and henceforth escaped poverty. This is an unusual event.

# 15

### On the Reward of Copying the Hoke-kyō and Holding a Service for a Mother in Revealing the Cause of Her Rebirth as a Cow[1]

Takahashi no muraji Azumabito 高橋連東人[2] was a very wealthy man in the village of Hamishiro, Yamada district, Iga province 伊賀國山田郡噉代里.[3] He copied the Hoke-kyō for his mother, making a vow, saying, "I want to invite a monk related to my vow by karma to hold a service for her salvation."[4] When he finished preparing a place for the service on the following day, he called a servant and said, "The first monk you happen to meet I will make the officiating monk. Don't overlook any monk who seems to be able to perform esoteric rites[5] and bring him to me."

The servant went first, in accord with his master's request, to the village of Mitani 御谷 in the same district.[6] There he found a mendicant[7] lying in the road, drunk, with a bag for a begging bowl at his elbow. His name is not known. He was sleeping so soundly that some mischievous person had shaved his head and hung a rope around him

---

9. Kichijō-tennyo is not exactly a bodhisattva because of its origin in the Hindu tradition, but it is one of Kannon's Tantric variations according to the *Asaba-shō* 阿娑縛抄, VI (*DBZ*, 40, 2087). Kyōkai, as well as lay devotees, perceived it as one of the bodhisattvas that was always ready to save them. Myōken is also identified with Kichijō-tennyo.

1. Cf. *Sanbō ekotoba* (II, 11), *Hokke kenki* (III, 106), *Konjaku monogatarishū* (XII, 25). A similar story is found in I.10.
2. Takahashi is the name of a native family, known to have served the Imperial Table Office (內膳司 *Naizenshi*).
3. Present Ayama-gun, Mie-ken 三重縣阿山郡.
4. 濟度 *saido*, to guide people across the sea of samsara and over to the other shore, that is, to salvation.
5. 修法 *shuhō, suhō,* or *zuhō.*
6. Unidentified.
7. 乞者.

like a surplice without waking him. Seeing him, the servant woke him with a greeting and asked him to visit his master.

On his arrival, the master greeted him with respect and faith and kept him inside the house for a day and a night, during which time he made a clerical robe in haste and offered it to the mendicant. The mendicant asked "Why have you treated me like this?" and the host replied, "I would like to ask you to expound the *Hoke-kyō*." Then the mendicant said, "I have no learning. I have simply stayed alive by reciting the *Hannya dharani*[8] and begging food." The host, however, repeated his entreaty. The mendicant thought to himself that the best way for him was a secret escape. Knowing that the mendicant intended to run away, the host had him watched.

That night, the mendicant had a dream. A red cow came to him, saying, "I am the mother of the master of this household. Among his cattle there is a red cow, whose calf is none other than I. Once in my former life, I stole property from my son, and now I am atoning for it in the form of a cow. I have confided this to you with respect and sincerity since you are going to preach on the Mahayana scripture[9] for me tomorrow. If you feel any doubt about my story, please prepare a seat at the back of the hall where you will preach tomorrow. You will find me seated there."

Awaking from this startling dream, the mendicant was very curious. The next morning he went up to the lecturer's seat, saying, "I am ignorant of Buddhist teachings. I came to take this seat in compliance with my host's entreaty. But I have one thing to tell you, which is a revelation that came to me in a dream." Then he told about the dream in detail. Whereupon the host stood up, prepared a seat, and called the cow, which took the seat and lay down. In sorrowful tears he said, "Indeed this is my mother! I had no idea! Now I will forgive her." The cow heard his words and sighed. When the service ended, the cow died suddenly. All the congregation cried so bitterly that there were echoes of weeping in the hall and in the garden. Nothing has ever been so miraculous as this. The son continued to accumulate merits for his mother.

We know that this miraculous event took place as a consequence of the son's extreme faith born of his feeling for his mother, and the mendicant's merits accumulated from reciting the divine dharani.

8. The dharani in the *Hannya shin-gyō*.
9. 大乗, in this case *Hoke-kyō*.

# 16

### On the Immediate Retribution of Good and Evil Because
### of Giving No Alms and Freeing Living Beings[1]

In the reign of Emperor Shōmu, there lived a wealthy man in the village of Sakata, Kagawa district, Sanuki province 讃岐國香川郡坂田里.[2] He and his wife had the same surname Aya no kimi綾君.[3] Next door to them lived an old widow and an old widower[4] without any family. They were extremely poor, having no clothes to wear nor food to eat. They used to come to the Aya no kimi's home to beg food at every meal. Once, out of curiosity, the husband got up secretly late at night, boiled rice, and fed his family,[5] but even then they appeared. All the family wondered about them.

The mistress said to her husband, "This man and woman are too old to work. I should like to have them in our household just for mercy's sake." Then he said, "If you want to feed them, give them some of your portion. The most meritorious deed of all is to save others by sacrificing one's own flesh. What I recommend to you will bring forth merit."

According to the master's suggestion, people in the household fed the old couple with part of their own portions. Among the household there was one servant who disliked the couple in spite of the master's words, however. Gradually other servants learned to dislike them and did not give them food. The mistress, therefore, fed them secretly from her portion. The troublesome servant falsely represented the matter to the master, saying, "Hungry and exhausted, we cannot work well in the field and are neglectful, for the mistress feeds the old ones by decreasing our portions." The mistress, however, kept them in food, even while the servant continued to slander her.

It happened that the ill-tempered servant went to sea to fish with a fisherman.[6] He saw ten oysters on the fishing rope, and he said to the

---

1. Cf. Konjaku monogatarishū (XX, 17).
2. Present Takamatsu-shi, Kagawa-ken 香川縣高松市.
3. Aya, a Japanese reading of 漢 Han; an immigrant family. See Aston, "Nihongi," I, 265.
4. 耆 okina, a man over sixty-six (Ryō no gige, "Koryō," Article 6) or sixty-five (Shoku Nihongi, XX, Tenpyō hōji 2:7:3), who was exempted from taxation.
5. 家口 keku, all members of the family; 口 is a numerary adjunct applied to men and animals.
6. The text appears to be corrupt at this point, for the subject of this sentence is the servant in the text, but it is likely that the master went out with the servant for fishing.

fisherman, "I would like to free these oysters." But the fisherman would not agree. Whereupon his companion pleaded earnestly, trying to convey Buddhist teachings to the fisherman, and argued, "Pious people build temples, so why do you object so much to freeing the oysters?" Eventually the fisherman yielded and said, "I want two and a half bushels[7] of rice in exchange for the ten oysters." Having paid the fisherman, he invited a monk to give a blessing and had the oysters returned to the sea.

One day the benefactor of the oysters went to the mountain with a servant to collect firewood.[8] He climbed a withered pine tree, fell from a branch, and died. His spirit, which possessed a diviner,[9] said, "Don't cremate me, but leave my corpse for seven days." In accord with this message, his corpse was carried from the mountain and placed outside, waiting for the appointed day.

On the seventh day he awoke and said to his family: "With five monks in front, and five lay brothers in the rear, I was going along a wide flat road as straight as a ruler. On both sides holy banners were raised, and a golden palace was in front. I asked them, 'What palace is this?' The lay brothers looked at each other, saying in whispers, 'This is the palace where your wife will be born. This palace was built as a reward for her merit of supporting the old ones. Do you know who we are?' I answered 'No.' Then, they revealed the fact, saying, 'You should know that the five monks and the five lay brothers are the ten oysters you paid for and set free.'

On either side of the palace gate stood a man with a horn on his forehead. They held up their swords ready to cut off my head, but the monks and lay brothers entreated them not to do so. Fragrant delicious food was served to both gatekeepers and all enjoyed the feast. During my seven days' stay inside I was so hungry and thirsty that my mouth was in flames. Then I was told, 'This is the penalty for your sin of disliking the old ones and not feeding them.' The monks and lay brothers escorted me back, and suddenly I awoke and found myself here."

After that the man gave alms as generously as the water moistens the land. The reward of saving living beings helps you, while the penalty of giving no alms returns to you in the form of hunger and thirst. We cannot help believing in the karmic retribution of good and evil.

7. Five *to* of rice; one *to* is 0.51 bushel. It is an exorbitant price for ten oysters.
8. In this story it is unclear whether the benefactor is the master or the servant.
9. 卜者 *kamnagi;* see Chap. II(3)a, n. 124.

# 17

*On Bronze Kannon Images Which Showed an Extraordinary Sign
in Their Transformation into the Form of a Heron*[1]

In the nunnery[2] of Okamoto in the village of Ikaruga, Heguri district, Yamato province 大和國平群郡鵤岡本尼寺,[3] there were twelve bronze statues of Kannon. (In the reign of the empress at the Palace of Owarida, it was a residence for Prince Regent Kamitsu-miya 上宮皇太子,[4] who made a vow and turned it into a nunnery.) In the reign of Emperor Shōmu, six bronzes were stolen, and they were sought without success. After that, many days and months passed.

There was a small pond to the west of the stagehouse of Heguri 平群驛.[5] One summer in June, some herdsmen near the pond saw the tip of a stake above the water. There was a heron on it. Seeing the heron, they gathered pebbles and rocks, trying to hit it, but it did not fly away. Tired of throwing stones, they went into the pond to catch it. Hardly did they reach it, when it dived under the water. When they looked closely at the stake on which the heron had rested, they saw golden fingers. When the stake was pulled out of the water, the fingers turned out to be bronze Kannons. The pond was thus named "Pond of the Bodhisattva" because of the discovery, and the herdsmen told the whole affair to the people.

Eventually the rumor reached the nunnery. The nuns came to see the Kannons, which they identified as the stolen ones although the gilding had fallen off. Surrounding the bronzes, the grieving nuns said, "We have missed our sacred images day and night, and now we are fortunate to be reunited by chance. We wonder what offenses caused you, our venerable masters,[6] to be stolen?" Then they prepared a palanquin, enshrined the images, and returned them to the temple. Clergymen and laymen in the crowd said, "They must have been stolen by those who forged coins, but the thieves eventually abandoned them, not knowing how to make use of them."

It was evident that the heron was not a real bird, but an incarnated

---

1. Cf. *Konjaku monogatarishū* (XVI, 13).
2. Identified as Hokki-ji 法起寺. See Fukuyama, *Narachō jiin*, 41–50.
3. See I.4, n. 7.
4. See I.4.
5. Unlocated. For the stage, see I.30, n. 6.
6. 大師; honorific title for Buddhas, bodhisattvas, and eminent monks.

Kannon. There is no room for doubt. The *Nehan-gyō*[7] says: "The dharma-body always exists even after the death of Buddha." This is nothing but the lesson of the present story.

# 18

## *On the Immediate Penalty of Being Given a Twisted Mouth and Death for Speaking Ill of the Monk, Devotee of the* Hoke-kyō[1]

In the Tenpyō era[2] there once lived a layman[3] in Sagaraka district, Yamashiro province,[4] whose name is unknown. At Koma-dera 高麗寺[5] in the same district there was a monk named Eijō 榮常[6] who used to recite the *Hoke-kyō* all the time. It happened that the monk and the layman had been playing *go* 碁[7] for some time. Whenever the monk put down a stone, he said, "This is the Venerable Eijō's hand of *go*." The layman mocked and mimicked him, deliberately twisting his mouth and saying, "This is the Venerable Eijō's hand of *go*." He went on and on this way. Then, all of a sudden, the layman's mouth was distorted. In fear, he left the temple holding his chin with his hands. He had hardly gone any distance before he fell on his back and died immediately. Witnesses said, "Though he did not persecute a monk, mocking and mimicking got him a twisted mouth and sudden death. What, then, must the penalty be if one vengefully persecutes a monk?"

The *Hoke-kyō* gives a passage to this effect: "A wise monk and a foolish monk cannot be discussed in the same breath. Similarly, a long-haired monk and a wise, unshaved layman cannot be treated alike and served with the same dishes. If one dares to do so, he will swallow an iron ball which is heated on red-hot copper and charcoal, and fall into hell."[8]

7. See Chap. II(3)b, n. 148.

1. Cf. *Konjaku monogatarishū* (XIV, 28). Similar to I.19.
2. (729–749).
3. 白衣; see I.19, n. 5.
4. See II.6, n. 2.
5. Once existed at present Kamikoma, Yamashiro-chō, Sōraku-gun, Kyoto-fu 京都府相樂郡山城町上狛.
6. Otherwise unknown.
7. See I.19, n. 4.
8. Unlocated in the *Hoke-kyō*.

# 19

## On the Visit to the Palace of King Yama by a Woman, Devotee of the Shin-gyō, and the Following Extraordinary Event[1]

Tokari no ubai 利苅優婆夷[2] came from Kawachi 河內 province. As her surname was Tokari no suguri 利苅村主,[3] she was called Tokari no ubai. With an innately pure heart she had faith in the Three Treasures[4] and used to recite the *Shin-gyō*[5] as a form of religious discipline. Her chanting was so beautiful that she was loved and appreciated by clergy and laity alike.

In the reign of Emperor Shōmu, this lay sister died while asleep, a sudden death without suffering, and went to King Yama.[6] Seeing her, the king stood up, made a seat, and spread a mat [for her], saying, "I have heard that you are very good at reciting the *Shin-gyō*. I was longing to hear you, and this is why I have invited you here for a short visit. Will you please recite the scripture? I am listening." She did so, and the king, delighted, rose from his seat and knelt to pay his respects to her, saying, "How noble! The rumor was true."

When three days had passed, the king said to her, "Now it is time for you to go home." When she came out of the palace, there stood three men in yellow robes.[7] They were delighted to see her, saying, "We met you only once before. We have longed to see you since we have not met for so long. What good luck brought you here! Hurry on home, and we will see you without fail in the east market of the capital of Nara[8] three days from today." Then she left them, returned home, and awoke.

On the morning of the third day she decided to go to the east market of the city because of the promise, but though she made her way there and waited all day, the three men did not come. Only a humble man came into the market by the east gate to sell Buddhist scriptures. He displayed them, calling out, "Will anybody buy some

1. Cf. *Konjaku monogatarishū* (XIV, 31).
2. The name Tokari may have originated with a local name in Kawachi province. *Ubai* is a transliteration of Skt. *upāsikā*, one who keeps the five precepts while remaining in lay status. The male counterpart is *ubasoku*.
3. *Suguri* is a title often conferred on immigrants.
4. 三寶 *sanbō*; see Chap. II(3)b.
5. *Hannya haramitsu shin-gyō* 般若波羅蜜心經; see Chap. II(1)a, n. 19.
6. 閻羅王; see Chap. II(1)c.
7. As it turns out later, they are the spirits of the scriptures she copied. Their yellow robes may signify scriptures which were written on yellow paper.
8. There was a market on each side of the capital.

scriptures?" Passing the sister, he went out of the city by the west gate. As she wanted to buy the scriptures, she sent for him to return, and, on opening them, she discovered that they were the two volumes of the *Bonmō-kyō* 梵網經[9] and the one volume of the *Shin-gyō* she had copied in the past. They had been stolen before the dedication ceremony, and she had looked for them unsuccessfully for many years. With forbearance and great joy in her heart, she asked the price of the man, whom she knew had stolen them, saying, "How much do you want?" He replied, "I want five hundred pieces[10] for each scroll." She bought them at this price.

It occurred to her that the three scrolls were the three men who had promised to meet her at the market. Thereupon she held a service to read these scriptures and deepened her faith in the law of causality. She recited the scriptures with even more devotion, never ceasing the recitation day and night.

How miraculous! Just as the *Nehan-gyō* says: "If a man does good deeds, his name will be noticed among heavenly beings; if he does evil deeds, his name will be recorded in hell."[11]

# 20

### *On the Mother Who Had a Bad Dream, with the Utmost Faith[1] Had a Scripture Recited, and Saved Her Daughter by an Extraordinary Sign[2]*

In the village of Yamamura in Sou upper district, Yamato province 大和國添上郡山村里,[3] there lived an aged mother[4] whose name is unknown. She had a married daughter who bore two children. Her son-in-law was appointed provincial magistrate,[5] and he took his family to his post. Several years passed.

9. *Bonmō-kyō* (*Brahmajālasūtra*) (*Taishō*, XXIV, No. 1484).
10. 文 *mon*.
11. See I.27, nn. 9, 10.

1. 至誠心; one of the three minds (至誠心、深心、廻向發願心) which lead to rebirth in the pure land. The Chinese monk Shan-tao 善導 (613–681) says that by the utmost faith is meant the essential sincerity which generates the physical act of prostration, the oral deed of praising Buddha, and the mental deed of meditating on Buddha with concentration (see the *Nihon ryōiki*, ed. by Kasuga and Endō, 236, n. 2). See his *Ōjō raisan* (*Taishō*, XLVII, 1980); also, I.22, n. 10.
2. Cf. *Sanbō ekotoba* (II,12).
3. See I.10, n. 2.
4. 長母; in order to differentiate the mother from her daughter 長 is added to 母.
5. 縣主宰 *agata no mikotomochi*, or 国司 *kuni no tsukasa*.

Once the old mother, who had stayed in the home village to take care of the household, received an omen in a dream concerning her daughter. Surprised and fearful, she wanted to have a scripture recited for her daughter, but she was too poor to ask a monk to do it. As her mind was never free of worry for her daughter, she finally thought of taking off her robe and washing it to offer it to the monk for his service. Then another omen appeared in a dream. In even greater fear she took off her skirt, cleaned it, and, as she had done before, gave it as an offering to the monk for reciting a scripture.

Meanwhile her daughter was living in the official residence for a provincial magistrate at her husband's post. It happened that her children were playing in the court, while she herself was inside the back quarters. The two children saw seven monks seated on the roof reciting a scripture. They called to their mother, saying, "Mother, seven monks are chanting a scripture on the roof. Hurry! Come and see them!" The chanting sounded like bees humming together. Wondering at this, the mother had scarcely come out of the rear building when its wall collapsed. All of a sudden, the seven monks disappeared. Greatly terrified and marveling at this accident, she thought to herself that heaven and earth had saved her from being crushed. Later, however, she heard from her mother who had sent a messenger to tell her about the evil omens and the subsequent services for the recitation of scriptures. She was so impressed with her mother's report that she professed her faith in the Three Treasures with the greatest awe.

Thus we know that the whole sequence of events was generated by the power of reciting scriptures and the determination of the Three Treasures to protect us.

# 21

*On the Clay Divine Image Which Showed an Extraordinary*
*Sign by Emanating Light from Its Legs and*
*Incurred an Immediate Reward*[1]

On a hill east of the capital of Nara[2] there was a temple named Konsu 金鷲.[3] In that mountain temple lived a man who was popularly called

1. Cf. *Konjaku monogatarishū* (XVII, 49), *Fusō ryakki* (Shō II, Shōmu), *Genkō shakusho* (XXVIII, Jizōshi), *Hōbutsu-shū* (V), *Kojidan* (III), etc. A famous story on the foundation of the original Tōdai-ji.
2. Present Kasugayama 春日山 area.
3. Or 金鐘寺 which was the old name of Hokke-dō, Tōdai-ji.

Konsu ubasoku[4] because he made his residence there. That temple has since become Tōdai-ji 東大寺.[5]

In the reign of Emperor Shōmu, before the establishment of the huge temple,[6] Konsu the Ascetic stayed there and lived a disciplined life. In the temple was enshrined a clay image of Shūkongōjin 執金剛神.[7] The ascetic never ceased to pray day and night, holding a rope tied to the legs of the image.[8]

It happened that light emanated from its legs and reached the imperial palace. In surprise and wonder, the emperor sent a messenger to discover its origin. The imperial messenger[9] traced the light back to the temple, where he found a lay brother prostrating himself before Buddha and confessing his offenses,[10] holding in his hand a rope tied to the legs of the divine image. The messenger went back immediately to report this to the emperor. The emperor sent for the ascetic, and asked, "What have you been praying for?" In reply he said, "I prayed that I might renounce the world and devote myself to the study of Buddhist teachings."[11] Therefore he was ordained[12] by an edict and adopted the name Konsu. The emperor admired his practice and made sufficient offerings to provide the four necessities.[13] People called him Bodhisattva Konsu, praising his discipline.

The image of Shūkongōjin which gave off the light still stands at the north door of Kensaku-dō 羂索堂[14] of Tōdai-ji.

The note says: How good is Konsu the Ascetic! He kindled a fire of faith in spring and made it flare up in the autumn. The light from the legs helped the fire to be recognized, and the emperor reverently revealed the sign of his faith in Buddha.[15] Indeed we learn from this story that no vow is made without obtaining a response.

4. Identified with Rōben 良辨 (689–773), who came from Ōmi province. Tradition says he was caught by an eagle and abandoned in front of Kasuga Shrine in Nara, where Giin 義淵 saved him and taught him the Hossō doctrines. In 733 Emperor Shōmu founded Konshō-ji for him, and after it was expanded into Tōdai-ji, he was in charge of the great temple. He became *sōjō* in 760. See I.9, n. 1, for the story of a child carried away by an eagle.

5. See Chap. I(1)c, for the construction of Tōdai-ji.

6. Its construction started in 747 and was completed in 749. Since the image of Lochana Buddha was dedicated in 752 (see I.Preface, n. 14), that is also taken as the year of the erection of Tōdai-ji.

7. Skt. Vajradhara, the guardian of dharma, originally a Vedic deity that was adopted in the Buddhist tradition; also an incarnation of Kannon.

8. This practice is called 綱引業 *tsunahiki-gyō* which became popular during the Heian period, particularly among those who aspired to rebirth in the pure land.

9. 勅信 *chokushin*.

10. 禮佛悔過 *raibutsu keka*; for *keka*, see Chap. II(1)a.

11. 佛法 *Buppō*.

12. 得度 *tokudo*; see Chap. I(1)d.

13. 四事 *shiji*, a shortened form of 四事供養 *shiji kuyō*, four kinds of offerings; shelter, clothing, food and drink, and flowers and incense.

14. Or 法華堂 Hokke-dō, 三月堂 Sangatsu-dō.

15. Refers to Emperor Shōmu.

# 22

*On the Stolen Bronze Buddha Which Gave an*
*Extraordinary Sign and Identified a Thief*[1]

In some part of Hine district, Izumi province 和泉國日根郡,[2] near a highway, there lived a thief whose name is unknown. Evil-natured, he lived by robbery and had no faith in the law of karmic causation. He would steal metal from temples to make into strips and sell.

In the reign of Emperor Shōmu, a Buddhist image of Jin'e-ji 盡惠寺[3] in that district was stolen by the robber. One day a man passed on horseback along the north side of the temple. He heard a voice crying, "Ouch! ouch!" The man on horseback, thinking someone was being hit, galloped forward in the direction of the voice, which faded out as he came closer. He stopped the horse to listen, but he heard nothing except the sound of metal being hammered. Therefore he passed on by the place. As he went further along, however, he heard the same cry. He could not bring himself to ride off; he returned but again he heard no cries, only the sound of hammering. Suspecting that there had been a murder or at least some evil scheme, he wandered about for a while and sent his attendant to peer secretly into the house. The attendant saw a man cutting off the limbs and chiseling the neck of a bronze Buddha that had been laid on its back.

On the spot he caught the man and asked him, "To which temple does this Buddha belong?" He said, "This is the Buddha of Jin'e-ji." At that, a messenger was sent to the temple to ask about the Buddha, and he learned that it had been stolen. The messenger reported the whole affair in detail. Both the monks and patrons of the temple came to the spot and, surrounding the broken Buddha, wailed, "How pitiful! How dreadful! What fault caused our great master[4] to suffer such a disaster? If the sacred image were at the temple, we would look up to it as our master. Since it is broken, what shall we revere as our master?"

The monks purified a palanquin to enshrine the broken Buddha, held a tearful funeral service[5] at the temple, and let the thief go with-

1. Cf. *Konjaku monogatarishū* (XII, 13).
2. Present Sennan-gun, Ōsaka-fu.
3. Unidentified.
4. *daishi*; see II.17, n. 6.
5. 殯 *mogari*, funeral rite before burial; see Chap. II(3)a. They treated the broken Buddha like a human being.

out punishment. But the man who had caught the thief sent him to court, where he was imprisoned.

We learn indeed that the Buddha performed a miracle in order to stop evil and that the Buddha's spirit responds to utmost devotion! In the twelfth volume of the *Nehan-gyō*[6] there is a passage which runs like this: "I have a high regard for the Mahayana teachings.[7] I killed a Brahman[8] who spoke ill of a Mahayana scripture.[9] Consequently I will not fall into hell hereafter." Another passage in the thirty-third volume of the same scripture[10] speaks to the same effect: "Those of the *ichisendai* 一闡提[11] shall perish forever. If you kill even an ant, you will be accused of the sin of killing; you will not, however, be accused of the sin of killing if you kill the *ichisendai*." (Because the *ichisendai* slanders the Three Treasures, fails to preach for all beings, and lacks a sense of gratitude, killing him is not a sin.)[12]

# 23

## On the Bronze Bodhisattva Miroku Which Was Stolen by a Thief and Revealed His Identity by a Miraculous Sign[1]

In the reign of Emperor Shōmu, an imperial messenger went round the city at night. When he was in the city at midnight, he heard wailing in the field covered with smartweed[2] south of the Kazuraki nunnery 葛木尼寺[3] in the capital of Nara. Something cried, "Ouch! Ouch!" On hearing this he proceeded in the direction of the cry, and found a thief breaking a bronze image of Bodhisattva Miroku 彌勒菩薩[4] with a stone. He caught and questioned the thief who confessed,

---

6. *Daihatsu nehan-gyō*, XII (*Taishō*, XII, 434c). 我 . . . 心重大乘聞婆羅門 誹謗方等 . . . 斷其命根 . . . 以是因緣 從是已來 不墮地獄.

7. 大乘 *daijō*; see I.23, n. 13.

8. A member of the top caste of the Hindu community which was in charge of sacrificial rites. As Buddha denied their spiritual authority, Buddhism was rejected by them.

9. 方等 *hōdō*; equal to *hōkō*, *daijō*.

10. *Daihatsu nehan-gyō*, XXXIII (*Taishō*, XII, 562b). See Chap. II(2)a. 一闡提輩 永斷滅 故以是義故 殺害蟻子 猶得殺罪 殺一闡提 無有殺罪.

11. Transliterated from Skt. *icchantika*; see Chap. II(2)a.

12. Kyōkai's note.

1. Cf. *Konjaku monogatarishū* (XVII, 25).

2. 蓼原 *tadehara*, the field of smartweed or a local name.

3. Located east of Daian-ji on the East Side of Nara. See *Shoku Nihongi*, XXXVI (Hōki 11:1:14); also, Fukuyama, *Narachō jiin*, 74–80.

4. Maitreya; see Chap. II(3)b, n. 131.

"This is the bronze of the Kazuraki nunnery." Returning the image to the nunnery, the messenger sent the thief to court, where he was imprisoned.

The dharma-body Buddha of the ultimate reality[5] has neither flesh nor blood. Why then did it suffer from pain? This took place only to show that dharma exists changeless. It is another miraculous event.

# 24

## On the Fiends, Messengers of King Yama, Who Canceled Death in Exchange for a Bribe[1]

Nara no Iwashima 楢磐嶋[2] lived at the Fifth Avenue, the Sixth Street, East Side of Nara 諾樂左京六條五坊,[3] that is, in the village west of Daian-ji 大安寺.[4] In the reign of Emperor Shōmu he got a loan of thirty *kan*[5] from the Sutara 修多羅 fund of Daian-ji,[6] went to the Tsuruga port in Echizen 越前都魯鹿[7] on business, and loaded the goods he had purchased on a boat to bring them home. On the way home he suddenly fell ill and got off the boat. Thinking he would go on alone, he hired a horse and set out.

When he reached Shiga-no-karasaki, Takashima district, Ōmi province 近江 [國] 高嶋郡磯鹿辛前,[8] he looked around and saw three men half a furlong[9] away running after him. At the Uji Bridge of Yamashiro 山代宇治椅,[10] they caught up and went along with him. Iwashima asked them, "Where are you going?" They replied, "We are messengers from the office of King Yama[11] sent for Nara no Iwashima." Then Iwashima said, "I am the very one you are sent for. But why do you want me?" The fiend messengers[12] answered, "When

---

5. 理法身 *ri-hosshin*; see Chap. II(3)b.

1. Cf. *Kongō hannya-kyō jikkenki* (I, Kyūgohen 13); *Sanbō ekotoba* (II, 14), *Konjaku monogatarishū* (XX, 19), *Genkō shakusho* (XXIX).
2. Since Iwashima lived in Nara, 楢 may be 諾樂 (奈良).
3. The southeast quarter of the capital.
4. Daian-ji was called Ōtsukasa-no-ōtera or Takechi-no-ōtera before its transfer to the capital of Nara in about 710 (see Chap. I(1)c). It was originally built by Emperor Tenmu 天武 in 674.
5. One *kan* consists of one thousand *mon*, pieces.
6. See Chap. I(1)c, nn. 65, 66, for Sutara-shū 修多羅宗. According to "Daianji garan engi" (*Nara ibun*, ed. by Takeuchi, I, 369), the Sutara fund was 1,668 *kan* and 61 *mon* in 747, the biggest at Daian-ji.
7. Present Tsuruga-shi, Fukui-ken 福井縣敦賀市.
8. The northern part of present Ōtsu-shi, Shiga-ken 滋賀縣大津市.
9. One *chō* 町 equals about 120 yards.
10. Located at present Uji-shi, Kyoto-fu. See I.12, n. 8.
11. 閻羅王闕.
12. 使鬼.

we looked for you at your home, we were told, 'He has gone on a business tour.' Therefore, we went to the port so that we might meet and catch you there, but a messenger from the Four Divine Guardians[13] implored us, saying, 'You should excuse him, since he is engaged in business with a loan from the temple.'[14] So we let you go free for a while. We have spent so many days trying to catch you that we feel hungry and exhausted. Do you have any food with you?" Iwashima answered, "I have only dried rice," and gave it to them to eat. The fiend messengers said, "Don't come any closer to us, or you will be made sick by our spirit.[15] You need not be afraid of us, though."

Eventually Iwashima took them home and gave them a feast. The fiends said to him, "We like the flavor of beef very much.[16] Will you serve us beef? We are the fiends who steal cows." So he told them, "I have two brindled cows. Will you let me go free if I offer them to you?" They said, "Well, we have eaten much of your food. If we release you because of your kind treatment, we shall be accused of a grave sin and be hit one hundred times with an iron stick. Do you by chance know anyone of the same age?" "No, I don't," he answered. Then one of the three fiends, after thinking a while, asked, "In which year were you born?" He answered, "I was born in the fifth year of the tiger."[17] Then the fiend said, "I heard that there is a diviner[18] who was born in the same year at the shrine of Izagawa 率川社.[19] He can be your substitute. We will take him instead. I urge you, however, to recite the *Kongō hannya-kyō*[20] one hundred times,[21]

13. 四王 *Shiō*, four deities who guard the four quarters of the world, that is, Dhṛtarāṣṭra 持國(E), Virūḍhaka 增長 (S), Virūpākṣa 廣目 (W), and Vaiśravaṇa 多聞 (N). See *Konkōmyō saishōō-kyō*, VI (*Taishō*, XVI, 427b–432c).

14. This indicates a belief that business conducted with the temple funds is an act to attain merit. In T'ang and later China, moneylending became a flourishing business of the temple. Michihata explains the presence of many legends on the penalties incurred by stealing the samgha property or not repaying the loan of the temple as one of the measures for self-protection taken by the monks. See his *Tōdai Bukkyōshi no kenkyū*, 539.

15. 氣 , vital force.

16. Animal sacrifice is made for an evil foreign deity (II.5) or hungry ghosts such as in this story.

17. 戊寅 *tsuchinoe-tora*; a combination of the Ten Stems and the Twelve Branches used as a device to indicate the year; in this case, the year of birth.

18. 相八卦讀 *sōhakkeyomi*; literally, one who can read the features of a house or man, and the eight trigrams (Ch. *pa kua* 八卦). Cf. Fung Yu-lan, *The History of the Chinese Philosophy*, 378–395.

19. Izagawa is the name of a brook which originates in Mt. Kasuga (see II.31, n. 2) and flows into the Saho River

20. *Kongō hannya haramitsu-kyō* 金剛般若波羅蜜經 (*Vajracchedikāprajñāpāramitāsūtra*) (*Taishō*, VIII, No. 235). See the *Vagaakkedikā* or *Diamond Cutter, Buddhist Mahāyāna Texts,* ed. by Cowell (*SBE*, XLIX, 109–144).

21. 百卷 ; literally, one hundred volumes, but translated here as one hundred times for it is a one-volume scripture.

invoking our names, so that we may escape whipping for the sin of accepting your offer of a cow. The first name is Takasamaro 高佐麻呂; the second, Nakachimaro 中知麻呂; the third, Tsuchimaro 槌麻呂." With this, they left him at midnight.

The next morning Iwashima found one of his cows dead. He went to Nantōin 南塔院[22] of Daian-ji and asked Novice Ninyō 仁耀[23] (at that time not yet ordained) to recite the *Kongō hannya-kyō* one hundred times. On his request Ninyō spent two days in reciting it. After three days the fiend messengers came to Iwashima, saying, "Owing to the power of the Mahayana scripture we escaped one hundred whipping strokes; besides, we were given half a bushel[24] more rice than the usual ration. How happy and grateful we are! Please be virtuous and hold services for our sake hereafter on every holy day."[25] Then all of a sudden they disappeared.

Iwashima was over ninety when he died.

As Te-hsüan 德玄[26] of T'ang China escaped the messenger of King Yama owing to the power of the *Hannya-kyō*, so did Iwashima of Japan because he was engaged in business with a loan from the temple fund. The same moral will be found in the story of a flower vendor who was born in Tōriten 忉利天,[27] or of Kikuta 掬多 who had once wanted to poison Buddha but whose good heart was restored by Buddha's omniscience.[28]

# 25

## *On the Fiend, Messenger of King Yama, Who Accepted the Hospitality of the One for Whom He Had Been Sent and Repaid It*[1]

In Yamada district, Sanuki province 讚岐國山田郡,[2] there lived a

22. Unidentified.
23. 沙彌仁耀 (d. 796) (Shiban, *Honchō kōsōden*, LXVI). He must have been in his late teens then, before ordination.
24. 一斗, 1 *to*.
25. 節 *sechi*, equal to 齋 *sai;* see I.24, n. 3.
26. Tou Te-hsüan 竇德玄, a high minister who lived in the reign of Kao-tsung (650–683) (*Kongō hannya-kyō jikkenki*, I).
27. Transliteration of Skt. *Trāyastriṃsa* meaning thirty-three heavens above Mt. Sumeru.
28. *Daishōgonron-kyō* 大莊嚴論經, XIII (*Taishō*, IV, 327c–333a).

1. Cf. *Myōhōki* (III, On Ma Chia-yün 馬嘉運), *Konjaku monogatarishū* (XX, 18), *Hōbutsushū* (VI).
2. Present Takamatsu-shi, or Kita-gun, Kagawa-ken 香川縣高松市, 木田郡.

woman whose name was Nunoshiki no omi Kinume 布敷臣衣女.[3] In the reign of Emperor Shōmu, she suddenly fell ill. Therefore, she laid all kinds of delicious offerings on both sides of her gate to give the deity of plagues a banquet as a bribe.[4]

There came a fiend, a messenger of King Yama, to seize her. Exhausted from searching for her, the fiend cast a covetous look at the offerings of delicacies and accepted them. Then he said to her, "As I have accepted your hospitality, I will repay your kindness. Do you know anyone of the same name as yours?" Kinume answered, saying, "Yes, there is another Kinume in Utari 鵜垂 district[5] of the same province." Thereupon, he took her to the other Kinume's home in Utari district to see her, and, taking out a one-foot chisel from his red bag, drove it into the latter's forehead and arrested her. The former Kinume of Yamada district went home in secret.

When King Yama, who had been waiting for them, examined her, he said, "This is not the Kinume I sent for. You have got the wrong person. Kinume, will you stay here for a while? Go and get the Kinume of Yamada district."

As he had failed in trying to conceal her, the fiend again went to Kinume of Yamada district to arrest her and came back with her. King Yama saw her and said, "*This* is the Kinume I sent for."

Meanwhile, Kinume of Utari district went home only to find her corpse had been cremated during her three-day absence. She came back and appealed to the king in grief, saying, "I have no body to enter into." Then, the king asked, "Is there the body of Kinume of Yamada district?" There was, whereupon the king said, "Go and take her body as yours."

In this way Kinume of Utari district came back to life in the body of Kinume of Yamada district. She said, "This is not my home. My home is in Utari district." At that her parents said, "You are our daughter. Why do you say such a thing?" She would not listen to them, however, and visited her own home, saying, "This is my real home." Her real parents disclaimed this, saying, "You are not our daughter. We have already cremated her." Thereupon, she explained in detail what King Yama had told her. Having heard her story, both sets of parents believed her and allowed her to inherit both fortunes. This is why the present Kinume had four parents and two inheritances.

There is sometimes merit in making offerings to a fiend as a bribe.

3. The Nunoshikis is a native family in Kinai.
4. This practice of making offerings of delicacies at the gate is also found in II.16. Its purpose is to bribe the fiends, executioners, or deities not to kill.
5. Present Ayauta-gun, Kagawa-ken 香川縣綾歌郡.

If you have anything, you should offer it.[6] This is another of the miraculous events.

# 26

## *On the Miraculous Sign of the Unfinished Log Which Was Cut out for Buddha Images but Abandoned*[1]

Dhyāna Master Kōtatsu 廣達,[2] whose secular name was Shimotsuke no asomi 下毛野朝臣,[3] was a man of Muza district, Kazusa province 上總國武射郡.[4] (Some say he was a man of Ahiru 畔蒜 district.)[5] In the reign of Emperor Shōmu, he went to the mountain called Kane no take, in Yoshino 吉野金峯,[6] and recited scriptures while walking around under the trees[7] in pursuit of the Buddha's path.

Now there was a horse-chestnut tree in the village of Tsuki in Yoshino district 吉野郡桃花里.[8] It was cut down to be made into Buddha images, but this was abandoned for many years. In this area there was a river named Akikawa 秋河.[9] It happened that the log was laid over the river so that men and animals could cross it.

Once Kōtatsu went to that village on an errand, and, upon crossing the bridge, heard a voice from under the bridge saying, "Ouch! Don't step on me!" Hearing this, he looked around in wonder, but he could not find anyone. As he did not dare to pass, he wandered around for a while close to the bridge, and, when he lifted it up, he found that it was an abandoned log cut for Buddha images. Struck with awe, he enshrined it in a purified place, paid homage to it in tears, and made a vow,[10] saying, "I will carve you into Buddha images since we have

6. The closing remarks imply that even making offerings as bribes is better than offering nothing, but this does not fit the story, for it was Kinume of Yamada who offered bribes, and Kinume of Utari who got four parents and two fortunes.

2. A monk of Gangō-ji, of the Hossō School. See the *Shoku Nihongi*, XXXII (Hōki 3:3:6). He was appointed as one of the ten *dhyāna* masters.
3. According to the *Shinsen shōjiroku*, the Shimotsuke family is descended from the imperial family.
4. Present Sanbu-gun, Chiba-ken 千葉縣山武郡.
5. Present Kimitsu-gun 君津郡.
6. See Chap. II(1)b; 1.28, n. 15.
7. 經行 *kyōgyō* or *kinhin*; after meditating in a sitting posture, ascetics walk around reciting scriptures.
8. Unlocated.
9. Present Shimoichi-gawa 下市川 which originates in Mt. Yoshino and flows into the Yoshino River.
10. 發誓願.

met by the work of interdependent causation.[11] He took the log to its appointed place, called upon the people to make offerings,[12] and directed the work of carving statues of Amida Buddha 阿彌陀佛,[13] Miroku Buddha 彌勒佛,[14] and Bodhisattva Kannon 觀音菩薩.[15] These are now enshrined in Oka-dō 岡堂,[16] in the village of Koshibe, Yoshino district 吉野郡越部村.[17]

Since a log does not have a mind, how can it cry? Doubtless this was nothing but the work of the Buddha's spirit.[18]

# 27

## On a Woman of Great Strength[1]

Owari no sukune Kukuri 尾張宿禰久玖利[2] was a governor of Nakashima district, Owari province 尾張國中嶋郡,[3] in the reign of Emperor Shōmu. His wife came from the village of Katawa in Aichi district 愛知郡片蘿里[4] of the same province (a granddaughter of the Venerable Dōjō of Gangō-ji).[5] She was faithful to her husband, and as gentle and delicate as glossed silk cloth. Once she wove fine hemp for her husband's robe. Its color and pattern were exquisite.

At that time the lord[6] who ruled that province was Wakasakurabe no Tau 稚櫻部任.[7] When the lord saw the beautiful robe on the district governor, he stripped him of it, saying, "It is too good for you to

11. 因緣 *in'en* or *innen*, the law of cause and effect.
12. He organized a *chishiki* or devotees' organization to carry out this project of making images. See Chap. I(1)d, nn. 110, 111.
13. See Chap. II(3)b, n. 132.
14. See Chap. II(3)b, n. 131. Doctrinally speaking, Maitreya is a bodhisattva, but there are many indications that he was considered a savior Buddha, much like Amida.
15. See Chap. I(1)a, n. 12.
16. Unlocated. See Fukuyama, *Narachō jiin*, 316.
17. Present Koshibe, Ōyodo-chō, Yoshino-gun, Nara-ken 奈良縣吉野郡大淀町越部.
18. 聖靈 *shōryō*; see Chap. II(3)b.

1. One of the Venerable Dōjō cycle related to I.3, II.4. Cf. *Konjaku monogatarishū* (XXIII, 18).
2. See the *Nihon shoki*, XXIX (Tenmu 1:12:2); Aston, "Nihongi," II, 367. The title of *sukune* was given to the Owari family.
3. Present Nakashima-gun, Aichi-ken 愛知縣中嶋郡.
4. See I.3, n. 3.
5. Kyōkai's parenthesis. For the Venerable Dōjō, see *ibid*.
6. 國守 a chief provincial magistrate.
7. According to the *Shinsen shōjiroku*, Wakasakurabe is the name of a native family, but this provincial magistrate is unknown.

wear," and would not return it. When the district governor's wife asked him what had happened to the robe, he said to her, "My lord took it away." Then the wife asked him, saying, "Do you miss it?" He replied, "Yes, I miss it very much."

Thereupon, the wife went to see the lord and implored, "I beg you to give the robe to me." The lord said, "What a crazy woman! Drive her away." Then, with two fingers, she picked up the bench where the lord was sitting, carried it outside the provincial office[8] with the lord on it, and tore into pieces the hem of his robe, still imploring, "I beg you to give the robe to me!" The lord was so terrified and embarrassed that he returned it to her. She brought it back home and, after cleaning it, folded it and put it away. She could crush a piece of bamboo into strips as fine as silk threads. At that the parents of the district governor were so terrified that they told their son, "Because of your wife you will incur the enmity of the lord and have some trouble," and they continued in panic, "She behaved like that even to the lord. If he decides to punish her for her offense, what shall we do? We cannot make our living." Therefore, they sent her back to her parents and abandoned her.[9]

Some time after that she happened to go out to the Kusatsu River 草津川[10] in the village to wash clothes. A merchant passed in front of her on a big boat heavily loaded with goods. The captain of the boat saw and teased her, treating her lightly. "Be quiet!" she said to him. "Those who play tricks on others get slapped on the cheek!" Angry at that, the captain stopped the boat and hit her, but she did not feel the pain. She drew the boat half way up the beach, leaving its stern sunk in the water. The captain hired men who lived near the ferry to lift the cargo out and then reload it in the boat. She said, "Because he had no manners, I pulled the boat up. Why do you people humiliate a humble woman like me?" She again dragged the loaded boat for about half a furlong. The sailors were struck with such awe that they knelt and said, "We were wrong. We are sorry." Therefore she forgave them. Even five hundred men could not pull the boat, and so it was evident that she had greater strength than five hundred men.

One scripture[11] has a passage to this effect: "If you make and offer

8. 國府 ko (ku) fu, a provincial office under the ritsuryō government which became an administrative, cultural, and military center of the province.

9. The law prescribes seven grounds for divorce of a wife by her husband as follows: childlessness; adultery; disobeying of parents-in-law; excessive talking; stealing; jealousy; serious disease (see Ryō no gige, "Ko-ryō," Article 28; Sansom, "Early Japanese Laws," Part Two, 142). In this case, the only possible grounds are disobeying of parents-in-law or excessive talking.

10. Unidentified.

11. Unidentified.

rice cakes to the Three Treasures, you will get the strength of Nārā-yaṇa,[12] who was as strong as diamond. . . ." Accordingly we learn that this woman was endowed with such strength because of having made big rice cakes to offer to the monks of the Three Treasures in her past life.

# 28

*On the Destitute Woman Who Prayed to the Sixteen-foot*
*Śākyamuni Buddha for a Share of Benefits*
*and Immediately Attained a Great Fortune*
*Brought by a Miraculous Event*[1]

In the reign of Emperor Shōmu, there lived a woman on the west side of Daian-ji[2] in the capital of Nara. She was extremely poor and, being without any means of livelihood, suffered from hunger. Having heard that the Sixteen-foot Buddha[3] of Daian-ji was ready to grant wishes immediately, she bought flowers, incense, and lamp oil, and went to make a petition before the Buddha, saying, "As I did not produce good causes in my previous lives, I am suffering from extreme poverty in my present body. Please give me some wealth to save me from dire poverty." She never ceased to pray for days and months.

One day she went as usual to pray to the Buddha for wealth, offered flowers, incense, and oil lamps, and went home to sleep. The next morning she got up to find four *kan* of coins[4] by the gate bridge. Attached was a plate which said that they were the Dai-sutaraku 大修多羅供 fund of Daian-ji.[5] In awe she sent them immediately to the temple. Thereupon, the monks of the Sutara seminar group checked the treasury and found that the seal was not broken but that four *kan* of coins were missing. So they put them back in the safe.

12. In the Buddhist tradition the name is used to refer to a legendary hero of great strength.

1. Cf. *Konjaku monogatarishū* (XII, 15).
2. See II.24, n. 4.
3. 丈六佛 ; see I.32, n. 6.
4. 四貫錢; see II.6, n. 6.
5. At Daian-ji there were five seminar groups, namely, Sutara, Sanron, Betsusanron, Ritsu, and Shōron. See II.24, n. 6. Each of them had its own office, treasury, and officers.

Again she went to the Sixteen-foot Buddha, offered flowers, incense, and lamps, and returned home to sleep. The next morning she found the four *kan* of coins in the garden. The attached plate said that they were from the Jō-sutaraku 常修多羅供[6] fund of Daian-ji. Therefore she sent them back to the temple. The monks of that group checked the iron safe, but it was sealed. When they opened it, they discovered that four *kan* of coins were missing. In wonder they sealed the safe.

As usual she went back to the Sixteen-foot Buddha, praying for a share of benefits, and came home to sleep. When she opened the door the next day, there were the four *kan* of coins in front of the threshold. The plate attached to them said they were from the *Jōjitsu-ron* 成實論[7] group fund of Daian-ji, so she sent them back to the temple. The monks of that seminar checked their safe, but it was sealed. When they opened it, they found exactly four *kan* of coins missing.

Accordingly, the treasurers of the six schools[8] got together in wonder, asking her, "Which practice have you been observing?" She answered, "Nothing in particular. As I am extremely poor with no means of livelihood, no one to depend on, and nothing to take recourse to, I have only been asking for a share of benefits." Hearing that, the monks consulted and said, "Since this is the money Buddha gave her, we won't keep it in our safe anymore." They returned the money to her. She made the gift of four *kan* of coins a step for further advancement,[9] attained a great fortune, and enjoyed a long life.

Indeed, we know this took place by the miraculous power of the Sixteen-foot Śākya and the woman's utmost devotion.

6. At both Daian-ji and Gufuku-ji there are Dai-sutara and Jō-sutara groups. According to Tamura, these groups were devoted to the study of the *Dai hannya-kyō;* the prefixes "Dai" and "Jō" are taken from the word 大乘 *daijō.* Since this scripture consists of six hundred volumes, Tamura maintains that the scripture was divided between the two groups (See Tamura, *Asuka Bukkyōshi kenkyū,* 129).

7. The group seems to be devoted to the study of the *Jōjitsu-ron* (*Taishō,* XXXII, No. 1616), although the "Daian-ji garan engi" does not have any record of such a group. Inoue Mitsusada infers that Sutara and Jōjitsu are the same and interchangeable ("Nanto rokushū no seiritsu," *Nihon rekishi,* No. 156, 11–12), but they seem to be separate groups with separate offices and treasuries. Since the Sanron group has the second largest fund at Daian-ji, it is possible that Kyōkai may have confused it with the Jōjitsu, since the two are similar in their tenets.

8. The Six Nara Schools came into existence between 747 and 751, from the latter years of Emperor Shōmu's reign to the beginning of Empress Shōtoku's reign. The six schools in this story may mean the Six Nara Schools (see Chap. I(1)c, n. 63), or the seminar groups which existed at Daian-ji at that time, five of which are recorded in the "Daianji garan engi," or in Kyōkai's general statement.

9. 増上緣 *zōjōen,* all causes which contribute to the emergence of a thing.

# 29

*On the Most Venerable Gyōgi, Who Accused a Woman of Having
Smeared Her Hair with Animal Oil Recognized
with His Penetrating Eye[1]*

In the village of Gangō-ji in the old capital,[2] there was once held a
service at which the Most Venerable Gyōgi[3] was invited to preach
Buddhist teachings for seven days. Accordingly, both clergymen and
laymen gathered to listen. In the congregation a woman whose hair
was smeared with animal oil, listened to the preaching. He saw and
accused her, saying, "That smell is offensive to me. Take the woman
whose hair is smeared with blood far away." Greatly ashamed, she
left the place.

Although our mediocre eyes[4] see only the hue of oil, the sage's
penetrating eye[5] sees real animal blood. He is an incarnation of the
Buddha,[6] the sage in disguise.[7]

# 30

*On the Extraordinary Sign of the Most Venerable
Gyōgi Who Perceived a Woman with a Child Loaded
with Past Enmity and Made Her Throw the
Child into the Stream[1]*

The Most Venerable Gyōgi opened up a canal from Naniwa, built
ferries, and preached Buddhist teachings to convert people. Clerical

1. One of the Venerable Gyōgi cycle. Cf. *Sanbō ekotoba* (II, 3), *Konjaku monogatarishū* (XVII,
36).
2. See I.3, n. 9.
3. See Chap. I(1)d.
4. 凡夫肉眼 *bonbu no nikugen;* physical eyes of ordinary men.
5. 聖人明眼 *shōnin no myōgen* (天眼 in the heading), sage's clairvoyance; see Chap. II(2)c,
n. 109.
6. 化身聖.
7. 隠身聖.

1. One of the Venerable Gyōgi cycle. Cf. *Konjaku monogatarishū* (XVII, 27).

and lay, high and low, all gathered to hear him. One day a woman from the village of Kawamata, Wakae district, Kawachi province 河內國若江郡川派里[2] came to the meeting with a child to hear the teachings. The child fretted and cried so much that she could not hear, and the child could not walk although he was over ten. Fretting and crying, he drank milk and ate incessantly. The venerable master said to her, "Come, my good woman—take your child outside and throw him into the stream!" Hearing that, the congregation whispered, "What causality[3] made such a compassionate sage to speak like that?" But the mother's affection prevented her from abandoning the child; still holding him, she listened to the preaching.

The next day she returned with the child to hear the teachings, and the child again cried so loudly that the audience could not hear. Accusing the mother, the venerable master said to her, "Throw the child into the stream!" Though troubled by doubts, the mother could not stand the loud cries and threw him into the deep stream. The child rose to the surface and, treading water and rubbing his hands together, he stared at her with big shining eyes and said with bitterness, "What a pity! I planned to exploit you by eating for three more years." Bewildered, the mother came back to her seat to hear the preaching. The venerable master asked her, "Did you throw away your child?" Whereupon she told him the whole sequence in detail. Then he explained, "In your previous existence you borrowed his things and did not return them, so he became your child and got back what you owed him by eating. That child was your creditor in your past life."

What a shame! We should not die without paying off our debts. Otherwise we reap the penalty without fail in our future life. Accordingly, the *Shutchō-gyō* says: "Because of a pennyworth debt of salt to the driver he was born as an ox and driven hard to carry a load of salt on his back to make up for his debt by labor."[4] This refers to the same type of thing.

---

2. Present Kawamata, Fuse, Higashi-ōsaka-shi 東大阪市布施川俣.

3. 因縁.

4. Not an exact quotation but a summary of a passage in the *Shutchō-gyō* (*Taishō*, VI, 425). There were two brothers; one chose to become an arhat, the other remained a layman who would never listen to his brother's preaching. Once the arhat met his brother born as an ox and loaded with burdens. The arhat told the driver of the ox that his brother had been born as an ox because of his debt of salt to the driver.

# 31

## On the Birth of a Girl with Sari in Her Hand Owing
## to Her Parents' Vow to Build a Pagoda[1]

Niu no atae Otokami 丹生直弟上[2] was a man of Iwata district, Tōtōmi province 遠江國磐田郡.[3] Although he made a vow to build a pagoda, he could not fulfill the vow for many years. He always regretted this and tried hard to find a way to do it. In the reign of Emperor Shōmu, a girl was born to Otokami, though he was seventy and his wife was sixty-two. The baby's left hand was clenched. In wonder, the parents tried to open it, but it was clenched more tightly than ever and never opened. Lamenting, they said, "It is a great shame for us to have given untimely birth to a crippled baby. But you are born to us as a result of the work of causality." And they nursed her with great care and never neglected her.

She grew up with fine features. At the age of seven she opened her fist to show it to her mother, saying, "Look at this!" When the mother looked at the child's palm, she found two pieces of *sari*,[4] the sacred ashes of Buddha. In joy and wonder she relayed the news to people everywhere. All were rapturous with joy. Provincial magistrates and district governors rejoiced, organized a devotees' association[5] to build a seven-story pagoda, and enshrined the *sari* in the pagoda during a dedication service. This is the pagoda of Iwata-dera 磐田寺[6] which stands in Iwata district now. At the completion of the pagoda, the child suddenly passed away.

This is what people mean when they say that a vow once made will be achieved and fulfilled without fail.

# 32

## On Rebirth as an Ox to Make up for the Unpaid
## Debt of Rice Wine for the Temple Fund[1]

In the reign of Emperor Shōmu, villagers of Mikami, Nagusa dis-

---

1. Cf. *Konjaku monogatarishū* (XII, 2).
2. Unknown.
3. Present Iwata-gun, Shizuoka-ken 靜岡縣磐田郡.
4. See Chap. II(2)b, n. 98.
5. 知識 *chishiki*; see Chap. I(1)d.
6. Unidentified.

1. Cf. *Konjaku monogatarishū* (XX, 22). Similar to I.10, 20; II.9, 15; III.26, etc.

trict, Kii province 紀伊國名草郡三上村,[2] organized a devotees' association to rotate the medical fund[3] of Yakuō-ji 藥王寺,[4] (now called
Seta-dera 勢多寺). At Okada no suguri Obame's 岡田村主姑女[5] this
medical fund was used to gain profits in a brewery.[6]

One day a brindled calf came to the temple and lay at the pagoda.
The men of the temple chased it away, but it came back again to lie
down and would not leave. In wonder they asked people, saying,
"To whom does this calf belong?" But no one claimed it as his own.
Therefore the monks caught, tied, and kept it. After it grew up it was
driven into the fields of the temple.

After five years, Okada no suguri Iwahito 岡田村主石人, a patron
of the temple, had a dream in which he was chased, thrust down, and
trampled by the same calf. He screamed in terror. Then the calf asked,
"Do you know me?" He answered "No." The calf released him,
stepped back, and knelt, saying in tears, "I am Mononobe no Maro
物部麿[7] of the village of Sakura 櫻村.[8] (He was popularly called Shio-
tsuki 鹽春. When he was alive, he shot at a boar and thought he had
hit it, though he had missed. Therefore, he ground salt[9] and brought
it to the spot to find not a boar but an arrow stuck in the ground.
Laughing at him, villagers named him "Shio-tsuki" [salt grinder],
which became his popular name). In my previous existence I borrowed ten gallons of rice wine from the medical fund of the temple
and died without repaying it. Because of that I was reborn as an ox
and driven hard to atone for my debt. My service was set for eight
years. As I have worked for five years, I have three more years to go.
Men of the temple have driven me so mercilessly, whipping my back,
that I have suffered greatly. I am telling you of my sad plight, for
you are the only one who has shown me mercy."

Iwahito asked, "How can I know if your story is true?" The ox
replied, "Please inquire of Ōomina of Sakura 櫻大娘[10] to find whether
or not my story is true. (Ōomina was Iwahito's sister, a mistress in
charge of the rice wine brewery.) In great wonder he visited his sister
to tell her the whole story in detail. Then she said, "That story is true.

2. Present Kaiso-gun, Wakayama-ken 和歌山縣海草郡.
3. 藥分 yakubun; the fund used to distribute medicine to people. Capital was accumulated
from the proceeds of rice and wine loans.
4. Judging from the name, it may have served as a medical center.
5. Since the title suguri was often conferred on immigrants, the Okada family may have
emigrated from the continent.
6. The temple made loans of rice and had the people brew wine, which was loaned again
to gain interest for medical expenses.
7. Unknown.
8. Unlocated.
9. He prepared the salt for the curing of the boar's flesh.
10. Meaning "Lady of Sakura village."

He did borrow ten gallons of rice wine and died without repaying it." When Jōtatsu 淨達,[11] a monk in charge of the temple household,[12] and patrons of the temple heard the story, they recognized the law of causality, and, moved by compassion, they held a service to recite scriptures for the ox. It disappeared at the end of eight years, and no one ever knew where it had gone; nor did it appear again.

We should remember that failure to pay debts will surely incur a penalty. Can you dare forget that? This is what the *Jōjitsu-ron* 成實論[13] has in mind when it says: "If man does not repay his debts, he will be reborn among such animals as oxen, deer, donkeys, and sheep in order to atone for his debts."

# 33

## *On a Woman Devoured by an Evil Fiend*[1]

In the reign of Emperor Shōmu a popular song spread all over the country:

Who asked you to be a bride,
Yorozu-no-ko of Amuchi-no-komuchi?
Namu, Namu.
Mountain ascetics inhale the breath,
Chanting formulas
Amashini, amashini.[2]

At that time there was a wealthy man who lived in the eastern part of the village of Amuchi, Tōchi district, Yamato province 大和國十市郡菴知村.[3] Kagamitsukuri no miyatsuko 鏡作造[4] was his surname. He had a daughter whose name was Yorozu-no-ko. She neither married nor made love. She was a beautiful girl, but, though men of

---

11. See *Shoku Nihongi*, III (Keiun 4:5:28); Snellen, "Shoku Nihongi," *JASJ*, Second Series, XI (December 1934), 239. A student monk who came back from Silla in 707.

12. 知寺僧 *chiji no sō*.

13. *Jōjitsu-ron*, VIII (*Taishō*, XXXII, 301).

1. Cf. *Konjaku monogatarishū* (XX, 37).

2. This song is hard to interpret, particularly the second half. Our translation depends on the *Nihon ryōiki* (*NKBT*). Its most interpretive and sensible explication is given by Kimoto Michifusa (*Jōdai kayō shōkai*) and quoted in the *Nihon ryōiki* (*NKBT*, 489).

. . . . . . . .
Namu, namu
The bridegroom came with decorated horses and oxen loaded with wine,
If Yorozu no ko had been wise, she would not have incurred her death.

3. Present Nikaidō, Tenri-shi Nara-ken 奈良縣天理市二階堂.

4. See *Nihon shoki*, XXIX (Tenmu 12:10:5). The title *muraji* was conferred on the Kagamitsukuri-no-miyatsuko family in 683. See Aston, "Nihongi," II, 361.

high rank proposed to her, she would not accept them. After several years, a man eventually came to propose with a present consisting of three carts loaded with pretty dyed silk cloths. She was happy at this and, becoming friendly with him, accepted his proposal and allowed him to enter the bedroom and consummate the marriage.

That night a voice was heard three times from the bedroom saying "It hurts!" Her parents heard, but ignored it and slept again, saying to each other, "She feels pain because she is not used to it."

The next morning because it grew late and she still did not get up, her mother knocked at the door of the bedroom, calling her daughter but getting no answer. Feeling uneasy, she opened the door and found her daughter completely eaten up except for her skull and one finger. Her parents were horrified and grieved at the sight. When they looked at the silk sent as a betrothal present, they discovered that it had turned into animal bones, and the three wagons into silverberry wood. People from all quarters came to hear and see what had happened, and all were filled with wonder. Her skull was put into a beautiful imported box, and the box was placed in front of the Three Treasures, where a vegetarian feast[5] was served on the first seventh morning.

Thus we suspect that an omen preceded the calamity. The song noted above was the omen. Some say that it was the mysterious work of a deity;[6] and others say she fell prey to a fiend.[7] On reflection, however, we know that this was a penalty for her past deeds. This is also an extraordinary event.

# 34

*On an Orphaned Girl Whose Devotion to the Bronze*
*Kannon Brought Her an Immediate Reward in a*
*Miraculous Event*[1]

In the neighborhood of Uetsuki-dera 殖槻寺 [2] on the West Side of Nara there was an orphaned girl. She was unmarried, and her name

5. 齋食 *saijiki*; see I.24, n. 3.
6. 神怪 *shinge*.
7. 鬼啖 *kitan*.

1. Cf. *Konjaku monogatarishū* (XVI, 8).
2. Or Kenpō-ji 建法寺, Kannon-ji 觀音寺. It was located next to Uetsuki Hachiman Shrine 植槻八幡宮, in present Yamato-kōriyama-shi 大和郡山市. See Fukuyama, *Narachō jiin*, 221–229.

is unknown. Her parents in their lifetime were very rich, built many houses and storehouses, and made a bronze Bodhisattva Kanzeon 觀世音菩薩,[3] two and a half feet high. They built a detached hall to enshrine the image and perform rites before it.

In Emperor Shōmu's reign the parents passed away, the slaves[4] ran away, and the cattle died. Thereupon, having lost her wealth and suffering from poverty, the girl stayed in the house and cried sorrowfully day and night. When she heard that Bodhisattva Kannon fulfilled the wishes of devotees, she offered flowers, incense, and lamps, holding the rope tied to the image[5] and praying for a good share of fortune, saying, "Since I am the only child, I have been all alone since the death of my parents. I have lost my fortune, and I am poor, lacking any means of livelihood. Will you please bring me a fortune immediately? Please give me a quick response!" Thus she wailed and prayed day and night.

In the same village there was a wealthy widower. He saw the girl and proposed to her through a go-between. She replied, "I am so poor that I am naked and have no clothes. How can I veil my face and go to talk with him?" The go-between reported her words to the widower, who said, "I know very well that she is poor and has no clothes. I only want to know if she accepts me." Therefore, the go-between visited the girl again to tell her the message, but again she said "No." Then the man forced his way in to call on and visit with her. Presently she accepted him and lay with him.

The next day it rained from morning till night. The rain kept him from leaving her, and he stayed for three days. Being hungry, he said, "I am hungry. Will you give me something to eat?" The wife said, "I will prepare a meal soon." She kindled fire in the stove and set an empty pot on the fire, crouching with her chin in her hands. Wandering in her empty house, she sighed sorrowfully, and after she had cleaned her mouth and washed her hands, she entered the sacred hall. In tears, holding the rope tied to the image, she implored, "Will you please save me from shame? Please bring me a fortune immediately." After that, she went out of the hall and crouched with her chin in her hands in front of the empty stove as before.

About four o'clock on that day there was a knock at the door, and somebody called to her. She went out and found the wet nurse of a

---

3. See Chap. I(1)a, n. 12.
4. 奴婢 *nuhi*; see Chap. I(1)a, n. 24.
5. See II.21, n. 8.

rich neighbor standing there. She had brought a big chest full of all kinds of food and drink, fragrant delicacies with nothing missing in metal bowls and on lacquered plates. She offered it to the wife, saying, "As we heard you have a guest, our master has prepared a present for you. Only please return the vessels when you have finished."

Greatly rejoicing, she was so overwhelmed with happiness that she took off her black robe to give to the messenger, saying, "I have nothing to offer you except my soiled clothes. Please accept this for your use." After the messenger put it on and left, she served the meal. At the sight the man wondered and looked at her face rather than at the feast.

After he had left the next day, ten rolls of silk and ten straw bags[6] of rice were sent from him with the following message: "Make your clothes out of the silk and wine out of the rice promptly." The girl visited the rich neighbors to thank them for their kindness, but the mistress said, "How funny you are! Or are you possessed by a spirit?[7] I do not know what you are talking about." The messenger, too, said, "I do not know either." Scolded by them, she went home and entered the hall to pay homage to the image as usual, and found her black robe draped on it. It was evident that this was a miracle of the Kannon. Therefore, she believed in the law of karmic causality and revered the image with increased faith. After that she gained a fortune as large as before and suffered from neither hunger nor sorrow. The couple enjoyed a long and happy life. This is a miraculous event.

# 35

*On the Penalty of Immediate Death from a Bad Disease for Hitting a Monk*[1]

Prince Uji 宇遅王 [2] was innately evil and had no faith in the Three Treasures. In the reign of Emperor Shōmu, this prince was traveling in Yamashiro 山背 [3] on an errand, accompanied by eight attendants.

6. 俵, one *hyō* contains 2.5 bushels of rice.
7. 鬼 *mono*.

1. Cf. *Genkō shakusho* (XXIX, 3).
2. Dates unknown. See *Shoku Nihongi*, XII (Tenpyō 9:9:28, 12:28); XIII (10:12:4). 從五位下宇治王爲中務大輔.
3. Present Kyoto-fu; see I.12, n. 6.

On his way to the capital of Nara, in Tsuzuki district 綴喜郡,[4] he met Taikyō 諦鏡,[5] a monk of Shimotsuke-dera 下毛野寺,[6] who had been traveling from Nara to Yamashiro. Taikyō happened to come upon the prince so suddenly that he could not find any place to which to retire and stood by the road, hiding his face with a hat.[7] Seeing this, the prince stopped his horse to have him whipped. Although the monk and his disciple ran into the rice paddy to escape, the attendants caught them and broke open the chests[8] they were carrying. Whereupon, the monk cried, "Why is there no guardian of dharma?"[9]

The prince had hardly moved on when he was attacked by a serious disease. He groaned loudly and leaped several feet off the ground. Seeing the prince suffering the attendants asked Taikyō to cure him, but Taikyō would not listen to them. They entreated him three times in vain. The monk asked, "Does he have pain?" To which they replied, "Yes, he is in great pain." Taikyō then said, "Let the unworthy prince suffer a thousand times, ten thousand times!"

At this, relatives of the prince addressed the emperor, saying, "Dharma Master Taikyō has cursed Uji," and they wanted to catch and kill him. Learning of their intention, the emperor did not allow them to do so. In three days the prince died, his body as black as ink. Again his relatives went to the emperor, saying, "'An eye for an eye.' We would like to take revenge by killing Taikyō, since Uji is already dead." The emperor addressed them, saying, "I am a monk, and so is Taikyō. How can a monk kill a monk? Taikyō is not responsible for Uji's incurring a calamity." Since the emperor had shaved his head, had been ordained, and followed the path of Buddha, he sided with the monk and would not let him be killed.[10]

The insane Prince Uji was so evil natured that the guardian of dharma punished him. The guardian of dharma is always present. How can we ignore this?

4. Present Tsuzuki-gun, Kyoto-fu 京都府綴喜郡.
5. Unknown.
6. An unlocated temple in Nara; it may be a family temple of the Shimotsuke family. See Fukuyama, *Naracho jiin*, 194–198. See also II.26, n. 3.
7. The *Sōni-ryō*, Article 19, states that monks and nuns must hide themselves when they meet a person of the Third Rank or higher on the road: they must stop their horse, salute, and pass on in case of meeting a person of the Fifth Rank or above or, if on foot, hide themselves. Monks were considered equal to persons of the Sixth Rank. Since Prince Uji had the Junior Fifth Rank, Lower Grade, Taikyō had to cover himself.
8. 蔵; the place to store valuables, or, in this case, Buddhist scriptures.
9. 護法 *gohō;* see II.1, n. 11.
10. Emperor Shōmu received the Mahayana bodhisattva precepts from Ganjin at the newly constructed ordination platform of Tōdai-ji and abdicated in 749. His clerical name is Shōman 勝満.

# 36

## *On the Wooden Image of Kannon Revealing Divine Power*[1]

In the reign of ex-Emperor Shōmu, the head of the image of Kannon, the attendant image on the east side of the Amida[2] in the golden hall of Shimotsuke-dera 下毛野寺[3] in the capital of Nara, fell off for no apparent reason. The patron of the temple discovered this and planned to repair it the next day. He came back to find that the head had returned to its place of its own accord, just as it had been before, and that now it gave off light.

Indeed we know that the dharma-body of wisdom[4] exists. This is a miraculous sign to bring the faithless to a realization of this.

# 37

## *On the Wooden Image of Kannon Which Revealed Divine Power, and Survived Fire*[1]

In the reign of Emperor Shōmu, a wooden image of Bodhisattva Shōkanjizai 正觀自在菩薩[2] was enshrined and venerated at a mountain temple of Upper Chinu, Izumi district, Izumi province 泉國泉郡珍努上.[3] Once a fire broke out and consumed the sacred hall. The wooden image of the Bodhisattva Kannon took about twenty steps out of the hall and lay down without sustaining any damage.

Indeed, we know that the Three Treasures shows its divine power although it cannot be recognized visually, having neither form nor mind.[4] This is the first of all wonders.

1. Cf. *Konjaku monogatarishū* (XVI, 11).
2. Kannon is made an attendant of Amida in the scriptures of the pure land school. See *Kanmuryōju-kyō* 觀無量壽經 (*Taishō*, XII, 265c).
3. See II.35, n. 6; Fukuyama, *Narachō jiin*, 194–198.
4. 理智法身 *richi-hosshin*; *dharmakāya* as embodiment of truth and wisdom. 理 often signifies the *tathatā*, supreme truth, true nature.

1. Cf. *Konjaku monogatarishū* (XVI, 12).
2. Kannon of the *Hoke-kyō*, *Muryōju-kyō*, *Kegon-gyō*, etc., in contrast to many Tantric variations of Kannon 變化觀音.
3. See II.2, n. 3.
4. 非色非心.

# 38

## On Rebirth as a Snake Because of Avarice[1]

In the reign of Emperor Shōmu, there was a monk who lived in a mountain temple of Maniwa 馬庭山寺[2] in the capital of Nara. When he was on the point of death, he said to his disciples, "After I die, you must not open the door of my room until three years have passed."

Seven times seven days after his death, a huge venomous snake was found lying at the door of the room. As the disciples understood why it had come, they counseled it, opened the door of the room, and found thirty *kan* of coins secretly stored there. With this money they recited scriptures, practiced good, and accumulated merits for the dead man.

Indeed we know that the dead monk returned in the form of a a snake to watch his hidden money because of his strong attachment to it. Here is an apt saying: "Even if you can see the top of Mt. Sumeru,[3] you can never see the top of Mt. Desire."

# 39

## On the Wooden Image of Yakushi Buddha Which Showed an Extraordinary Sign, Washed away in the Water and Buried in the Sand[1]

Between Suruga province 駿河國[2] and Tōtōmi province 遠江國[3] there flowed the river Ōigawa 大井河. Beside the river was the village of Uda 鵜田, which is in Harihara district 榛原郡, Tōtōmi province.[4] In the third month in the spring of the fifth year of the dog, the second

---

1. Cf. *Konjaku monogatarishū* (XX, 24).
2. Fukuyama locates it in the precincts of Tōdai-ji, near Maniwa no saka along the Saho River 佐保川. See his *Narachō jiin*, 277.
3. A cosmic mountain which stands in the center of the world. Taishakuten 帝釋天 resides on its summit.

1. Cf. *Konjaku monogatarishū* (XII, 12), *Genkō shakusho* (XXVIII).
2. Present Shizuoka-ken 靜岡縣.
3. Present Shizuoka-ken.
4. Unidentified.

year of the Tenpyō hōji era, in the reign of Emperor Ōhi 大炊天皇[5] who resided at Nara Palace, a voice crying, "Take me out! Take me out!" was heard from the sand on the beach at the village of Uda.

At that time a monk was traveling in Tōtōmi province, and, when he happened to pass the spot, he heard the voice calling persistently to be let out. The monk answered and could hear the voice coming from under the sand. Suspecting that some dead person buried there might have come to life, he dug and found a wooden image of Yakushi Buddha 藥師佛, six feet five inches high, with both ears missing. In tears, he paid homage to it, saying, "Great Master, what offense caused you to be a victim of flood? As I was destined by karma to find you, will you please let me repair you?"

He organized devotees,[6] invited a sculptor to fix the ears of the Buddha, and built a hall in the village of Uda to enshrine and venerate it. It is now called Uda-dō 鵜田堂. Clergy and laymen all revered this Buddha, for it gave off light, revealing a miraculous sign, and generously granted their wishes.

It was similar to the sandalwood statue made by Uten 優塡[7] which stood up to pay homage to Buddha, or the wooden image of Tinglan's mother[8] which moved as if alive as tradition says.[9]

# 40

## *On the Evil-loving Man Who Was Killed with Swords*
## *and Thus Got an Immediate Death Penalty*[1]

Tachibana no asomi Naramaro 橘朝臣諾樂麻呂[2] was a son of Prince Kazuraki 葛木王.[3] With overweening ambition he planned to usurp

5. Emperor Jun'nin (r. 758–764). This event took place in 758.
6. 知識 *chishiki*; see Chap. I(1)d, nn. 110, 111.
7. Udayana, king of the Kushan Empire, patron of Buddhism.
8. See I.17, n. 11.
9. *Shōkyō yōshū*, XV (*Taishō*, LIV, 74). 昔優塡初刻栴檀 . . .皆現寫眞容工圖妙相 故能流光動瑞 . . .丁蘭溫凊竭誠 木母以之變色. See Haraguchi, "*Nihon ryōiki* shutten goku kanken," *Kuntengo to kunten shiryō*, No. 34 (December 1966), 53–67.

1. Cf. *Shoku Nihongi*, XX (Tenpyō hōji 1:7:2, 3, 4). Similar to II.1, 35 and III.36 in the sense that men of high status and influence were punished as a consequence of their bad deeds and that none of these events are recorded in court histories.
2. Naramaro planned a rebellion against Fujiwara no Nakamaro (see III.38) with the support of Empress Kōken and Empress dowager Kōmyō. The rebellion failed and he died in 757.
3. (d. 757). In 736 Prince Kazuraki succeeded to his mother's surname and called himself Tachibana no Moroe 橘諸兄. He became Chancellor of the Senior First Rank, but was forced to resign by Fujiwara no Nakamaro in 756 and died in the following year. See *Shoku Nihongi*, XIX (Tenpyō shōhō 8:2:2).

the throne and summoned rebels to consult with him on the possibilities for a rebellion. He painted a monk's figure as a target and tried to shoot out the pupils of its eyes.[4] He loved to do evil deeds, but none was more evil than this.

Once a slave[5] of Naramaro went to Nara hills 諾樂山[6] to hunt birds with a hawk and found many young foxes there. He caught and skewered them with a stick, leaving the stick standing at the opening of the fox hole. Now, this man had a baby. The mother fox, seeking revenge, turned itself into the baby's grandmother. She took the baby in her arms and carried it to the entrance of the hole, threading it on a skewer and leaving it standing at the entrance as the man had done to her children.

Even a humble animal has the means to repay an evil deed. Immediate retribution lies at hand. How can we live without compassion? Merciless deeds will incur merciless revenge. Thus, Naramaro fell into disgrace with the emperor and was put to death not long after. We learn, therefore, that his evil deed in the above story was an omen of his fate of being killed by the sword. This is also a miraculous event.

# 41

## On a Woman Who Survived Violation of a Big Snake Owing to the Power of Drugs[1]

In the village of Umakai, Sarara district, Kawachi province 河內國更荒郡馬甘里,[2] there was a girl from a wealthy family. In Emperor Ōhi's reign, in the fourth month in the summer of the sixth year of the boar, the third year of the Tenpyō hōji era,[3] the girl climbed a mulberry tree to pick leaves. A large snake crawled up the tree after

4. According to Kitayama, the monk may be Gyōgi who sided with Fujiwara no Nakamaro. This is why Kyōkai wrote about the retribution of Naramaro as well as Prince Nagaya who was also opposed to Nakamaro. See Kitayama, *Nihon kodai seijishi*, 269–330.

5. 奴 *yakko*, the same as *nuhi*; see Chap. I(1) a, n. 24.

6. Nara-yama, present Sahosaki kyūryō 佐保佐紀丘陵; hills north of Nara between Nara Basin and Kyoto Basin.

1. Cf. *Konjaku monogatarishū* (XXIV, 9). Buddhist adaptation of the snake-lover theme which is also found in II.8, 12. According to Fujisawa Morihiko, a similar legend is found in the tradition of a tribe in Taiwan (see his *Nihon densetsu kenkyū*, IV, 43). A condensed translation of this story is given by D. L. Philippi, "Ancient Tales of Supernatural Marriage," *Today's Japan*, V (No. 3, 1960), 19–23.

2. Present Kita-kawachi-gun, Ōsaka-fu.

3. 759.

her. When a passerby saw it and warned her, she was frightened and fell to the ground. The snake, too, dropped down after her, wrapping itself around her and creeping into her vagina while she lay unconscious. Seeing this, her parents sent for a doctor of medicine[4] and brought their daughter home with the snake on the same bedding, placing it in the yard. Then the doctor burned three sheaves (which means a bundle three feet high) of millet stalks[5] and put the ashes into hot water to get fourteen gallons of liquid, which were boiled down to nine gallons and added to ten bunches of chopped-up boar's hair. After that, the people hung her on stakes by her head and two feet, and poured the prepared brew into the vaginal opening. When they had poured in five gallons of the brew, the snake came out and was killed and thrown away. The snake's eggs were white just like frog's eggs, and approximately two and a half gallons of them came out of the vagina, with boar's hairs sticking to them. When the people had poured in nine gallons of brew, all the snake eggs came out.

The girl, who had fainted, woke up and began to speak. At the inquiry of her parents she answered, "I felt I was dreaming, but now I am awake and all right." Since drugs work effectively, we should deal with them very carefully. After three years she died, having been violated by a snake again.

When man dies and leaves his parents, spouse, and children, he will say, "After death I will not fail to see you again in my next life." According to the law of karmic causality, one is reborn as a snake, horse, cow, dog, or bird, or falls in love with a snake[6] because of evil deeds in the past, or is born in the form of a ghostly creature. Sensual attachments are not all the same.

A scripture[7] describes it in this way: Once, when Buddha and Ānanda[8] were passing a cemetery, a man and wife were making offerings at the tomb and wailing their attachment to the dead. The man cried out of his love for his mother[9] while the wife wept.[10] Buddha heard the woman crying and lamented aloud. Ānanda asked Buddha, "Why are you lamenting, Tathāgata?" Buddha said to him, "This

4. 藥師 kusushi; see Chap. II(3)a, n. 125; II.7, n. 15.
5. 稷藁三束 awakibi wara sanzoku.
6. Or "makes love as a snake."
7. Unidentified.
8. Śākyamuni's favorite disciple. As he accompanied the Master for more than twenty years, he played an important role in relaying Śākyamuni's teachings.
9. There is some confusion in the relationships of the people involved. Although the text depicts a couple and a woman in this passage, the following words of Buddha are about a couple.
10. The woman cried for her present father-in-law and former husband.

woman had a son in her previous existence. She was so attached to him that she kissed his penis. After three years she contracted a serious disease, and at the last moment she caressed him, kissing his penis and saying, "I will see you in my future existences." She was reborn as the daughter of a neighbor, eventually became the wife of her own son, and is now crying over the ashes of her former husband. Since I know the chain of causation,[11] I am lamenting."

Another scripture[12] gives this story: Once there was a child who was very light and could run as fast as a flying bird. His father loved him so much that he cared for him as he would care for his own eyes. Once when the father saw the child's agility, he commented, "Good for you, my child! You run as fast as a fox!" Then the child died, and was later reborn in the form of a fox.

You should think only of good analogies and not bad ones, for you will incur retribution [for what you say].

# 42

*On the Destitute Woman Whose Devotion to the Image*
*of the Thousand-armed Kannon Brought a Great Fortune*
*in Response to Her Wish for a Share of Benefits*[1]

Amanotsukai Minome 海使茨女[2] lived at the Ninth Street, Second Avenue, on the East Side of Nara 諾樂左京九條二坊. She had given birth to nine children, and, as she had no means of livelihood, she was extremely poor. She had been praying to the Thousand-armed Kannon[3] of Anaho-dera 穴穗寺[4] for a share of fortune for nearly a year.

In the reign of Emperor Ōhi 大炊, on the tenth of the tenth month in the winter of the tenth year of the hare, the seventh year of the Tenpyō hōji era,[5] her sister happened to visit her and left a chest made of

11. 本末事.
12. Unidentified.

1. Cf. *Konjaku monogatarishū* (XVI, 10). Similar to II.28, 34.
2. Unknown.
3. Senju Kannon 千手觀音; see Chap. II(3)b, nn. 138, 139, 141.
4. Although the text has 向穗, Kariya maintains that it is a compiler's or copier's mistake to replace 穴 with 向. However, Fukuyama says it should be read as 向穗積寺 and that 積 has been left out since the *Konjaku* gives this name. The Hozumi-dera existed in the city of Nara. See Fukuyama, *Narachō jiin*, 313–315.
5. 743, in the reign of Emperor Jun'nin.

leather, the legs of which were soiled with horse dung. The sister said, "Will you keep it for awhile? I will be back shortly." Having waited for the sister's return in vain, the woman went to her brother to inquire about it, but he said, "I know nothing about it."

Then she opened the chest out of curiosity and found a hundred *kan* of coins in it. When she bought flowers, incense, and oil, and went to Kannon to offer them as usual, she noticed that its feet were soiled with horse dung. Thereupon, she suspected that the money was given by the Bodhisattva. It was discovered after three years that a hundred *kan* of coins had disappeared from the construction fund donated to Senju-in 千手院.⁶ Thus it was evident that the leather chest contained the money of the temple. Indeed, we know that the money was the gift of the Kannon to her.

The note says: Happy was the mother of the Amanotsukai family. In the morning she had looked at her hungry children, shedding tears of blood, while in the evening she had burned incense, praying for Kannon's power. She had been given the money as a reward for her faith and was able to put an end to her worries; Kannon fulfilled her wishes, letting the springs of great fortune flow to allow her to bring up her children with enough food and clothes.

Indeed, we know that the merciful one⁷ came to her aid to repay her continual offerings. The *Nehan-gyō* gives this relevant passage: "By loving the child, the mother is reborn into Bonten 梵天."⁸ This is a miraculous event.

6. A temple to enshrine Senju Kannon.
7. 慈子, man of mercy.
8. The Brahama's heaven, first and lowest of the four *dhyāna* heavens.

# NIHONKOKU GENPŌ ZEN'AKU RYŌIKI

## VOLUME III

by Kyōkai

Monk of Yakushi-ji
on the West Side of Nara

## CONTENTS

Thirty-nine Stories on the Karmic Retribution of Good and Evil

Preface     221

1. On the Tongues of the Reciters of the *Hoke-kyō* Which Did Not Decay in the Skulls Exposed to the Elements     223
2. On the Mutual Revenge for Killing by Being Reborn as a Fox and a Dog     225
3. On a Monk Who Received an Immediate Reward because of his Devotion to the Eleven-headed Kanzeon Image     226
4. On a Monk Who Was Saved from Drowning in the Sea by Reciting a Mahayana Scripture     227
5. On Bodhisattva Myōken's Incarnation as a Deer to Detect a Thief     229
6. On the Fish Which a Monk Wanted to Eat and Which Turned into the *Hoke-kyō* to Defend Him against Popular Abuse     230
7. On a Narrow Escape from Death with the Protection of the Wooden Kannon Image     231
8. On a Miraculous Appearance of Bodhisattva Miroku in Response to the Vow     232
9. On King Yama Showing an Extraordinary Sign and Advising That People Practice Good     233
10. On the *Hoke-kyō* Copied with Devotion and Reverence Surviving a Fire     235
11. On a Blind Woman Whose Sight Was Restored Owing to Her Devotion to the Wooden Image of Yakushi Buddha     236
12. On a Blind Man Whose Sight Was Restored Owing to His Chanting of the Name of Nichimanishu of the Thousand-armed Kannon     237
13. On a Man Who Made a Vow to Copy the *Hoke-kyō* and

Who Was Saved from a Dark Pit Devoid of Sunlight
Owing to the Power of His Vow   238

14. On Receiving an Immediate Penalty of Violent Death
because of Hitting the Reciter of the Dharani of the
Thousand-armed Kannon   239

15. On Receiving an Immediate Penalty of Violent Death
because of Hitting a Begging Novice   241

16. On a Licentious Woman Whose Children Cried for Milk,
Receiving an Immediate Penalty   242

17. On an Extraordinary Sign of an Unfinished Clay Image
Groaning   244

18. On the Immediate Penalty of Violent Death for a
Licentious Scripture Copier Who Copied the *Hoke-kyō*   245

19. On a Girl Born of a Flesh Ball Who Practiced Good and
Enlightened People   246

20. On Immediately Getting a Twisted Mouth by Speaking Ill
of a Woman Copying the *Hoke-kyō*   248

21. On a Monk Whose Blind Eye Was Cured by Having the
*Kongō hannya-kyō* Recited   249

22. On Being Repaid Good and Evil for Copying the *Hoke-kyō*
and for Exploiting Others with Heavy Scales   250

23. On the Immediate Repayments of Good and Evil in Return
for a Vow to Copy the *Dai hannya-kyō* and for the Use of
the Temple Property   252

24. On Being Born as a Monkey for Keeping Men from
Seeking the Way   253

25. On Being Saved by Reciting the Name of Śākyamuni
Buddha While Drifting on the Ocean   255

26. On Receiving the Immediate Penalty of Violent Death for
Collecting Debts by Force and with High Interest   257

27. On an Extraordinary Sign of a Skull Shown to the Man
Who Removed a Bamboo Shoot from Its Eye and Prayed
for It   259

28. On an Extraordinary Sign Shown by the Sixteen-foot-high
Image of Miroku, the Neck of Which Was Bitten by Ants   261

29. On the Immediate Penalty of Violent Death Incurred by
an Ignorant Man Who Broke a Wooden Buddha Image a
Village Child Had Made in Playing   262

30. On the Monk Who Accumulated Merits by Making
Buddhist Images and Showed an Extraordinary Sign at the
End of His Life   263

31. On a Woman Who Gave Birth to Stones and Enshrined
Them as Kami   265

32. On a Fisherman Netting Fish Who Was Almost Drowned
in the Sea but Saved Owing to His Devotion to
Bodhisattva Myōken   266

33. On the Immediate Penalty of Violent Death for
Persecuting a Humble, Begging Novice   267

34. On Gaining an Immediate Cure of a Bad Disease for Being
    Ordained and Practicing Good     270
35. On Being Penalized for Abusing an Official's Authority
    and Ruling Unrighteously     271
36. On Receiving a Penalty for Building a Lower Pagoda and Taking
    down the Banners of the Temple     273
37. On Receiving a Penalty for Doing Evil because of Ignorance of
    the Law of Karmic Causation     274
38. On the Appearance of Good and Evil Omens Which Were
    Later Followed by Their Results     276
39. On the Rebirth as a Prince of a Monk Who Excelled in
    Both Wisdom and Discipline     283

# Preface to Volume III[1]

The Inner Scriptures[2] show how good and evil deeds are repaid, while the Outer Writings[3] show how good and bad fortunes bring merit and demerit. If we study all the discourses Śākyamuni made during his lifetime, we learn that there are three periods: first, the period of the true dharma (shōbō 正法), which lasts five hundred years; second, the period of the counterfeit dharma (zōbō 像法), lasting a thousand years; and third, the period of the degenerate dharma (mappō 末法), which continues for ten thousand years. By the fourth year of the hare, the sixth year of the Enryaku era,[4] seventeen hundred and twenty-two years have passed since Buddha entered nirvana.[5] Accordingly, we live in the age of the degenerate dharma following the first two periods. Now in Japan, by the sixth year of the Enryaku era, two hundred and thirty-six years have elapsed since the arrival of the Buddha, Dharma, and Samgha.[6] Flowers bloom without voice, and cocks cry without tears. In the present world those who practice good are as few as flowers on rocky hills, but those who do evil are as plentiful as weeds in the soil. Without knowing the law of karmic retribution, one offends as easily as a blind man loses his way. A tiger is known by its tail.[7] Those devoted to fame, profit, and killing doubt the immediate repayment of good and evil which occurs as quickly as a mirror reflects. One who is possessed of an evil spirit is like one who holds a poisonous snake; the poison is always there ready to appear.

The great power of karmic retribution reaches us as quickly as sound echoes in a valley.[8] If we call, the echo never fails to answer, and this is the way karmic retribution works in this life. How can we fail to be more careful? It is useless to repent after spending a lifetime in vain. Who can enjoy immortality since you are given a limited life? How can you depend on your transient life as being eternal? We are already in the age of the degenerate dharma.[9] How can we live with-

---

1. The Shinpukuji manuscript lacks the first ten lines of the preface. The only extant manuscript which has this paragraph is the Maeda manuscript, and thus this portion is called "Unknown Passage of the Maeda Manuscript." For a discussion of it, see Chap. I(1)b. It consists of one hundred and seventy-seven characters, translated as the first paragraph.

2. 內經 naikyō; see I.Preface, n. 1.

3. 外典 geten; see I. Preface, n. 2.

4. 787.

5. See Chap. I(1)b, n. 36. The date around 480 B.C. is accepted by most modern scholars.

6. 538 or 552. There is an indication that Kyōkai adopts 552 as the year for the official introduction of Buddhism to Japan.

7. The text may be corrupt.

8. See Chap. I(2)a, n. 139; I.Preface, n. 24.

9. 末劫 matsugō; 劫 kō, an abbreviated transliteration of Skt. kalpa, an astronomical length of time.

out doing good? My heart aches for all beings. How can we be saved from calamity in the age of the degenerate dharma? If we offer monks only a handful of food, the merit of our good deed will save us from the calamity of hunger. If we keep a precept of nonkilling for a day, we will be saved from the calamity of sword and battle.

Once there was a full-fledged monk who lived on a mountain and practiced meditation. At every meal he shared his food with a crow which came to him every day. After a vegetarian meal, he chewed a toothpick,[10] cleaned his mouth, washed his hands and played with a stone. The crow was behind the hedge when he threw the stone. He hit the crow without knowing that it was there. The crow died on the spot, its head crushed into pieces, and was reborn as a boar. The boar lived in the same mountain as the monk. It happened to go to the place above his hut, rooting about among the rocks for food, whereupon one of the rocks rolled down and killed the monk. Although the boar had no intention of killing him, the rock rolled down by itself. A sin committed by an action which is neither good nor bad[11] will in turn generate the same kind of action. In the case of intentional murder, how is it possible to escape the penalty? A deluded mind produces the seed and fruit of evil; an enlightened mind produces the seed of good to attain Buddhahood.

I, the mediocre monk Kyōkai, have not studied enough to ask questions in the manner of the Tendai Sage.[12] Nor am I sufficiently enlightened to answer in the manner of holy and eloquent men.[13] My efforts are like bailing water out of the ocean with a shell or looking at the sky through a straw. Though I am not an eminent monk who transmits the light of dharma[14] I try hard to meditate on it, following the path to the pure land and directing the mind toward enlightenment. I repent of my previous misdeeds and pray for future good. By editing these stories of miraculous events I want to pull the people forward by the ears, offer my hand to lead them to good, and show them how to cleanse their feet of evil. My sincere hope is that we may all be reborn in the western land of bliss, leaving no one on the earth, and live together in the jeweled palace in heaven, abandoning our earthly residence.

10. See I.26, n. 5.
11. 無記 muki. This story may have originated in the Bonmō-kyō bosatsukaihon-sho 梵網經菩薩戒本疏 (Taishō, XL, 611), according to Haraguchi ("Nihon ryōiki shutten goku kanken," Kuntengo, No. 34, 61–62).
12. 天台智者; see Chap. I(1)b, n. 51.
13. 神人辯者.
14. 傳燈良匠.

# I

*On the Tongues of the Reciters of the* Hoke-kyō
*Which Did Not Decay in the Skulls Exposed
to the Elements*[1]

In the reign of Empress Abe 帝姫阿倍天皇[2] who governed Ōya-shima[3] at Nara Palace, there was a monk, Dhyāna Master Eigō 永興[4] in the village of Kumano in Muro district, Kii province 紀伊國牟妻郡熊野村.[5] He taught and guided the people by the sea. His contemporaries revered him as a bodhisattva, respecting his self-discipline.[6] As he lived in a place south of the imperial capital, he was called the Bodhisattva of the South 南菩薩.[7]

Once a *dhyāna* master came to the bodhisattva. He had with him a copy of the *Hoke-kyō* (written with very small characters in one scroll),[8] a pewter pitcher, and a stool made of rope.[9] He used to recite the *Hoke-kyō* constantly. After one year or so, he thought of leaving Dhyāna Master Eigō, and with a bow presented his stool as an offering, saying, "I am leaving you and going into the mountains to cross over to Ise province 伊勢國.[10] Hearing this, the master gave him one bushel of ground dry glutinous rice, and had two lay brothers accompany him to see him on his way. After having been escorted for a day, he gave them his *Hoke-kyō*, bowl, and ground dry rice, and sent them back, while he continued with only twenty yards of hemp rope and a pewter pitcher.

After two years had passed, the villagers of Kumano went up to a mountain by the upper stream of the Kumano to cut down trees

1. This section consists of two independent stories on the same motif of the "singing skull." See Chap. II(1)b, n. 41, and (3)a. Cf. *Konjaku monogatarishū* (XII, 31), *Genkō shakusho* (XXIX, 3).

2. Teiki Abe no sumeramikoto, that is, Empress Kōken 孝謙 (r. 749–757) or Shōtoku 稱德 (r. 764–770), twice enthroned. It is hard to know whether this story should be dated in her first or second reign.

3. See II.1, n. 3.

4. See III.2, nn. 3, 4, 5. Also see the *Shoku Nihongi*, XXXII (Hōki 3:3:6). He was appointed as one of the ten *dhyāna* masters in 772.

5. In the vicinity of present Shingū-shi, Wakayama-ken 和歌山縣新宮市.

6. 行 *gyō*.

7. Minami no bosatsu.

8. Kyōkai's note.

9. Monks are allowed to possess and carry scriptures, a begging bowl, a pitcher of water for drinking and washing, a stick, a toothpick, a stool made of rope, etc. in traveling. In the Mahayana tradition, the number of such items is eighteen (十八物 *jūhachimotsu*).

10. Present Mie-ken 三重縣.

to build a boat. They heard a voice reciting the *Hoke-kyō*, and it did not stop for days and months. Listening to the voice reciting the scripture, the boat builders felt faith and reverence arising, and, with their rationed food as an offering, they looked everywhere for the reciter. Although they could find no trace of him, the voice reciting the scripture went on as before.

After half a year, they returned to the mountain to draw out the boat. Again they heard the voice continuously reciting the scripture. They reported this to Dhyāna Master Eigō, and, as he also wondered about it, he went to the mountain and heard it for himself. After a search he discovered a corpse hanging over a cliff, its feet tied with a hemp rope, that of a man who had jumped to his death. Beside the corpse there was a pewter pitcher. It was evident that the corpse was that of the monk who had left him. At the sight Eigō wailed in sorrow and went back.

After three more years, villagers came to him, saying, "The voice has never ceased to recite the scripture." Eigō went back to collect the bones, and, when he looked at the skull, he found that the tongue was still alive and had not even begun to decay in the course of three years.

Indeed we know that this event occurred because of the mysterious power of the Mahayana scripture, and the merits of the late monk who had recited it.

The note says: What a noble thing it was for the *dhyāna* master to reveal a miraculous sign of the Mahayana scripture in his flesh-and-blood body by reciting the *Hoke-kyō* constantly! Though he flung himself from a cliff and was exposed to the elements, his tongue alone did not decay. Needless to say, he is sacred and not ordinary.

Also, on Kane-no-take 金峯 in Yoshino[11] there was a *dhyāna* master who went from peak to peak reciting the scripture. Once he heard a voice reciting the *Hoke-kyō* and *Kongō hannya-kyō* ahead of him. He stopped to listen to it, and, in searching in the bushes, he found a skull. Though it had been exposed to the elements for a long time, its tongue had not decayed but retained its life. The *dhyāna* master enshrined it in a purified place, saying to the skull, "By the law of causation I met you," and made a shelter above it with grass, living beside it to recite the scripture and hold services six times a day.[12] As he recited the *Hoke-kyō* the skull joined him, and its tongue vibrated. This is also a miraculous event.

11. Or Kinpu-sen in present Yoshino-gun, Nara-ken 奈良縣吉野郡.
12. 六時行道 *rokuji gyōdō*. See II.13, n. 6.

# 2

## *On the Mutual Revenge for Killing by Being Reborn as a Fox and a Dog*

Dhyāna Master Eigō was a monk[1] of Kōfuku-ji 興福寺[2] on the East Side of Nara. His secular name was Ashiya-no-kimi 葦屋君 family,[3] or Ichiki 市往 family,[4] according to one tradition. He came from Teshima district in Settsu province 攝津國手嶋郡.[5] He lived a disciplined life in the village of Kumano in Muro district, Kii province 紀伊國牟婁郡熊野村.[6]

Once a sick man in the village came to the temple where he lived, and asked him to cure his disease. As long as he chanted a formula, the patient was cured. If he stopped, however, the disease would return at once. Thus many days passed, and the man was not cured. Making a vow to cure the patient at any cost, the monk continued chanting the formula. Then, possessed by a spirit, the patient said, "I am a fox. I won't surrender easily, so don't try to force me!" The monk asked, "Why?" The patient replied, "This man killed me in his previous life, and I am taking revenge on him. If he dies eventually, he will be reborn as a dog and kill me." In amazement, the *dhyāna* master tried to teach and counsel the spirit, but it did not loosen its hold and finally killed the patient.

A year later, one of his disciples lay in the same room where the patient had been. A visitor tied his dog to a post and came to see the *dhyāna* master. Barking, the dog struggled to free itself from the leash and chain and tried to run away. Amazed, the master said to his visitor, "Set him free to find out the cause." As soon as the dog was released, it ran into the room of the sick disciple and came out with a fox in its mouth. Although the visitor tried to restrain the dog, it would not release the fox but bit it to death.

It was evident that the dead person had been reborn as a dog to take revenge on the fox. Ah! Revenge knows no limits. For King

---

1. 沙門 *shamon*; see Chap. I(1)a, n. 4.
2. It stands in the present Nara Park, Nara-shi 奈良市奈良公園. See I.6, n. 10.
3. The *Shinsen shōjiroku* lists it as an immigrant family in Settsu province.
4. The *Shinsen shōjiroku* says that the family is descended from a prince of Paekche.
5. Present Toyono-gun, Ōsaka-fu 大阪府豊能郡.
6. See III.1, n. 5.

Virūḍhaka 毗瑠璃王[7] killed ninety-nine million and nine hundred thousand men of the Śākyas to revenge the past. If vengeance is used to requite vengeance, then vengeance will never end, but will go on rolling like the wheel of a cart. Forbearance[8] is the virtue of the man who restrains himself by taking his enemy as a teacher and not seeking revenge. Accordingly, enmity is nothing but the teacher of forbearance. This is what the scripture[9] means when it says: "Without respect for the virtue of forbearance one would kill even one's own mother."

# 3

## On a Monk Who Received an Immediate Reward Because of His Devotion to the Eleven-headed Kanzeon Image[1]

The Venerable Bensō 辯宗[2] was a monk of Daian-ji.[3] As he was innately eloquent, he used to address the Buddha on behalf of devotees[4] and won many patrons[5] and popularity.

In the reign of Empress Abe, Bensō borrowed thirty *kan* of coins from the Sutaraku fund of the temple[6] for his own use and could not repay them. The officials of the temple[7] pressed him for repayment. As he had no means of repaying, he went up to a mountain temple of Hatsuse 泊瀬[8] and paid homage to the Eleven-headed Bodhisattva Kannon.[9] Holding the rope tied to the hand of the Bodhisattva Kannon, he prayed, saying, "I have spent the money from the Sutara fund of Daian-ji, but have no means to repay it. I beseech

7. The prince of King Prasenajit. Because of his mother's low status, he was humiliated at Kapilavastu, the castle of the Śākyas. Later, when he was enthroned, he gained revenge on the Śākyas by exterminating them. See *Zōitsu agon-gyō* 增一阿含經, XXVI (*Taishō*, II, 692).
8. 忍辱 *ninniku*, a translation of Skt. *kṣānti*, one of the six kinds of bodhisattvas' self-discipline. See I.6, n. 7.
9. Unidentified.

1. Cf. *Konjaku monogatarishū* (XVI, 27), *Hase-dera reigenki* (III).
2. Unknown.
3. See I.32, n. 6.
4. 白堂 *byakudō*; a kind of mediator who verbally formulates the devotees' wishes to the Buddha.
5. 檀越 *taniochi*; see I.7, n. 18.
6. See II.24, n. 6.
7. 維那 *ina*, one of the *sangō* 三綱, samgha officials. See Chap. I(1)d, n. 84.
8. Present Hase-dera, Hatsuse-machi, Shiki-gun, Nara-ken.
9. See Chap. II(3)b, nn. 137, 142.

you to give me the money." He chanted the name of Kannon and prayed. The officials followed him there to ask for repayment. He answered them, saying, "Please wait for a moment. I am praying to the Bodhisattva for the money for repayment. It won't take long."

At that time Prince Fune 船親王,[10] led by a good cause, came to the mountain temple and held a service. Holding the rope tied to the image, Bensō continued praying, "Please give me the money so that I may repay it at once." Hearing this, the prince asked Bensō's disciple, "What makes him pray like that?" The disciple told him about the whole affair. When the prince heard it, he gave the money to repay the debt.

Indeed we know that this was brought about by the great compassion of the Kannon and the utmost devotion of the monk.

# 4

## On a Monk Who Was Saved from Drowning in the Sea by Reciting a Mahayana Scripture

In the capital of Nara there was a fully qualified monk[2] whose name is unknown. He used to recite a Mahayana scripture[3] and lived as a layman, supporting his family by lending money. His only daughter married and lived separately with her husband. In the reign of Empress Abe, her husband was appointed an official in Mutsu province.[4] Therefore, he borrowed twenty *kan* of money from his father-in-law to outfit himself and went off to his new post. After many years, he repaid only the principal but not the interest, which had become as much as the principal in the course of time. Meanwhile the father-in-law asked for repayment. The son developed a secret hatred of him and looked for a chance to kill him. The father-in-law, however, did not know this and urged him, as usual, to repay the debt.

10. Or 船王, son of Prince Toneri 舎人親王, and a grandson of Emperor Tenmu; exiled to Oki because of his involvement in Nakamaro's rebellion. See III.38.

1. Cf. *Sanbō ekotoba* (II, 15), *Fusō ryakki* (VI, Genmyō), *Konjaku monogatarishū* (XIV, 38).
2. 大僧 *daisō*.
3. 方廣經典; see Chap. II(1)a, n. 8.
4. Mutsu is larger than other provinces, comprising present Fukushima, Miyagi, Iwate, and Aomori. Jō 掾 is a provincial magistrate of the third class (local magistrates are 守, 介, 掾, 目, 史生).

One day the son said to his father-in-law, "I would like to take you to Mutsu province." The latter agreed and got on board a ship for Mutsu. Plotting with the sailors, the son tied his father-in-law up and threw him into the sea. When he went home, he said to his wife, "As your father wanted to see you, I took him on the ship for the voyage. Before long we ran into a storm at sea, and the ship[5] sank. Your father, being beyond any means of rescue, was drowned. He drifted on the sea before he sank under the water, while I barely saved myself." The wife, greatly dejected by this news, wailed and said, "How unhappy I am to lose my father! Did my idea of inviting him cause me to lose my treasure? It would be easier to find a jewel on the bottom of the sea than to see him and collect his bones. What a pity!"

Meanwhile, the monk sank into the water, reciting a Mahayana scripture with utmost devotion, and found that the water left a hollow space allowing him to crouch safely on the bottom. After two days and nights another ship bound for Mutsu province sailed by. The sailors noticed the tip of a rope drifting on the sea, and, seizing it, pulled up the monk on the other end. He looked as well as ever. The sailors, therefore, wondered greatly and asked him, "Who are you?" He answered, "I am so and so. I met robbers and was thrown into the sea with my limbs bound with a rope." Then they asked him again, "Venerable Master, by what magic could you survive without being drowned in the water?" He said, "I am always reciting a Mahayana scripture. No doubt its mysterious power has saved me." Thus he never revealed his son-in-law's name. He asked then, "Will you take me to a port in Mutsu?" Accordingly, they took him there.

As for the son-in-law in Mutsu province, he held a service for the drowned father, making an offering to the Three Treasures. The father, who had been wandering and begging there, happened to attend the service with a group of self-ordained monks[6] and received an offering of food while his face was covered. When the son-in-law held out offerings for the monks, the drowned father put his hands out to receive them. The startled son-in-law shrank back in horror, his eyes shifting restlessly and his face flushing. He hid himself, stricken with terror. The smiling father-in-law showed no anger but only forbearance, never revealing the evil deed. Owing to the hollow space in the water, he did not drown; nor was he eaten by a poisonous fish, but remained safe in the sea. Indeed we know that this was

5. 驛船 ekisen; government boats for transportation. Cf. I.30, n. 6.
6. 自度 jido.

caused by the miraculous power of a Mahayana scripture and the protection of various Buddhas.

The note says: How good he was to be tolerant and not to accuse his son-in-law of his evil deed! Indeed he was the very model of fortitude. This is what the *Jōagon-gyō*[7] means when it says: "To requite vengeance with vengeance is like trying to put out a fire with hay, but to requite vengeance with mercy is like putting out a fire with water."

# 5

## On Bodhisattva Myōken's Incarnation as a Deer
## to Detect a Thief

In Asuka district, Kawachi province 河内國安宿郡,[1] there was a mountain temple of Shidehara 信天原山寺.[2] It was a place to offer lamps to Bodhisattva Myōken 妙見菩薩,[3] and every year lamps were offered from provinces around the capital.[4]

In the reign of Empress Abe, the devotees' association[5] held the usual celebration of offering lamps[6] to the Bodhisattva and made offerings of money and valuables to the monk in charge of the temple.[7] At that time his disciple stole five *kan* of money from the offerings and hid it. Later the disciple went to the spot to retrieve the money and discovered nothing but a dead deer with an arrow in it. Therefore, he went to the village of Inoue-dera 井上寺[8] near the city of Kawachi to get men to help him bring down the deer. When he led them to the spot, there was no deer but the five *kan* of money. In this way the thief was discovered.

Indeed, we know that the deer was not real but had been a temporary manifestation of the Bodhisattva. It is a miraculous event.

7. Kariya says that this passage is found not in the *Jōagon-gyō* but *Bonmō-kyō koshakki*, III (*Taishō*, XL, 712).

1. Present Minami-kawachi-gun, Ōsaka-fu 大阪府南河内郡.
2. Unidentified.
3. See Chap. II(3)b, n. 133.
4. 畿内 Kinai; see Chap. I(1)a, n. 3.
5. 知識 chishiki.
6. 燃燈 nentō.
7. 室主 muronushi.
8. Or Fukō-ji 普光寺, Torisaka-dera 鳥坂寺.

# 6

*On the Fish Which a Monk Wanted to Eat and Which*
*Turned into the Hoke-kyō to Defend Him*
*Against Popular Abuse*[1]

On Mt. Yoshino there was a mountain temple called Amabe-no-mine 海部峯.[2] In the reign of Empress Abe, a fully qualified monk lived an ardent life of self-discipline there. When he became too exhausted and weak to move around, he had a desire to eat fish and said to his disciple, "I would like to have fish. Will you go and get some for me to eat?" According to the master's wish, the disciple went to the seacoast of Kii province, bought eight fresh gray mullet,[3] and returned with them in a small chest.

On the way he happened to meet three familiar patrons of the temple who asked him, "What are you carrying in the chest?" The acolyte[4] answered, "This is the *Hoke-kyō*." However, the water from the fish dripped out of the chest, and it smelled. The laymen realized that it was not the scripture. Soon they came to the neighborhood of the market of Uchi in Yamato province大和國内市.[5] They rested beside the acolyte and pressed him, saying, "What you are carrying is not the scripture. It is fish." He replied, "It is not fish. It is nothing but the scripture." Then they forced him to open the chest. Having found it impossible to refuse, he opened it and discovered that the eight fish had turned into eight scrolls of the *Hoke-kyō*. At the sight the laymen were stricken with awe and wonder and left him.

One of them, however, was still suspicious, and, wanting to find out about the whole affair, followed him in secret. When the acolyte returned to the mountain temple, he reported to his master in detail what the laymen had done. Listening to him, the master felt wonder and joy in learning that heaven had protected him, and he ate the fish. Thereupon, the layman who had witnessed the whole series of events, prostrated himself on the ground and said to the *dhyāna* master,

1. Cf. *Sanbō ekotoba* (II, 16), *Konjaku monogatarishū* (XII, 37), *Genkō shakusho* (XII), *Hokke kenki* (I, 10).
2. Located at present Higashi-yoshino-mura, Yoshino-gun, Nara-ken 奈良縣吉野郡東吉野村.
3. 鯔 *nayoshi*, or *bora* in contemporary Japanese. See Sekine Shinryū, *Narachō shokuseikatsu no kenkyū*, 159–160, for its references in other documents.
4. 童子 *warawa;* see I.3, n. 8.
5. Unidentified.

"Fish turn into the *Hoke-kyō* when a sage eats them.[6] Because of our ignorant and wicked minds, we disturbed and accused him without knowing the law of causality. Will you please forgive our sin? From now on I acknowledge you as a great master and will serve you with reverence and offerings." After that he became a great patron of the temple and made offerings to the master.

Indeed, we know that the master saved himself through his devotion to dharma. As to his food, even poison turns into honeydew; eating fish is no offense for him. For fish is turned into a scripture, and heaven in sympathy prepares a way for him. This is also a miraculous event.

# 7

## *On a Narrow Escape from Death with the Protection of the Wooden Kannon Image*

Ōma Yamatsugi 大眞山繼[1] of the Senior Sixth Rank, Upper Grade, was of the village of Ogawa, Tama district, Musashi province 武藏國多磨郡小河鄉.[2] His wife was a woman of the Shiragabe family.[3] Yamatsugi became a soldier and was sent to the frontier to conquer the hairy men.[4] While he was away, his wife made a wooden image of Kannon and worshipped it with great devotion and reverence, praying for her husband's safety. Untouched by disasters, he came home and served the Kannon with his wife, grateful for its protection.

Several years passed after that time. In the reign of Empress Abe, in the twelfth month of the first year of the dragon, the eighth year of the Tenpyō hōji era, Yamatsugi was involved in the rebellion of Nakamaro 仲麿,[5] and was one of thirteen men sentenced to death.

6. Cf. I.5, n. 20. This means that even a forbidden food is all right for a sage who is free from precepts.

1. Unknown.
2. Present Akita-machi, Nishi-tama-gun, Tokyo-to 東京都西多摩郡秋多町.
3. See I.29, n. 2; also, *Shoku Nihongi*, XXXVIII (Enryaku 4:5:3). The Shiragabe family changed its name to Magabe because of the similarity to Emperor Shirakabe 白壁天皇.
4. 毛人 Emishi, indigenous people of the northeastern part of Japan, ethnically different from the people of the Yamato court.
5. Fujiwara no Nakamaro 藤原仲麿, later known as Emi no Oshikatsu 惠美押勝 (706–764), who rebelled against ex-Empress Kōken and Dōkyō and was executed. After this event, Kōken was re-enthroned as Empress Shōtoku. See III.38, n. 4.

When twelve of the men had been beheaded, he had a strange vision: the wooden image of Kannon he had worshipped so devotedly accused him, saying, "Oh, why do you stay in such a filthy place?" and transfixed his body with its leg from head to toe, making his body a girdle of its leg.

At the moment when the executioner was about to behead him, after ordering him to stretch out his neck, an imperial messenger hurried in, asking, "Is there a man named Ōma Yamatsugi among these?" "Yes, he is about to be beheaded," was the answer. Whereupon the messenger said, "Don't kill him. He is to be exiled to Shinano province."[6]

He was exiled, but, before long, was recalled and appointed an assistant governor[7] of Tama district. On his neck could still be seen a scar from a cut inflicted by the sword at the moment he was to have been executed. It was Kannon that saved him from being beheaded. For you will be filled with great delight and saved from calamity with Kannon's help if your faith arises and your devotion deepens owing to the merit you have accumulated.

# 8

## On a Miraculous Appearance of Bodhisattva Miroku
## in Response to the Vow

In the village of Oe, Sakata district, Ōmi province 近江國坂田郡遠江里,[1] there lived a wealthy man, whose name is unknown. Once he made a vow to copy the *Yuga-ron* 瑜伽論,[2] but many years passed, and the vow was not fulfilled. Finally the man fell on bad times and lost his means of livelihood. He left home, abandoning his family, and lived a life of discipline in pursuit of happiness. Remembering his unfulfilled vow, he was always thinking how he might achieve it.

In the reign of Empress Abe, in the ninth month in the autumn of the third year of the horse, the second year of the Tenpyō jingō era,[3]

6. Present Nagano-ken 長野縣.
7. 少領 *shōryō*; see I.30, n. 3.

1. Present Azai-chō, Higashi-azai-gun, Shiga-ken 滋賀縣東淺井郡淺井町.
2. *Yugashiji-ron* 瑜伽師地論 (*Taishō*, XXX, No. 1579). (Skt. *Yogācārabhūmiśāstra*). Maitreya's discourse translated by Hsüan-tsang 玄奘 and a major text for the Hossō School.
3. 766, in the reign of Empress Shōtoku.

he went to a mountain temple and stayed for several days. In its precincts there was a bush. All of a sudden, an image of Bodhisattva Miroku 彌勒菩薩[4] appeared[5] on the bark of a branch of the bush. When the ascetic saw it, he walked around the bush and prayed fervently.

At the news people came to see the image. Some donated bags of rice, while others gave money and clothing. With these donations he was able to copy one hundred scrolls of the *Yuga-ron* and hold a dedication ceremony, although the image vanished some time before.

Indeed we know that Miroku high in Tosotsuten 兜率天[6] came down in response to his vow so that he could attain deep faith and happiness here below in this land bound by suffering.[7] How can one doubt it?

# 9

In the reign of Empress Abe, Fujiwara no asomi Hirotari 藤原朝臣 廣足[2] was suddenly taken ill, and, in order to cure the illness, he went to live at a mountain temple of Makihara, Uda district, Yamato province 大和國菟田郡眞木原.[3] He kept the eight precepts and quietly practiced calligraphy with a brush at the desk till the evening of the seventeenth of the second month in the second year of the Jingo keiun era.[4] His young attendant, thinking he was asleep, shook him and tried to waken him, saying, "It is time to worship the Buddha since the sun has set." Still he remained motionless. The attendant shook

4. Maitreya; see Chap. II(3)b, n. 131. The Hossō School traditionally chose Maitreya as the focus of devotion.
5. 化生 *keshō;* one of the four kinds of birth. See I.21, n. 5.
6. A combination of a transliteration of Skt. Tuṣita and a translation of *deva,* 天; the fourth of the six heavens of the world of desire. Tradition says Maitreya resides and preaches in its inner palace waiting to descend to this world at the end of the age of degenerate dharma.
7. 願主下在 苦縛凡地 in contrast to the heavens.

1. Cf. *Jizō reigenki* (VI, 20). *Uji shūi monogatari* (VI, 1). On the theme "visit to the other world," this tale resembles I.30; II.5, 7, 16, 19; III.36, 37. See also Chap. II(1)b, c.
2. Unknown.
3. Kariya says that the remains of the temple are found near Kōsui Pass, north of present Haibara-chō, Uda-gun, Nara-ken 奈良縣宇陀郡榛原町.
4. 768.

him harder, and he dropped his brush and fell flat on his back with his arms and legs folded, not breathing. Upon close inspection he was found to be dead. In awe and terror the attendant ran home to inform his family and relatives of his death. At the news they prepared for a funeral, but they went to the temple three days later and found him restored to life and cured of the illness, waiting for them.

He answered their inquiries in this way: "There came men with moustaches growing straight up, clad in red robes and armor and equipped with swords and halberds. They called to me, saying, 'The Office[5] has suddenly summoned you,' and, with a halberd at my back urged me to accompany them. They forced me to hurry all the way, with one in front and two in the rear escorting me.

"Ahead of us there was a deep river; the water being black as ink, did not run but stood still. A good-sized young branch was placed in the middle of the stream, but it was not long enough to reach both sides of the river. The messenger said to me, 'Follow me into the stream and ford it by following in my footsteps.' Thus he guided me across.

"There was a many-story pavilion in front of us that was shining brightly and gave off light. Curtains made of precious stone beads closed four sides of the building, so that I could not see the face of the person sitting inside. One messenger ran inside and addressed him, saying, 'Here he is.' A voice answered, 'Let him in.'

"When I was led in, the curtain was moved, and the king asked me, 'Do you know the woman standing behind you?' Turning around, I saw my wife who had died in childbirth. I replied, 'This is none other than my wife.' Then the king said to me, 'I have summoned you because of this woman's appeal. She has already suffered three of her six years of punishment, and she has three more years to go. She implored me to let her share the rest of her suffering with you since she died in childbirth.'

"I said, 'I will copy, expound, and recite the *Hoke-kyō* and hold services in order to save her from suffering.' Then my wife addressed the king, saying, 'Please take his word and let him go back to the world at once.' Agreeing with her, the king said to me, 'Go back to the world immediately and practice good.'

"When I reached the gate of the palace, as he had directed me, I was curious to know who had summoned me, and, turning around, asked, 'I would like to know who you are.' Thereupon, he said, 'I am King Yama, also called Bodhisattva Jizō in your country.'[6] Then he stroked

5. 閻 *mikado*; see II.24, n. 11.
6. See Chap. II(1)c, n. 55.

my neck with his right hand, saying, 'You will never meet disaster, since I have marked you with a charm. Lose no time in going home.' One finger of his hand was about ten yards around."[7]

This is the report of Hirotari no asomi. For the sake of his deceased wife, he copied, expounded, and recited the *Hoke-kyō*, held services, and accumulated many posthumous merits in order to atone for her suffering and save her. This is an extraordinary event.

# IO

## *On the* Hoke-kyō *Copied with Devotion and Reverence Surviving a Fire*[1]

Muro no shami 牟婁沙彌 was of the Enomoto 榎本 family,[2] being self-ordained without a clerical name. He was popularly called the Novice of Muro, for he came from Muro district in Kii province 紀伊國牟婁郡.[3] Living in the village of Arata in Ate district 安諦郡荒田村,[4] he shaved his head and face and wore a surplice, but he led a householder's life, following a vocation to earn his livelihood.[5] He made a vow to copy the *Hoke-kyō* as it should be done, and, in a state of purification, he started copying it by himself.[6] After every bodily function he purified himself by bathing, and, when six months had passed, he finished copying. After the dedication ceremony he put the *Hoke-kyō* in a lacquered leather chest, which he placed in a high niche in his living room for occasional reading.

In the summer of the sixth year of the cock, the third year of the Jingo keiun era,[7] at noon on the twenty-third of the fifth month, a fire broke out and destroyed his whole house. In the raging flames only the chest containing the scripture remained unharmed. When he

---

7. 十抱餘 ; see Chap. II(1)c, n. 60.

1. Cf. *Konjaku monogatarishū* (XII, 29), *Myōhōki* (I, On a Nun of Hotung).
2. The *Shinsen shōjiroku* lists the Enomoto family as being descended from kami.
3. Present Higashi- and Nishi-muro-gun, Wakayama-ken 和歌山縣 東, 西牟婁郡.
4. Present Arida-gun, Wakayama-ken 和歌山縣有田郡.
5. See Chap. I(1)d.
6. Copying the *Hoke-kyō* is one of the five devotional practices recommended in it; upholding, reading, reciting, expounding, and copying it are regarded as adequate means to spread its teaching, although there are evidences that copying was added in the later stage of its compilation. Dedication ceremonies of copied scriptures became a popular means to attain merit. See Kiyota Jakuun, "*Hoke-kyō* no shosha ni tsuite," *Mikkyō bunka*, No. 71/72 (April 1965), 160–171.
7. 769.

opened the chest, he found the color of the scripture brilliant and its characters distinct. People came from all quarters to see it and could not help wondering at it.

Indeed, we know that the same manifestations of power took place here as in the case of the scripture being copied properly by a highly disciplined nun of Hotung 河東練行尼, or as in the case of the daughter of Wang Yü 王與女 in the time of the Ch'en dynasty being saved from fire by reciting the scripture.[9]

The note says: How praiseworthy was this member of the Enomoto family for accumulating merits by his great devotion and by copying the Ekayana scripture![10] The guardian deity of dharma performed a miracle in the flames. This is an effective story for converting the minds of nonbelievers and an excellent guide for stopping offenses of the evil-minded.

# I I

### On a Blind Woman Whose Sight Was Restored Owing to Her Devotion to the Wooden Image of Yakushi Buddha[1]

There was a wooden image of Yakushi-nyorai 藥師如來[2] in Tadehara-dō 蓼原堂[3] in the village of Tadehara, south of the pond of Koshida 越田池 in the capital of Nara.[4] In the reign of Empress Abe, a blind woman lived in the village. She was a widow whose only daughter was seven years old. She was so poor that she could not get food, and almost starved to death. She said to herself, "My poverty comes not only from my deeds in this life but from those in my previous lives.[5] I had better practice good with faith rather than die of hunger in vain."

Asking her daughter to lead her, she went to the hall and prayed to

8. See *Myōhōki*, I (*Taishō*, LI, 789).
9. Source unknown.
10. 一乘經, that is, *Hoke-kyō* which expounds the Ekayana teaching that all vehicles are reduced into one vehicle on the ultimate level. See I.Preface, n. 16; III.38, n. 42.

1. Cf. *Konjaku monogatarishū* (XII, 19), *Genkō shakusho* (XXIX, 3).
2. *Bhaiṣajyaguruvaiḍūryaprabhatathāgata*; see Chap. II(3)b, n. 135.
3. Unidentified.
4. It may be located in the southern outskirts of the capital.
5. 宿業; see I.8, n. 4.

the image of Yakushi Buddha for restoration of her sight, saying, "I do not care for my life, only for my daughter's. Both of us are about to die. I entreat you to give me sight!" A patron of the temple who was present saw her and, in sympathy, opened the door of the hall to let her pay homage to the image and recite its name.[6]

Two days later the daughter saw something pink and as sticky as gum suddenly oozing from the breast of the image. She told her mother about it. The mother, who wanted to eat it, said to her child, "Will you take some and put it in my mouth?" It was delicious, and all at once her eyes were opened.

Indeed we learn that any vow will be fulfilled if made with utmost devotion. This is an extraordinary event.

# I2

## On a Blind Man Whose Sight Was Restored Owing to His Chanting of the Name of Nichimanishu of the Thousand-armed Kannon[1]

In a village east of Yakushi-ji 藥師寺[2] in the capital of Nara, there was a blind man whose eyes were open, but he could not see. He was devoted to Kannon and meditated on Nichimanishu 日摩尼手[3] to restore his eyesight. During the day he used to sit at the eastern gate of Yakushi-ji, spread a handkerchief, and chant the name of Nichimanishu. Passersby and sympathizers put money, rice, and cereal on the handkerchief. At other times he sat in the marketplace doing the same thing. When he heard the temple bell at noon, he would go to the temple to beg food from the monks and in this way he lived for many years.

In the reign of Empress Abe, two strangers came to him, saying, "In sympathy for you we have come to cure your eyes." After they

6. 稱禮 shōrai.

1. Cf. Konjaku monogatarishū (XVI, 23).
2. See Editor's Preface, n. 4.
3. The Thousand-armed Kannon has forty arms in addition to the regular two, and each of them has twenty-five spheres of existence; hence, the figure 1,000 is arrived at. Nichimanishu or Nisshōmanishu 日精摩尼手 is the eighth right arm of the forty, which holds the jewel of the sun, a symbol of Kannon's cosmic significance. It gives off light continuously. Senju-sengen-kanzeon-bosatsu-daihishin-darani says, "The blind man should recite [the following mantra] in the name of Nisshōmanishu . . ." (Taishō, XX, 111a).

had treated both his eyes, they said, "We will come back here without fail in two days. Don't forget to wait for us." Before long both his eyes grew bright and he recovered his eyesight. On the promised day he waited for them, but they never returned.

The note says: How good it was for a blind man to recover his eyesight in this present life and to travel far along the Great Way,[4] having thrown away his cane, seeing clearly and acting firmly. Indeed, we know that it happened because of the power of Kannon and the great devotion of the blind man.


# 13

*On a Man Who Made a Vow to Copy the* Hoke-kyō *and Who Was Saved From a Dark Pit Devoid of Sunlight Owing to the Power of His Vow*[1]

In Aita district, Mimasaka province 美作國英多郡,[2] there was a state-owned iron mine. In the reign of Empress Abe, a provincial magistrate drafted ten workmen and had them enter the iron mine to dig out ore. All of a sudden, the entrance to the mine caved in. Surprised and terrified, the workmen made a rush for the exit, and nine of them barely managed to escape. Before the last man got out, the entrance was blocked. The magistrate and people, high and low, grieved for him, for they thought he had been crushed to death in the landslide. Wailing in grief, his family painted an image of Kannon and copied the scriptures to give merits to the dead man, thus completing the seventh day service.[3]

The man, however, was sealed in the pit alone, saying to himself, "I have not yet fulfilled my vow which I made recently to copy the *Hoke-kyō*. If my life is saved, I will fulfill it without fail." In the dark pit he felt regret and sorrow greater than he had ever experienced.

Meanwhile he noticed that the door of the pit opened a little and

4. 太方 *taihō*; the path of Buddha.

1. Cf. *Myōhōki* (I, On a Servant in Yeh 鄴下人), *Sanbō ekotoba* (II, 17), *Hokke kenki* (III, 108), *Fusō ryakki* (VI, Genmyō), *Konjaku monogatarishū* (XIV, 9).
2. Or Agata district; present Aita-gun, Okayama-ken 岡山縣英多郡.
3. Or "seventh day services" which are usually continued for seven seven-day periods during which the dead person's future existence is decided. But from the following story we choose "seventh day service" as more probable than a longer period.

a ray of sunlight came in. A novice[4] entered through the opening and brought him a bowl filled with delicacies, saying, "Your family made offerings of food and drink so that I might save you. I have come to you since you have been wailing in grief." So saying, he went out. Not long after he had gone, a hole opened above the man's head, and sunlight flooded the pit. The opening was about two feet square and fifty feet high.

At the same time, about thirty men who had come into the mountain to collect vines passed near the hole. The man at the bottom of the pit saw them pass and cried, "Take my hand." The workmen in the mountain heard what sounded like the hum of a mosquito. Out of curiosity they dropped a vine into the pit with a stone at the end of the vine. The man took hold of it and pulled. It was evident that there was someone at the bottom. They made a rope and a basket of vines, tied lengths of vine rope to the four corners of the basket, and lowered it into the pit with a pulley set up at the opening. When the man at the bottom got into the basket, they pulled him up and sent him home.

Nothing could surpass the joy of his family. The provincial magistrate asked him, "What good did you do?" The man told him the whole story. Greatly moved, the magistrate organized a devotees' association[5] to cooperate in copying the *Hoke-kyō* and held a dedication ceremony.

This took place owing to the divine power of the *Hoke-kyō* and the favor of Kannon.[6] There is no doubt about this.

# I4

## On Receiving an Immediate Penalty of Violent Death Because of Hitting the Reciter of the Dharani of the Thousand-armed Kannon[1]

In Kaga district, Echizen province 越前國加賀郡,[2] there was an of-

---

4. An incarnated Kannon.
5. 知識 *chishiki.*
6. This story is a rare case of Kannon and *Hoke-kyō* combined in one story.

1. Cf. *Sanbō ekotoba* (II, 8).
2. Present Kawakita-gun and Ishikawa-gun, Ishikawa-ken 石川縣河北郡, 石川郡. Since Kaga district became Kaga province in 823, this story offers one evidence for dating the compilation of the *Nihon ryōiki* before 823. See *Ruijū sandai-kyaku*, V (Kōnin 14:2:3).

ficial in charge of vagrants.[3] He hunted for them and made them work on temporary projects, forcing them to pay production and labor taxes. At that time there was a man registered in the capital of Nara, whose name was Ono no asomi Niwamaro 小野朝臣庭麿 .[4] He became a lay brother and recited the dharani of the Thousand-armed Kannon. He led a life of self-discipline, wandering in the mountains in that district.

In the spring of the sixth year of the cock, the third year of the Jingo keiun era,[5] on the twenty-seventh of the third month, the official[6] was in the village of Mimakawa 御馬河里[7] in that district about noon. He came across the ascetic and said to him, "Where do you come from?" The man replied, "I am practicing the path; I am not a layman." In anger the official accused him, saying, "No, you are a vagrant. Why didn't you pay your taxes?" Though the official bound and hit him to force him to work, the ascetic refused and sorrowfully quoted a proverb to him, saying, "There is a proverb that says: 'When lice from the clothes climb up to the head, they turn black; when lice from the head go down to the clothes, they turn white.' I carry the dharani on the top of my head and scriptures on my back so that I may not be persecuted by lay people. Why did you hit and humiliate one who upholds Mahayana teachings? They have a miraculous power, as I will now demonstrate."[8]

The official bound the scripture called the *Senju-kyō* 千手經[9] with a rope and dragged it along the ground. His house was about half a mile[10] from the spot where he had hit the ascetic. When he reached his house and wanted to get down from the horse, he was immobilized and could not dismount. At that instant he flew through the sky with his horse until he was suspended over the spot where he had hit the

3. 浮浪人 *ukarebito*; those who left their registered place of birth to evade taxation; no longer under the control of the *ritsuryō* government, they sought the protection of powerful nobles and local gentry or pretended to be monks and nuns. The first prohibition against the practice is recorded in 709. See *Shoku Nihongi* IV (Wadō 2:10:14); VI (Reiki 1:5:1 and Yōrō 1:5:17, 4:3:17, 4:5:21). See Naoki, "Nara jidai ni okeru furō ni tsuite," *Shirin*, XXXIV (No. 3, 1951), 19–39.

4. The Ono family is descended from the imperial family, according to the *Shinsen shōjiroku*. See *Nihon shoki*, XXIX (Tenmu 13:11:1); Aston, "Nihongi," II, 366.

5. 769.

6. The official who hunted vagrants was often of the local gentry, and he made them work for him.

7. Present Mima-machi, Kanazawa-shi 金澤市三馬町.

8. This may also be translated as follows: "If you have a miraculous power, please demonstrate it now." In this case, it is addressed to the scriptures and not to the official.

9. See n. 11, below, and also Chap. II(3)b, n. 138.

10. 一里; 1 *ri* was 0.41 mile, although 1 *ri* equals 2.45 miles according to the present standards of measurement.

ascetic. About noon on the following day he fell to the ground after having been in the air for one day and one night. His body was broken into pieces, just like a bagful of scattered needles. Everyone who witnessed it was filled with terror and awe.

The *Senju-kyō*[11] gives a relevant passage: "Great divine dharani[12] can bring branches, blossoms, and fruit even to a dead tree. To speak ill of this dharani means to speak ill of Buddhas as numerous as the grains of sand of the River Ganges. . . ." A Mahayana scripture[13] has a passage to the same effect: "The sin of speaking ill of wise men is equal to that of destroying temples and pagodas in eighty-four thousand counties."[14]

# 15

## On Receiving an Immediate Penalty of Violent Death
## Because of Hitting a Begging Novice

Inukai no sukune Maoyu 犬養宿禰眞老[1] lived in the village of Saki, north of the Imperial Mausoleum of Ikume 活目陵北之佐岐村[2] in the capital of Nara. Innately evil-minded, he hated mendicants. In the reign of Empress Abe, a novice went to Maoyu's door to beg food. Far from making an offering, Maoyu robbed him of his surplice and accused him, saying, "What kind of monk are you?" The mendicant replied, "I am a self-ordained monk."[3] Maoyu chased him away, and the mendicant left, filled with ill will.

That evening Maoyu cooked some carp in soup and chilled it until it was set.[4] The next morning at about eight o'clock he awoke and tasted the carp while still in bed. When he was about to drink some rice wine, however, he vomited black blood and fell on his side as

11. 千手千眼觀世音菩薩廣大圓滿無礙大悲心陀羅尼經 (*Taishō*, XX, III).
12. 大神咒 *daishinju*; in this case, Senju dharani or Daihishin dharani.
13. 方廣經 *Hōkō-kyō*.
14. Unlocated.

1. The Inukai family was originally in charge of hunting and guarding public granaries.
2. Emperor Suinin's mausoleum was located on the Third Street, Third Avenue, on the West Side of Nara, and the Village of Saki is at present Saki-machi, Nara-shi 奈良縣佐紀町, not far from Yakushi-ji.
3. 自度 *jido*.
4. When the soup is chilled, it becomes gelatinous.

though in a trance, his breathing stopped; as though asleep, his life came to an end.

Indeed, we learn that an evil mind is a sharp sword which kills the bearer; an angry mind is an evil fiend which incurs calamities; greediness causes the suffering of a hungry fiend; avarice is an impenetrable bush to block the offering of compassion. When you see a mendicant, you should be merciful and happy and make spiritual and material offerings. Therefore, the *Jōbu-ron* 丈夫論[5] gives this passage: "Those who are greedy value even mud more than gold and jewels, while those who are merciful offer gold and jade, caring less for them than grass and trees. At the sight of a mendicant they cannot bear to say they have no alms and wail in sorrow. . . ."

# 16

## *On a Licentious Woman Whose Children Cried for Milk, Receiving an Immediate Penalty*

Yokoe no omi Naritojime 横江臣成呂女[1] was from Kaga district, Echizen province 越前國加賀郡.[2] Innately licentious, she used to keep company with many men. She died before completing the best years of her life,[3] and many years passed.

Dharma Master Jakurin 寂林,[4] who was from the village of Noo, Nagusa district, Kii province 紀伊國名草郡能應里,[5] left his home and traveled to other provinces, practicing the teachings and seeking the path. He came to the village of Uneda in Kaga district 加賀郡畝田村[6] and stayed there for some years. In the reign of Emperor Shirakabe 白壁,[7] who governed Ōyashima 大八嶋[8] at Nara Palace, on the night

5. *Daijōbu-ron*, I (*Taishō*, XXX, 260). This quotation shows more identity with the *Shokyō yōshū* than the original text. See *Shokyō yōshū*, X (*Taishō*, LIX, 93). 又丈夫論云 若慳心多者 雖復泥土重於金玉 若悲心多者 雖施金玉輕於草木 若慳心多者喪失財寶心大憂惱 . . . 富慳貪者 生餓鬼中 受無量苦 . . . 菩薩心念施無有財物 見人乞時 不忍言無 悲苦墮淚 . See also III.33, n. 21.

1. Unknown. Naritojime seems to be her first name.
2. See III.14, n. 2.
3. 丁齡; from twenty-one to sixty. See *Ryō no gige*, "Ko-ryō," Article 6.
4. Unknown.
5. Present Yamaguchi-mura, Kaisō-gun, Wakayama-ken 和歌山縣海草郡山口村.
6. Present Ōno, Ishikawa-gun, Ishikawa-ken 石川縣石川郡大野.
7. Emperor Kōnin 光仁 (r. 770–780).
8. See II.1, n. 3.

of the twenty-third of the twelfth month, in the winter of the seventh year of the dog, the Hōki era,[9] he had a dream: He was heading toward the east along the path in front of Prince Shōtoku's palace at Ikaruga, Yamato province.[10] The path was like a mirror, about half a furlong wide,[11] and as straight as a plumb line, with a grove of trees on one side. Jakurin stopped to look into the grove and found a large naked woman crouching there. Both her breasts were swollen as big as a mound oven and hanging down with pus oozing from them. Kneeling, she grasped her knees with her hands, looked at her sick breasts, and said, "How painful my breasts are!"

Jakurin asked her, "Who are you?" She replied, "I am the mother of Yokoe no omi Narihito 横江臣成人 in the village of Uneda in Ōno, Kaga district, Echizen province. In the prime of life I was licentious and used to keep company with many men, abandoning my little ones so that I could lie with men. For days they were hungry for my breasts. Among them, Narihito was the hungriest. I received a penalty of this disease of swollen breasts because of my sin of letting my little ones go hungry for milk." He asked her, "How can you be released from this sin?" She answered, "If Narihito learns of it, he will forgive my sin."

Awaking from the dream, Jakurin was amazed; filled with wonder, he went round the village inquiring about the man. One man answered, "I am the very one you are seeking." Jakurin told him about the dream. On hearing it, he said, "I lost my mother at such a young age that I do not remember her. But I have an elder sister who may know the situation well." When he asked his sister, she said, "The story is true. Our mother had such good features that she was loved by men, kept company with them, and begrudged giving her breasts to us."

Thereupon, all the children grieved and said, "We don't bear her a grudge. Why does our loving mother suffer for this sin?" They made Buddhist images and copied scriptures in order to atone for her sin. After the ceremony was over, she appeared to Jakurin once more in a dream, saying, "I am now released from my sin."

Indeed, we learn that a mother's tender breasts, though capable of bestowing great benefit, can, on the contrary, become a source of sin if she begrudges offering them to her little ones.

9. 770.
10. See I.4, n. 7.
11. 1 *chō*; see II.24, n. 9.

# 17

*On an Extraordinary Sign of an Unfinished Clay*
*Image Groaning*[1]

Novice Shingyō 沙彌信行[2] came from the village of Mike, Naka district, Kii province 紀伊國那賀郡彌氣里.[3] His secular name was Ōtomo no muraji Oya 大伴連祖.[4] He renounced the householder's life, ordained himself, shaved his head, and wore a surplice, looking for what might bring happiness.[5] In that village there was a temple,[6] called Yamamuro-dō of Mike 彌氣山室堂 by the villagers who had built it for themselves. (Its formal name was Jishi-zenjō-dō 慈子禪定堂, Maitreya's Meditation Hall.)[7] Inside there were two unfinished clay images. They were the attendants of Bodhisattva Miroku, and their broken limbs were placed in the bell hall. The patrons of the temple discussed the matter and said, "We will keep them in some pure place in the mountain."

Novice Shingyō used to live in that hall and strike the bell. Seeing the unfinished images, he felt uneasy and tied the fallen limbs to the images with threads, stroking their heads and saying again and again, "I hope that some sage[8] will come to complete them."

Many years passed. In the reign of Emperor Shirakabe, in the middle of the seventh month in the autumn of the eighth year of the boar, the second year of the Hōki era,[9] a voice was heard after midnight, groaning "How painful! How painful!" It was feeble and hardly audible, sounding like a woman's voice giving a long, drawn out groan. At first Shingyō thought that a traveler going across the mountain had suddenly been taken ill and was staying in the temple. He got up immediately and went around the temple looking for a sick person, but he found no one there. Although wondering at this event, he said nothing about it. The groan of someone suffering, however, did not cease at night. When Shingyō could endure it no longer, he got up and

---

1. Similar to II.22, 23; III.28, etc. See Chap. II(3)b.
2. Unknown.
3. Present Wakayama-shi 和歌山市.
4. Oya may be the first name or a copyist's error. The Maeda manuscript does not have this script.
5. That is, good deeds, attainment of merit.
6. 道場 *dōjō*.
7. Kyōkai's note.
8. 聖人 *shōnin*, an eminent monk.
9. 771.

searched again, locating the groan in the bell hall. He discovered that it was the images groaning, and Shingyō at once marveled and grieved at the discovery.

At that time Monk Hōkei 豊慶[10] of Gangō-ji[11] on the East Side of Nara was staying in the temple. Shingyō surprised the monk by knocking on the door of his room and saying, "Venerable Master, please get up and listen to me!" Then he described in detail how the images were groaning. Thereupon the two monks, together moved by great wonder and grief, organized a devotees' association and completed the clay images for dedication. A service was held to enshrine them. They are the attendants of Miroku enshrined in Mike-dō. (The one on the left is Bodhisattva Daimyōshō 大妙聲菩薩, while the one on the right is Bodhisattva Hōonrin 法音輪菩薩.)[12]

Indeed, we learn through this event that any vow will be achieved and fulfilled without fail. This is also a miraculous event.

# 18

*On the Immediate Penalty of Violent Death for a*
*Licentious Scripture Copier Who Copied*
*the* Hokke-kyō[1]

Tajihi the Scripture Copier came from Tajihi district, Kawachi province 河內國丹治比郡.[2] As his surname was Tajihi, he was given such a popular name. In that district there was a temple[3] called Nonaka-dō 野中堂.

In the sixth month in the summer of the eighth year of the boar, the second year of the Hōki era,[4] a man made a vow to copy the *Hoke-kyō* and invited the copier to the temple. Female devotees gathered in the temple to add purified water to the ink for copying scriptures, and it happened that the sky suddenly clouded over and there was a shower in the afternoon. The temple was so cramped that those who sought

10. Or Hōkyō.
11. See I.3, n. 9.
12. Kyōkai's note.

1. Cf. *Konjaku monogatarishū* (XIV, 26).
2. Present Minami- and Kita-kawachi-gun, Ōsaka-fu 大阪府南, 北河內郡.
3. See III, 17, n. 6.
4. 771.

shelter from the shower filled it, and the copier and the women were sitting in the same place Then the scripture copier, driven by strong lust, crouched behind one of the girls, lifted her skirt, and had intercourse with her. As his penis entered her vagina, they died together embracing each other. The girl died foaming at the mouth.

Indeed, we learn that this was the punishment given by the Guardian of dharma.[5] However intensely your body and heart may burn with the fire of lust, do not, because of the promptings of a lewd heart, commit a filthy deed. A fool indulging in lust is just like a bug jumping into a fire. Therefore, a preceptive scripture[6] says, "A thoughtless youth easily feels lust."[7] Or the *Nehan-gyō*,[8] expressing the same idea, says: "If you know what the five kinds of desire[9] are, you will not find any pleasure in them. Nor will you remain a slave to them even momentarily. It is just like a dog chewing on a meatless bone, never knowing satisfaction."

# 19

*On a Girl Born of a Flesh Ball Who Practiced Good
and Enlightened People*[1]

The wife of Toyobuku no Hirogimi 豐服廣公,[2] in the village of Toyobuku, Yatsushiro district, Higo province 肥後國八代郡,[3] became pregnant, and, about four o'clock in the morning on the fifteenth of the eleventh month in the winter of the eighth year of the boar, the second year of the Hōki era,[4] she gave birth to a flesh ball.[5] It looked like an egg. Not taking this as a good omen, the man and wife put it in a vessel and stored it in a cave in the mountain.[6] After seven days

---

5. 護法 *gohō;* see II.1, n. 11.

6. 律 *ritsu,* a translation of Skt. *vinaya.*

7. *Konpon sabatabu-ritsu-sho* 根本薩婆多部律攝. See Haraguchi, "*Nihon ryōiki* shutten goku kanken," *Kuntengo,* No. 34 (December 1966), 53–54.

8. *Daihatsu nehan-gyō,* XXII (*Taishō,* XII, 496), *Bonmō-kyō koshakki* (*Taishō,* XL, 705). See Haraguchi, "*Nihon ryōiki*," 54.

9. 五欲 *goyoku,* five kinds of desire which arise out of attachment to the five objects: color/form, sound, smell, taste, and touch.

1. Cf. *Sanbō ekotoba* (II, 4); *Hokke kenki* (III, 98); *Genkō shakusho* (XVIII).

2. Present Toyobuku-mura, Shimomashiki-gun, Kumamoto-ken 熊本縣下益城郡豐服村.

3. Unknown. Hirogimi may be the first name, although *kimi* is originally an honorific title such as Lord.

4. 771.

5. 肉團 *shishimura;* see Chap. II(2)b, n. 96; also, nn. 21, 22, below.

6. "A cave in the mountain" may signify the womb of mother earth to which the dead go back and from which new life comes out.

they returned to the cave and discovered that a girl had been born of the flesh ball, breaking through its covering. The parents took her home, and her mother nursed her. There was no one in the province who did not wonder at this.

After eight months had passed she suddenly grew very large, but her head and neck were joined without any chin, in a form different from other people, and she was three and a half feet high. Endowed with wisdom, she was by nature brilliant. Before she was seven, she recited the *Hoke-kyō* and the Eighty-volume *Kegon-gyō* 八十花嚴.[7] She was reserved and never boasted. Eventually she decided to renounce the world, shaved her head, and wore a surplice. Prompted by her faith, she practiced good and enlightened people. She had such a good voice that it could lead her audience to become merciful. In her deformed body there was no vagina but only an opening for urine. Foolish laymen mocked her, calling her Saru-hijiri 猴聖,[8] False-sage.

On one occasion a monk of the provincial temple in Takuma district 託磨郡,[9] and a monk of Daijin-ji 大神寺 at Yahata, Usa district, Buzen province 豐前國宇佐郡矢羽田,[10] became envious of the nun, and said to her, "Your teachings are false."[11] They looked down at her, mocking and making a fool of her. A divine man[12] flew down from the sky and made as though to impale them with a halberd. They screamed in terror and eventually died.

When the Most Venerable Kaimyō 戒明[13] of Daian-ji[14] was appointed as a superior provincial preceptor[15] of Tsukushi province 筑紫國[16] about the seventh or eighth year of the Hōki era, Sagano kimi Kogimi 佐賀君兒公,[17] of the Senior Seventh Rank, Upper Grade, a governor of Saga district of Hizen province 肥前國佐賀郡,[18] held a

---

7. There are two major texts of *Avatamsakasūtra* in Chinese: *Daihōkōbutsu kegon-gyō* (60 vols.) (*Taishō*, IX, No. 278) and *Daihōkōbutsu kegon-gyō* (80 vols.) (*Taishō*, X, No. 279).

8. See Chap. II(2)c.

9. Present Izumi-chō, Kumamoto-shi 熊本市出水町.

10. Or Miroku-dera which was once located in the precincts of Usa Hachiman Shrine, in Usa-machi, Usa-gun, Ōita-ken 大分縣宇佐郡宇佐町.

11. 外道 *gedō;* originally refers to non-Buddhists and their teachings, but it is also used in a pejorative sense, meaning followers of the wrong teachings.

12. 神人 *shinjin;* guardian of dharma in a human form.

13. A monk of Daian-ji who specialized in the *Kekon-gyō*, studied in China in the Hōki era (770–780), and died in the Enryaku era (782–805).

14. See I.32, n. 6.

15. 大國師 *daikokushi; kokushi* is a provincial preceptor who is in charge of the samgha in the province. See Chap. I(1)a, n. 21; d, n. 79. Since Tsukushi (see below) is a big province, *dai* is added to the title.

16. Formally includes Chikuzen and Chikugo 筑前, 筑後, but often means present Kyūshū as a whole.

17. Unknown. Probably of the local gentry.

18. Present Saga-gun, Saga-ken 佐賀縣佐賀郡.

retreat with Dharma Master Kaimyō to lecture on the Eighty-volume *Kengon-gyō*. The nun was seated in the audience, never missing a lecture.

Seeing her, the lecturer said accusingly, "Who is that nun un-scrupulously seated among the monks?"[19] In reply she said, "Buddha promulgated the right teaching out of his great compassion for all sentient beings. Why do you restrain me in particular?" Then she asked a question by quoting a verse from the scripture, and the lecturer could not interpret it. In amazement, all the famous wise men ques-tioned and examined her, but she never failed. In that way they could not interpret it. In amazement, all the famous wise men ques-tioned and examined her, but she never failed. In that way they learned that she was an incarnation of Buddha, and named her Bod-hisattva Sari.[20] Clergy and laymen revered her and made her their master.

In Buddha's lifetime, ten eggs born from Sumanā, a daughter of Sudatta, a wealthy man of Śrāvastī, opened to produce ten men, all of whom renounced the world to become arhats.[21] The wife of a wealthy man of Kapilavstu became pregnant and gave birth to a flesh ball, which opened after seven days to bring forth one hundred children, all of whom renounced the world to become arhats.[22] Even in a country as small as ours, there is an excellent example which is similar. This is also an extraordinary event.

# 20

## *On Immediately Getting a Twisted Mouth by Speaking Ill of a Woman Copying the* Hoke-kyō[1]

In the village of Hani, Nakata district, Awa province 粟國名方郡 埴村,[2] there was a woman whose surname was Imbe no obito 忌部首.[3]

---

19. Although the *Sōni-ryō* allows monks to visit a nunnery and nuns to visit a monastery on occasions of religious ceremonies or lecture meetings, this passage is an indication that Bud-dhist studies were generally confined to monks and institutions were dominated by men. See Chap. II(2)b, n. 98.
20. See Chap. II(2)b, n. 98.
21. See *Kengu-kyō* 賢愚經, XIII (*Taishō*, IV, 440).
22. *Senjū hyakuen-gyō* 撰集百緣經, VII (*Taishō*, IV, 237ab).

1. Cf. *Konjaku monogatarishū* (XIV, 27). Similar to I.19; II.18.
2. Present Ishii-chō, Myōzai-gun, Tokushima-ken 德島縣名西郡石井町.
3. The Awa Imbe 阿波忌部 families, which lived in present-day Oe-gun, were orginally in charge of traditional religious affairs.

(Her name was Tayasuko 多夜須子.)[4] In the reign of Emperor Shira-kabe,[5] she was copying the *Hoke-kyō* at Sonoyama-dera 菀山寺[6] in Oe district 麻殖郡[7] when Imbe no muraji Itaya 忌部連板屋[8] of the same district spoke ill of her, pointing out her mistakes. Immediately he was inflicted with a twisted mouth and a distorted face, which never returned to their normal state.

The *Hoke-kyō* says: "If you speak ill of a devotee of this scripture, none of your organs will work well, and you will be dwarfed, ugly, feeble limbed, blind, deaf, and hunchbacked." Speaking to the same effect, it also says: "If you reveal the mistakes of a devotee of this scripture, you will contract leprosy in this world, whether what you say is true or not."[9] Therefore, be reverent and have faith in the *Hoke-kyō*. Praise its power. Do not speak ill of others' faults, for you may incur a great disaster if you do.

# 21

## *On a Monk Whose Blind Eye Was Cured by Having the* Kongō hannya-kyō *Recited*[1]

The Venerable Chōgi 長義[2] was a monk of Yakushi-ji on the West Side of Nara. In the third year of the Hōki era,[3] Chōgi lost the sight in one of his eyes. Five months elapsed. Day and night he was ashamed and grieved, and he invited many monks to recite the *Kongō hannya-kyō*[4] for three days and nights. His eye was then cured, and he could see as distinctly as before.

How great is the miraculous power of the *Hannya*![5] For, if a vow is made with profound faith, it will never remain unfulfilled.

---

4. Kyōkai's note. Tayasuko is her first name.
5. Emperor Kōnin.
6. Unlocated.
7. Present Oe-gun, Tokushima-ken.
8. Unknown. See *Shoku Nihongi*, XXIX (Jingo Keiun 2:7:14).
9. *Myōhōrenge-kyō* (*Taishō*, IX, 62). See also I.19, n. 7.

1. Cf. *Konjaku monogatarishū* (XIV, 33). Similar to I.8; III.11, 12, etc.
2. Unknown.
3. 772, in the reign of Emperor Kōnin.
4. See II.24, n. 20.
5. Refers to the above scriptures.

# 22

## On Being Repaid Good and Evil for Copying the
## Hoke-kyō *and for Exploiting Others with Heavy Scales*[1]

Osada no toneri Ebisu 他田舍人蝦夷[2] was a man of the village of Atome, Chīsagata district, Shinano province 信濃國小縣郡跡目里.[3] He was very rich, and would lend money and rice. He copied the *Hoke-kyō* twice, and each time he held a ceremony to recite it. After further thought, he was not satisfied with this; he reverently copied it once again, but did not hold another ceremony.

At the end of the fourth month in the summer of the tenth year of the ox, the fourth year of the Hōki era,[4] Ebisu died suddenly. His family conferred and said, "Since his birth was in the year of fire,[5] we won't cremate him." Instead they consecrated the ground on which to build a tomb, while providing temporary burial.[6]

Seven days had passed after his death when he was restored to life and related a story as follows: "There were four messengers who accompanied and guided me. At first we crossed in a field and then came to a steep hill. When we had climbed the slope, I saw a tall zelkova tree. Standing there and looking over the path ahead, I saw many men sweeping the road with brooms and heard them saying, 'We are sweeping and purifying the road along which a man who copied the *Hoke-kyō* will pass.' When I reached them, they stood by and bowed to me. In front of me there was a deep river about a hundred and twenty yards wide. There was a bridge over the river. Many men were repairing it, saying, 'We are repairing the bridge which a man who copied the *Hoke-kyō* will cross.' When I reached them, they stood by and bowed to me.

"Having crossed the bridge to the other side, I saw a golden palace, in which a king was seated. Near the bridge, the road was three-

---

1. Karmic retribution of good and evil is exemplified in one person who visited the land of the dead. Similar to II.5, 16; III.23, 37.

2. The family name Osada is found in Suruga, Shinano, etc. Toneri is used like a *kabane*, and Ebisu is the first name, probably originating from a common noun for people in the eastern part of Japan.

3. Present Chīsagata-gun, Nagano-ken 長野縣小縣郡.

4. 733, in the reign of Emperor Kōnin.

5. 丙 *hinoe;* the third of the Ten Stems, which is associated with fire, one of the Five Elements. See Chap. II(3)a, n. 119.

6. 殯 *mogari.*

forked.[7] The first way was wide and flat; the second was somewhat overgrown with grass; the third was obstructed by thick bushes. The messengers forced me to take the third one, and one of them entered the palace, saying, 'We have brought him.' The king saw me, and said, 'This is the man who copied the *Hokke-kyō*.' Pointing to the second way, he said to the messengers, 'Take him that way.'

"The four men accompanied me to a hot iron pillar, which they made me hold while they pushed a scorching iron net against my back. After three nights, they made me hold a copper pillar, pushing a scorching copper net against my back. After three days, the objects were still as hot as burning charcoal. Though the iron and copper were hot, they were not unbearable, merely uncomfortable. Though they were heavy, they were not unbearable, but certainly not light. Led by my past evil deeds, I was attracted to them, only wanting to hold them and bear the burden.

"When six days had passed, I left the place. Three monks asked me, 'Do you know why you suffered?' I replied, 'No, I don't.' Then they asked me, 'What good did you perform?' I said, 'I made three copies of the *Hoke-kyō*, one of which has not yet been dedicated.' They took out three tablets, two made of gold, one of iron.[8] Then they took out two scales; one weighed on the heavy side by one quart of rice,[9] the other on the light side by one quart. Then they said to me, 'Checking our tablets, we have learned that you made three copies of the *Hoke-kyō*. Though you copied a Mahayana scripture, you committed a grave sin. You were summoned here because you used the lighter-weight scale for lending rice,[10] but the heavier-weight scale for collecting debts. Now, go home immediately.'

"On my way back, I saw many men sweeping the road with brooms and repairing the bridge as before and heard them saying, 'The man who copied the *Hoke-kyō* will return from the palace of King Yama.' When I had crossed the bridge, I realized that I had been restored to life."

After that he paid homage to the copied scripture, and recited it with greater faith in the service. Indeed, we learn that doing good brings luck and doing evil brings disaster. The effects of good and evil never disappear, and the repayment of these two takes place at the same time. One should only practice good and never do evil.

7. 衢 *chimata*; for the symbolism of the three paths, see Chap. II(1)c, n. 57. Since Kyōkai never uses *sanzu* 三塗(途), it seems that the term and idea were not familiar to Kyōkai.
8. Merits were recorded on the tablets. Cf. III.22, n. 10; III.38, n. 34.
9. About a quart of rice is obtained from a sheaf of rice stalks.
10. 出擧 *suiko*; see I.23, n. 9.

# 23

### On the Immediate Repayments of Good and Evil in Return
### for a Vow to Copy the Dai hannya-kyō and for the Use
### of the Temple Property[1]

Ōtomo no muraji Oshikatsu 大伴連忍勝[2] came from the village of
Omuna, Chīsagata district, Shinano province 信濃國小縣郡孃里.[3] The
Ōtomo-no muraji family got together and built a hall in the village
to serve as the family temple.[4] Because Oshikatsu wanted to copy
the *Dai hannya-kyō* 大般若經,[5] he made a vow and collected donations.
Having shaved his head and face, put on a surplice, and received the
precepts, he lived in the temple, practicing the path.

In the third month in the spring of the first year of the tiger, the
fifth year of the Hōki era,[6] he was accused of a crime and beaten to
death by the patrons[7] of the temple. (The patrons were of the same
family[8] as Oshikatsu.) This family conferred and said, "Since murder
is involved, we will wait for a judgment." Accordingly they did not
cremate him on the spot but made a tomb and arranged the corpse
for a temporary burial. After five days, however, he was restored to
life, and told this story to his family:

"Five messengers accompanied me and made me hurry along.
Ahead of us there was a very steep slope. Having reached the top of
the slope, I stopped to look around and saw three broad paths. The
first was flat and wide, the second covered with grass, and the third
blocked with thick bushes. In the center of the three-forked road[9] a
king was seated, to whom the messengers spoke, saying, 'We have
brought him.' Pointing to the flat path, he said to them, 'Take him
this way.' Surrounding me, the king's messengers went on that path.

"At the end of the way, there was a big kettle. The steam rose
from it like a sheet of flame, and the water boiled with the thunderous

1. Cf. *Konjaku monogatarishū* (XIV, 30).
2. Unknown. For the Ōtomo no muraji family, see I.5, n. 2.
3. Present Ueda-shi, Nagano-ken 長野縣 上田市.
4. 氏寺 *uji-dera*; see Chap. I(1)d.
5. *Maka hannya haramita-kyō* (*Taishō*, VIII, No. 223) or *Dai hannya haramita-kyō*, 600 vols.
(*Taisho*, V, VI, VII, No. 220).
6. 774, in the reign of Emperor Kōnin.
7. 檀越 *taniochi*.
8. 氏 *uji*; see Chap. I(1)d, n. 112.
9. See III.33, n. 7.

roar of breaking waves. But when they threw me into it alive, the kettle turned cold and broke into four pieces.

"Three monks came out then, and asked me, 'What good have you done?' I answered, 'I haven't practiced any good, but I made a vow once to copy six hundred volumes of the *Dai hannya-kyō*, although I haven't fulfilled it yet.' Then they took out three iron tablets[10] for checking and said to me, 'It is true that you made a vow and renounced the world to practice the way. In spite of those good deeds you brought destruction on yourself by using property belonging to the temple. Now, go back to fulfill the vow and atone for the loss of the temple property.' Suddenly released, I came back by the three-forked broad way, coming down the slope, and I realized at once I had been restored to life. I incurred this karmic retribution because of the effort shown in making the vow and because of my use of temple property, and hell has nothing to be blamed for."

This is what the *Dai hannya-kyō*[11] means when it says: "One *mon*, if multiplied for twenty days, will make 1,740,003,968 *mon*.[12] Therefore, don't steal or use even one *mon*."

# 24

## *On Being Born as a Monkey for Keeping Men from Seeking the Way*[1]

On the mountain named Mikamu-no-take, in Yasu district, Ōmi province 近江國野州郡御上嶺,[2] there was a shrine called the abode of Taga no Ōkami 陁我大神.[3] It was endowed with six families' holdings as its private property. Near the shrine there was a temple.

During the Hōki era,[4] in the reign of Emperor Shirakabe, the Venerable Eshō 惠勝[5] of Daian-ji was staying at the temple for a

---

10. See III.22, n. 8.

11. Unlocated.

12. This calculation does not seem to be corrects since it amounts to 524, 288 on the twentieth day, and 536,870,912 on the thirtieth day, which is the reading in the Maeda manuscript.

1. Cf. *Fusō ryakki* (Shō II, Kōnin), *Genkō shakusho* (IX).

2. Or Mikami-yama 三上山, Ōmi Fuji 近江富士, located in present Yasu-chō, Yasu-gun, Shiga-ken

3. Taga Shrine located in present Taga-chō, Inukami-gun, Shiga-ken 滋賀縣犬上郡多賀町, although Izanagi and Izanami are enshrined now.

4. (770–780).

5. Unknown.

retreat when he had a dream in which a man appeared, saying, "Please read the scriptures for me." When he awoke from his sleep, he wondered about the dream.

The next day a tiny white monkey appeared and came to him, saying, "Stay at this temple and recite the *Hoke-kyō* for me." The monk asked the monkey, "Who are you?" Whereupon the monkey replied, "I was the king of a state in the eastern part of India. In my state about one thousand men (it means about one thousand and not thousands)[6] became followers of monks, neglecting agricultural matters. Therefore, I suppressed them, saying, 'There should not be so many followers.' At that time I limited the number of followers, but not the acts carried out in pursuit of the path. Even if I did not suppress the practice of the teaching, however, to prevent men from following monks was a sin. This is why I was reborn as a monkey and the kami of this shrine. Please stay here and recite the *Hoke-kyō* so that I may be released from this life."[7]

The monk said, "Then you must make offerings." The monkey answered, "I have nothing to offer." To which the monk replied, "In this village there is a lot of unhulled rice. Give the rice to me as an offering so that I may recite the scripture." The monkey said, "Though the government officials gave the rice to me, the person in charge of it regards it as his own and would never let me have it for my use." ('A person in charge of it' means the priest at the shrine.) The monk said, "How can I recite the scripture without any offering?" The monkey answered, "In that case I will join a group of several monks in Asai district 淺井郡[8] who are going to read the *Rokkan-shō* 六卷抄."[9] (Asai district is in the same province. The *Rokkan-shō* is the title of the preceptual writing.)

This monk, in wonder and doubt, went to the Venerable Manyo 滿預[10] of Yamashina-dera 山階寺,[11] who was a patron, and told him what the monkey had asked. The latter, disbelieving it, said, "These are merely the words of a monkey. I do not believe what you say. Nor will I accept nor admit the monkey into the group."

---

6. Kyōkai's note.

7. The idea that a kami is a sentient being and needs to hear dharma to be saved is well exemplified in this story. For its significance in Japanese religious history, see Chap. I(1)d.

8. Present Higashi-Azai-gun and Iga-gun, Shiga-ken 滋賀縣 伊賀郡, 東淺井郡.

9. *Shibunritsu sanhan hoketsu gyōji-shō* 四分律刪繁補闕行事抄 (*Taishō*, XL, No. 1804, 1–156), edited by Tao-hsüan 道宣.

10. Unknown. He seems to have been a monk of Yamashina-dera and at the same time a patron of the temple in Ōmi, where he was invited to lecture on the *Rokkan-shō*.

11. Fujiwara no Kamatari founded it in Yamashina in 669, and it was later transferred to the new capital of Nara in 710, where it was renamed Kōfuku-ji 興福寺.

When he was preparing for the recitation of the *Rokkan-shō*, an acolyte and a lay brother came to him in haste, saying, "There was a tiny white monkey at the hall. Then we saw the great hall eighteen yards long[12] fall down in pieces, along with all the Buddha images and residential quarters." He went out to discover that all had been destroyed as reported. Thereupon, Manyo conferred with Eshō, built a hall fourteen yards long,[13] and, believing the words of the monkey which revealed him as the Great Kami of Taga, accepted the monkey among the audience for the recitation of the *Rokkan-shō* according to the request of the Great Kami. From that time until the vow was fulfilled, there was never any trouble.

Those who keep men from practicing good are penalized by being reborn as a monkey. Therefore, you must not prevent monks from telling followers to hold services, for you will be penalized.

When Rahula was a king in his previous existence, he prevented a self-enlightened monk[14] from begging. As the latter could not enter the former's kingdom, he was hungry for seven days. Owing to this sin Rahula had to stay in his mother's womb for six years before his next birth.[15] This story teaches us the same lesson.

# 25

## On Being Saved by Reciting the Name of Śākyamuni Buddha While Drifting on the Ocean[1]

Ki no omi Umakai 紀臣馬養[2] was a man[3] from the village of Kibi, Ate district, Kii province 紀伊國安諦郡吉備鄉.[4] Nakatomi no muraji Ojimaro 中臣連祖父麿[5] was a boy[6] from the village of Hamanaka,

12. 九間大堂; since one *ken* is about two yards, nine *ken* is eighteen yards. *Ken* is a basic unit in Japanese architecture, and the size of the hall often becomes its name such as 三十三間堂, Thirty-three *ken* Hall.
13. 七間堂.
14. 獨覺.
15. *Daichido-ron*, XXVIII (*Taishō*, XXV, 182).

1. Cf. *Konjaku monogatarishū* (XII, 14).
2. The Ki family is listed in the *Shinsen shōjiroku* as one descended from the imperial family; residents of Kii province.
3. 長男 *chōnan* may mean 丁, men from twenty-one to sixty (see *Ryō no gige*, "Ko-ryō," Article 6).
4. Present Kibi-chō, Arida-gun, Wakayama-ken 和歌山縣有田郡吉備町.
5. The Nakatomi family is a priestly family which traditionally served the kami. The powerful Fujiwara was a branch of this family.
6. 小男 *shōnan* is a boy between four and six (cf. n. 3, above).

Ama district 海部郡濱中郷[7] in the same province. Kinomaro no asomi 紀萬侶朝臣[8] lived at a port in Hidaka district 日高郡[9] in the same province, using a net to catch fish. Umakai and Ojimaro were given an annual payment for their labor by Maro no asomi, and both were driven hard day and night to catch fish by net.

In the reign of Emperor Shirakabe, on the sixth of the sixth month in the summer of the second year of the hare, the sixth year of the Hōki era,[10] it suddenly blew hard and rained in torrents, so that the water flooded the port and floated various timbers and logs into the sea. Maro no asomi sent Umakai and Ojimaro to collect driftwood. Both man and boy made the collected timber into a raft on which they rode, trying to row against the current. The sea was extremely rough, breaking the ropes that held the raft together, and immediately the raft broke apart and drifted out of the port into the sea. The man and the boy each got hold of a piece of wood and drifted to sea on it. Both of them were ignorant, but they never ceased wailing, "Śākya-muni Buddha, please deliver us from this calamity!"

After five days, the boy was eventually cast by the waves onto the beach at a salt makers' village, Tamachino no ura, in the south-western part of Awaji province 淡路國田町野浦,[11] in the evening. The other man, Umakai, was cast onto the same spot early in the morning on the sixth day. The local people, having asked them why they had been cast by the waves onto the shore, learned what had happened and took care of them out of pity, reporting it to the provincial magistrate.[12] When he heard, he came to see them and gave them food because he was sympathetic.

In grief, the boy said, "As I have followed a man who kills, my suffering is immeasurable. If I go home, I shall be driven to begin killing again and never be able to stop." Thus he stayed at the pro-vincial temple in Awaji province 淡路國,[13] becoming a follower of the monk of that temple.

Umakai, however, went home after two months. When his family saw his face and protruding eyes, they wondered and said, "He was drowned in the sea. The seventh seventh day[14] has passed, and we

7. Present Shimotsu-chō, Kaisō-gun, Wakayama-ken 和歌山縣海草郡下津町.
8. Unknown. For the Ki family see n. 2, above.
9. Present Hidaka-gun, Wakayama-ken 和歌山縣日高郡.
10. 775, in Emperor Kōnin's reign.
11. Takeda and Itabashi read this "Minami omota no ura, Awaji province" 淡路國南面田野浦, while Endō and Kasuga suggest that 三原 might be replaced with 南西.
12. 國司 kokushi or kuni no tsukasa.
13. Located at present Mihara-chō, Mihara-gun, Hyōgo-ken 兵庫縣三原郡三原町.
14. 七々日, that is, the forty-ninth day, the last day of the funeral rites.

have already offered a vegetarian feast[15] to thank the Buddha for his benevolence. How could he come back alive so unexpectedly? Is it a dream, or is he a ghost?'' Thereupon, Umakai told his family in detail what had happened, and they were sorrowful as well as happy. Awakened and disillusioned with the world, he entered the mountains to practice dharma. Those who saw or heard of him could not but marvel at the event.

The sea being full of danger, it was owing to the power of Shaka-nyorai[16] and the deep faith of those who drifted on the sea that they could survive the peril. The immediate repayment of our deeds is as sure as in this instance, and how much more certain repayment in future lives will be!

# 26

*On Receiving the Immediate Penalty of Violent*
*Death for Collecting Debts by Force and*
*with High Interest*[1]

Tanaka no mahito Hiromushime 田中眞人廣虫女[2] was the wife of Oya no agatanushi Miyate 小屋縣主宮手,[3] of Outer Junior Sixth Rank, Upper Grade, a governor[4] of Miki district, Sanuki province 讃岐國 美貴郡.[5] She gave birth to eight children and was very rich. Among her possessions were cattle, slaves, money and rice,[6] and fields. However, she lacked faith and was so greedy that she would never give away anything. She used to make a great profit by selling rice wine diluted with water. On the day when she made a loan, she used a small measuring cup, while on the day she collected, she used a big measuring cup. Or, when she lent rice, she used a lightweight scale, but, when she collected it, she used a heavyweight scale.[7] She did not

15. 齋食 *saijiki*; see I.24, n. 3.
16. 釋迦如來, Śākyamuni Tathāgata.

1. Similar to I.10, 20; II.9, 15, 32, the motif of rebirth in the form of an ox or a cow as a penalty.
2. Unknown.
3. Unknown. *Agatanushi* is a title.
4. 大領 *dairyō*.
5. Present Miki-chō, Kita-gun, Kagawa-ken 香川縣木田郡三木町.
6. 稻錢 loaned with interest.
7. 小斤 *shōgon*, 大斤 *daigon*; see I.23, n. 9; I.30, n. 10.

show any mercy in forcibly collecting interest, sometimes ten times and sometimes a hundred times as much as the original loan. She was strict in collecting debts, never being generous. Because of this, many people worried a great deal and abandoned their homes to escape from her, wandering in other provinces. There has never been anybody so greedy.

On the first of the sixth month in the seventh year of the Hōki era,[8] Hiromushime took to her bed and was confined there for many days. On the twentieth of the seventh month she called her husband and eight sons to her bedside and told them about the dream she had experienced.

"I was summoned to the palace of King Yama, and told of my three sins: the first one consists of using much of the property of the Three Treasures and not repaying it; the second, of making great profits by selling diluted rice wine; the third, of using two kinds of measuring cups and scales, giving seven-tenths for a loan and collecting twelve-tenths for a debt. 'I summoned you because of these sins. I just want to show you that you should receive a penalty in this life,' said the king."

She passed away on the same day she told of the dream. They did not cremate her for seven days, but called thirty-two monks and lay brothers to pray to Buddha for her for nine days. On the evening of the seventh day she was restored to life and opened the lid of the coffin. When they came to look in it, the stench was indescribable. Her body above the waist had already turned into an ox with four inch horns on the forehead; her two hands had become ox hooves, with the nails cracked like the insteps of an ox hoof. The lower body below the waist was human in form. She did not like rice but grass, and, after eating, ruminated. She did not wear any clothes, lying in her filth. Streams of people from the east and west hurried to gather and look at her in wonder. In shame, grief, and pity, her husband and children prostrated themselves on the ground, making numerous vows. In order to atone for her sin, they offered various treasures to Miki-dera 三木寺,[9] and seventy oxen, thirty horses, fifty acres of fields, and four thousand rice bundles to Tōdai-ji 東大寺.[10] They wrote off all debts. At the end of five days she died after the provincial and district magistrates had seen her and were about to send a report to

---

8. 776, in Emperor Kōnin's reign.

9. Since the temple was named after the local name, it might be founded by local magistrates. She is said to have used the temple property, which may belong to Miki-dera.

10. See Chap. I(1)c.

the central government. All the witnesses in that district and province grieved over and worried about her.

She did not know the law of karmic retribution, being unreasonable and unrighteous. Thus we know that this is an immediate penalty for unreasonable deeds and unrighteous deeds. Since the immediate penalty comes as surely as this, how much more certain will be the penalty in a future life.

One scripture[11] says: "Those who don't repay their debts will atone for them, being reborn as a horse or an ox." The debtor is compared to a slave, the creditor to a master. The former is like a pheasant, the latter a hawk. If you make a loan, don't use excessive force to collect the debt, for, if you are unreasonable, you will be reborn as a horse or an ox and made to work by your debtor.

# 27

*On an Extraordinary Sign of a Skull Shown to the Man*
*Who Removed a Bamboo Shoot from Its Eye*
*and Prayed for It[1]*

In the reign of Emperor Shirakabe, at the end of the twelfth month in the winter of the fifth year of the horse, the ninth year of the Hōki era,[2] Homuchi no Makihito 品知牧人,[3] from the village of Ōyama, Ashida district, Bingo province 備後國葦田郡大山里,[4] traveled to the Fukatsu Market, Fukatsu district 深津郡深津市[5] in the same province, to shop for the new year's celebration.

Since it grew dark while he was still on the road, he slept in the bamboo grove at Ashida in Ashida district.[6]

In the place he chose to spend the night, he heard a plaintive voice say, "How my eye hurts!" Hearing it, he could not sleep all night, though he lay curled up on the ground.

11. A summary of a passage from the *Jōjitsu-ron*. See II.32, n. 12.

1. Similar to I.12, III.1, the motif of the "grateful dead." See Chap. II(2)a.
2. 778, in Emperor Kōnin's reign.
3. Homuchi is the family name; Makihito, the given name.
4. Present Ashina-gun, Hiroshima 廣島縣蘆品郡.
5. Present Fukayasu-gun, Hiroshima-ken 廣島縣深安郡.
6. Present Fuchū-shi, Hiroshima-ken 廣島縣府中市.

The next morning he discovered a skull with a bamboo shoot growing up through the eye socket. He pulled out the bamboo, releasing the skull from suffering, and offered it his dried rice, saying, "May I attain good fortune."

At the market his shopping proceeded as he had wished. He wondered if, in response to his prayer, the skull was repaying his kindness. On the way back from the market he stayed overnight in the same bamboo grove. Then the skull appeared as a live being, saying, "I am Ananokimi no Otogimi 穴君弟君[7] of the village of Yanakuni, Ashida district 葦田郡屋穴國郷,[8] and I was killed by my wicked uncle Akimaru 秋丸. Whenever the wind blew, my eye would hurt terribly. Thanks to your compassion, my suffering has been removed. I have attained immense joy, and I will never forget your kindness. Being overcome with happiness, I would like to repay you for your kindness. On New Year's Eve[9] will you visit my home in the village of Yanakuni where my parents live? That night is the only time I can repay your kindness."

More and more Makihito's wonder increased, and he kept it a secret. On New Year's Eve he went to the house. Taking his hand, the spirit led him into the house where they shared the offerings made there and ate together. The spirit wrapped the rest of the offerings and gave them to Makihito, together with some treasures. Then the spirit suddenly disappeared.

When the parents, who had come to the place to worship the spirits, saw Makihito, they were surprised and asked him why he had come. Whereupon he told them the whole story in detail. They seized Akimaru and asked why he had killed Otogimi, saying to him, "According to your story, on the way to the market with our son you met a creditor and forsook our son because that man pressured you for the return of the debt. You asked, 'Did he come home?' We answered, 'Not yet. We haven't seen him.' Why does the story we have heard differ from your story?"

Shaken to the bottom of his heart, Akimaru the robber could not conceal the facts, and he eventually said, "Toward the end of last year, I went to the market with Otogimi in order to shop for New Year's Day. He brought a horse, cloth, cotton, and salt with him. As it got dark on the way, we stopped at the bamboo grove, where I killed him in secret and took his belongings. I went to the Fukatsu

7. *Kimi* is an honorific title.
8. Unlocated.
9. For cosmic renewal rites at the end of the year, see Chap. II(1)a.

market to sell his horse to a man from Sanuki province 讚岐國,[10] and now I am using the rest of his things myself."

Having heard this, the parents said, "Ah! Our dear son was killed by you and not by robbers!" Since sons of the same parents are as close to them as a reed to a rush, they concealed the brother's sin, banishing him but not making it public. They thanked Makihito and offered him more food and drink. When he returned, he related this story.

Even a skull exposed to the sun is like this! It repays a food offering with good fortune and benevolence with benevolence. Therefore, how could a man forget benevolence? This is what the *Nehan-gyō*[11] means when it says: "Man repays benevolence which he has received with benevolence."[12]

# 28

### *On an Extraordinary Sign Shown by the Sixteen-foot-high Image of Miroku, the Neck of Which Was Bitten by Ants*[1]

In the village of Kishi, Nagusa district, Kii province 紀伊國名草郡 貴志里,[2] there was a temple, called Kishi-dera 貴志寺. It was so named because villagers of Kishi had built it with their donations.

In the reign of Emperor Shirakabe,[3] a lay brother lived in this temple. Once he heard groans and a voice saying, "What pain! What pain!" It sounded like it was an old man. Early in the evening[4] he thought that a traveler had come to stay at the temple because of illness. He got up to make the rounds of the temple, looking for the person, but he could not find him. At that time there was timber for a pagoda, but it had never been used. It had been left to lie on the ground and decay for a long time. The lay brother wondered whether what he had heard had been the groaning sound of the spirit of the

---

10. Present Kagawa-ken 香川縣.
11. Unlocated in the *Nehan-gyō*.
12. 受恩報恩.

1. Similar to II.17, 22, 23, 26; III.17.
2. In the present city of Wakayama.
3. Emperor Kōnin.
4. From sunset to about eight o'clock.

pagoda, and the painful groan was heard every night. When he could endure no longer, he got up to look for the sufferer, but there was still nobody around. At dawn, however, the groaning was far more intense than usual, echoing through heaven and earth. He wondered again if it were the spirit of the pagoda.

When he arose early the next morning and looked around the temple, he discovered that the head of the sixteen-foot image of Miroku 彌勒[5] had been severed and had fallen to the ground. About a thousand large ants were gathered there, devouring the head. Having seen this, he reported it to the patrons of the temple. In grief, they repaired the image and held a dedication ceremony with reverence.

It is said that the Buddha statue is not alive, so how could it suffer and be sick? Indeed, we learn that this was the manifestation of the Buddha's mind. Even after the death of Buddha, the dharma-body always exists, eternal and unchangeable. You should not doubt any further.

# 29

## On the Immediate Penalty of Violent Death Incurred by an Ignorant Man Who Broke a Wooden Buddha Image a Village Child Had Made in Playing[1]

In the village of Hamanaka, Niki, Ama district, Kii province 紀伊國海部郡仁嗜濱中村,[2] there was an ignorant man whose name is unknown. Born ignorant, he did not know the law of causation.

There was a path running along the mountain[3] between Ama 海部 and Ate 安諦.[4] It was called Tamasaka 玉坂.[5] If one climbs the mountain from Hamanaka, traveling due south, he will reach the village of Hata 秦里.[6] Once a child of that village went into the mountain to collect firewood and played by that mountain path, carving a piece

5. Maitreya; see Chap. II(3)b, n. 131.

1. Probably written as an illustration for the second chapter of the *Hoke-kyō*, "Hōben-bon" 方便品 (Kern, *Saddharma*, Chap. II, "Skillfulness").
2. In the vicinity of present Shimotsu-shi, Wakayama-ken 和歌山縣下津市.
3. One of the Nagamine Mts. 長峰山脈, forming the boundary between Kaisō-gun and Arida-gun.
4. See III.10, n. 4.
5. Unidentified.
6. Present Hata, Shimotsu-shi 下津市畑.

of wood into a Buddha image and piling stones into a pagoda. He placed the image in the stone pagoda and occasionally played there, making offerings.

In the reign of Emperor Shirakabe, an ignorant man laughed at the statue carved by the child in his play, chopping and breaking it with an axe. Hardly had he gone any distance when he threw himself on the ground, bleeding from the nose and mouth with both eyes plucked out, dying in an instant like the disappearance of an illusion.

Indeed, we learn that the Guardian of dharma[7] is present. How could we not revere it? The *Hoke-kyō* explains it thus: "If children draw an image of Buddha with a twig, brush, or fingernail in their play, they will all attain Buddhahood. Or if they raise one hand and bow to worship a Buddha-image, they will attain the supreme stage of Buddhahood."[8] Therefore, be pious and faithful.

# 30

## *On the Monk Who Accumulated Merits by Making Buddhist Images and Showed an Extraordinary Sign at the End of His Life*

Elder Master Kanki's 觀規 secular name was Mimana no Kanuki 三間名干岐.[1] He was from Nagusa district, Kii province 紀伊國名草郡.[2] He was naturally gifted in carving. He was such a learned monk that he fulfilled the role of a speaker in a ceremony[3] and was influential among the people. He supported his family by agricultural work.

In the village of Noo 能應村[4] in Nagusa district, there was a temple which his ancestors had built. It was formerly called Miroku-dera 彌勒寺,[5] but popularly referred to as Noo-dera. In the reign of Em-

---

7. 護法 *gohō*.
8. See Chap. II(1)c, n. 53; also, Katō, trans., *Myōhō-renge-kyō*, 57–58.

1. Mimana 任那 is the name of the estate held by the Yamato court from the fourth century to 562. Kanuki is a popular name for ancient Korean royal families. Cf. *Nihon shoki*, XVII (Keitai 23 : 4); Aston, "Nihongi," II, 19: "Konomata Kanki 己能末多干岐, King of Imna, came to the court."
2. Present Kaisō-gun, Wakayama-ken.
3. 得業 *tokugō*; monks who have accomplished the task in one of the three great ceremonies of the southern capital, that is, Yuima-e and Hokke-e of Kōfuku-ji 興福寺維摩會, 法華會 and Saishō-e of Yakushi-ji 藥師寺最勝會.
4. Present Yamaguchi-mura 山口村.
5. Although the temple is named after Maitreya, it does not seem to be dedicated to Maitreya. However, it may have enshrined Maitreya when founded.

peror Shōmu, he made a vow to carve a sixteen-foot Śākya[6] and its attendants;[7] he completed them in the sixth year of the sheep, the tenth year of the Hōki era, in the reign of Emperor Shirakabe,[8] and placed them in the golden hall of Noo-dera, holding a dedication ceremony. Then he made another vow to carve a ten-foot wooden statue of the Eleven-headed Bodhisattva Kannon,[9] but he did not complete the work. Having spent years without many helpers, he he was too old and weak to carve it himself. When he was over eighty, he passed away in bed at Noo-dera on the eleventh day of the second month, in the spring of the tenth year of the boar, the first year of the Enryaku era, in the reign of Emperor Yamabe 山部[10] who governed Ōyashima at Nagaoka Palace.[12]

After two days he was restored to life and called his disciple Myōki 明規,[13] saying, "I forgot to say one word and, since I could not endure it, I came back to the world." Then he had an elevated seat made on the floor, a rug spread on it, and a meal prepared. He invited Musashi no suguri Tarimaro 武藏村主多利丸[14] of the devotees' organization,[15] had him sit on the seat while he himself served the meal, and ate facing his guest. When it was over, he arose and, leading Myōki and all his relatives, knelt to pay homage to Tarimaro, saying, "I, Kanki, have used up my share of life, dying suddenly without completing the statue of Kannon. Luckily, having this good opportunity, I am wondering how I can express my hope. I beg you in your benevolence to complete the sacred image. If this moderate wish of mine is granted even in part, I will gain great fortune in the future and you will gain the merits for an immediate reward. As I had no control over my sincere wish, I dared to come back to make such a bold request. In awe and fear I am appealing to you in reverence."

Thereupon, Tarimaro as well as Myōki and the others grieved and wailed, saying to him, "We will be sure to complete the work you have told us about." Hearing this, the monk was delighted and stood up, clasping his hands in veneration.

6. 釋迦丈六; see I.32, n. 6.
7. 脇士 kyōji; Bodhisattvas Mañjuśrī and Samantabhadra.
8. 779, in the reign of Emperor Kōnin.
9. 十一面觀音; see Chap. II(3)b, n. 137.
10. 782, in the reign of Emperor Kanmu.
11. See II.1, n. 3.
12. Located at present Otokuni-gun, Kyoto-fu 京都府乙訓郡. Nagaoka was the capital from 784 to 794.
13. Unknown.
14. Unknown.
15. 知識 chishiki; see Chap. I(1)d, n. 110.

Two days later, on the fifteenth of the same month, he called Myōki and said to him, "Today is the anniversary of Buddha's entry into nirvana,[16] and I, too, will end my life." Myōki was about to say that the master was right, but, out of love for his dear master, he lied, saying, "No, the anniversary has not come yet." Looking at the calendar, the master said, "Today is the fifteenth. How could you lie by saying that the day had not come, my child?"

Having asked for hot water, he washed himself. He changed his clothes, knelt to clasp his hands in veneration, held an incense burner, faced to the west, and died at four in the afternoon of the same day.[17] In accord with his wish, the Buddhist artist Tarimaro had already completed the statue and held the dedication ceremony to report to Buddha how the statue came to be made. It is now found in the pagoda of Noo-dera.

The note says: How praiseworthy the Most Venerable Mimana no Kanuki is for keeping the Buddha's mind inside and manifesting an average form outside, living a mundane, householder's life and yet not defiling his jewel of the precepts.[18] At his last moment he faced to the west, and his devotion to the vow made his spirit work out an extraordinary sign. Indeed, we know that this is sacred and not ordinary.

# 31

## On a Woman Who Gave Birth to Stones and Enshrined Them as Kami[1]

In the village of Kusumi, Mizuno, Katakata district, Mino province 美濃國方縣郡水野鄉楠見村,[2] there was a woman whose surname was

---

16. 佛涅槃 Butsu-nehan; the fifteenth of the second month is regarded as the date of Śākyamuni's entry into nirvana.

17. This is the typical manner of death for those who have faith in rebirth in the western pure land. Cf. I.22.

18. 戒珠 kaishu, virtue of self-discipline.

1. One of the legends on the birth and growth of stones. See Yanagita Kunio, "Seiseki densetsu," Teihon Yanagita Kunio shū, V, 493–498.

2. Present Nagara, Gifu-shi 岐阜市長良. For the significance of this story, see Chap. II(2)b.

Agata-no-uji 縣氏.[3] She was over twenty but unmarried, and she became pregnant without any sexual intercourse. At the end of the second month in the spring of the tenth year of the boar, the first year of the Enryaku era, in the reign of Emperor Yamabe,[4] she gave birth to two stones after a three-year pregnancy. They measured five inches in diameter. One was blue and white mixed together, while the other was pure blue. They grew year after year.[5]

In Atsumi 淳見 district,[6] next to Katakata district, there was a great kami, whose name was Inaba 伊奈婆.[7] The deity took possession of a diviner[8] and spoke through him, saying, "The two stones which were born are my own children." Therefore, they were enshrined at the girl's residence in a sacred place surrounded with a hedge.[9]

We have never heard a story like this from ancient times until today. This is also a miraculous event in our country.

# 32

## On a Fisherman Netting Fish Who Was Almost Drowned in the Sea but Saved Owing to His Devotion to Bodhisattva Myōken[1]

Kurehara no imiki Nanimomaro 吳原忌寸名妹丸[2] was of the village of Hata, Takechi district, Yamato province 大和國高市郡波多里.[3] From his childhood he used to make nets and catch fish. On the evening of the nineteenth day of the eighth month, in the autumn of the first year of the rat, the second year of the Enryaku era,[4] he went out

3. The *Sandai jitsuroku* 三代實錄 gives the same name as a local gentry family.
4. 782, in the reign of Emperor Kanmu.
5. See Chap. II(2)b.
6. Present Inaba-gun, Gifu-ken 岐阜縣稻葉郡.
7. Inaba Shrine 稻葉神社 is located in this district.
8. 卜者 *kamnagi*.
9. 忌籬 *imigaki;* or *igaki*, the hedge which marks the holy precincts of a shrine.

1. Similar to III.35.
2. Unknown. Since the name *imiki* was often conferred on immigrant families, the Kurehara family may have immigrated from China.
3. Present Hata, Takechi-mura, Takechi-gun 高市郡高市村畑.
4. Enryaku 2 is the tenth year of the boar 癸亥, and Enryaku 3 the first year of the rat 甲子 (784).

upon the sea between Iwataki Island 伊波多岐嶋[5] in Ama district in Kii province 紀伊國海部郡 and Awaji province 淡路國[6] to cast a net and catch fish. There were nine fishermen in three boats. All at once a gale came up, destroying the three boats and drowning all the men except him.

Floating on the water, Nanimomaro devoted his heart to Bodhisattva Myōken,[7] making a vow and saying, "If you save my life, I will make a statue of Myōken as tall as I am." He floated on the sea and battled the waves, exhausting himself and nearly losing consciousness, being more asleep than awake. He awoke on a bright moonlit night to discover himself lying on the grass on the beach of Kata 蚊田浦濱,[8] Ama district, Kii province. Having been saved, he took his own measurements and made a statue as tall as himself.

Ah, how miraculous! When the gale destroyed the boats and waves drowned his friends, he was the only one that survived. Therefore, he made a statue as tall as he was. Indeed, we learn that he was saved by the great help of Myōken and the power of his devotion.

# 33

*On the Immediate Penalty of Violent Death for*
*Persecuting a Humble, Begging Novice*[1]

Ki no atae Yoshitari 紀直吉足[2] was popularly called Lord Hashi no iegimi 橋家長[3] in the village of Wake, Hidaka district, Kii province 紀伊國日高郡別里.[4] He was innately evil natured and did not believe in the law of karmic causation. In the fifth month in the summer of the second year of the ox, the fourth year of the Enryaku era,[5] a provincial official who was making the rounds of the district to give out

5. It may be Tomogashima 友島 off the coast of Kada, Kaisō-gun, Wakayama-ken 和歌山縣 海草郡加太.
6. Present Awajishima, Hyōgo-ken 兵庫縣淡路島.
7. See Chap. II(3)b, n. 133.
8. See n. 5, above.

1. Similar to I.29; II.1, 35; III.14, 15; etc.
2. The *Shinsen shōjiroku* lists the Kii family in Kinai as descended from kami.
3. See I.10, n. 3.
4. Present Hidaka-gun, Wakayama-ken.
5. 785, in the reign of Emperor Kanmu.

loans of government rice[6] came to that district to distribute them to all.

There was a self-ordained monk[7] who was called Ise no shami 伊勢 沙彌.[8] Reciting the divine names of the Twelve Yakṣa[9] of the *Yakushi-gyō* 藥師經,[10] he went around the village begging. He followed the official who was distributing the rice and came to the gate of the evil man. At the sight of the mendicant, the latter did not offer anything, but persecuted him by scattering the rice he had been carrying and also stripped him of his surplice. The mendicant ran away and hid himself in the residential quarters of Wake-dera 別寺.[11] The evil man gave chase and caught him there, brought him back to his own door, picked up a big stone, took aim at the mendicant's head and said, "Recite the divine names of the Twelve Yakṣa, and bind me with a charm." The mendicant refused, but the evil man pressed him harder. The abuse was so unbearable that the mendicant recited them once and ran away. Not long after that, the evil man fell to the ground and died.

There should be no doubt that the man was punished by the Guardian of dharma. Even a self-ordained monk deserves to be regarded with tolerance, for sages live hidden among ordinary monks.[12] Do not try to pick holes in a person who has no obvious faults as if you were blowing back the hair to search for a scar. If you try to find faults, even those who are in the three preliminary stages[13] or the ten stages[14] in the bodhisattva's ascent have some. If you look for virtues, even those who speak ill of dharma or prevent good have something worthy of praise.

Accordingly, the *Jūrin-gyō* 十輪經[15] says: "As an orchid, even if it has withered, excels other flowers, so monks, even if they violate

6. 正税 *shōzei*; see I.23, n. 9, for the government loan system of rice as one form of taxation.
7. 自度 *jido*.
8. Since self-ordained monks did not have clerical names, they were often called after their native place. See I.27; III.10.
9. 十二藥叉, 十二神將 Jūni yasha or Twelve Divine Generals; attendants of Yakushi-nyorai 藥師如來, who protect ascetics.
10. *Yakushi rurikō nyorai hongan kudoku-kyō* 藥師瑠璃光如來本願功德經 (*Taishō*, XIV, No. 450).
11. Unidentified.
12. 隱身聖人交凡中故. See I.4, n. 14.
13. 三賢 *sangen*; in the Mahayana tradition there are three preliminary stages preceding the ten stages (see n. 14, below) in the practice of bodhisattvas. Although scriptures differ in the details, the most generally accepted theory is found in the fifty-two stages of the *Yōraku hongō-kyō* 瓔珞本業經 (*Taishō*, XXIV, No. 1485).
14. 十地 *jūji*; see I.Preface, n. 15.
15. *Daijō daijū Jizō jūrin-gyō* (*Taishō*, XIII, No. 411).

precepts, excel non-Buddhists. To talk about a monk's faults such as whether he violates or keeps the precepts, whether he recognizes or does not recognize the precepts, or whether he has or has not faults is a graver sin than that of letting the bodies of innumerable Buddhas bleed."[16]

According to a certain commentary,[17] this means: "Even if you cause the Buddha-body to bleed, you cannot block the Buddha's teaching. However, if you talk about a monk's faults, you will destroy many men's faith, arouse their cravings, and block the Buddha's path. Therefore, the bodhisattva desires to look for virtues but not faults."

The Zōbō ketsugi-kyō 像法決疑經[18] says, "In the future secular officials should not make monks pay taxes. If they do, they will commit an immeasurable sin. Laymen should not ride on the cattle belonging to the Three Treasures. Nor should they whip slaves[19] and the six kinds of domestic animals belonging to the samgha.[20] Nor should they accept the greetings of the slaves of the Three Treasures. If they do, they will all be punished. . . ."

Or another commentary[21] puts it this way: "Those who are greedy value even mud more than gold and jewels, and misers begrudge a gift, even when they are asked for dirt, never making offerings, being stingy of their wealth, and fearing that their accumulated wealth will become known to others. When they pass away, leaving their bodies, they join the group of hungry fiends who lament their pangs of hunger."

Speaking of wealth, it is shared by five parties: first, government officials who might come and ask for it unreasonably; second, robbers who might come to steal it; third, water which might wash it away; fourth, fire which might destroy it suddenly; fifth, wicked children who might waste it unreasonably.[22] Therefore, a bodhisattva is very happy to make offerings.

---

16. This quotation is closer to a passage in the Bonmō-kyō koshakki (Taishō, XL, 706) than to the original text of the Jūrin-gyō (Taishō, XIII, 741).

17. 義解 gige; unidentified.

18. Zōbō ketsugi-kyō (Taishō, LXXXV, 1337). The quotation differs a little from the original text; the original passage depicts the age of degenerate dharma which is coming, but the quoted passage is changed into a warning to secular officials.

19. 奴婢 nuhi; see Chap. I(1)a, n. 24.

20. The six domestic animals are the horse, ox, sheep, dog, pig, and fowl.

21. Daijōbu-ron (Taishō, XXX, 260b). See III.15, n. 5; also Haraguchi, "Nihon ryōiki," 59–60.

22. Kariya gives a passage of the Dai-hōshak-kyō 大寶積經 (Taishō, XII, No. 352) as the possible source of this statement, although there are slight differences. 一切財業 五家水火盜賊怨家債 主縣官惡子分耳.

# 34

*On Gaining an Immediate Cure of a Bad Disease for*
*Being Ordained and Practicing Good*[1]

Kose no Asame 巨勢姶女[2] was a woman from the village of Haniu, Nagusa district, Kii province 紀伊國名草郡埴生里.[3] In the eighth year of the ox, the fifth year of the Tenpyō hōji era,[4] she contracted a serious disease, which caused a growth as big as a melon on her neck. The pain almost killed her, and it was not cured for years. She thought to herself, "This disease was brought to me by my deeds not only in this life, but also in previous lives.[5] In order to be healed, I had better atone for my sins by practicing good." Thus, she shaved her head, was ordained, put on a surplice, and lived in Ōtani-dō 大谷堂[6] in the village, reciting the *Shin-gyō*[7] and practicing the path intently.

When fifteen years had passed, an ascetic named Chūsen 忠仙[8] came to the temple to live with her. In sympathy with her, he tried to cure her disease by reciting a formula, making a vow, and saying: "In order to cure this disease, I will recite the *Yakushi-gyō*[9] and the *Kongō hannya-kyō*[10] three thousand times, the *Kanzeon-gyō*[11] ten thousand times, and the *Kannon sanmai-kyō*[12] one hundred times."

Fourteen years later, he finished reciting the *Yakushi-gyō* two thousand and five hundred times, the *Kongō hannya-kyō* one thousand times, and the *Kanzeon-gyō* two hundred times. He was constantly chanting the Senju dharani.[13] Twenty-eight years passed from the time she contracted the disease, but the scriptures had not yet been recited as many times as had been vowed. About eight o'clock in the morning, on the twenty-seventh of the eleventh month, in the winter

---

1. The motif is miraculous healing; similar to I.8; III.11, 12, 21.
2. The Kose family is listed in the *Shinsen shōjiroku* as descendants of the imperial family.
3. Present Kaisō-gun, Wakayama-ken. Haniu is unidentified.
4. 761, in the reign of Emperor Jun'nin.
5. 宿業; see I.8, n. 4.
6. A small private temple unidentified.
7. *Hannya haramitsu shin-gyō;* see Chap. II(1)a, n. 19.
8. Unknown.
9. *Yakushi rurikō nyorai hongan kudoku-kyō*, 1 vol. (*Taishō*, XIV, No. 450).
10. *Kongō hannya haramitsu-kyō*, 1 vol.; see II.24, n. 20.
11. Chap. xxv of the *Hoke-kyō* (*Taishō*, IX, 56c–58b).
12. *Kanzeon bosatsu juki-kyō* 觀世音菩薩授記經 , 1 vol. (*Taishō*, XII, No. 371).
13. See III.14, n. 11.

of the sixth year of the Enryaku era,[14] her growth opened and discharged the pus of its own accord, and it was healed as she had prayed.

Indeed, we learn that it took place owing to the miraculous power of the Mahayana divine formula and the accumulated merits of the sick person and the ascetic. This is what people mean when they say that the all-embracing compassion[15] brings a miraculous sign to the pious, and mysterious knowledge of the ultimate principles of voidness[16] reveals a clear manifestation to men of deep faith.

# 35

## *On Being Penalized for Abusing an Official's Authority and Ruling Unrighteously*[1]

In the reign of Emperor Shirakabe, a man by the name of Hi no kimi 火君[2] of Matsura district, Hizen province in Tsukushi 筑紫肥前國松浦郡,[3] died suddenly and reached the land of Yama. When the king checked, it turned out that his death was premature, and he was sent back home.

On his way back he saw a hell which looked like a boiling kettle in the ocean. In it something black like a stump that was sinking and rising as the water boiled called to him, saying, "Wait! I have something to tell you." It sank as the water boiled, and then it came again to the surface, saying, "Wait! I have something to tell you."

After this had happened three times, the object spoke a fourth time, saying "I am Mononobe no Komaro 物部古丸[4] from Harihara district in Tōtōmi province 遠江國榛原郡.[5] During my life I worked as an official[6] for many years in charge of transporting hulled rice and took other people's property unrighteously. Because of this sin, I have been suffering here. I pray that you will copy the *Hoke-kyō* for me so that I may be excused from my sin."

14. 787, in Emperor Kanmu's reign.
15. 無緣大悲 the great mercy of Buddha and the bodhisattvas, Kannon in particular.
16. 無相妙智 as expounded in the *Hannya-kyō*.

1. Cf. *Genkō shakusho* (XXIX).
2. Probably of the local gentry. See *Nihon shoki*, XIX (Kinmei 17:1): "The Lord of Hi in Tsukushi was sent to escort a prince of Paekche."
3. Matsuura-gun is now divided into two parts, one in present Saga-ken, the other in present Nagasaki-ken.
4. Unknown.
5. Present Harihara-gun, Shizuoka-ken.
6. 綱丁 *gōchō*, a transportation master.

When Hi no kimi came back from the Land of the Dead,[7] he wrote a precise report of what he had seen and heard and sent it to the local government.[8] Having received this report, the local government in turn forwarded it to the central government. As the central government did not take it seriously, the grand secretary[9] did not bother to report it to the emperor, ignoring it for twenty years.

When Sugano no asomi Mamichi 菅野朝臣眞道[10] of the Junior Fourth Rank, Upper Grade, was appointed head secretary,[11] he noticed the report, and presented it to Emperor Yamabe.[12] Having heard this, the emperor inquired of Assistant Executive Sekyō 施曉僧頭,[13] saying, "Are we, living beings in this world, released from suffering after twenty years in hell?" Sekyō answered, "Twenty years on earth is only the beginning of the suffering in hell, because one hundred years in this world corresponds to one day and night in hell.[14] This is why he is not yet released."

Upon hearing this, the emperor made a sign of repentence and sent his messenger to Tōtōmi province to investigate Komaro's case. Having asked about Komaro's deeds, he discovered that the report was true. The emperor grieved over this, believing it, and summoned four scripture copiers to copy the *Hoke-kyō* for Komaro on the seventh of the third month in the beginning of the fifteenth year of the Enryaku era.[15] He organized a devotees' association to support this work, inviting the prince regent, ministers, and officials in number equal to the 69,384 characters of the scripture.[16] Also, the emperor held an elaborate service at a private temple in the capital of Nara,[17] to recite that scripture with the Most Venerable Zenshu 善珠[18] as lecturer[19]

7. See Chap. II(1)b, for 黃泉(國) Yomi (no kuni).

8. 太宰府 Dazaifu; the local government which controlled all of Kyūshū and the islands of Iki and Tsushima.

9. 大辨官 *daiben no tsukasa*, the secretary under *daijō daijin*, of the Junior Fourth Rank, Upper Grade. See *Ryō no gige*, "Kan'i-ryō," Article 9.

10. Of an immigrant family. The title was conferred on him in 790; he died in 814.

11. The head secretary is called *sadaiben* 左大辨. See *Nihon kōki* (Enryaku 16:3:11).

12. Emperor Kanmu.

13. 施曉僧都 who was appointed junior assistant executive 少僧都 in 797.

14. See Chap. II(1)c, n. 60.

15. 796.

16. The number of all the Chinese characters of the *Hoke-kyō*.

17. 平城宮野寺; unidentified. One theory maintains that it is a private temple in contrast to the state temples of Nara; another, that it is a temple transferred from Nara to Kyoto by Emperor Kanmu.

18. (724–797) a monk of Akishino-dera and Kōfuku-ji who devoted himself to the study of the Yuishiki doctrines. Five out of his twenty writings are extant. See III.39. See also Inoue Mitsusada, *Nihon Jōdokyō seiritsushi*, 75–81. Inoue traces Zenshu's faith in the pure land to the Kegon School of Silla.

19. 講師 *kōji*.

and Assistant Executive Sekyō as reciter,[20] giving merits to Komaro to save his spirit from suffering.

Ah! How deplorable he was who, without knowing the law of karmic causation, ruled unrighteously like a fox who borrows a tiger's skin and its power and who was eventually punished for his inordinately mean heart! The law of causation never fails to work.

# 36

### On Receiving a Penalty for Building a Lower Pagoda and Taking down the Banners of the Temple[1]

Fujiwara no asomi Nagate 藤原朝臣永手[2] of the Senior First Rank was Chancellor[3] in the reign of Emperor Shirakabe who resided at Nara Palace. In the first year of the Enryaku era, his son Ieyori 家依[4] of the Junior Fourth Rank, Upper Grade, had a bad dream about his father, and said to him, "More than thirty soldiers came to summon you, Father. Since this is an ill omen, you should pray to ward off disaster."

In spite of this warning, his father would not follow his advice. Meanwhile, he died. Then Ieyori succumbed to a long disease and invited monks and lay brothers to protect him with formulas, but was not healed. At that time one *dhyāna* master among those attending him made a vow, saying, "I live a life of discipline according to the Buddha's teaching so that I may save other living beings. Now I offer my life in exchange for my patient's. If the Buddha's teaching is true, please let the patient live!" Not caring for his own life, he put hot charcoals on his hand to burn incense, walked round the Buddha, chanting dharani, and suddenly began to run around and roll on the ground.

---

20. 讀師 *tokuji.*

1. Cf. *Genkō shakusho* (XXIX), *Shoku Nihongi*, XXXI (Hōki 2:2:22).
2. ·He served Emperor Shōmu, Empress Kōken, Emperor Jun'nin, Empress Shōtoku, and Emperor Kōnin. See *Shoku Nihongi*, XXXI (Hōki 2:2:22). When he died, he was the Senior Minister of the Senior First Rank. Since, according to the *Ryō no gige*, ministers belong to the Second Rank, there is some confusion in the *Shoku Nihongi* as well as the *Nihon ryōiki*. The title of Chancellor was conferred by Emperor Kōnin posthumously. The *Nihon ryōiki* is incorrect in dating his death in 782 or later.
3. 太政大臣.
4. (?–785).

Then the patient talked, being possessed by a spirit, saying, "I am Nagate. I had the banners of Hokke-ji 法花寺[5] taken down and later was responsible for the pagodas of Saidai-ji 西大寺[6] having four corners instead of eight and five stories instead of seven. Because of this sin, I was summoned to the Office of King Yama, who made me hold a pillar of fire and drove bent nails into my hands, interrogating and beating me. Then the palace filled with smoke. When the king asked, 'What smoke is this?' there was a reply, 'This is the smoke of the incense from the hand of the monk who has been attending Ieyori, Nagate's son, suffering from disease.' Thereupon, the king released me and sent me back to the world. My body, however, has perished, and I have nothing to live in, and must float about in the air." All at once, the patient, who had not been eating, asked for food and recovered from his disease, leaving his sickbed.

Speaking of the banners of the temple, they are good causes for being born as a Buddhist universal king 轉輪王.[7] On the other hand, a pagoda is a treasury to store the Buddha's remains in the past, present and future. Accordingly, this man committed sins by taking down the banners of the temple and lowering the proposed height of the pagoda. How could we not be in awe? This is a recent instance of immediate repayment.[8]

# 37

*On Receiving a Penalty for Doing Evil because of*
*Ignorance of the Law of Karmic Causation*[1]

Saheki no sukune Itachi 佐伯宿禰伊太知[2] of the Junior Fourth Rank,

5. Located at present Hokkeji-chō, Nara-shi 奈良市法華寺町. Founded by Empress Kōmyō 光明皇后 in 741 as the headquarter of all provincial nunneries.
6. Located at present Saidaiji-chō, Nara-shi 奈良市西大寺町 and founded by Empress Shō-toku in 765. There were two five-storied pagodas at Saidai-ji.
7. See Chap. II(2)a, n. 79. Banners were symbols of royalty in India and later were used as symbols of the Buddhist dharma.
8. As shown (n. 1, above), this story differs greatly from the court history in its assessment of Nagate. In the court history he is a loyal and wise minister, but in the *Nihon ryōiki* he is a destroyer of the Three Treasures and hence made to suffer in hell. This story is intended to show that even a man of great influence and high status is not free from karmic retribution.

1. Similar to III.35 as to the motif of suffering in hell reported by a visitor to hell; similar to III.36 as to the hero politically lauded but religiously criticized.
2. Or 伊多智, 伊達, who won crucial wars against Nakamaro in 764 and was promoted to the Junior Sixth Rank (*Shoku Nihongi*, XXVI, Tenpyō jingo 1 : 1 : 7), and Junior Fourth Rank, Upper Grade (*ibid.*, XXXI, Hōki 2 : 3 : 1) in 771.

Upper Grade, lived in the reign of the emperors who resided at Nara Palace.[3]

Once a man from the capital went to Chikuzen 筑前[4] and died of a sudden illness, arriving at the palace of King Yama. Though he did not see anybody, he heard the voice of a man who was being beaten echoing through the earth. At every lash of the whip, he cried, "What pain! What pain!"

The king asked his clerks,[5] saying, "When he was in the world, what good did he do?" The clerks answered, "He made one copy of the *Hoke-kyō*." Then the king said, "Atone for his sins by balancing them against the scrolls of the scripture."[6] When they matched the scrolls with his sins, the scrolls were outnumbered without any comparison. Then they matched the 69,384 characters of the scripture[7] with his sins, but still the latter outnumbered the former, and he could not be saved. Thereupon, the king clapped his hands in surprise, saying "Although I have seen many people who committed sins and suffered, I have never seen a man who committed so many sins."

The man from the capital secretly asked a person beside him, "Who is the man being beaten?" The answer was, "This is Saheki no sukune Itachi." When he returned from the Land of the Dead[8] unexpectedly and was restored to life, he remembered the name very well and sent a report on the Land of the Dead to the local government.[9] The government, however, did not believe it. Therefore, he took an opportunity to go up to the capital by boat and gave a report on how Lord Itachi had labored and suffered in the palace of King Yama. At this news, his family was deeply troubled, saying, "From his death to seven times the seventh day[10] we practiced good and applied the merits to his benevolent spirit. How can we think of him suffering severely, having fallen in an evil state?" Then they made another copy of the *Hoke-kyō*, revered and dedicated it in order to save his spirit from suffering. This is also an extraordinary event.

3. He must have lived in the reigns of Emperor Shōmu, Empress Kōken (Shōtoku), and Emperor Kōnin.
4. Present Fukuoka-ken 福岡縣, the northern part of Tsukushi.
5. 諸史 *shoshi*, probably the same as 書史, clerks in charge of records.
6. The *Hoke-kyō* consists of either seven or eight scrolls or volumes.
7. See III.35, n. 17.
8. See Chap. II(1)b.
9. Dazaifu; see III.35, n. 8.
10. The forty-ninth day, the end of the funeral rites.

# 38

## On the Appearance of Good and Evil Omens Which
## Were Later Followed by Their Results[1]

It is said that before good and evil events occur they are preceded be some forms of songs which spread throughout the countryside. Thereupon, all the people under heaven hear them and sing them to communicate the message.

Ex-Emperor Shōhō-ōjin-shōmu, who had governed the country for twenty-five years at Nara Palace,[2] called High Councilor[3] Fujiwara no asomi Nakamaro 藤原朝臣仲麿[4] close to the throne and decreed, "It is my desire to make my daughter, Princess Abe 阿陪內親王,[5] and Prince Funado 道祖親王[6] rule over the country. What do you think of this? Do you agree with my decree?" In reply Nakamaro said, "It is an excellent idea," thus expressing his consent.

Thereupon the emperor made him drink the divine wine[7] and swear, saying to him, "You must swear an oath that, if you forget my decree, both heaven and earth shall hate you and bring you great disaster." Therefore, Nakamaro swore, saying, "If I do not follow Your Majesty's decree in the future, deities in heaven and earth shall hate and get angry with me, and I shall incur great disaster which will destroy my body and take away my life." After swearing this oath, he drank the divine wine, and the ceremony was over. Later, when the emperor passed away, Nakamaro followed his wish according to the decree and made Prince Funado the Prince Regent.

1. This story consists of two parts; the first part illustrates the mysterious correspondence between natural phenomena and human events, while the second part is an account of Kyōkai's own experience. The latter has an autobiographical quality, although it is more symbolic than factual. The Maeda manuscript omits the first part. For the motif, see Chap. I(1)a; Chap. II(1)a.

2. Emperor Shōmu (r. 724–749).

3. 大納言 dainagon.

4. Or 惠美押勝 (706–764). For his biography, see Shoku Nihongi, XXV (Tenpyō hōji 8:9:18); Kishi Toshio, Fujiwara no Nakamaro. He became Chanellor of the Junior First Rank in 760.

5. (718–770). The eldest daughter of Emperor Shōmu and Empress Kōmyō, and a cousin to Nakamaro; she became Princess Regent at the age of twenty-one. In 749, when she was enthroned as Empress Kōken 孝謙, Nakamaro was made High Councillor of the Senior Third Rank.

6. 道祖王 (d. 757). In 756 ex-Emperor Shōmu died, and, according to his last wishes, Prince Funado was appointed Prince Regent on the same day. However, Empress Kōken and Nakamaro replaced him with Prince Ōhi 大炊 in the next year. See Shoku Nihongi, XIX (Tenpyō shōhō 8:5:2, 9:3:29, 9:4:4). He joined in the rebellion against Nakamaro and Empress Kōken and was executed in 757. See II.40.

7. 祈御酒 ukei no misake, used in the ritual to swear before the kami.

When the empress dowager[8] and Empress Abe[9] resided at Nara Palace, all the people under heaven sang a song which said:

A young prince, who passes away at such a young age,
Like a dead fish floating on the water:
When will your life be taken? Oh, poor flatfish!
When will your life be taken?

Then, on the eighteenth day of the eighth month, in the ninth year of the Tenpyō shōhō era, the reign of Empress Abe and the empress dowager, the name of the era was changed from Tenpyō shōhō to Tenpyō hōji.[10] In the same year Prince Regent Funado was captured at the palace, imprisoned, and executed. Together with him were killed Prince Kifumi 黄文王,[11] Prince Shioyaki 鹽燒王,[12] and their families.

Again in the tenth month in the eighth year of the Hōji era, Emperor Ōhi 大炊 [13] was attacked by ex-Empress Abe and dethroned, retiring to Awaji province 淡路國. Also killed were Nakamaro and his family. The song quoted in the above was an omen of the fatal destiny of these princes.

Also in the reign of the empress dowager there was a song which circulated among the people in the country:

Don't be contemptuous of monks because of their robes.
For under their skirts are hung garters and hammers.[14]
When the hammers erect themselves,
The monks turn out to be awesome lords.

Or, there was another song that went like this:

Lie down along
The dark valley of my thighs
Till you become a man.

In the reign of Empress Abe, in the beginning of the second year of the snake, the first year of the Tenpyō jingo era, Dharma Master

8. Empress Kōmyō (700–760).
9. Empress Kōken.
10. 757. It is said the four characters 天平大平 appeared on the canopy of the empress' bedroom. This event may be interpreted as a political measure to smooth over the replacement of the prince regent.
11. The son of Prince Nagaya (see II.1), he was executed with Prince Funado.
12. Prince Funado's brother, who escaped accusation because he did not participate in the rebellion. In 764, however, Nakamaro supported him as successor to the throne, and he and Nakamaro were executed as rebels against the court. Kyōkai is mistaken in adding his name to those who were killed in Nakamaro's rebellion.
13. (r. 758–764). Grandson of Emperor Tenmu, married to Nakamaro's daughter-in-law and thus supported by Nakamaro. He was exiled to Awaji after Nakamaro's unsuccessful rebellion, but he tried to escape and died an unnatural death in 765.
14. Garters refer to the monks' political involvement; hammers to their love affairs.

Dōkyō 道鏡 of the Yuge 弓削 family[15] had intercourse with the empress on the same pillow, hearing the affairs of state and ruling over the country together. The above songs were a prediction of his relations with the empress and his control over state affairs.

Also in the reign of the empress dowager, there was a song that went like this:

Look straight at the root of the tree,
And you will find the most venerable master
Standing satiated and fat.

It is evident that this was a prediction of the participation in state affairs of Dharma Master Dōkyō as Dharma King 法皇 and Dharma Master Ingō 韻興[16] of the Kamo 鴨 family as spiritual councillor.[17]

Or, in the reign of ex-Emperor Shōhō-ōjin who governed the country at Nara Palace for twenty-five years, this song was sung by people all over the country:

The morning sun is shining over Sakurai 櫻井,[18]
West of the Toyura-dera 豊浦寺,
A white jewel sinks at Sakurai;
A good jewel sinks at Sakurai.
Therefore, my house will prosper.

Later, in the reign of Empress Abe, on the fourth day of the eighth month in the seventh year of the dog, the fourth year of the Jingo keiun era,[19] Emperor Shirakabe ascended to the throne, and on the first of the tenth month of the same year, when a turtle was presented from Tsukushi province, the era name was once again changed, this time to Hōki, and thus he ruled over the country. Therefore, we learn that the song was a sign of the reign of Emperor Shirakabe.

Or, in the reign of Empress Abe, all over the country, men sang:

Don't trample on the slope of Yabe 山部坂[20]
Which faces the imperial palace,
Though it is the earth.

After the circulation of this song, on the fifteenth day of the fourth month in the eighth year of the cock, the first year of the Ten'ō[21]

15. (705?–772). He came from Wakae district, Kawachi province 河内國若江郡 studied under Giin 義淵 and Rōben 良弁 (see II.21, n. 4), was put in charge of the court chapel, and won the empress' favor. See Yokota Ken'ichi, Dōkyō.
16. Or Ongō; appointed senior assistant executive in 766, of the Kamo-no-asomi family.
17. 法臣參議.
18. The name of a well. See Shoku Nihongi, XXXI (Hōki 1:10), for another version of this song.
19. 770 (Jingo keiun 4, Hōki 1).
20. Yabe-saka faces Fujiwara Palace. It implies Prince Yamabe.
21. 781.

era, in the reign of Emperor Shirakabe, Emperor Yamabe ascended to the throne to rule over the country. Therefore, it is clear that the song was a prediction of his reign.

In the reign of Emperor Yamabe, on the night of the eighth of the eleventh month, in the first year of the rat, the third year of the Enryaku era,[22] all heavenly stars moved and flew about wildly from eight in the evening to four in the morning. On the eleventh of the same month, the emperor with Prince Regent Sawara 早良[23] moved the palace from Nara 諾樂 to Nagaoka 長岡.[24] The flight of the heavenly stars was a sign that the imperial palace would be moved.

On the night of the fifteenth day of the ninth month, the second year of the ox, the following year,[25] the moon looked dark all night in the lightless sky. At ten o'clock on the evening of the twenty-third of the same month, Fujiwara no asomi Tanetsugu 藤原朝臣種繼,[26] Minister of Ceremony[27] of the Senior Third Rank, was killed by an arrow in a residential quarter of Nagaoka Palace by Ojika no sukune Kozumi 雄鹿宿禰木積 and Hahaki no Mochimaro 波々岐將丸, imperial guards.[28] The disappearance of the moonlight was an omen of the death of Lord Tanetsugu.

In the reign of the same emperor, at six in the evening on the fourth of the ninth month in the autumn of the fourth year of the hare, the sixth year of the Enryaku era,[29] Monk Kyōkai, stricken with remorse, grieved over himself, lamenting and saying:

"Ah! What a shame! Born in this world, I know no way to make a living. Because of karmic causation[30] I am bound by the net of

22. 784, in the reign of Emperor Kanmu.

23. (d. 785). Emperor Kōnin's second son and Emperor Kanmu's brother, he was made prince regent in 781, but was deposed and exiled to Awaji province, dying on the way (see n. 26, below). As his spirit terrified the imperial family and the Fujiwaras, he was given a posthumous title of emperor and ceremonially reburied.

24. The capital from 784 to 799, located at present Mukō-machi, Otokuni-gun, Kyoto-fu 京都府乙訓郡向日町.

25. 785, in Emperor Kanmu's reign.

26. (737–785). A grandson of Fujiwara no Umakai 藤原宇合, a member of the Shikike 式家 branch of the Fujiwara family and named after the title Shikibukyō (see n. 26, below) conferred on Umakai. He was favored by Emperor Kanmu and was put in charge of the construction of the capital of Nagaoka. Prince Regent Sawara was deposed because of involvement in his assassination. See *Shoku Nihongi*, XXXVIII (Enryaku 4:9:23, 24); *Nihon kiryaku* (Enryaku 4:9:23, 24).

27. 式部卿 the minister of ceremony had charge of court ceremonies, advancement and conferring ranks, appointment and assessment of local officials, qualifying examination of government officials, etc.

28. They are unknown imperial guards 近衛舍人.

29. 787. See Chap. I(1)a, for the following autobiographical passage.

30. 等流果 *tōruka*, the result of a past cause, where the result is of the same quality as the cause, but in this passage it means karmic causation in general.

lust, enveloped in cravings, combining death and life, running in all directions, and burning my body alive. Remaining in the secular life, I have no means to support my family and am without food, salt, clothes, or firewood. My mind is never at rest, worrying about the things I need. As I am hungry and freezing in the daytime, so at night I am hungry and freezing. For in my previous lives I did not practice almsgiving. How mean my heart is! How low my deeds are!"

Then at midnight, while sleeping, he had a dream: a mendicant came to his door, recited the scripture, and preached, saying:

"If you practice the good of the upper grade,[31] you will become seventeen feet tall; if you practice the good of the lower grade,[32] you will become ten feet tall."

Having heard this, Kyōkai looked around to see the mendicant and discovered that he was Novice Kyōnichi of the village of Awa in Kusumi, Nakusa district, Kii province 紀伊國名草郡楠見粟村.[33] Looking at him closely, he found a wooden tablet[34] about twenty feet long and one foot wide. On the tablet there were two marks, one at the height of ten feet, and the other at the height of seventeen feet. Seeing this, Kyōkai asked, "Are they marking the heights of those who practice the good of the upper and lower grades?" The answer was, "Yes, they are."

Thereupon Kyōkai was stricken with remorse, making a sign of repentance, and said, "Thus one gets great height by practicing the good of the upper and lower grades. I am only about five feet tall, for I did not practice the good of even the lower grade before. How foolish I was!" Repenting, he grieved and lamented. Having heard his remark, all who stood by said, "You are right!"

Then Kyōkai made an offering to the mendicant of a few cups of white rice which he was about to cook. The mendicant received it with a blessing[35] and immediately took out a scroll to give to Kyōkai, saying, "Copy this scroll, for it is an excellent scripture to guide people." Kyōkai looked at it and discovered that it was the *Shokyō yōshū*,[36] which is as good as the mendicant had said. In grief, Kyōkai

31. 上品善 *jōbon no zen*.
32. 下品善 *gehon no zen*.
33. Present Nagusa-gun, Wakayama-ken.
34. A provincial magistrate's messenger or King Yama's messenger carries the same type of tablet but not as big as this. See II.10, n. 5; III.22, n. 8; III.23, n. 10.
35. 咒願 *jugan;* a short prayer, blessing, or vow expressed in short phrases. See II.8, n. 9; II.12, 16.
36. See Chap. I(1)a, n. 14.

said, "What shall I do? I have no paper to copy it on." The mendicant took out some used paper and gave it to Kyōkai, saying, "Copy it on this paper. In the meantime I will visit other places for begging and come back here." Then he went away, leaving the tablet and the scripture.

Thereupon Kyōkai said, "This novice does not usually beg food. Why is he doing it now?" Somebody answered, "Because he has many children. As he does not have any way to support them, he is begging."

This is the dream I had, and I am not sure what it means. I suspect it is none other than a revelation of Buddha. The novice may be an incarnation of Kannon. As one who is not yet ordained is called a novice; so is Kannon, who remains in the stage of self-discipline[37] in order to save all sentient beings in spite of having attained enlightenment. Begging shows the thirty-three incarnations of Kannon illustrated in the "Chapter on the All-Sided One."[38] "The seventeen feet of the upper grade" is the result of all virtues in the pure land. Ten feet is a complete number, for it is perfect, while seven feet is incomplete, for it is imperfect. "The ten feet of the lower grade" is the result of the cravings in this world and heaven. "Being stricken with remorse, making a sign of repentance" means that one has been endowed with good causes,[39] and by adding wisdom and practice one may make up for sins in previous lives and gain benefits. Repentance, shaving oneself, wearing a surplice, and showing remorse help destroy sins and gain benefits. "I am only about five feet tall" may be analyzed as follows: "five" refers to the five ways of being, and "about" means tentative orientation[40] to the upper or lower spheres according to the working of the mind. For "about" does not designate a specific number, and it does not give an exact height.[41] Therefore, it is the cause for five different modes of being.

Offering white rice to a mendicant refers to practicing good by vowing to make a Buddha image and copy a scripture in order to

37. 　位 *in'i*; literally the stage in which bodhisattvas accumulate causes to become Buddhas. Buddhahood is called 果位 *kai*, the stage of consequences.
38. *Myōhōrenge-kyō*, "Kanzeon bosatsu fumon-bon" (*Taishō*, IX, 57 a–c).
39. 種子 *shushi* or *shuji*; meaning, literally, seeds. As plants grow from seeds, so consequences arise from causes. According to the teaching of the Hossō School, the seeds are stored in the *ālayavijñāna*. See Chap. I(1)a, n. 6.
40. Only the Maeda manuscript has 不定種性 *fujō no shujō*, meaning tentative potentiality. For *shujō*, see Chap. II(2)a, n. 63.
41. 非尺非丈.

get the great white bullock-cart.[42] The mendicant's acceptance of them with a blessing means that Kannon accepted the prayer. Giving a scripture is interpreted as adding wisdom to the path seekers by giving new seeds for good. Taking out used paper implies that good seeds of wisdom covered and hidden for a long time in the past will be revealed by practicing the good dharma. "I will visit other places for begging and come back here" may be paraphrased as "Kannon's boundless compassion will fill the world and save all sentient beings, and Kyōkai's wish will be granted with fortune and benefits given." "He does not usually beg food" means that Kyōkai has not sensed anything till he makes a vow. "Why is he doing it now?" may be interpreted that benefits will finally be given to him according to his wish. "He has many children" means that there are many sentient beings to guide and teach. "He does not have any ways to support them" means that those who lack potentiality are not oriented for enlightenment. "He is begging to support them" means that they are getting seeds in this world and heaven.

Again Kyōkai had another dream on the night of the seventeenth of the third month, in the spring of the second year of the ox, the seventh year of the Enryaku era.[43]

In the dream, Kyōkai died, and his corpse was burned with firewood. Thereupon his spirit watched his corpse burn, but it did not burn as he wished. Therefore, he took a stick to skewer his corpse and broil it. He said to others who were buring their corpses, "Burn as well as I do." His legs, knees, joint bones, elbows, head and other parts were all burned and fell off. Then Kyōkai's spirit cried aloud, putting his mouth to the ear of a bystander to tell him his wish, but his voice sounded hollow and the bystander did not answer. Then Kyōkai thought that he could not hear his voice as the spirit of the dead was voiceless.

43. See Myōhōrenge-kyō (Taishō, IX, 12b–13c); Katō, trans., Myōhō-renge-kyō, 82–100; Kern, Saddharma, 72–76. This is the most famous parable of the Hoke-kyō: Once there was an old, rich householder who had a great mansion with one door. Suddenly his house was swept by a blaze while he was outside but his children were playing inside. In order to make them run out of the house, the father called them saying that bullock-carts, goat-carts, and deer-carts were ready for them. When they rushed out of the house safely, thanks to the father's skill in means, he gave them only bullock-carts, saying that he would give them only the greatest vehicles. In China this parable gave rise to a debate. One party maintains that the bullock-cart is bodhisattvayāna, the goat-cart pratyekabuddhayāna, and the deer-cart śrāvakayāna. (The house is the world of karma and samsara, and Buddha uses skillful means to save all beings.) Therefore, the bullock-cart is Mahayana, which the Hoke-kyō teaches. The other party says the bullock-cart and the great cart are different, and that there are four kinds of carts altogether. The above three are the teachings of skill in means and the fourth cart is the true teaching of Buddha.

43. 788, the year of his second dream.

44. For an interpretation of this dream, see Chap. I(1)a.

This dream has not been interpreted yet.[44] He only suspects that it is a sign of attaining longevity or an official rank. He hopes that by waiting he will learn the meaning of the dream in the future.

Then, on the thirteenth day of the twelfth year in the winter of the second year of the boar, the fourteenth year of the Enryaku era,[45] Kyōkai was given the Junior Rank of Transmission of Light.[46] In the fourth and fifth months in the summer of the sixteenth year of the Enryaku era, in the reign of the same emperor residing at Nara Palace,[47] a fox came to Kyōkai's room to cry every night. The fox also dug a hole in the wall of the hall built by Kyōkai[48] and entered inside the hall, soiling the seat of the Buddha with filth and crying in the daytime. Two hundred and twenty days or so passed, and Kyōkai's son died.[49]

Again, about the eleventh and twelfth months of the sixth year of the hare, the eighteenth year, a fox cried, and at times the sound of a cicada was heard. In the following year, the seventh year of the dragon, on the twelfth of the first month, Kyōkai's horse died, and on the twenty-fifth of the same month another horse died. Accordingly, it is evidnet that an omen of disaster appears first, and disaster comes later. Kyōkai, however, has not studied the *yin-yang tao* 陰陽道 of Huang Ti 黃帝,[50] nor understood the profound truth of the Tendai Sage 天台智者,[51] and he is stricken with disaster without knowing how to evade it, worrying and grieving without looking for the way to do away with disaster. We must work hard for discipline, and maintain a sense of awe.

# 39

## *On the Rebirth as a Prince of a Monk Who Excelled in Both Wisdom and Discipline*[1]

The secular name of Dhyāna Master Saka Zenshu 尺善珠禪師[2] was

45. 794.
46. 傳燈住位 *Dentō jū-i*; see Chap. I(1)a, n. 5.
47. 797, in Emperor Kanmu's reign. 平城宮 Nara Palace should read Heian Palace.
48. The translation follows the Maeda manuscript which has "wall" 私造堂壁, but other manuscripts lack the last character.
49. See Chap. I(1)a, nn. 22, 23.
50. 軒轅黃帝 Kenioni Kōtei; 軒轅 Hsien-yüan is a name for Huang Ti, or the Yellow Emperor, which probably originated with his home district in Honan. See Chap. I(1)b, n. 52.
51. See Chap. I(1)b, n. 51.

1. Cf. *Fusō ryakki* (Shō II, Kanmu), *Genkō shakusho* (II).
2. See III.35, n. 18.

Ato no muraji 跡連.[3] He was named after his mother's family, Ato no uji. In his childhood he lived with his mother in the village of Shikishima, Yamanobe district, Yamato province 大和國山邊郡磯城嶋村.[4]

After ordination,[5] he worked so hard at study and practice that he excelled in both wisdom and discipline. He was respected by high and low and revered by monks and laity. He made it his vocation to preach dharma and guide people. Thereupon, the emperor appointed him chief executive[6] out of respect for his deeds and virtues. This monk had a large birthmark on the right side of his chin.

In the seventeenth year of the Enryaku era, in the reign of Emperor Yamabe who ruled at Nara Palace,[7] when Dhyāna Master Zenshu was about to pass away, a diviner[8] was called to give an oracle about his life after death, as was the practice of the people at that time, by means of boiling rice.[9] Then the divine spirit, having possessed the diviner, said, "I will enter the womb of Tajihi no omina 丹治比嬢女,[10] a wife of the emperor of Japan, to be reborn as a prince. You shall know his identity owing to the same birthmark as mine on the prince's face."

In the eighteenth year of the Enryaku era, after Dhyāna Master Zenshu had passed away, Tajihi no omina gave birth to a prince. As the prince had the same birthmark as the late Dhyāna Master Zenshu, he was named Prince Daitoku 大德親王, Prince of Great Virtue. He died after three years, however. When the diviner was called, the prince's spirit said through the diviner, "I am none other than Dhyāna Master Zenshu. I have lived as a prince for a while. Hold a service and burn incense for me."

Therefore, it was evident that the Most Venerable Zenshu was born again in the form of a human being, a prince. This is the meaning of the saying in the Buddhist scripture: "Man is born in various families according to his status."[11]

In Kamino district in Iyo province there was a mountain called

3. 阿都 (Fusō ryakki), 安部 (Genkō shakusho).
4. The northern part of present Sakurai-shi, Nara-ken.
5. 得度 tokudo; see Chap. I(1)c, for the ordination system.
6. 僧正 sōjō; see Chap. I(1)c.
7. 797, in Emperor Kanmu's reign. Therefore, Nara Palace is incorrect (see III.38, n. 47). Fusō ryakki dates his death in 796.
8. 卜者 kamnagi; see Chap. II(3)a, n. 124.
9. 飯占 iura.
10. A daughter of Tajihi no Nagano of the Junior Second Rank; in 797 (Enryaku 16) the Junior Third Rank was conferred on her, and she was made a wife to Emperor Kanmu.
11. Abidaruma kusha-ron (Taishō, XXIX, 124a). 人家家 謂於人趣 生二三家 證圓寂.

Iwazuchi-yama 石槌山.¹² The name was derived from that of the Kami of Iwazuchi who lived on the mountain.¹³ It was so high that ordinary persons could not reach the summit. Only men pure in mind and deed could climb up and live there.

In the reign of ex-Emperor Shōhō-ōjin-shōmu who ruled over the country for twenty-five years at Nara Palace, and also in the reign of Empress Abe who ruled for nine years at the same palace, there lived a monk of pure deed, studying and disciplining himself. He was named Bodhisattva Jakusen 寂仙菩薩¹⁴ and called Bodhisattva because his contemporaries, clerical and lay, revered his pure life.

In the second year of the Tenpyō hōji era, that is, the fifth year of the dog, the ninth year of the empress' reign, Dhyāna Master Jakusen realized he was about to die and put down his words to give to his disciples, saying, "Twenty-eight years after my death, I shall be reborn as a prince whose name is Kamino 神野; you may know that the prince is I, Jakusen."

Twenty-eight years passed by. In the fifth year of the Enryaku era, in the reign of Emperor Yamabe who ruled over the country at Heian Palace, a prince who was named Prince Kamino was born to the emperor. This is none other than present Emperor Kamino,¹⁵ who has been ruling the country for fourteen years.

Accordingly, we know he is a sage emperor. Then, how do we know he is a sage? People say, "The imperial law does not fail to kill a murderer. This emperor, however, makes us realize what Kōnin 弘仁, 'spreading benevolence,' the name of his era, means; he governs us, saving our lives by replacing killing with exile. Therefore it is evident that he is a sage emperor."

Some speak ill of him, saying that he is not a sage emperor. They say, "We do so because there have been droughts and plagues in the country during his reign.¹⁶ There have also been many disasters of heaven and earth,¹⁷ and famines.¹⁸ And he keeps hunting dogs, going out to hunt birds, boars, and deer. So he does not have compassion."

12. The highest mountain in Shikoku, situated at present Nii- and Shūsō-gun, in Ehime-ken 愛媛縣新居, 周桑郡.

13. On the top of the mountain there is Iwatsuchibiko Shrine where Iwatsuchibiko no kami (deity of rock and earth) who was born of Izanagi and Izanami is enshrined. See *Kojiki*, I (*NKBT*, 56); Philippi, trans., *Kojiki*, 55.

14. *Montoku jitsuroku* (Kashō 3 : 5). 伊豫國神野郡 昔有高僧 名灼然 稱爲聖人 有弟子名上仙 住止山頂 精進練行.

15. Emperor Saga (786–842). A great patron of the arts who composed poems in Chinese, favored Kūkai, and was good in calligraphy. For Kūkai, see Chap. I(1), nn. 8, 89.

16. They occurred in Daidō 4, Kōnin 3, 8, 10, 11, 13, etc. See *Nihon kiryaku*, *Ruijū kokushi*.

17. Typhoon (Daidō 4, Kōnin 4); flood (Kōnin 4, 5, 6, 7); earthquake (Kōnin 9).

18. (Daidō 5; Kōnin 3, 4, 8, 10, 11, 13, 14).

Their charge, however, is not right. Everything in the country he reigns over belongs to him, and we cannot claim as our own even a piece of earth the size of a needle point. All are at the will of the emperor. How could we accuse him of such things? Even in the reign of the sage emperors Yao 堯 and Shun舜, there were also droughts and plagues. So we should refrain from such abuse.[19]

## POSTSCRIPT

According to what I had heard, I selected oral traditions and put down miraculous events, dividing them into good and evil. By conferring the merits obtained in writing this work on all beings who are going astray, I pray to be born in the western land of bliss[20] with them all!

*DAINIHONKOKU-GENPŌ-ZEN'AKU-RYŌIKI*
Volume III
Written by Monk Kyōkai of the Junior Rank of
Transmission of Light at Yakushi-ji
on the West Side of Nara

19. See Chap. II(2)a.
20. 西方安樂國 ; see Chap. I(1)a, n. 16.

Appendixes    Bibliography    Index

# Appendix A

## Chronology[a]

| Emperor | Reign | Date | Event | Reference |
|---|---|---|---|---|
| Yūryaku 雄略 | 456–479? | 7 (463) | Chīsakobe no Sugaru catches the thunder | I.1 |
| Kinmei 欽明 | 539–571 | 13 (552)? | King Syöng-myöng of Paekche presents a Buddha image and Buddhist scriptures | I.P, 5; III.P |
| | | 14 (553) | Strange music heard, Buddha image made | I.5 |
| Bitatsu 敏達 | 572–585 | 14 (585) | Mononobe no Moriya burns the temple | I.5 |
| | | | | I.5 |
| Yōmei 用明 | 585–587 | 2 (587) | Soga no Umako destroys Mononobe no Moriya | I.5 |
| Sushun 崇峻 | 587–592 | | | |
| Suiko 推古 | 592–628 | | | I.8 |
| | | 1 (593) | Prince Shōtoku was appointed Prince Regent | I.4, 5 |
| | | 9 (601) | Prince Shōtoku builds Ikaruga Palace | I.4 |
| | | 21 (613) | The prince meets a beggar at Kataoka | I.4 |
| | | 29 (621) | The prince dies | I.5 |
| | | 32 (624) | The beginning of the *Sōgō system* | I.5 |
| Jomei 舒明 | 629–641 | | | |
| Kōgyoku 皇極 | 642–645 | 2 (643) | Soga no Iruka destroys Yamashiro no Ōe, Prince Shōtoku's heir | I.5 |
| | | | An eagle carries away a baby | I.9 |
| Kōtoku 孝德 | 645–654 | Taika 大化 1 (645) | The Soga family destroyed | I.5 |
| | | 2 (646) | Dōtō builds the Uji Bridge | I.12 |
| | | Hakuchi 白雉 4 (653) | Dōshō goes to T'ang China | I.22 |
| | | 5 (654) | A lay woman becomes a heavenly saint | I.13 |
| Saimei 齊明 | 655–661 | 6 (660) | Silla and T'ang China attack Paekche | I.14 |
| | | | Dōshō returns from study abroad | I.22 |
| | | 7 (661) | Japan sends a force to support Paekche | I.7 |
| Tenchi 天智 | 661–671 | 2 (663) | The Japanese force lost; Paekche destroyed | I.17 |
| | | 7 (668) | Ōmi-ryō promulgated (?) | |
| Kōbun 弘文 | 671–672 | | | |
| Tenmu 天武 | 673–686 | 9 (681) | The emperor vows to build Yakushi-ji | |

[289]

## Appendix A—*continued*

| Emperor | Reign | | Date | Event | Reference |
|---|---|---|---|---|---|
| Jitō<br>持統 | 686–697 | | 3 (689)<br>6 (692) | *Asuka-kiyomihara-ryō* promulgated<br>Ōmiwa no Takechimaro admonishes the empress not to make a trip in spring | <br>I.25 |
| | | | 8 (694) | The court moved to the capital of Fujiwara | |
| Monmu<br>文武 | 697–707 | | 3 (699) | E no Ozunu exiled to Izu | I.28 |
| | | | 4 (700) | Dōshō's cremation | I.22 |
| | | Taihō<br>大寳 | 2 (702) | The *Taihō-ritsuryō* promulgated | |
| | | Keiun<br>景雲 | 2 (705) | Kashiwade no omi Hirokuni visits the other world | I.30 |
| Genmei<br>元明 | 707–715 | Wadō<br>和銅 | 3 (710)<br>5 (712) | The capital shifted to Nara<br>The *Kojiki* completed | |
| Genshō<br>元正 | 715–724 | Yōrō<br>養老 | 1 (717)<br>2 (718)<br>4 (720) | Gyōgi's movement denounced<br>Gyōzen returns from China<br>The *Nihon shoki* completed<br>Government permits given to monks and nuns to authorize their status | <br>I.6 |
| Shōmu<br>聖武 | 724–749 | | | | II.2–4, 6, 8, 11–14, 16–19, 22–34, 37, 38 |
| | | Jinki<br>神龜 | 4 (727) | A prince born and an amnesty given but he dies in the following year | I.32 |
| | | Tenpyō<br>天平 | 1 (729) | Prince Nagaya abused and kills himself | II.1 |
| | | | 10 (738) | Prince Uji appointed Vice-minister of Central Affairs | II.35 |
| | | | 12 (740) | Rōben founds the Kegon School in Japan | II.21 |
| | | | 15 (743) | The emperor vows to build the Lochana Buddha statue | I.P, 5 |
| | | | 17 (745) | Gyōgi is appointed great chief executive | II.7 |
| | | | 21 (749) | Gyōgi dies | II.7 |
| | | Tenpyō kanpō<br>天平感寳 | 1 (749) | The Lochana Buddha of Tōdai-ji completed | I.P |
| Kōken<br>孝謙 | 749–758 | Tenpyō shōhō<br>天平勝寳 | 2 (750) | Ōtomo no Akamaro reborn as an ox | II.9 |
| | | | 6 (754) | A wicked man experiences hell<br>Ganjin comes from China | II.10 |
| | | | 8 (756) | Ex-Emperor Shōmu dies<br>Prince Funado appointed Prince Regent | III.38 |
| | | Tenpyō hōji<br>天平寳字 | 1 (757) | Rebellion of Tachibana no Naramaro<br>The *Yōrō-ritsuryō* promulgated | II.40;<br>III.38 |

## Appendix A—*continued*

| Emperor | Reign | | Date | Event | Reference |
|---|---|---|---|---|---|
| Jun'nin 淳仁 | 758–764 | Tenpyō hōji | 2 (758) | Yakushi Buddha's miraculous sign | II.39 |
| | | | 3 (759) | A girl attacked by a snake | II.41 |
| | | | 5 (761) | Healing by reciting scriptures | III.34 |
| | | | 7 (763) | Thousand-armed Kannon's miraculous sign | II.42 |
| | | | 8 (761) | Rebellion of Fujiwara no Nakamaro | III.7 |
| | | | | Emperor Jun'nin exiled to Awaji | III.38 |
| Shōtoku 稱德 | 764–770 | | | | III.1–6, 11–13, 15 |
| | | Tenpyō jingo 天平神護 | 1 (765) | Dōkyō appointed Dhyāna Master Chancellor | III.38 |
| | | | 2 (766) | Dōkyō appointed Dharma King | III.38 |
| | | | | Budhisattva Miroku's miraculous sign | III.8 |
| | | Jingo keiun 神護景雲 | 2 (768) | Fujiwara no Hirotari's visit to the other world in which Jizō is mentioned | III.9 |
| | | | 3 (769) | A miraculous sign of the *Hoke-kyō* | III.10 |
| | | | | An officer persecutes an ascetic | III.14 |
| Kōnin 光仁 | 770–781 | | | | III.20, 24, 28, 29 |
| | | Hōki 寳龜 | 1 (770) | Dōkyō exiled | |
| | | | | Jakurin saves a licentious woman | III.16 |
| | | | 2 (771) | Fujiwara no Nagate dies | III.37 |
| | | | | A miraculous sign of a Buddhist image | III.17 |
| | | | | A licentious act punished | III.18 |
| | | | | Saru Hijiri born of a ball of flesh | III.19 |
| | | | 3 (772) | A miraculous sign of the *Kongō hannya-kyō* | III.21 |
| | | | 4 | Osada no toneri Ebisu visits the other world | III.22 |
| | | | 5 | Ōtomo no muraji Oshikatsu visits the other world | III.23 |
| | | | 6 | Fishermen saved by an invocation | III.25 |
| | | | 7 | Tanaka no mahito Hiromushime dies and changes into an ox | III.26 |
| | | | 9 | A skull repays a given favor | III.27 |
| | | | 10 | Kanki carves Buddha-images | III.30 |
| Kanmu 桓武 | 781–806 | Ten'ō 天應 | 1 (781) | Emperor Kanmu enthroned and Prince Sawara, his brother, appointed Prince Regent | III.38 |
| | | Enryaku 延暦 | 1 (782) | Kanki dies | III.30 |
| | | | | A woman gives birth to two stones, descendents of Inaba no Kami | III.31 |
| | | | 2 (783) | Bodhisattva Myōken saves a fisherman | III.32 |
| | | | 3 (784) | The capital shifted to Nagaoka | III.38 |
| | | | | Fujiwara no asomi Tanetsugu assassinated | III.38 |
| | | | 4 (785) | An official punished for persecuting a mendicant | III.33 |

## Appendix A—*continued*

| Emperor | Reign | | Date | Event | Reference |
|---|---|---|---|---|---|
| | | | | Prince Sawara dies violently | III.38 |
| | | | 5 (786) | Jakusen (d. 758) born as Prince Kamino | III.39 |
| | | | 6 (787) | Kyōkai's first dream | III.38 |
| | | | | Saichō establishes a temple on Mt. Hiei | |
| | | | 7 (788) | Kyōkai's second dream | III.38 |
| | | | 13 (794) | The capital shifted to Kyoto from Nagaoka | III.38 |
| | | | 15 (796) | Emperor Kanmu holds a service for Mononobe no Komaro | III.35 |
| | | | 16 (797) | The *Shoku Nihongi* completed | |
| | | | | Kyōkai's son dies | III.38 |
| | | | 17 (798) | Zenshu dies | III.39 |
| | | | 18 (799) | Prince Daitoku born | III.39 |
| | | | 19 (800) | Kyōkai's horses die | III.39 |
| | | | 24 (805) | Saichō returns from China | |
| Heizei 平城 | 806–809 | Daidō 大同 | 1 (806) | Kūkai returns from China | |
| Saga 嵯峨 | 809–823 | Kōnin 光仁 | 5 (814) | The *Shinsen shōjiroku* compiled | |
| | | | 7 (816) | Kūkai founds a temple on Mt. Kōya | |
| | | | 13 (822) | The *Nihon ryōiki* completed (?) | III.39 |
| | | | 14 (823) | Saichō dies | |

ᵃ This tabulation makes use of dates cited in the *Nihon shoki* and *Shoku Nihongi* whenever possible, since the dating in the *Nihon ryōiki* is less accurate.
ᵇ P, here, means Preface.

# Appendix B

## Imperial Family Lineage[a]

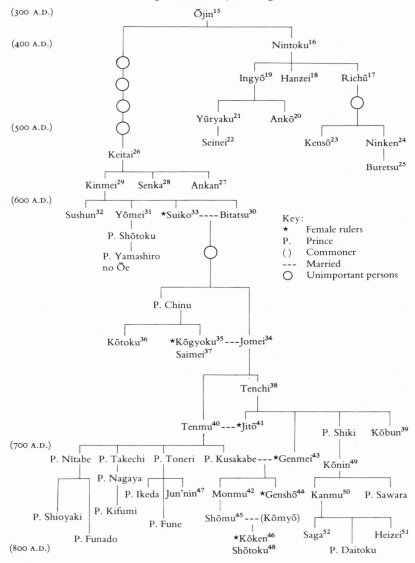

(300 A.D.)     Ōjin[15]

(400 A.D.)     Nintoku[16]

Ingyō[19]   Hanzei[18]   Richū[17]

Yūryaku[21]     Ankō[20]

(500 A.D.)     Seinei[22]     Kensō[23]    Ninken[24]

Buretsu[25]

Keitai[26]

Kinmei[29]   Senka[28]   Ankan[27]

(600 A.D.)     Sushun[32]   Yōmei[31]   ★Suiko[33]----Bitatsu[30]

P. Shōtoku

P. Yamashiro no Ōe

P. Chinu

Kōtoku[36]    ★Kōgyoku[35]---Jomei[34]
Saimei[37]

Tenchi[38]

Tenmu[40]---★Jitō[41]    P. Shiki   Kōbun[39]

(700 A.D.)     P. Nitabe   P. Takechi   P. Toneri   P. Kusakabe---★Genmei[43]

Kōnin[49]

P. Nagaya

P. Ikeda | Jun'nin[47]   Monmu[42]   ★Genshō[44]   Kanmu[50]   P. Sawara

P. Shioyaki   P. Kifumi

P. Fune   Shōmu[45]---(Kōmyō)

P. Funado     Saga[52]    Heizei[51]

(800 A.D.)     ★Kōken[46]    P. Daitoku
Shōtoku[48]

**Key:**
★     Female rulers
P.     Prince
( )    Commoner
---   Married
○    Unimportant persons

[a] The numbers designate the order of succession to the throne based on the *Nihon shoki*, the only exception being Emperor Kōbun. The absence of a line between names indicates that the same ruler was enthroned twice, using different names each time.

[ 293 ]

# Appendix C

## Translated Ranks and Titles

| English | Japanese | Sanskrit | Reference |
|---------|----------|----------|-----------|
| acolyte | *dōji* 童子 | *kumāra* | I.3, n.8 |
| ascetic | *gyōja* 行者 | | I.11, n.9 |
| assistant officer | *sakan* 佐官 | | Chap. I, n.78 |
| chief executive | *sōjō* 僧正 | | Chap. I(1)d |
| dean | *gakutō* 學頭 | | Chap. I(1)c |
| dharma king | *hōō* 法王 | *dharmarāja* | Chap. I, n.18 |
| dharma master | *hōshi* 法師 | | I.3, II.35, etc. |
| *dhyāna* master | *zenji* 禪師 | | I.7, n.2 |
| director | *teranushi* or *teraju* 寺主 | *vihārasvāmin* | Chap. I, n.84 |
| elder master | *rōsō* 老僧 | | III.30 |
| full-fledged monk | *biku* 比丘 | *bhikṣu* | I.5, n.32 |
| full-fledged nun | *bikuni* 比丘尼 | *bhikṣunī* | |
| great chief executive | *daisōjō* 大僧正 | | II.7, n.18 |
| lay brother | *ubasoku* 優婆塞 | *upāsaka* | Chap. I, n.91 |
| lay sister | *ubai* 優婆夷 | *upāsikā* | II.19, n. 2 |
| lecturer | *kōji* 講師 | | Chap. I. n.21 |
| monk | *shamon* 沙門 | *śramaṇa* | Chap. I, n.4 |
| | *sō* 僧 | *saṃgha* | Chap. I, nn.4, 17 |
| (the) Most Venerable | *daitoku* 大德 | *bhadanta* | I.5, n.43 |
| novice (monk) | *shami* 沙彌 | *śrāmaṇera* | Chap. I, n.10 |
| novice (nun) | *shamini* 沙彌尼 | *śramaṇerikā* | I.35, n.3 |
| nun | *ama* 尼 | | III.10 |
| preceptor | *risshi* 律師 | | Chap. I(1)c |
| presiding officer | *jōza* 上座 | *sthāvira* | Chap. I, n.84 |
| provincial preceptor | *kokushi* 國師 | | Chap. I, nn.21, 79 |
| provost | *(tsu) ina* (都)維那 | *karmadāna* | Chap. I, n.84 |
| scripture copier | *kyōji* 經師 | | III.18 |
| secretary | *hōzu* 法頭 | | Chap. I(1)c |
| supervisor | *sōzu* 僧都 | | Chap. I(1)c |
| venerable master | *daishi* 大師 | | II.17, n.6 |
| (the) Venerable | *-shi* 師 | | |

# Appendix D

## Buddhist Scriptures Quoted
## or Referred to in the *Nihon ryōiki*

| No. | Title in the *Nihon ryōiki* | Full or correct title | *Taishō* vol. | Where cited | Quoted or referred |
|---|---|---|---|---|---|
| 1 | *Bonmō-kyō* 梵網經 | Same | XXIV | II.19 | R[a] |
| 2 | *Dai hannya-kyō* 大般若經 | *Dai hannya haramita-kyō* 大般若波羅蜜多經 | V, VI, VII | III.23 | R |
| 3 | *Dai hannya-kyō shō* 大般若經抄 | Same | | II.7 | R |
| 4 | *Dai hōdō-kyō* 大方等經 | *Daihōdō daijik-kyō* 大方等大集經 | XIII | I.20 | IQ[b] (BK)[c] |
| 5 | *Daijik-kyō* 大集經 | *Daihōdō daijik-kyō* 大方等大集經 | XIII | II.9 | IQ (BK) |
| 6 | *(Dai) jōbu-ron* (大)丈夫論 | Same | XXX | I.29; III.15 | Q[d] |
| 7 | *Daijō-kyō* 大乘經 | ? | | I.30 | R |
| 8 | *Fushigikō bosatsu-kyō* 不思議光菩薩經 | *Fushigikō bosatsu shosetsu-gyō* 不思議光菩薩所說經 | XIV | II.7 | IQ (BK) |
| 9 | *Ganshi kakun* 顔氏家訓 | Same | | I.11 | IQ (SY)[e] |
| 10 | *Hannya dharani* 般若陀羅尼 | in *Hannya haramitsu shin-gyō* 般若波羅蜜心經 | VIII | II.15 | R |
| 11 | *Hannya kenki* 般若檢記 | *Kongō hannya-kyō jikkenki* 金剛般若經集驗記 | | I.Preface | R |
| 12 | *Hoke-kyō* 法華經 | *Myōhōrenge-kyō* 妙法蓮華經 | IX | I.11, 18, 28 II.3, 6, 15 III.1, 6, 9, 10, 13, 18, 19, 22, 24, 35, 37 I.19; II.18; III.20, 29 | R R R Q |
| 13 | *Hoke-kyō sho* 法華經疏 | *Hokke gisho* 法華義疏 | LXI | I.4 | R |
| 14 | *Hōkō-kyō* 方廣經 | ? | | I.8, 10; III.4 III.14 | R Q |
| 15 | *Ichijō-kyō* 一乘經 | *Myōhōrenge-kyō* 妙法蓮華經 | IX | III.10 | R |
| 16 | *Jōagon-kyō* 長阿含經 | Same | I | III.4 | IQ (BK) |
| 17 | *Jōjitsu-ron* 成實論 | Same | XXXII | II.32 | Q |
| 18 | *Jūrin-gyō* 十輪經 | *Daijō daijū Jizō jūrin-gyō* 大乘大集地藏十輪經 | XIII | III.33 | IQ (BK) |

[295]

| No. | Title in the *Nihon ryōiki* | Full or correct title | *Taishō* vol. | Where cited | Quoted or referred |
|---|---|---|---|---|---|
| 19 | *Jūrin-gyō gige* 十輪經義解 | ? | III.33 | | Q |
| 20 | *Kannon-bon* 觀音品 | *Myōhōrenge-kyō:* Fumon-bon 妙法蓮華經普門品 | IX | II.15 | R |
| 21 | *Kannon sanmai-kyō* 觀音三昧經 | *Kanzeon bosatsu juki-kyō* 觀世音菩薩授記經 | XI | III.34 | R |
| 22 | *Kanzeon-kyō* 觀世音經 | See title 20 | IX | I.30; III.34 | R |
| 23 | *Kegon-gyō*, 80 vols. 華嚴經 | *Daihōkōbutsu kegon-gyō* 大方廣佛華嚴經 | X | III.19 | R |
| 24 | *Kongō hannya-kyō* 金剛般若經 | *Kongō hannya haramitsu-kyō* 金剛般若波羅蜜經 | VIII | II.24; III.1, 21, 34 | R |
| 25 | *Kujakuō juhō* 孔雀王咒法 | in *Kujakuō ju-kyō* 孔雀王咒經 | XIX | I.28 | R |
| 26 | *Kyōman-gyō* 憍慢經 | ? | | II.1 | Q |
| 27 | *Kyōron* 經論 | *Daijōbu-ron* 大丈夫論 | XXX | III.33 | Q |
| 28 | *Myōhōki* 冥報記 | Same | XXX | I.P. | R |
| 29 | *Nehan-gyō* 涅槃經 | *Daihatsu nehan-gyō* 大般涅槃經 | XII | I.20 | R |
| | | | | I.27, 29; II.10, 13, 17, 19, 22, 42; III.18, 27 | Q |
| 30 | *Ritsu* 律 | *Konponsabatabu ritsushō* 根本薩婆多部律攝 | | III.18 | IQ (BK) |
| 31 | *Rokkan shō* 六卷抄 | *Shibunritsu sanhan hoketsu gyōjishō* 四分律刪繁補闕行事抄 | XL | III.24 | R |
| 32 | *Saishōō-kyō* 最勝王經 | *Konkōmyō saishōō-kyō* 金光明最勝王經 | XVI | II.5 | Q |
| 33 | *Senju dharani* 千手陀羅尼 | in *Senju sengen kanzeon bosatsu kōdai enman muge daihishin darani-kyō* 千手千眼觀世音菩薩廣大圓滿無礙大悲心陀羅尼經 | XX | III.34 | R |
| 34 | *Senju-kyō* 千手經 | See title 33 | XX | III.14 | Q |
| 35 | *Shin-gyō* 心經 | *Hannya haramitsu shin-gyō* 般若波羅蜜心經 | VIII | II.19 | R |
| 36 | *Shin hannya-kyō* 心般若經 | See title 35 | VIII | I.14 | R |
| 37 | *Shin hannya-kyō sho* 心般若經疏 | See title 35 | VIII | II.7 | R |
| 38 | *Shōjin nyomon-kyō* 精進女問經 | *Mukushōjin nyomon-kyō* 無垢精進女問經 | XIV | I.13 | Q |
| 39 | *Shokyō yōshū* 諸經要集 | Same | LIV | III.38 | R |

| No. | Title in the *Nihon ryōiki* | Full or correct title | *Taishō* vol. | Where cited | Quoted or referred |
|-----|------|------|------|------|------|
| 40 | *Shōman-gyō sho*<br>勝鬘經疏 | Same | LXI | I.4 | R |
| 41 | *Shutchō-gyō*<br>出曜經 | Same | IV | II.30 | Q |
| 42 | *Urabon-kyō sho*<br>盂蘭盆經疏 | ? | | II.7 | R |
| 43 | *Vinaya-kyō*<br>鼻奈耶經 | Same<br>毘奈耶經 | XXIV | II.5 | IQ (SY) |
| 44 | *Yakushi-gyō*<br>藥師經 | *Yakushi nyorai hongan-kyō*<br>藥師如來本願經 | XIV | III.33, 34 | R |
| 45 | *Yugaron*<br>瑜伽論 | *Yugashijiron*<br>瑜伽師地論 | XXX | III.8 | R |
| 46 | *Zen'aku inga-kyō*<br>善惡因果經 | Same | LXXXV | I.18 | IQ (SY) |
| | | | | II.10 | Q |
| 47 | *Zōbō ketsugi-kyō*<br>像法決疑經 | Same | LXXXV | III.33 | Q |

[a] R : Referred
[b] IQ : Indirect quotation
[c] BK : *Bonmō-kyō koshakki*
[d] Q : Quoted
[e] SY : *Shokyō yōshū*

# Appendix E

## Chronological List of Major Japanese Works of Legendary Literature during the Heian-Kamakura Periods

| Date | Author | Title | Vols. | Tale |
|------|--------|-------|-------|------|
| 810–823 | Kyōkai<br>景戒 | *Nihon ryōiki*<br>日本靈異記 | 3 | 116 |
| 848–892 | Gishō<br>義昭 | *Nihon kanryōroku*<br>日本感靈錄 | 2 | 73 |
| 984 | Minamoto no Tamenori<br>源爲憲 | *Sanbō ekotoba*<br>三寶繪詞 | 3 | 62 |
| 983–988 | Yoshishige no Yasutane<br>慶滋保胤 | *Nihon ōjō gokurakuki*<br>日本往生極樂記 | 1 | 42 |
| 1040–1043 | Chingen<br>鎭源 | *Dainihon Hoke-kyō kenki*<br>大日本法華經驗記<br>or *Honchō Hokke kenki*<br>　本朝法華驗記 | 3 | 129 |
| 1094–1169 | Kōen<br>皇圓 | *Fusō ryakki*<br>扶桑略記 | 30 | — |
| 1097–1098 | Ōe no Masafusa<br>大江匡房 | *Honchō shinsenden*<br>本朝神仙傳 | 1 | ? |
| 1101–1111 | Ōe no Masafusa | *Zoku honchō ōjōden*<br>續本朝往生傳 | 1 | 42 |
| 1106–1110 | ? | *Konjaku monogatarishū*<br>今昔物語集 | 31<br>(8, 18, 21<br>extinct) | 1103<br>(originally<br>ca. 1200) |
| 1110 | ? | *Hyakuza hōdan kikigakishō*<br>百座法談聞書抄 | | 20<br>(originally<br>ca. 300) |
| 1123 | Miyoshi no Tameyasu<br>三善爲康 | *Shūi ōjōden*<br>拾遺往生傳 | 3 | 95 |
| 1126–1131 | ? | *Kohon setsuwashū*<br>古本説話集 | 2 | 70 |
| 1134 | ? | *Uchigikishū*<br>打聞集 | 1 | 27 |
| 1137–1139 | Miyoshi no Tameyasu | *Goshūi ōjōden*<br>後拾遺往生傳 | 3 | 75 |
| 1139 | Renzen<br>蓮禪 | *Sange ōjōki*<br>三多往生記 | 1 | 53 (58?) |
| 1151 | Fujiwara no Munetomo<br>藤原宗友 | *Honchō shinshū ōjōden*<br>本朝新修往生傳 | 1 | 41 |
| 1170–1195 | Nakayama no Sadachika<br>中山定親 | *Mizukagami*<br>水鏡 | 3 | |
| 1179 | Taira no Yasuyori<br>平康頼 | *Hōbutsushū*<br>寶物集 | 6 (1, 2, 3,<br>6, 7, 9) | ? |
| 1185 | Fujiwara no Kenshō<br>藤原顯昭 | *Shūchū-shō*<br>袖中抄 | 20 | — |
| 1200–1212 | ? | *Hase-dera Kannon kenki*<br>長谷寺觀音驗記 | 2 | 52 |
| 1212–1221 | ? | *Ujishūi monogatari*<br>宇治拾遺物語 | 2 (2, 15) | 197 |

## Appendix E—*continued*

| Date | Author | Title | Vols. | Tale |
|------|--------|-------|-------|------|
| 1212–1215 | Minamoto no Akikane<br>源顯兼 | *Kojidan*<br>古事談 | 6 | ? |
| 1216 | Kamo no Chōmei<br>鴨長明 | *Hosshinshū*<br>發心集 | 3 (3, 5, 8) | 102 |
| 1219–1220 | Jien<br>慈圓 | *Gukanshō*<br>愚管抄 | 7 | — |
| 1252 | Rokuhara no<br>Nirozaemon<br>六波羅二臈左衞門 | *Jikkinshō*<br>十訓抄 | 10 | 282 |
| 1254 | Tachibana no Narisue<br>橘成季 | *Kokon chomonshū*<br>古今著聞集 | 20 | 726 |
| 1243–1255 | Saigyō?<br>西行 | *Senjūshō*<br>撰集抄 | 9 | 117 |
| 1283 | Mujū<br>無住 | *Shasekishū*<br>沙石集 | 10 | 120 |
| 1322 | Shiren<br>師練 | *Genkō shakusho*<br>元亨釋書 | 30 | — |
| 1354–1358 | (Agui in)<br>安居院 | *Shintōshū*<br>神道集 | 10 | 50 |

# Selected Bibliography

This bibliography includes all cited works and works which were consulted and found relevant. For the convenience of Western readers, a limited number of helpful works and translations were added.

## (1) TEXTS OF THE *Nihon Ryōiki*

Endō Yoshimoto 遠藤嘉基 and Kasuga Kazuo 春日和男, ed. and annot. *Nihon ryōiki* 日本靈異記 (*NKBT*, 70). Tokyo: Iwanami shoten, 1967.

Furuta Shōkin 古田紹欽, ed. *Nihon ryōiki* 日本靈異記. *Koten kenkyū* 古典研究, suppl. (February 1939).

Harada Toshiaki 原田敏明 and Takahashi Mitsugu 高橋貢, trans. (modern Ja.). *Nihon ryōiki* (*Tōyō bunko* 東洋文庫, 97). Tokyo: Heibonsha, 1967.

Itabashi Tomoyuki 板橋倫行, ed. *Kōyaku Nihon ryōiki* 校譯日本靈異記. Tokyo: Shunyōdō, 1929.

———, ed. and annot. *Nihon ryōiki* (*Kadokawa bunko* 角川文庫). Tokyo: Kadokawa shoten, 1957.

Kariya Ekisai 狩谷棭齋, ed. *Kōhon Nihon ryōiki* 校本日本靈異記. Edo: Bankyūdō, 1816. Reprinted in *Gunsho ruijū* 群書類從, XVI, Book 447. Tokyo: Keizai zasshisha, 1894; *Kariya Ekisai zenshū* 狩谷棭齋全集, I (*Nihon koten zenshū* 日本古典全集, First Series, 11). Tokyo: Nihon koten zenshū kankōkai, 1925; *Gunsho ruijū*, XXV. Tokyo: Zoku gunsho ruijū kanseikai, 1929; *SGR*, XIX. Tokyo: Naigai shoseki, 1932.

———. *Nihon ryōiki kōshō* 日本靈異記攷證. Reprinted in *Kariya Ekisai zenshū*, II. Edo: Bankyūdō, 1821. See above.

Koizumi Michi 小泉道, ed. and annot. *Kōchū Shinpukujibon Nihon ryōiki* 校註眞福寺本日本靈異記. *Kuntengo to kunten shiryō* 訓點語と訓點資料, suppl. No. 22, June 1962.

Kurano Kenji 倉野憲司. trans. (modern Ja.) *Nihon ryōiki* (*Koten Nihon bungaku zenshū*, I). Tokyo: Chikuma shobō, 1960.

*Maeda-bon Nihon ryōiki* (*Sonkyōkaku sōkan*, 19). Photostatic copy. Ikutoku zaidan, 1931.

Matsuura Teishun 松浦貞俊, ed. and annot. *Nihon ryōiki* (*Zoku Nihon koten dokuhon*, II). Tokyo: Nihon hyōronsha, 1944.

———. *Nihon ryōiki* (*Atene bunko*). Tokyo: Kōbundō, 1956.

Ōya Tokujō 大屋德城, ed. *Kōfukuji Nihon ryōiki* 興福寺日本靈異記. Kyoto: Benridō, 1934.

Satō Kenzō 佐藤謙三, ed. *Kōhon Nihon ryōiki*. Tokyo: Meiseidō, 1943.

Takase Shōgon 高瀬承嚴, ed. *Nihonkoku genpō zen'aku ryōiki* 日本國現報善惡靈異記 (*Kokuyaku issaikyō*: shidenbu, XXIV). Tokyo: Daitō shuppansha, 1938.

Takeda Yūkichi 武田祐吉, ed. and annot. *Nihon ryōiki* (*Nihon koten zensho*). Tokyo: Asahi shinbunsha, 1950.

## (2) WORKS IN WESTERN LANGUAGES

Akanuma, Chizen. "On the Triple Body of the Buddha." *Eastern Buddhist*, IV (No. 1, 1922), 1–29.

# Selected Bibliography

Anesaki, Masaharu. "Prayer (Buddhist)." *Encyclopaedia of Religion and Ethics*. Ed. by James Hastings. New York: Charles Scribner's Sons, 1913–1927.

Ashikaga, Enshō. "Notes on Urabon." *JAOS* (No. 71, 1951), 71–75.

Aston, W. G., trans. "Nihongi, Chronicles of Japan," 2 vols., *TPJA*, suppl. 1 (1896).

Bachofen, J. J. *Myth, Religion, and Mother Right*. Trans. by Ralph Manheim (Bollingen Series, LXXXIV). Princeton, N. J.: Princeton University Press, 1967.

Bader, Clarisse. *Women in Ancient India*. Trans. by Mary E. R. Martin. London: Kegan Paul, Trench, Trubner, & Co., 1925. (*La femme dans l'Inde Antique*, 1867).

Beaseley, W. G. "Traditions of Historical Writings in China and Japan." *TASJ*, Third Series, VII (November 1959), 169–186.

Bohner, Hermann. "Kamatari-den." *Monumenta Nipponica*, IV (No. 1, 1941), 207–244.

———. "Kōbō Daishi." *Monumenta Nipponica*, VI (No. 1–2, 1943), 266–313.

———. "Legenden aus der Frühzeit des Japanischen Buddhismus." *Mitteilungen der Deutschen Gesellschaft für Natur- und Völkerkunde Ostasiens*, XXVII (1934).

———. "Shōtoku taishi," *Mitteilungen der Deutschen Gesellschaft für Natur- und Völkerkunde Ostasiens*, XVIII (1936).

Brandon, S. G. F. *The Judgement of the Dead*. New York: Charles Scribner's Sons, 1969.

Buchanan, D. C. "Inari: Its Origin, Development, and Nature." *TASJ*, Second Series, XXI (December 1935).

Burlingame, Eugene Watson. *Buddhist Legends*, 3 vols. (Harvard Oriental Series, 28–30). Cambridge, Mass.: Harvard University Press, 1921.

Chavannes, Edouard. *Le T'ai chan*. Paris: Earnest Leroux, 1910.

Chou, Yi-liang, "Tantrism in China." *HJAS*, VIII (No. 3–4, March 1945), 241–332.

Conze, Edward. *Buddhist Scriptures*. Baltimore, Md.: Penguin Books, 1959.

———. *Buddhist Wisdom Books: The Diamond Sutra. The Heart Sutra*. London: Allen & Unwin, 1958.

———. *The Large Sutra on Perfect Wisdom*. London and Madison: Luzac & Co., 1961–1964.

———. *Thirty Years of Buddhist Studies*. Oxford, Eng.: Bruno Cassirer, 1967.

Cowell, E. G., ed. *Buddhist Mahāyāna Texts* (*SBE*, XLIX). Oxford, Eng.: Clarendon Press, 1894. New York: Dover Publications, 1969.

Davidson, J. Leroy. *The Lotus Sutra in Chinese Art: A Study in Buddhist Art to the Year 1000*. New Haven, Conn.: Yale University Press, 1954.

Dumézil, George. "The Three Last Voyages of Il'Ja of Murom." In *Myths and Symbols*, 153–162. See Kitagawa.

Earhart, H. Byron. "Shugendō, the Tradition of En no Gyōja, and Mikkyō Influences." In *Studies of Esoteric Buddhism and Tantrism*. Kōyasan: Kōyasan University Press, 1965, pp. 297–317.

———. *A Religious Study of the Mount Haguro Sect of Shugendo. An Example of Japanese Mountain Religion* (Monumenta Nipponica Monograph). Tokyo: Sophia University, 1970.

Eliade, Mircea. *Birth and Rebirth*. Trans. by Willard R. Trask. New York: Harper & Brothers, 1958.

———. *The Myth of the Eternal Return*. Trans. by Willard R. Trask. New York: Pantheon Books, 1954. (*Cosmos and History*. Harper Torchbook, 1959).

———. *Myths, Dreams, and Mysteries*. Trans. by Philip Mairet. New York: Harper & Brothers, 1960.

———. "Methodological Remarks on the Study of Religious Symbolism." *In The History of Religions: Essays in Methodology*. Ed. by M. Eliade and J. M.

Kitagawa. Chicago: University of Chicago Press, 1959, pp. 86–107.

———. *Patterns in Comparative Religion*. Trans. by Rosemary Sheed. New York: Sheed & Ward, 1958.

———. *Shamanism*. Trans. by Willard R. Trask. New York: Pantheon Books, 1964.

———. *Yoga: Immortality and Freedom*. Trans. by Willard R. Trask. (Bollingen Series, LVI). Princeton, N.J.: Princeton University Press, 1958, 1969.

Ellwood, Robert. "Harvest and Renewal at the Grand Shrine of Ise." *Numen*, XV (No. 3, November 1968), 165–190.

Evans-Wentz, W. Y., ed. *Tibetan Yoga and Secret Doctrines*. London: Oxford University Press, 1935 (Paperback, 1967).

Florents, K. See Satow.

Forster, John S. "Uji Shūi Monogatari (Selected Translation)." *Monumenta Nipponica*, XX (No. 1–2, 1965), 135–208.

Frank, Bernard. "Un recueil de jurisprudence surnaturelle; remarques sur le chapitre demonologique du Konjaku monogatari." *Asiatische Studien* (No. 1/2, 1953), 47–57.

Fung Yu-lan. *A History of Chinese Philosophy*, 2 vols. Trans. by Derk Bodde. Princeton, N. J.: Princeton University Press, 1953.

Gonda, J. *Ancient Indian Kingship from the Religious Point of View* (reprinted from *Numen*, III [1956], IV [1957]). Leiden: E. J. Brill, 1966.

Goodrich, L. C., ed. *Japan in the Chinese Dynastic Histories*. South Pasadena, Calif.: P. D. and Ione Perkins, 1951. See Tsunoda.

Groot, J. J. M. de. *The Religious System of China*, 6 vols. Leiden: E. J. Brill, 1892–1910; Taipei: Literature House, 1964.

Guenther, Herbert V. "Tantra and Revelation." *History of Religions*, VII (No. 4, May 1968), 279–301.

Hanayama, Shinshō. "Prince Shōtoku and Japanese Buddhism." *Philosophical Studies of Japan*, IV (1963), 23–48.

Hartmann, Gerda. *Beiträge zur Geschichte der Göttin Lakṣmī*. Leipzig: Otto Harrascowitz, 1933.

Hoffmann, Helmut. *The Religions of Tibet*. Trans. by Edward Fitzgerald. New York: Macmillan, 1961.

Hori, Ichirō. *Folk Religion in Japan*. Ed. by Joseph M. Kitagawa and Alan L. Miller. Chicago: University of Chicago Press, 1968.

———. "On Concept of *Hijiri* (holy-man)." *Numen*, V (No. 2–3, 1958), 128–160, 199–231.

Horner, Isaline Blew, trans. *The Collection of Middle Length Sayings*, 3 vols. London: Luzac & Co., for Pali Text Society, 1954–1959.

———. *Women Under Primitive Buddhism*. London: George Routledge & Sons, 1930.

Hurvitz, Leon. "*Chih-i*." *Mélanges chinois et bouddhiques*, XII (1960–1962), 1–372.

Ishida, Eiichirō. "Mother-son Deities," *History of Religions*, IV (No. 1, 1964), 30–52.

Jones, S. W., trans. *Ages Ago: Thirty-seven stories from the Konjaku Monogatari Collection*. Cambridge, Mass.: Harvard University Press, 1959.

Kaltenmark, Max, trans. *Le Lie-sien Tchouan*. Paris: Université de Paris, 1953.

Kamstra, J. H. *Encounter or Syncretism*. Leiden: E. J. Brill, 1967.

Katō, Bunnō, trans. *Myōhō-renge-kyō: The Sutra of the Lotus Flower of the Wonderful Law*. Tokyo: Kōsei shuppansha, 1971.

Kern, H. *Saddharma-Puṇḍarika or the Lotus of the True Law*. (*SBE*, XXI). Oxford, Eng.: Clarendon Press, 1884; New York: Dover Publications, 1963.

Kitagawa, Joseph M. "Gohei Hasami—A Rite of Purification of Time at Mt. Kōya." *Proceedings of the XIth International Congress of the International Association for*

the History of Religions, II. Leiden: E. J. Brill, 1968, pp. 173–174.
———, ed. Myths and Symbols: Studies in Honor of Mircea Eliade. Chicago: University of Chicago Press, 1969.
———. Religion in Japanese History. New York: Columbia University Press, 1966.
Lamotte, Etienne. "Mañjuśrī." T'oung Pao, XLVIII (1960), 1–95.
Laufer, Berthold. Jade. South Pasadena, Calif.: P. D. & Ione Perkins in cooperation with the Westwood Press & W. M. Hawley, 1946 (originally published in 1912 from the Field Museum of Natural History).
Lee, Peter H. Lives of Eminent Korean Monks (Harvard-Yenching Institute Studies, XXV). Cambridge, Mass.: Harvard University Press, 1969.
Legge, James, trans. A Record of Buddhist Kingdoms. Oxford, Eng.: Clarendon Press, 1886. New York: Dover Publications, 1965.
———. The Texts of Taoism, 2 vols. (SBE, XXXIX, XL). Oxford, Eng.: Clarendon Press, 1891; New York: Dover Publications, 1962.
Levy, Howard S., trans. The Dwelling of Playful Goddess. Tokyo: Dai Nippon insatsu, 1965.
Liebenthal, Walter. "The Immortality of the Soul in Chinese Thought." Monumenta Nipponica, VIII (1952), 327–396.
———. "One-mind-dharma." In Tsukamoto hakushi shōju kinen Bukkyō shigaku ronshū. Kyoto: Tsukamoto hakushi shōju kinenkai, 1961, pp. 41–47.
———. "Shih Hui-yüan's Buddhism as Set Forth in His Writings." JAOS, LXX (1950), 243–259.
Long, Charles H., ed. See Kitagawa.
Mallman, Maric-Thérèse de. Etude iconographique sur Mañjuśrī. Paris: Ecole Française d'Extreme-Orient, 1964.
———. Introduction à l'étude d'Avalokiteçvara. Paris: Civilisations du sud, S.A.E.P., 1948.
Matsunaga, Alicia Orloff. The Buddhist Philosophy of Assimilation (Monumenta Nipponica Monograph). Tokyo: Sophia University, 1969.
Max-Müller, Friedrich, trans. Dhammapada (SBE, X). Oxford, Eng.: Clarendon Press, 1924.
———, ed. Sacred Books of the East (SBE), 49 vols. Oxford, Eng.: Clarendon Press, 1879–1927.
Mayer, Fanny Hagin. "Religious Elements in Japanese Folk Tales." Studies in Japanese Culture, 1–16. Ed. by Joseph Roggendorf. See Roggendorf.
Mibu, Taishun. "On the Thought 'kṛtajña' or '知恩' in Buddhism," IBK, XIV (No. 2, March 1966), 951–961.
Monden, Louis. Signs and Wonders. New York: Desclee Co., 1966.
Moor, Charles A., ed. The Japanese Mind. Honolulu: East-West Center Press, 1967.
Mus, Paul. "Thousand-Armed Kannon: A Mystery or a Problem?" IBK, XII (No. 1, January 1964), 438–470.
Nobel, Johannes. Suvarṇaprabhāsottama-sūtra, 2 vols. Leiden: E. J. Brill, 1958.
Nott, S. C., ed. The Mahābhārata. Trans. by P. C. Roy. New York: Philosphical Library, 1956.
Ouwehand, C. Namazue and Their Themes. Leiden: E. J. Brill, 1964.
Philippi, Donald L. "Ancient Tales of Supernatural Marriage." Today's Japan, V (No. 3, March-April 1960), 19–23.
———, trans. Kojiki. Tokyo: University of Tokyo Press, 1968.
———, trans. Norito. Tokyo: Institute for Japanese Culture and Classics, Kokugakuin University, 1959.
Pierson, J. L., trans. The Manyōsū, 20 vols. Leiden: E. J. Brill, 1929–1963.
Poussin, Louis de la Vallée. L'Abhidharmakośa de Vasubandhu, 6 vols. Paris: P. Geuthner, 1923–1931.

# Selected Bibliography

————. "The Three Bodies of a Buddha." *JRAS* (October 1906), 934–977.

Rahder, J. "Miscellany of Personal Views of an Ignorant Fool." *Acta Orientalia*, XV (1936), 173–230; XVI (1937), 59–77.

Reischauer, A. K., trans. "Genshin's Ojo Yoshu: Collected Essays on Birth into Paradise." *TASJ*, Second Series, VII (December 1930), 16–97.

Reischauer, Edwin O., trans. *Ennin's Diary: The Record of a Pilgrimage to China in Search of the Law*. New York: Ronald Press, 1955.

Rhys Davids, C. A. F., *Psalms of the Early Buddhists: 1. Psalms of the Sisters*. London: Pali Text Society, 1909.

Rhys Davids, T. W., trans. *Buddhist Suttas* (*SBE*, XI). London: Clarendon Press, 1881; New York: Dover Publications, 1969.

————, and C. A. F. Rhys Davids, trans. *Dialogues of the Buddha*, 3 vols. London: Oxford University Press, 1899–1921.

Roggendorf, Joseph. *Studies in Japanese Culture* (Monumenta Nipponica Monograph). Tokyo: Sophia University, 1963.

*Sacred Books of the East*. See Max-Müller.

Sansom, George B. *A History of Japan to 1334*. Stanford, Calif.: Stanford University Press, 1958, 1964³.

————. "Early Japanese Law and Administration." Parts One and Two. *TASJ*, Second Series, IX (December 1932), 67–109; XI (December 1934), 117–149.

————. "The Imperial Edicts in the *Shoku Nihongi*." *TASJ*, Second Series, I (1923/24), 5–39.

Satow, E., and K. Florents. "Ancient Japanese Rituals." *TASJ*, reprint of II (December 1927), 5–143.

Shih, Robert, trans. *Biographies des moines éminents (Kao Seng Tschouan) de Houei-kiao*. Louvain: Institut Orientaliste, 1968. (The first three books are translated).

Smith, D. Howard. "Chinese Concept of the Soul." *Numen*, V (1958), 165–179.

Smith, Robert. "On Certain Tales of the *Konjaku Monogatari* as Reflections of Japanese Folk Religion." *Asian Folklore Studies*, XXV (1966), 221–233.

Snellen, J. B. "Shoku Nihongi." *TASJ*, Second Series, XI (December 1934), 151–239; XIV (June 1937), 209–278.

Soothill, E., trans. *The Lotus of the Wonderful Law*. Oxford, Eng.: Clarendon Press, 1930.

Suzuki, D. T. *Outlines of Mahāyāna Buddhism*. London: Luzac and Co., 1907; New York: Schocken Books, 1963.

Thomas, Edward J. *The History of Buddhist Thought*. London: Routledge & Kegan Paul, 1933, 1951².

Thompson, Stith. *The Folktale*. New York: Holt, Rinehart and Winston, 1946.

————. *Motif-Index of Folk-literature*, 6 vols. Helsinki: Academia Scientiarum Fennica, 1932–1936 (revised and enlarged edition, Bloomington: Indiana University Press, 1956).

Tsuda, Sōkichi. "The Idea of Kami in Ancient Japanese Classics." *T'oung Pao*, LII (No. 4–5, 1966). 293–304.

————. "On the Stages of the Formation of Japan as a Nation and the Origin of the Belief in Perpetuity of the Imperial Family." *Philosophical Studies of Japan*, IV (1963), 49–78.

Tsunoda, Ryūsaku, trans. *Japan in the Chinese Dynastic Histories*. See Goodrich.

Ui, Hakuju. "A Study of Japanese Tendai Buddhism." *Philosophical Studies of Japan*, I (1959), 33–74.

Visser, M. W. de. *Ancient Buddhism in Japan*, 2 vols. Leiden: E. J. Brill, 1935.

————. *The Bodhisattva Ti-tsang (Jizō) in China and Japan*. Berlin: Oesterheld & Co., 1914.

————. *The Dragon in China and Japan*. Amsterdam: Johannes Müller, 1913.

————. "The Fox and the Badger in Japanese Folklore." *TASJ*, XXXVI (No. 3, 1908), 1–159.

Waddell, L. A. "The *Dhāraṇī* Cult in Buddhism, Its Origin, Deified Literature and Images." *Ostasiatische Zeitschrift*, I (No. 2, July 1912), 155–195.

————. "The Indian Buddhist Cult of Avalokita and His Consort, Tārā 'the Saviouress,' Illustrated from the Remains in Magadha." *JRAS* (1894), 51–89.

Ware, James R., trans. *Alchemy, Medicine, Religion in the China of A.D. 320:* Cambridge, Mass.: MIT Press, 1966.

Watters, Thomas, trans. *On Yuan Chwang's Travels in India*, 2 vols. Edited by T. W. Rhys Davids and S. W. Bushell. London: Royal Asiatic Society, 1904–1905 (reprinted in China, 1938).

Wayman, Alex. "Significance of Dreams in India and Tibet." *History of Religions*, VII (No. 1, August 1967), 1–12.

————. "Studies in Yama and Māra." *Indo-Iranian Journal*, III (1959), 44–73, 112–131.

Wright, Arthur F. "Biography and Hagiography: Hui-chiao's *Lives of Eminent Monks*." In *Silver Jubilee Volume of the Zinbun-kagaku Kenkyūsyo, Kyōto University* (1954), pp. 383–432.

Yen chih-t'ui. *Family Instructions for the Yen Clan*. Trans. by Teng ssu-yü. (Monographies du T'oung Pao, IV). Leiden: E. J. Brill, 1968.

Zaehner, R. C. *The Dawn and Twilight of Zoroastrianism*. London: Weidenfeld and Nicolson, 1961.

————. *The Teaching of the Magi*. London: George Allen & Unwin; New York: Macmillan Co., 1956.

Zürcher, Erik. *Buddhist Conquest of China*. Leiden: E. J. Brill, 1959.

## (3) WORKS IN NON-WESTERN LANGUAGES

The following list excludes all Buddhist scriptures compiled in the *Shinshū Taishō daizō-kyō*. See Appendix D.

Aida Hanji 會田範治. *Chūkai Yōrō-ryō* 註解養老令. Tokyo: Yūshindō, 1964.

Akamatsu Chijō 赤松智城 and Akiba Takashi 秋葉隆. *Chōsen fuzoku no kenkyū* 朝鮮巫俗の研究. Tokyo: Ōsakayagō shoten, 1938.

Akizuki Kan'ei 秋月觀瑛. "Rikuchō Dōkyō ni okeru ōhōsetsu no hatten" 六朝道教における應報説の發展. *Hirosaki daigaku jinbunshakai* 弘前大學人文社會, no. 33 (1964), 26–60. Reprinted in the *Chūgoku kankei ronsetsu shiryō* 中國關係論説資料, I (1964), Part One, 386–403.

Amemiya Shōji 雨宮尚治. "Enpō-bon *Nihon ryōiki*" 延寶本日本靈異記. *Ōtani gakuhō* 大谷學報, XX (No. 2, June 1939), 33–44.

————. "Kōya-bon kei *Nihon ryōiki shōkō*" 高野本系日本靈異記小考. *Ōtani gakuhō* 大谷學報, XVI (No. 3, October 1935), 51–73.

————. "*Nihon ryōiki* ni tsuite" 日本靈異記について. *Kokugo kokubun* 國語國文, IV (No. 5, 1934), 68–89.

————. "*Shukyō yōshū konzō-ron* kanken" 衆經要集金藏論管見. *Kokugo to Koku bungaku* 國語と國文學, No. 227 (March 1943), 49–60.

*Asaba-shō* 阿娑縛抄 (*DBZ*, 35–41). See *Dainihon Bukkyō zensho*.

Asai Endō 淺井圓道. "Dengyō Daishi to Hokke shisō no renkan" 傳教大師と法華思想の連關. In *Hoke-kyō no shisō to bunka*, 569–597. See Sakamoto.

Bukkyō bungaku kenkyūkai 佛教文學研究會, ed. *Bukkyō bungaku kenkyū* 佛教文學研究, 8 vols. Kyoto: Hōzōkan, 1963–1970.

*Bungaku* 文學, II (No. 5, 1934). A special number on legendary literature.

# Selected Bibliography

Chingen 鎮源. *Honchō Hokke kenki* 本朝法華驗記. (*ZGR*, VIII A, Book 194), also called *Dainihon Hoke-kyō kenki* 大日本法華經驗記. See *Zoku gunsho ruijū*.

*Dainihon Bukkyō zensho* 大日本佛教全書 (*DBZ*), 160 vols. Tokyo: Bussho kankōkai, 1912–1922.

*Dainihon zokuzō-kyō* 大日本續藏經, 750 books. Kyoto: Zōkyō shoin, 1905–1912.

*Dengyō Daishi zenshū* 傳教大師全集, 5 vols. Shiga Hieizan tosho kankōkai, 1926–1927.

Etani Ryūkai 惠谷隆戒. "Gangō-ji Chikō no *Muryōju-kyō ronshaku* no kenkyū" 元興寺智光の無量壽經論釋の研究. In *Hikata hakushi koki kinen ronbunshū*, 561–576. See Hikata hakushi. . . .

*Fudoki* 風土記 (*NKBT*, 2). Ed. by Akimoto Kichirō 秋本吉郎. See *Nihon koten bungaku taikei*.

Fujino Michio 藤野道生. "Zen'in-ji kō" 禪院寺考. *Shigaku zasshi* 史學雜誌, LXVI (No. 9, September 1957), 1–43.

Fujisawa Morihiko 藤澤衞彥. *Nihon densetsu kenkyū* 日本傳説研究, 4 vols. Tokyo: Mikasa shobō, 1935.

————. *Nihon minzokugaku zenshū* 日本民俗學全集, 8 vols. Tokyo: Akane shobō, 1959–1961.

Fujita Kōtatsu 藤田宏達. "Tenrin jōō ni tsuite" 轉輪聖王について. In *Miyamoto Shōson kyōju* . . ., 145–156. See Hanayama.

Fujiwara no Kenshō 藤原顯昭. *Shūchū-shō* 袖中抄 (*Nihon kagaku taikei* 日本歌學大系, betsukan II). Tokyo: Kazama shobō, 1957–1958.

Fujiwara no Munetomo 藤原宗友. *Honchō shinshū ōjōden* 本朝新修往生傳 (*ZGR*, VIII, Book 199). See *Zoku gunsho ruijū*.

Fukui Kōjun 福井康順. *Tōyō shisō no kenkyū* 東洋思想の研究. Tokyo: Risōsha, 1965.

————. *Tōyō shisōshi kenkyū* 東洋思想史研究. Tokyo: Shoseki bunbutsu ryūtsūkai, 1960.

Fukushima Kōichi 福島行一. "Nihon ryōiki ni arawareta Kyōkai no kangaekata" 日本靈異記に現れた景戒の考え方. *Heian bungaku* 平安文學, 99–138. See Keiō. . . .

Fukuyama Toshio 福山敏男. *Narachō jiin no kenkyū* 奈良朝寺院の研究. Kyoto: Takakiri shoin, 1948.

Funabashi Issai 舟橋一哉. *Gō no kenkyū* 業の研究. Kyoto: Hōzōkan, 1954.

Fuse Kōgaku 布施浩岳. *Hoke-kyō seishinshi* 法華經精神史. Kyoto: Heirakuji shoten, 1954.

*Fusō ryakki*. See Kōen.

Futaba Kenkō 二葉憲香. *Kodai Bukkyō shisōshi kenkyū* 古代佛教思想史研究. Kyoto: Nagata bunshōdō, 1962.

*Genkō shakusho*. See Shiren.

Gishō 義昭. *Nihon kanryōroku* 日本感靈錄 (*ZGR*, XXVB, Book 717). See *Zoku gunsho ruijū*.

Gotō Yoshio 後藤良雄. "*Myōhōki* no shōdōsei to *Ryōiki*" 冥報記の唱導性と靈異記. *Kokubungaku kenkyū* 國文學研究. XXV (March 1962), 84–90.

Gotō Taiyō 後藤大用. *Kanzeon bosatsu no kenkyū* 觀世音菩薩の研究. Tokyo: Sankibō busshorin, 1958.

*Gunsho ruijū* 群書類從, 19 vols. Tokyo: Keizai zasshisha, 1893–1902.

Haga Yaichi 芳賀矢一. *Kōshō Konjaku monogatarishū* 攷證今昔物語集, 3 vols. Tokyo: Fuzanbō, 1913, 1914, 1921.

Hanayama Shinshō 花山信勝. *Hokke gisho no kenkyū* 法華義疏の研究 (*Tōyō bunko ronsō* 東洋文庫論叢, XVIII, I). Tokyo: Tōyō bunko, 1933.

———— and others, ed. *Miyamoto Shōson kyōju kanreki kinen ronbunshū: Indogaku Bukkyōgaku ronshū* 宮本正尊教授還曆記念論文集印度學佛教學論集. Tokyo: Sanseidō, 1954.

# Selected Bibliography

Haraguchi Hiroshi 原口裕. "*Nihon ryōiki* shutten goku kanken" 日本靈異記出典語句管見. *Kuntengo to kunten shiryō* 訓點語と訓點資料, No. 34 (December 1966), 53–67.

Hashikawa Tadashi 橋川正. "*Ryōiki no kenkyū*" 靈異記の研究. *Geibun* 藝文, XIII (No. 3, 1922), 187–203. Reprinted in his *Nihon Bukkyō bunkashi no kenkyū* 日本佛教文化史の研究. Tokyo: Chūgai shuppan, 1924.

Hayashi Rokurō 林睦郎. *Kōmyō kōgō* 光明皇后 (*Jinbutsu sōshō* 人物叢書, 79). Tokyo: Yoshikawa kōbunkan, 1961.

Higo sensei koki kinen ronbun kankōkai 肥後先生古稀記念論文刊行會, ed. *Nihon bunkashi kenkyū* 日本文化史研究. Tokyo: Kōbundō, 1969.

Hikata Ryūshō 干潟龍祥. *Honjōkyōrui no shisōshiteki kenkyū* 本生經類の思想史的研究. Tokyo: Sankibō busshorin, 1954.

———. *Jātaka gaikan* ジャータカ概觀. Tokyo: Suzuki zaidan, 1961.

Hikata hakushi koki kinenkai 干潟博士古稀記念會, ed. *Hikata hakushi koki kinen ronbunshū* 干潟博士古稀記念論文集. Fukuoka: 1964.

Hirabayashi Harunori 平林治德 and others, ed. *Nihon setsuwa bungaku sakuin* 日本説話文學索引. Tokyo: Nihon shuppansha, 1943.

Hirakawa Akira 平川彰. *Ritsuzō no kenkyū* 律藏の研究. Tokyo: Sankibō busshorin, 1960.

———. *Shoki Daijō Bukkyō no kenkyū* 初期大乘佛教の研究. Tokyo: Shunjūsha, 1968.

Hirano Kunio 平野邦雄. "Nihon kodai ni okeru *uji* no seiritsu to sono kōzō" 日本古代における「氏」の成立とその構造. *Kodaigaku* 古代學, XII (No. 1, May 1965), 21–49.

Honda Hitoshi 本田濟. "Seijin" 聖人. *Ōsaka shiritsu daigaku bungakubu kiyō: jinbun kenkyū* 大阪市立大學文學部紀要人文研究, XIX (No. 10, 1968), 28–37. Reprinted in *Chūgoku kankei ronsetsu shiryō* 中國關係論説資料, IX (1968), Part One, 50–54.

Hori Ichirō 堀一郎. *Nihon jōdai bunka to Bukkyō* 日本上代文化と佛教. Tokyo: Hōzōkan, 1940.

———. *Wagakuni minkan shinkōshi no kenkyū* 我國民間信仰史の研究, 2 vols. Tokyo: Sōgensha, 1953, 1955.

Horiike Shunpō 堀池春峰. "Ubasoku kōshinge to shukke nyūshisho" 優婆塞貢進解と出家入試所. *Nihon rekishi* 日本歴史, No. 114 (1957), 25–32.

Ienaga Saburō 家永三郎. *Jōdai Bukkyō shisōshi kenkyū* 上代佛教思想史研究. Tokyo: Meguro shoin, 1942. Revised edition (Kyoto: Hōzōkan, 1966).

———. *Nihon Bukkyōshi: Kodaihen* 日本佛教史 古代篇. Kyoto: Hōzōkan, 1966.

———, ed. *Nihon Bukkyō shisō no tenkai* 日本佛教思想の展開. Kyoto: Heirakuji shoten, 1956.

Iida Mizuho 飯田瑞穗. "Ono no Imoko *Hoke-kyō* shōrai setsuwa" 小野妹子法華經將來説話. *Nihon kodaishi ronshū* 日本古代史論集, I, 435–478. See Sakamoto Taro. . . .

Ikeda Kikan 池田龜鑑. "*Nihon ryōiki* no itsubun wa hatashite gisaku naruka" 日本靈異記の佚文は果して僞作なるか. *Kokubungaku tōsa* 國文學踏査, I (December 1931). Reprinted in *Monogatari bungaku* 物語文學, II (*Ikeda Kikan senshū* 池田龜鑑選集). Tokyo: Shibundō, 1968.

Ikeda Suetoshi 池田末利. "Tendō to tenmei, Part One" 天道と天命. *Hiroshima daigaku bungakubu kiyō* 廣島大學文學部紀要, XXVIII (No. 1, 1968), 24–39. Reprinted in *Chūgoku kankei ronsetsu shiryō* 中國關係論説資料, X (1968), Part One, 68–75.

Inaya Yūsen 稻谷祐宣. "Nara jidai no mikkyō kyōten to Kūkai" 奈良時代の密教經典と空海. *Mikkyō bunka* 密教文化, No. 73 (June 1965), 52–59.

Inobe Jūichirō 井野部重一郎. "Hōkō-ji to Gangō-ji no idō ni tsuite" 法興寺と元興寺

の異同について. *Shoku Nihongi kenkyū* 續日本紀研究, VII (No. 1, 1960), 1–13.

Inoue Kaoru 井上薫. *Gyōki* 行基 (*Jinbutsu sōsho* 人物叢書, 24). Tokyo: Yoshikawa kōbunkan, 1959.

——. "Hijiri-kō" ひじり考. *Historia* ヒストリア, I (September 1951), 24–32.

——. *Narachō Bukkyōshi no kenkyū* 奈良朝佛教史の研究. Tokyo: Yoshikawa kōbunkan, 1966.

——. *Nihon kodai no seiji to shūkyō* 日本古代の政治と宗教. Tokyo: Yoshikawa kōbunkan, 1961.

Inoue Mitsusada 井上光貞. "Nanto rokushū no seiritsu" 南都六宗の成立. *Nihon rekishi* 日本歴史, No. 156 (1961), 2–14.

——. *Nihon Jōdokyō seiritsushi no kenkyū* 日本淨土教成立史の研究. Tokyo: Yamakawa shuppansha, 1957.

——. *Nihon kodai kokka no kenkyū* 日本古代國家の研究. Tokyo: Iwanami shoten, 1967.

Iryǒn 一然. *Samguk yusa* (Ja. *Sangoku iji*) 三國遺事. Kyoto: Chōsen gakkai, 1929.

Ishida Mizumaro 石田瑞麿. *Ganjin* 鑑眞. Tokyo: Daizō shuppansha, 1958.

——. *Nihon Bukkyō ni okeru kairitsu no kenkyū* 日本佛教における戒律の研究. Tokyo: Zaike Bukkyōkai, 1963.

Ishida Mosaku 石田茂作. *Nara jidai bunka zakkō* 奈良時代文化雜攷. Tokyo: Sōgensha, 1944.

——. *Shakyō yori mitaru Narachō Bukkyō no kenkyū* 寫經より見たる奈良朝佛教の研究 (*Tōyō bunko ronsō* 東洋文庫論叢, XI). Tokyo: Tōyō bunko, 1930.

Ishii Ryōsuke 石井良助. *Nihon hōseishi gaisetsu* 日本法制史概説. Tokyo: Sōgensha, 1948, 1960 (revised).

Itabashi Tomoyuki 板橋倫行. "Nihon ryōiki no senjutsu nenji ni tsuite" 日本靈異記の撰述年時について. *Kokugo to kokubungaku* 国語と國文學, VII (No. 2, February 1930), 132–142.

——. "Ryōiki Enryaku yonen izen gensensetsu ni tsuite" 靈異記延暦四年以前原撰說について. *Bungaku* 文學, III, (No. 6, 1935), 757–764.

——. "Shaba no bungaku" 沙婆の文學. *Bungaku*, XXI (No. 11, 1953), 54–62.

Itō Tasaburō 伊東多三郎, ed. *Kokumin seikatsushi kenkyū* 國民生活史研究, IV. Tokyo: Yoshikawa kōbunkan, 1960.

Iwabuchi Etsutarō 岩淵悦太郎. "Nihon ryōiki ni mietaru *Hannya kenki* towa nanika" 日本靈異記に見えたる般若檢記とは何か. *Kokugo to kokubungaku* 國語と國文學, XII (No. 8, 1935), 61–67.

Iwamoto Yutaka 岩本裕. *Bukkyō setsuwa kenkyū josetsu* 佛教說話研究序說. (*Bukkyō setsuwa kenkyū* 佛教說話研究, I). Kyoto: Hōzōkan, 1967.

——. *Mokuren densetsu to Urabon* 日蓮傳說と盂蘭盆. Kyoto: Hōzōkan, 1968.

Iwasaki Koyata hakushi shōju kinenkai 岩崎小彌太博士頌壽記念會, ed. *Nihon shiseki ronshū* 日本史籍論集, I. Tokyo: Yoshikawa kōbunkan, 1969.

Jien 慈圓. *Gukanshō* 愚管抄 (*NKBT*, 86), ed. by Okami Masao 岡見正雄 and Akamatsu Toshihide 赤松俊秀. See *Nihon koten bungaku taikei*.

Kajiyama Yūichi 梶山雄一. "Eon no hōōsetsu to shinfumetsuron" 慧遠の報應說と身不滅論. *Eon kenkyū—kenkyūhen* 慧遠研究—研究篇, 89–120. See Kimura.

Kamimura Shinjō 上村眞肇. "Chūgoku Tendai to Hokke shisō no renkan" 中國天臺と法華思想の連關. In *Hoke-kyō no shisō to bunka*, 550–555. See Sakamoto.

Kamo no Chōmei 鴨長明. *Hosshinshū* 發心集. Ed. by Yanase Kazuo 簗瀬一雄. Tokyo: Kazama shobō, 1956.

Kanaoka Shūyū 金岡秀友. "Konkōmyō-kyō no teiōkan to sono Shina-Nihonteki juyō" 金光明經の帝王觀とその支那・日本的受容. *Bukkyō shigaku* 佛教史學, VI (No. 4, October 1957), 21–32.

Kanda Hideo 神田秀夫. "Kiki-Fudoki-Ryōiki no ushi to kikajin" 記紀・風土記・

靈異記の牛と歸化人. *Kokugo to kokubungaku* (November 1961), 14–26; (December 1961) 13–26.

Katayose Masayoshi 片寄正義. *Konjaku monogatarishū no kenkyū* 今昔物語集の研究, 2 vols. Tokyo: Sanseidō, 1943.

———. *Konjaku monogatarishū-ron* 今昔物語集論. Tokyo: Sanseidō, 1944.

Katō Totsudō 加藤咄堂. *Kannon shinkōshi* 觀音信仰史 (*Kannon zenshū* 觀音全集, VII). Tokyo: Yūkōdō, 1940.

Kawaguchi Hisao 川口久雄. *Heianchō Nihon Kanbungakushi no kenkyū* 平安朝日本漢文學史の研究. Tokyo: Meiji shoin, 1959.

———. "Nihon setsuwa bungaku to gaikoku bungaku tono kakawari" 日本說話文學と外國文學とのかかわり. *Kokubungaku kaishaku to kanshō* 國文學解釋と鑑賞, XXX (No. 2, 1965), 59–63.

Kazue Kyōichi 數江教一. *Nihon no mappō shisō* 日本の末法思想. Tokyo: Kōbundō, 1961.

Keiō gijuku daigaku kokubungaku kenkyūkai 慶應義塾大學國文學研究會, ed. *Heian bungaku* 平安文學 (*Kokubungaku ronsō* 國文學論叢, III). Tokyo: Shibundō, 1959.

Kenshin gakkai 顯眞學會, ed. *Umehara Kangaku koki kinen ronbunshū* 梅原勸學古稀記念論文集. Kyoto: Kenshin hōrin monjo dendōbu, 1955.

Kikuchi Takeshi 菊地武. "*Nihon ryōiki* butten kō" 日本靈異記佛典考. *Nihon shiseki ronshū*, I, 241–263. See Iwasaki.

Kimoto Michifusa 木本通房. *Jōdai kayō shōkai* 上代歌謠詳解. Tokyo: Musashino shoin, 1942.

Kimura Eiichi 木村英一, ed. *Eon kenkyū—ibunhen* 慧遠研究—遺文篇. Tokyo: Sōbunsha, 1960.

———, ed. *Eon kenkyū—kenkyūhen* 慧遠研究—研究篇. Tokyo: Sōbunsha, 1962.

Kishi Kunio 岸邦男. *Fujiwara no Nakamaro* 藤原仲麻呂 (*Jinbutsu sōsho* 人物叢書, 153). Tokyo: Yoshikawa kōbunkan, 1969.

Kitayama Shigeo 北山茂夫. *Narachō no seiji to minshū* 奈良朝の政治と民衆. Kyoto: Takakiri shoin, 1948.

———. *Nihon kodai seijishi no kenkyū* 日本古代政治史の研究. Tokyo: Iwanami shoten, 1959.

——— and Yoshinaga Noboru 吉永登, ed. *Nihon kodai no seiji to bunka* 日本古代の政治と文化. Tokyo: Aoyama shoin, 1956.

Kiyota Jakuun 清田寂雲. "*Hoke-kyō* no shosha ni tsuite" 法華經の書寫について. *Mikkyō bunka* 密敎文化, No. 71/72 (April 1965), 160–171.

Kobayashi Taichirō 小林太市郎. "Narachō no Senju Kannon" 奈良朝の千手觀音. *Bukkyō bijutsu* 佛敎美術, XXV (1955), 55–80.

———. "Shin-Tō no Kannon" 晉唐の觀音. *Ibid.*, X (1950), 3–46.

———. "Tōdai no Daihi Kannon" 唐代の大悲觀音. *Ibid.*, XX (1953), 3–27; XXI (1954), 89–109; XXII (1954), 3–28.

Kobayashi Tomoaki 小林智昭. *Mujōkan no bungaku* 無常感の文學. (*Atene shinsho* アテネ新書). Tokyo: Kōbundō, 1959.

Kodaigaku kyōkai 古代學協會, ed. *Kanmuchō no shomondai* 桓武朝の諸問題. Ōsaka: Kodaigaku kyōkai, 1962.

*Kodai kayōshū* 古代歌謠集 (*NKBT*, 3). Ed. by Tsuchihashi Hiroshi 土橋寬 and Konishi Jin'ichi 小西甚一. See *Nihon koten bungaku taikei*.

Kōen 皇圓. *Fusō ryakki* 扶桑略記 (*SZKT*, XII). See *Shintei zōho kokushi taikei*.

Koizumi Michi 小泉道. "Ekisai no Ryōiki kōshō no hotei" 掖齋の靈異記攷證の補訂. *Kokugo kokubun* 國語國文, XXIX (No. 5, 1960), 44–57.

———. "Kōya-bon *Nihon ryōiki* kō" 高野本日本靈異記考. *Ibid.*, XXI (No. 10, 1952), 11–21.

# Selected Bibliography

————. "Kyōkai gensen ni arazaru *Nihon ryōiki* futatsu" 景戒原撰にあらざる日本靈異記二つ. *Ibid.*, XXIV (No. 6, 1955), 45–54.

————. "*Ryōiki* no Kōya-bon o megutte" 靈異記の高野本をめぐって. *Ibid.*, XXV (No. 8, 1956).

————. "*Ryōiki* no shohon o megutte" 靈異記の諸本をめぐって. *Kuntengo to kunten shiryō* 訓點語と訓點資料, No. 34 (December 1966), 18–38.

*Kojiki* 古事記 (*NKBT*, 1). Ed. by Kurano Kenji 倉野憲司. See *Nihon koten bungaku taikei.*

Kojima Noriyuki 小島憲之. *Jōdai Nihon bungaku to Chūgoku bungaku* 上代日本文學と中國文學, 3 vols. Tokyo: Hanawa shobō, 1962–1965.

*Kokubungaku* 國文學, III (No. 11, November 1958). A special number on legendary literature.

Ko Hung 葛洪. *Pao p'u-tzu* 抱朴子 (*SPTK*). Shanghai: Commercial Press, 1927 (reprint of the Ming edition).

Koten isan no kai 古典遺産の會, ed. *Ōjōden no kenkyū* 往生傳の研究. Tokyo: Shindokushosha, 1968.

*Koten kenkyū* 古典研究, IV (No. 2, February 1939). A special number on *Nihon ryōiki.*

————, VIII (No. 5, May 1942). A special number on religious literature.

Kubo Noritada 窪德忠. "Dōkyō to shugendō" 道教と修驗道. *Shūkyō kenkyū* 宗教研究, XXXVI (No. 2, December 1962), 25–48.

Kubota Osamu 久保田収. "Shōtoku taishi Kannon keshinsetsu no genryū" 聖德太子觀音化身說の源流. *Mikkyō bunka* 密教文化, No. 32 (February 1956), 42–53.

Kurabayashi Masatsugu 倉林正次. *Kyōen no kenkyū: Bungakuhen* 饗宴の研究 (文學篇). Tokyo: Ōfūsha, 1969.

Kurano Kenji 倉野憲司. *Koten to jōdai seishin* 古典と上代精神. Tokyo: Shibundō, 1942.

————. "*Nihon ryōiki kō*" 日本靈異記攷. *Bungaku* 文學, II (No. 12, 1934), 751–765.

————. "*Nihon ryōiki ni tsuite*" 日本靈異記について. *Bungaku* 文學, III (No. 12, 1935), 79–84.

Kurosawa Kōzō 黑澤幸三. "Kaniman-ji engi no genryū to sono seiritsu" 蟹滿寺緣起の源流とその成立. *Kokugo to kokubungaku* 國語と國文學, No. 535 (September 1968), 14–24.

*Lü-shih ch'un ch'iu* 呂氏春秋 (*SPTK*). Shanghai: Commercial Press, 1929 (reprint of the Ming edition).

Maeda Egaku 前田惠學. "Ryokō no tochū tasekai ni sōgū suru monogatari kō" 旅行の途中他世界に相遇する物語考. *IBK*, VI (No. 1, January 1958), 196–200.

————. "Indo Bukkyō ni arawareta tasekai no kenkyū" 印度佛教に現われた他世界の研究. In *Bungaku ni okeru higan hyōshō no kenkyū.* See Ueda.

Makita Tairyō 牧田諦亮. *Chūgoku kinsei Bukkyōshi kenkyū* 中國近世佛教史研究. Kyoto: Heirakuji shoten, 1957.

Manabe Kōsai 眞鍋廣濟. *Jizōson no sekai* 地藏尊の世界. Tokyo: Aoyama shoin, 1959.

————. *Jizō-bosatsu no kenkyū* 地藏菩薩の研究. Kyoto: Sanmitsudō shoten, 1960.

*Manyōshū* 萬葉集 (*NKBT*, 4–7). Ed. by Takagi Ichinosuke 高木市之助 and others. See *Nihon koten bungaku taikei.*

Masuda Fukutarō 增田福太郎. *Chūgoku no zokushin to hō-shisō* 中國の俗信と法思想. Kyoto: Sanwa shobō, 1966.

Masuda Katsumi 益田勝實. *Kodai setsuwa bungaku* 古代說話文學 (*Iwanami kōza: Nihon bungaku*, 1). Tokyo: Iwanami shoten, 1958.

————. *Setsuwa bungaku to emaki* 說話文學と繪卷. Tokyo: San'ichi shobō, 1960.

Matsubayashi Hiroyuki 松林弘之. "Chōsen sangoku teiritsu jidai no Bukkyō" 朝鮮

# Selected Bibliography

三國鼎立時代の佛教. *Bukkyō shigaku* 佛教史學, XIV (No. 1, 1968).

Matsumura Takeo 松村武雄. *Nihon shinwa no kenkyū* 日本神話の研究, 4 vols. Tokyo: Baifūkan, 1954–1958.

Matsunaga Yūkei 松長有慶. "Gokoku shisō no kigen" 護國思想の起源. *IBK*, XV (No. 1, December 1966), 69–78.

Mibu Taishun 壬生台舜. "Bukkyō ni okeru on no gogi" 佛教における恩の語義. *Shūkyō kenkyū* 宗教研究, IX (No. 1, January 1961), 200–203.

Michihata Ryōshū 道端良秀. *Bukkyō to Jukyō rinri* 佛教と儒教倫理. (*Sāra sōsho* サーラ叢書, 17). Kyoto: Heirakuji shoten, 1968.

———. *Tōdai Bukkyōshi no kenkyū* 唐代佛教史の研究. Kyoto: Hōzōkan, 1957.

Minamoto no Akikane 源顯兼. *Kojidan* 古事談 (*SZKT*, XVIII). See *Shintei*. . . .

Minamoto no Tamenori 源爲憲. *Sanbō ekotoba* 三寶繪詞. See Takase Shōgon and Yamada Yoshio.

Miyamoto Shōson 宮本正尊, ed. *Bukkyō no konpon shinri* 佛教の根本眞理. Tokyo: Sanseidō, 1956.

Miyoshi no Tameyasu 三善爲康. *Shūi ōjōden* 拾遺往生傳 (*ZGR*, VIII, Book 196).

———. *Goshūi ōjōden* 後拾遺往生傳 (*ZGR*, VIII, Book 197). See *Zoku*. . . .

Mizuno Kōgen 水野弘元. "Go-setsu ni tsuite" 業説について. *IBK*, II (No. 2, March 1954), 110–120.

Mizutani Kōshō 水谷幸正. "Ichisendai kō" 一闡提攷. *Bukkyō daigaku kenkyū kiyō* 佛教大學研究紀要, XL (1961), 63–107.

Mochizuki Kankō 望月歡厚, ed. *Kindai Nihon no Hokke Bukkyō* 近代日本の法華佛教. Kyoto: Heirakuji shoten, 1968.

*Montoku (tennō) jitsuroku* 文德實錄 (*SZKT*, III). See *Shintei*. . . .

Mujū 無住. *Shasekishū* 沙石集 (*NKBT*, 85). See *Nihon koten*. . . .

Murakami Toshio 村上俊雄. *Shugendō no hattatsu* 修驗道の發達. Tokyo: Unebi shobō, 1943.

Murakami Yoshimi 村上嘉實. *Chūgoku no sennin* 中國の仙人 (*Sāra sōsho* サーラ叢書, 2). Kyoto: Heirakuji shoten, 1956.

Murayama Shūichi 村山修一. "Jōdai no onmyōdō" 上代の陰陽道. In *Kokumin seikatsushi kenkyū*, IV, 131–133. See Itō.

———. *Shinbutsu shūgō shichō* 神佛習合思潮 (*Sāra sōsho*, 6). Kyoto: Heirakuji shoten, 1956.

Nagai Yoshinori 永井義憲. *Nihon Bukkyō bungaku* 日本佛教文學. Tokyo: Hanawa shobō, 1963.

———. *Nihon Bukkyō bungaku kenkyū* 日本佛教文學研究, 2 vols. Tokyo: Toshima shobō, 1966.

Nagao Gajin 長尾雅人 and Nozawa Jōshō 野澤靜訟, ed. *Yamaguchi hakushi kanreki kinen Indogaku Bukkyōgaku ronsō* 山口博士還暦記念印度學佛教學論叢. Kyoto: Hōzōkan, 1955.

Nakagawa Osamu 中川收. "Shōtoku-Dōkyō seiken no keisei katei" 稱德・道鏡政權の形成過程. *Nihon rekishi* 日本歷史, No. 196 (1964), 41–55.

Nakamura Akizō 中村明藏. "Ubasoku ni tsuite" 優婆塞について. *Shoku Nihongi kenkyū* 續日本紀研究, VII (No. 11, 1960), 274–281.

Nakamura Hajime 中村元. *Jihi* 慈悲 (*Sāra sōsho*, 1). Kyoto: Heirakuji shoten, 1968.

Nakamura Kyōko 中村恭子. *Ryōi no sekai: Nihon ryōiki* 靈異の世界―日本靈異記 (*Nihon no Bukkyō* 日本の佛教, 2). Tokyo: Chikuma shobō, 1967.

Nakano Gishō 中野義照. "Genshi Bukkyō ni okeru tenrin jōō" 原始佛教における轉輪聖王. *Mikkyō bunka* 密教文化, No. 32 (February 1956), 4–19.

Nakao Toshihiro 仲尾俊博. "Dengyō Daishi Saichō no ningenkan" 傳教大師最澄の人間觀. *Bukkyō no ningenkan*, 188–203. See Nihon Bukkyō gakkai.

Nakayama no Sadachika 中山定親. *Mizukagami* 水鏡 (*SZKT*, XXIA). See *Shintei*. . . .

# Selected Bibliography

Nakayama Tarō 中山太郎. *Nihon fujo-shi* 日本巫女史. Tokyo: Ōokayama shoten, 1930.

Nanba Toshinari 難波俊成. "*Sōni-ryō no kōsei to seiritsu ni tsuite*" 僧尼令の構成と成立について. *Bukkyō shigaku* 佛教史學, XIII (No. 2, September 1967), 104–120.

Naoki Kōjirō 直木孝次郎. "Chīsakobe no seishitsu ni tsuite" 小子部の性質について. *Shoku Nihongi kenkyū* 續日本紀研究, VII (No. 9, September 1960), 225–228.

——. *Jitō tennō* 持統天皇 (*Jinbutsu sōsho* 人物叢書, 41). Tokyo: Yoshikawa Kō-bunkan, 1960.

——. "Kura no moto no gogi ni tsuite," 倉下の語義について. *Shoku Nihongi kenkyū*, VII (No. 7, July 1955), 178–181.

——. "Nara jidai ni okeru furō ni tsuite" 奈良時代における浮浪について. *Shirin* 史林, XXXIV (No. 3, 1951), 19–39.

——. *Nihon kodai heiseishi no kenkyū* 日本古代兵制史の研究. Tokyo: Yoshikawa kōbunkan, 1968.

——. *Nihon kodai no shizoku to tennō* 日本古代の氏族と天皇. Tokyo: Hanawa shobō, 1964.

——. "Ryōiki ni mieru dō ni tsuite" 靈異記にみえる堂について. *Shoku Nihongi kenkyū*, VIII (No. 12, 1960), 295–300.

*Nara* 寧樂, XIII (August 1930). A special number on the study of Kannon.

Nihon Bukkyō gakkai 日本佛教學會, ed. *Bukkyō ni okeru gyō no mondai* 佛教における行の問題. Kyoto: Heirakuji shoten, 1965.

——, ed. *Bukkyō ni okeru kai no mondai* 佛教における戒の問題. Kyoto: Heirakuji shoten, 1967.

——, ed. *Bukkyō ni okeru shin no mondai* 佛教における信の問題. Kyoto: Heirakuji shoten, 1963.

——, ed. *Bukkyō ni okeru shō no mondai* 佛教における證の問題. Kyoto: Heirakuji shoten, 1966.

——, ed. *Bukkyō no ningenkan* 佛教の人間觀. Kyoto: Heirakuji shoten, 1968.

*Nihon chimei jiten* 日本地名辭典. Ed. by Watanabe Hikaru 渡邊光 and others. Tokyo: Asakura shoten, 1967–1968.

*Nihon kiryaku* 日本紀略 (*SZKT*, X, XI). See *Shintei*. . . .

*Nihon kōki* 日本後紀 (*SZKT*, III). See *Shintei*. . . .

*Nihon koten bungaku taikei* 日本古典文學大系 (*NKBT*), 100 vols. Tokyo: Iwanami shoten, 1957–1963.

*Nihon shoki* 日本書紀 (*NKBT*, 67, 68). Ed. by Sakamoto Tarō 坂本太郎 and others. See *Nihon koten*. . . .

Nihon shūkyōshi kenkyūkai 日本宗教史研究會, ed. *Fukyōsha to minshū to no taiwa* 布教者と民衆との對話 (*Nihon shūkyōshi kenkyū*, II). Kyoto: Hōzōkan, 1968.

Nishi Yoshio 西義雄, ed. *Daijō bosatsudō no kenkyū* 大乘菩薩道の研究. Kyoto: Heirakuji shoten, 1968.

Nishida Nagao 西田長男. *Jinja no rekishiteki kenkyū* 神社の歷史的研究. Tokyo: Heirakuji shoten, 1968.

Nishio Kōichi 西尾光一. *Chūsei setsuwa bungakuron* 中世說話文學論. Tokyo: Hanawa shobō, 1963.

Nomura Yōshō 野村耀昌. "Kindai ni okeru Myōken shinkō" 近代における妙見信仰. In *Kindai Nihon no Hokke Bukkyō*, 201–246. See Mochizuki.

——. *Shūbu hōnan no kenkyū* 周武法難の研究. Tokyo: Azuma shuppan, 1968.

*Norito* 祝詞 (*NKBT*, 1). Ed. by Takeda Yūkichi 武田祐吉.

Ōchō Enichi 横超慧日. "Jōdo kyōten ni okeru josei" 淨土經典における女性. *Hikata hakushi koki kinen ronbunshū*, 371–387. See Hikata hakushi. . . .

Ogata Yuishō 緒方惟精. "*Nihon ryōiki ni okeru ōhō shisō*" 日本靈異記における應報思想. *Kokubungaku kō* 國文學攷, No. 28 (1962), 26–35.

Okamura Keishin 岡村圭眞. "Keika ajari to no deai" 惠果阿闍梨との出會い. *Mikkyō bunka* 密教文化, Nos. 77–78 (November 1966), 138–154.

Ono Genmyō 小野玄妙, ed. *Bussho kaisetsu daijiten* 佛書解說大辭典, 12 vols. Tokyo: Daitō shuppansha, 1933.

Ōno Tatsunosuke 大野達之助. "Nara Bukkyō no Sutara-shū no kyōgaku keitō" 奈良佛教の修多羅宗の教學系統. *Nihon rekishi* 日本歴史, No. 174 (1962), 10–13.

Ōoka Minoru 大岡實. *Nanto shichidaiji no kenkyū* 南都七大寺の研究. Tokyo: Chūō-kōron bijutsu shuppan, 1966.

Ōe no Masafusa 大江匡房. *Honchō shinsenden* 本朝神仙傳 (*Shiseki shūran* 史籍集覽, revised edition, XXVI). Ed. by Tsunoda Bun'ei 角田文衞. Tokyo: Sumiya shobō, 1967.

———. *Zoku honchō ōjōden* 續本朝往生傳 (*Gunsho ruijū*, IV, Book 66). See *Gunsho ruijū*.

Orikuchi hakushi kinenkai 折口博士記念會, ed. *Orikuchi Shinobu zenshū* 折口信夫全集, 31 vols. Tokyo: Chūōkōronsha, 1954–1957.

Ōsaka rekishi gakkai 大阪歴史學會, ed. *Ritsuryō kokka no kiso kōzō* 律令國家の基礎構造. Tokyo: Yoshikawa kōbunkan, 1960.

Ōya Tokujō 大屋德城. *Nara Bukkyōshi-ron* 寧樂佛教史論. Kyoto: Tōhō bunken kankōkai, 1937.

Renzen 連禪. *Sange ōjōki* 三外往生記 (*ZRG*, VIII, Book 198). See *Zoku*. . . .

*Ruijū kokushi* 類從國史 (*SZKT*, V, VI). See *Shintei*. . . .

*Ruijū sandaikyaku* 類從三代格 (*SZKT*, XXV). See *Shintei*. . . .

*Ryō no gige* 令義解 (*SZKT*, VII). See *Shintei*. . . .

Saichō 最澄. *Kenkai-ron* 顯戒論 (*Dengyō Daishi zenshū*, I). See *Dengyō Daishi zenshū*.

Sakaguchi Genshō 阪口玄章. *Nihon Bukkyō bungaku josetsu* 日本佛教文學序說. Tokyo: Keibunsha, 1935.

Sakai Kōhei 坂井衡平. *Konjaku monogatarishū no shin kenkyū* 今昔物語集の新研究. Tokyo: Sanseidō, 1923.

Sakamoto Tarō and others, ed. *Nihon shoki*. See *Nihon shoki*.

Sakamoto Tarō hakushi kanreki kinenkai 坂本太郎博士還暦記念會, ed. *Nihon kodaishi ronshū* 日本古代史論集, 2 vols. Tokyo: Yoshikawa kōbunkan, 1962.

Sakamoto Yukio 坂本行男, ed. *Hoke-kyō no shisō to bunka* 法華經の思想と文化. Kyoto: Heirakuji shoten, 1965.

Sakurai Mitsuru 櫻井滿. "Mei no chikara: Naka no sumeramikoto o megutte" 姪の力一中皇命をめぐって. *Kokugo to kokubungaku*, XLII (No. 12, December 1965), 23–33.

Sasaki Kentoku 佐々木憲徳. "Bukkyō no on shisō o kiwamete Jōdomon no sore ni oyobu" 佛教の恩思想を究めて淨土門のそれに及ぶ. *Umehara Kangaku koki kinen ronbunshū*, 19–47. See Kenshin gakkai.

Sato Akio 佐藤亮雄, ed. *Hyakuza hōdan kikigakishō* 百座法談聞書抄. Tokyo: Nan'undō Ōfusha, 1963.

Satō Tetsuei 佐藤哲英. "Dengyō Daishi no Daijō sōdan" 傳教大師の大乗僧團. In *Bukkyō kyōdan no kenkyū*, 351–396. See Yoshimura.

Sawada Mizuho 澤田瑞穂. *Jigokuhen* 地獄變. Kyoto: Hōzōkan, 1968.

Sawada Takio 澤田多喜男. "Tong chang-shu tenjin sōkansetsu shitan" 董仲舒天人相關說試探. *Nihon bunka kenkyūsho kiyō* 日本文化研究所紀要, III (1967), 293–312. Reprinted in *Chūgoku kankei ronsetsu shiryō* 中國關係論說資料, VIII (1967), Part One, 428–438.

Seki Akira 關晃. *Kikajin* 歸化人 (*Nihon rekishi shinsho* 日本歴史新書). Tokyo: Shibundō, 1956.

Sekine Shinryū 關根眞隆. *Narachō shokuseikatsu no kenkyū* 奈良朝食生活の研究. Tokyo: Yoshikawa kōbunkan, 1969.

# Selected Bibliography

Shiban 師蠻. *Honchō kōsōden* 本朝高僧傳 (*DBZ*, 102). See *Dainihon Bukkyō zensho*.

Shida Jun'ichi 志田諄一. "Chisakobe no seikaku ni tsuite" 小子部の性格について. *Nihon rekishi* 日本歴史, No. 214 (March 1966), 66–79.

———. "Kōgyokuchō no mondai ni tsuite: kisetsu ihen-kaii no kisai yori mita" 皇極朝の問題について—季節異変怪異の記載よりみた. *Shoku Nihongi kenkyū* 續日本紀研究, VII (No. 5, 1960), 106–112.

Shigematsu Akihisa 重松明久. "Ōjōden no kenkyū" 往生傳の研究. *Nagoya daigaku bungakubu kenkyū ronshū* 名古屋大學文學部研究論集, XXIII (1960), 1–124.

*Shinkō gunsho ruijū* 新校群書類從 (*SGR*), 24 vols. Tokyo: Naigai shoseki, 1932.

*Shinsen shōjiroku* 新撰姓氏錄 (*Gunsho ruijū*, XVI, Book 448). See *Gunsho ruijū*.

*Shintei zōhō kokushi taikei* 新訂增補國史大系 (*SZKT*), 66 vols. Ed. by Kuroita Katsumi 黑板勝美. Tokyo: Yoshikawa kōbunkan, 1929–1966.

Shiren 師鍊. *Genkō shakusho* 元亨釋書 (*DBZ*, 101). See *Dainihon Bukkyō zensho*.

*Shoku Nihongi* 續日本紀, 2 vols. (*SZKT*, II). See *Shintei*. . . .

Sogabe Shizuo 曾我部靜雄. *Ritsuryō o chūshin toshita Nitchū kankeishi no kenkyū* 律令を中心とした日中関係史の研究. Tokyo: Yoshikawa kōbunkan, 1968.

Sonoda Kōyū 薗田香融. "Saichō to Kūkai" 最澄と空海. In *Nihon Bukkyō shisō no tenkai*, 33–57. See Ienaga.

———. "Suiko" 出擧. *Ritsuryō kokka no kiso kōzō*, 397–466. See Ōsaka. . . .

Sugahara Masako 菅原征子. "Kodai Tōgoku ni okeru Kannonzō no zōryū" 古代東國における觀音像の造立. *Bukkyō shigaku* 佛教史學, XIII (No. 4, June 1968), 14–41.

Suzuki Shūji 鈴木修二. "*Konjaku monogatarishū* ni okeru byōsha to chiryōsha" 今昔物語集における病者と治療者. *Nihon rekishi* 日本歴史, No. 243 (August 1968), 92–105.

Tachibana no Narisue 橘成季. *Kokon chomonshū* 古今著聞集 (*NKBT*, 84). Ed. by Nagazumi Yasuaki 永積安明 and Shimada Isao 島田勇雄.

Taira no Yasuyori 平康頼. *Hōbutsushū* 寶物集 (*Koten bunko*, 258). Ed. by Yoshida Kōichi 吉田幸一. Tokyo: Koten bunko, 1969.

*Taishō shinshū daizōkyō* 大正新脩大藏經. Ed. by Takakusu Junjirō 高楠順次郎 and Watanabe Kaigyoku 渡邊海旭 (*Taishō*), 100 vols. Tokyo: Taishō issaikyō kankōkai, 1922–2932.

Takao Giken 高雄義堅. *Chūgoku Bukkyōshi-ron* 中國佛教史論. Kyoto: Heirakuji shoten, 1953.

Takase Shigeo 高瀬重雄. *Kodai sangaku shinkō no shiteki kōsatsu* 古代山岳信仰の史的考察. Tokyo: Kadokawa shoten, 1969.

Takase Shōgon 高瀬承嚴. *Sanbō ekotoba* 三寶繪詞. Tokyo: Morie shoten, 1932.

Takeda Chōshū 竹田聽州. *Sōsen sūhai* 祖先崇拜 (*Sāra sōsho*, 8). Kyoto: Heirakuji shoten, 1957.

Takeuchi Rizō 竹內理三, ed. *Nara ibun* 寧樂遺文, 2 vols. Tokyo: Tōkyōdō, 1943–1944.

Tamura Enchō 田村圓澄. *Asuka Bukkyōshi kenkyū* 飛鳥佛教史研究. Tokyo: Hanawa shobō, 1969.

———. *Nihon Bukkyō shisōshi kenkyū: Jōdokyōhen* 日本佛教思想史研究・淨土教篇. Kyoto: Heirakuji shoten, 1959.

Tanaka Takashi 田中卓. *Sumiyoshi taisha shi* 住吉大社史, I. Ōsaka: Sumiyoshi taisha hōsankai, 1963.

*Teihon Yanagita Kunio shū* 定本柳田國男集, 35 vols. Tokyo: Chikuma shobō, 1962–1964.

Toganoo Shōun 栂尾祥雲. *Mandara no kenkyū* 曼荼羅乃研究. Kōyasan: Kōyasan daigaku shuppanbu, 1927.

Tokiwa Daijō 常盤大定. *Busshō no kenkyū* 佛性の研究. Tokyo: Meiji shoin, 1944.

Tokushi Yūshō 禿氏祐祥. "*Nihon ryōiki* ni inyō seru kyōkan ni tsuite" 日本靈異記

に引用せる經卷について. *Bukkyō kenkyū* 佛教研究, I (No. 2, February 1937), 51–65.

Torao Toshiya 虎尾俊哉. *Handen shūjuhō no kenkyū* 班田收授法の研究. Tokyo: Yoshikawa kōbunkan, 1961.

Tsuchihashi Shūkō 土橋秀高. "Jukai girei no hensen" 授戒儀禮の變遷. *Bukkyō kyōdan no kenkyū*, 205–282. See Yoshimura.

Tsukishima Hiroshi 築島裕. *Heian jidaigo shinron* 平安時代語新論. Tokyo: Tokyo daigaku shuppankai, 1969.

*Tsuda Sōkichi zenshū* 津田左右吉全集, 33 vols. Tokyo: Iwanami shoten, 1963–1966.

Tsuji Zennosuke 辻善之助. *Nihon Bukkyōshi: Jōseihen* 日本佛教史上世篇. Tokyo: Iwanami shoten, 1944.

*Tsukamoto hakushi shōju kinen Bukkyōshigaku ronshū* 塚本博士頌壽記念佛教史學論集. Kyoto: Tsukamoto hakushi shōju kinenkai, 1961.

Tsukamoto Zenryū 塚本善隆. *Chūgoku Bukkyō tsūshi* 中國佛教通史, I. Tokyo: Suzuki zaidan, 1968.

———. "Kinsei Shina taishū no nyoshin Kannon shinkō" 近世支那大衆の女身觀音信仰. In *Yamaguchi hakushi kanreki kinen Indogaku Bukkyōgaku ronsō*, 262–280. See *Yamaguchi hakushi.* . . .

Tsumoto Ryōgaku 津本了學. "*Nihon ryōiki* ni mieru shido no shami ni tsuite" 日本靈異記にみえる私度の沙彌について. *Ryūkoku daigaku ronshū* 龍谷大學論集, No. 348 (December 1954), 37–46.

Tsuruoka Shizuo 鶴岡静夫. *Kantō kodai jiin no kenkyū* 關東古代寺院の研究. Tokyo: Kōbundō, 1969.

———. *Nihon kodai Bukkyōshi no kenkyū* 日本古代佛教史の研究. Tokyo: Bungadō shoten, 1962.

*Uchigikishū* 打聞集 (photostatic copy). Tokyo: Koten hozonkai, 1927.

Uchiyama Toshihiko 內山俊彦. "Kandai no ōhō shisō" 漢代の應報思想. *Tokyo Shina gakuhō* 東京支那學報, No. 6 (1960), 19–32.

Ueda Yoshifumi 上田義文 and others, ed. *Bungaku ni okeru higan hyōshō no kenkyū* 文學における彼岸表象の研究. Tokyo: Chūō kōronsha, 1959.

Uematsu Shigeru 植松茂. *Kodai setsuwa bungaku* 古代說話文學. Tokyo: Hanawa shobō, 1964.

Uno Yukio 宇野幸雄. "Kodai ni okeru seiji to shūkyō no kankei" 古代における政治と宗教の關係. *Nihon rekishi* 日本歷史, No. 82 (March 1955), 19–23.

Watanabe Shōkō 渡邊照宏. "Udāyaṇa ō to Rudrāyaṇa ō" Udāyaṇa 王と Rudrā-yaṇa 王. *Hikata hakushi koki kinen ronbunshū*, 81–95. See *Hikata hakushi.* . . .

Watanabe Tsunaya 渡邊綱也 and Nishio Kōichi 西尾光一, ed. *Uji shūi monogatari* 宇治拾遺物語 (*NKBT*, 27). See *Nihon koten.* . . .

Yabuki Keiki 矢吹慶輝. *Sangaikyō no kenkyū* 三階教の研究. Tokyo: Iwanami shoten, 1927.

Yagi Atsuru 八木充. *Ritsuryō kokka seiritsu katei no kenkyū* 律令國家成立過程の研究. Tokyo: Hanawa shobō, 1968.

Yagi Tsuyoshi 八木毅. "*Nihonkoku genpō zen'aku ryōiki* to *Myōhōki* ni tsuite" 日本國現報善惡靈異記と冥報記について. *Gobun* 語文, No. 25 (March 1965), 15–24.

Yamada Yoshio 山田孝雄, ed. and annot. *Sanbō ekotoba ryakuchū* 三寶繪詞略注. Tokyo: Hōbunkan, 1941.

——— and others, ed. *Konjaku monogatarishū* 今昔物語集 (*NKBT*, 22–26).

Yamaguchi Susumu 山口益. *Seshin no Jōgō-ron* 世親の成業論. Kyoto: Hōzōkan, 1951.

*Yamaguchi hakushi kanreki kinen Indogaku Bukkyōgaku ronsō*. 山口博士還曆記念印度學佛教學論叢. Kyoto: Hōzōkan, 1955.

Yamazaki Hiroshi 山崎宏. "Tō no Dōsen no kantsū ni tsuite" 唐の道宣の感通に

# Selected Bibliography

ついて. *Tsukamoto hakushi shōju kinen Bukkyōshigaku ronbunshū*, 895–906. See *Tsukamoto hakushi. . . .*

────. *Shina chūsei Bukkyō no tenkai* 支那中世佛教の展開. Tokyo: Shimizu shoten, 1942.

────. *Zui-Tō Bukkyōshi no kenkyū* 隋唐佛教史の研究. Kyoto: Hōzōkan, 1967.

Yanagita Kunio. See *Teihon. . . .*

Yanase Kazuo 簗瀬一雄. See Kamo.

Yokota Ken'ichi 横田健一. *Dōkyō* 道鏡 (*Jinbutsu sōsho*, 18). Tokyo: Yoshikawa kōbunkan, 1963.

Yoshida Akira 吉田晶. "8, 9 seiki ni okeru shisuiko ni tsuite" 8, 9 世紀における私出擧について. In *Ritsuryō kokka no kiso kōzō*, pp. 467–514. See *Ōsaka. . . .*

────. *Nihon kodai shakai kōseishi-ron* 日本古代社會構成史論. Tokyo: Hanawa shobō, 1968.

Yoshimura Shūki 吉村修基, ed. *Bukkyō kyōdan no kenkyū* 佛教教團の研究. Kyoto: Hyakkaen, 1968.

Yoshioka Gihō 吉岡義豐. "Shoki Dōkyō no shuitsu shisō to Bukkyō" 初期道教の守一思想と佛教. *Taishō daigaku kenkyū kiyō* 大正大學研究紀要, No. 53 (1968), 61–84. Reprinted in *Chūgoku kankei ronsetsu shiryō* 中國關係論說資料, IX (1968), Part One, 200–212.

Yoshishige no Yasutane 慶滋保胤. *Nihon ōjō gokurakuki* (*Gunsho ruijū*, IV, Book 66; *SGR*, III). See *Gunsho ruijū* or *Shinkō. . . .*

*Yūki kyōju shōju kinen Bukkyō shisōshi ronshū* 結城教授頌壽記念佛教思想史論集. Tokyo: Daizō shuppan, 1964.

*Zoku gunsho ruijū* 續群書類從 (*ZGR*), 70 vols. Tokyo: Zoku gunsho ruijū kanseikai, 1923–1930.

# Index

*Abhidharmasārahrdaya*, translation of, 31
Amaterasu Ōmikami, 53, 69 and 69 n83
Amida (deity), 55, 71, 85, 88, 89
Ascetics (*gyōja*), 54–55, 84
Asuka-no-tera (Hōkō-ji; temple), 15
*Avādana* story, 36 and 36 n153
Avalokiteśvara (deity), 5n12, 52, 86–87.
　See also Kannon

Bitatsu, Emperor, 40
Bodhisattva, 5n12, 33, 53
*Bon* festival (July 15), 46 and 46n10
Brahmans, 66
Buddha, three bodies of (*trikāya*), 88–89
Buddha-nature, doctrine of (or *Tathāgata-garbha*), 62
Buddhist movements, popular, 18–29

*Cakravartin* (*tenrin jōō*), idea of, 66
Chanjang (Korean preceptor), 39
Chikō (monk), 13, 76–77, 79
Chinese Buddhist literature, influence of, 34–40
*Chuang-tzu* (Taoist classic), 52
Confucius, 77
Cosmological theories, 14 and 14n52, 32, 45–49, 55, 62
Cremation, 81–83

*Daihōdō daijik-kyō* (scripture), 12–13
*Daihōkō jūrin-gyō*, 58
*Daijōbu-ron*, 57
*Dainihon Hoke-kyō kenki* (Records of Wonders Related to the *Hoke-kyō* in Japan), 43
Dead: veneration for, 46–47; belief in spirits of, 80–84. *See also* Hell; Paradise
Decrees, concerning Buddhist temples and monks, 7–8
*Dentō jū-i* (Kyōkai's clerical rank), 3 and 3n5
Desire and passion, as cause of misery, 63–64
Dharani, 13 and 13n47, 34, 71, 84
Dharma, 7n18, 49, 76, 88–89; three stages of, 9, 11–14
Dharma King, 7 and 7n18
Diviners, 83–84
Dōji (monk), 11–13, 25, 86
Dōjō, Venerable (monk), 73, 74
Dōkyō (monk), 7, 13, 65–66

Dōshō, Venerable (monk), 24, 25, 58, 81
Dōtō (Buddhist scholar), 46–47
Dreams, Kyokai's, and decision to pursue spiritual life, 4–6

E no Ozunu, 27 and 27n118, 39–40, 54, 78, 82
Eigō, Dhyāna Master, 77
Emperor, significance of, in Japanese tradition, 68
Empresses, large number of, 68–69
Enlightenment, 6–7, 14n50, 61, 63
Enryaku era, 9–10
Era names, practice of using, influence of Chinese system on, 47–48
Eschatological ideas, first reference to, in Japan, 9–10, 13, 14

*Fudoki* (Topographic Records), 41, 50
Fuji, Mt., 54, 55
Fujiwara no asomi Hirotari, 58
Fujiwara no Kamatari, 17
*Fusō ryakki* (Concise Chronicle of Japan), 44

Gangaku (monk), 77–78, 82
Gangō-ji (temple), 73
Ganjin (Chinese monk), 21, 22, 87
Genbaryō (bureau), 19, 21
Genbō (monk), 86
Gigaku (Korean monk), 78
*Gohei hasami*, rite of, 49
Golden Peak, Mt. (Kane no take), 54
*Gukanshō* (Miscellany of Ignorant Views), 44
"Gushi" (A Fool's Idea), 11–12
Gyōgi (monk), 24–25, 40, 43, 78; compared with Chikō, 76–77; legends about, 79–80

*Han shu* (History of Former Han Dynasty), 34
*Hannya kenki* (A Collection of Miraculous Stories concerning the *Kongō hannya-kyō*), 36, 37–38
*Hannya shin-gyō*, 49, 56
Hell, 50–51, 52, 55–60. *See also* Other world
*Hijiri*, defined, 77–79
Himiko, 69 and 69n84
Hinayana precepts, 22
Hirokuni, 41
Hitokotonushi no kami, 27 and 27n119, 54
*Hoke-kyō* (Buddhist scripture), 23, 57, 59, 78,

# Index

83; power of, to promote welfare of state, 28; references to karma in, 33–34; Kyōkai's familiarity with, 35; popularity of, 37; Records of Wonders Related to, 43; and ascetic practices, 53–54; influence of, on Kyōkai, 62; on salvation for women, 70–71, 73; legends, 84–85, 86, 87–88

*Hokke gisho* (Prince Shōtoku's commentary on the *Hoke-kyō*), 88

*Hokke kenki*, 43 and 43n181, 87–88

*Honchō kōsō-den* (Biographies of Eminent Monks in Japan), 3

*Hosshinshū* (Collection of Tales for Awakening Faith), 44

Hossō School, 24

*Hou-Han shu* (History of Later Han Dynasty), 34

Hsi Ch'ao, 30

Hsin-hsing, 10–11

Huang Ti (Yellow Emperor), 14 and 14n52, 77

Hui-yüan, 39–40; "San-pao lun" (Treatise on the Three Ways of Karmic Retribution), 30–31, 32, 33

*Hyakuza hōdan kikigakishō* (Summary Notes of One Hundred Lectures on Dharma), 43

Ichisendai, concept of, 61, 64, 90

Ienaga Saburō, on the Three Treasures, 89–90

Inoue Mitsusada, 69

Ise, Grand Shrine of, 28, 69n83

Iwazuchi, Mt., or Iwazuchi-yama (mountain), 54, 55

Izanagi, 53

Izanami, 53

Jakusen, Dhyāna Master, 67, 77

Japanese legendary literature, 40–44

Jātaka literature, 30, 36 and 36n153

Jitō, Empress, 15, 19, 65, 81

Jizō (the Bodhisattva Ksitigarbha), 58

Judgment after death, 55–56

*Jūichimen kanzeon shinju-kyō* (scripture), 86

Kamakura period, 44, 65

Kami, 27 and 27nn117–128, 49, 54

*Kamnagi* (diviner), 83–84

Kaneaki, Prince, 43

Kaniman-ji cycle (legends), 63

Kanki (monk), 58

Kanmu, Emperor, 7, 51

Kannon, 5 and 5n12, 6, 34, 52, 55, 89; acquired feminine features, 76; legends, 84–88; Eleven-headed and Thousand-armed, 86–87

*Kannon-gyō* (chapter on Kannon of the *Hoke-kyō*), 86

Kanroku (Kwal-leuk; Korean monk), 18–19

*Kao-seng chuan* (Biographies of Eminent Monks), 31

Karma, doctrine of, 5 and 5n11, 6, 14n50, 50, 60, 91; samsara and, 29–34

Karmic retribution, 30–33, 58, 80; theme of early Chinese works, 36, 38; clarified in the *Nihon ryōiki*, 42, 60

Katayose Masayoshi, on "utmost devotion," 64–65

Kawara-no-tera (Gufuku-ji; temple), 15

*Keka* (rite of repentance), 45–46, 49

Kichijōten (deity), 46n6, 85

Kii province, 3

Kinai, origin of most legends of *Nihon ryōiki*, 3

Kinmei, Emperor, 40

Kōfukuji manuscript of the *Nihon ryōiki*, 9

*Kojiki* (historical records), 34, 38, 40, 41, 50

*Kongō hannya-kyō jikkenki* (collection of stories about *Kongō hannya-kyō*), 37–38

Kōnin, Emperor, 7, 10, 40, 51

*Konjaku monogatarishū* (Collection of Tales Present and Past), 43, 65

Konsu, the Ascetic, 77

Korea, transmission of Buddhism to Japan from, 16

Kōya(san) manuscript of the *Nihon ryōiki*, 4, 9

Kuan-yin, 5n12, 87. *See also* Kannon

Kūkai (monk), 4, 22, 23

Kumano, Mt., 55

Kumārajīva, his "Treatises on the Past, Present, and Future," 31

Kyōkoku (Keikoku; monk), 8

Kyōnichi (novice monk), 4, 5, 6, 36

Kyoto, capital transferred from Nara to, 7

Lao-tzu, 77

Legends: Korean Buddhist, 39; "non-Buddhist," in *Nihon ryōiki*, 73–74

Literature: Jātaka, 30; influence of Chinese Buddhist, 34–40; Japanese legendary, 40–44

Lochana Buddha, Great, 15, 24

"Lu-shan Yüan-kung hua" (legend), 39

Maeda (-ke) manuscript of the *Nihon ryōiki*, 9, 59–60

"Maeda (-ke) -bon itsubun" (Unknown Passage of the Maeda Manuscript), 9–10, 11–14

Maitreya (deity), 53–54, 55, 85n131, 87–88

Man: what makes him human, 60–68; ideal image of, 76–80. *See also* Woman

"Mandate of Heaven," 30 and n130

Mañjuśrī (deity), 39, 53–54, 55, 67, 77

Mantra, 34, 84

*Manyōshū*, 40

# Index

*Mappō* consciousness, 10–11
Maro (attendant), 46–47
Meditation, 71
Merit (Skt. *punya*), 61
Minamoto no Tamenori, 43
Miroku (bodhisattva), 85 and 85n131. *See also* Maitreya
*Mogari*, practice of, 81
Monks and nuns, *see* Samgha
Monmu, Emperor, 15, 51
Motherly love, 75–76
Moto-yakushi-ji (temple), 15
Mountains, ascetic practices in, 51, 53–55
*Muryōju-kyō* (scripture), 86
*Myōhōki* (Record of Invisible Work of Karmic Retribution), 10–11, 36–37, 38, 81
Myōken (bodhisattva), 85

Nachi, Mt., 55
Nāga, King, daughter of, 71, 73
Nagaya, Prince, 65, 82–83
Nara, 3, 4, 7–8, 15; Schools, Six, 16–18
*Nehan-gyō* (scripture), 35, 57, 61–62, 88; influence of, on Kyōkai, 64; on salvation for women, 70–72
*Nidāna* story, 36 and 36n153
*Nihon kanryōroku* (Japanese Record of Miraculous Events), 42
*Nihon ōjō gokurakuki* (Biographies of the Japanese Who Were Born in the Land of Bliss), 43
*Nihon shoki* (historical records), 34, 41–42; on the official introduction of Buddhism, 11, 40; influence of, on Kyōkai, 38; on Prince Shōtoku, 39, 78; idea of other world in, 50
*Ninnō hannya-kyō* (Buddhist scripture), 28
Nintoku, Emperor, 67
Nirvana, 6 and 6n13, 33, 53

Odae, Mt., 39
*Ōharae* (rite of purification), 45, 46, 49
*Ōjōden* series, 44, 58, 87
*On*, concept of, 62–63
*Onmyōdō*, 84 and 84n127
Ordinances concerning monks and nuns, *see* *Sōni-ryō*
Ordination system, 21–23
Orikuchi Shinobu, 68–69
Other world, symbolism of visit to, 49–55. *See also* Hell; Paradise
Ōtomo family, 26
Ōtsukasa-no-ōtera (Takechi-no-ōtera; temple), 15

Paradise, 50, 51, 55–60. *See also* Other world
Potalaka, Mt. (Ch. Po-t'o-lo shan; Jap. Fudarakusan), 52

Repaying kindness, theme of, 62–63
Rites of cosmic renewal, 45–49

Sacred, versus secular, 79
Saga, Emperor, 9, 67
Sages, 77–79
Saichō (monk), 21, 22, 23, 25; identified, 4; on the eschatological idea, 13; and Mahayana samgha, 28–29; on clergy and laity, 64
*Saishōō-kyō* (*Kichijō-keka*; Buddhist scripture), 23, 28, 45–46
Śākyamuni, 29, 45, 66, 76, 89; teachings of, 9, 14, 70, 76; and nirvana, 11, 33; on repaying kindness, 62; on enlightenment, 63; power of, 65, 90; as great sage, 77; relics of, 83; stories on, 85; *Hoke-kyō* influential in Japanese understanding of, 88
Samgha, 7 and 7n17, 8; state control of, 18–29
Samghadeva, 31
*Samguk yusa*, 39
Samsara, doctrine of, 50, 60; karma and, 29–34
*San-pao*, theory of, 30–31
*Sanbō ekotoba* (Notes on Pictorial Presentations of the Three Treasures), 43
Śāriputra (Śākyamuni's disciple), 71
Saru-hijiri (bodhisattva), 77
Schools and seminars, Buddhist, 16–18
Sect of the Three Stages, *see* Dharma, three stages of
*Senju sengen darani-kyō* (scripture), 86
Shakanyorai, 65
Shasekishū (Collection of Sand and Stone), 44
Shiban, 3, 4
*Shih chi* (Records of the Historian), 34
*Shin-gyō*, 78
Shingon (monk), 58, 63, 79
Shingon School, 49, 67
*Shinji kan-gyō* (scripture), 63, 67
Shinpukuji manuscript of the *Nihon ryōiki*, 9
*Shōbō nenjo-kyō*, 63
*Shoku Nihongi* (historical work), 12, 38, 40–41, 83
*Shokyō yōshū* (Chu-ching yao-chi; Essentials of All Sūtras), 6, 36, 38
Shōmu, Emperor, 15–16, 22, 28, 82, 87; and Gyōgi, 24–25; as incarnation of Mañjuśrī, 39, 67; reign of, 51
Shōtoku (Kōken), Empress, 7 and 7n19, 51, 65–66
Shōtoku, Prince, 43, 67, 88; legend about, 39–40, 52, 55; anecdote of his meeting with a beggar, 77–78, 82; on the Three Treasures, 89–90
Shun, Emperor, 67, 77

# Index

Soga family, 19, 25

*Sōgō-sei* (a supervisory system for monks and nuns), 18

Sōgō system, 18–21, 29

*Sōni-ryō* (Ordinances concerning Monks and Nuns), 8, 18, 29, 37, 84; described, 20, 23–25

Suiko, Empress, 5, 18–19

*Suminoe no taisha jindaiki* (Ancient History of the Great Shrine of Suminoe), 41–42

Sutara-shū (school), 16–17

Symbolism of visit to other world, 49–55

Taga, Great Kami of, 28, 56

T'ai, Mt., 51

Taika Reform, 69

Tajimamori (legendary hero), 49

Tajō (or Tarajō; Korean monk), 84

Takamagahara (name for other world), 50

Tamura Enchō, 11

T'ang-lin, 32, 37

Tantric scriptures, 86–87

*Tao-seng ko* (laws concerning Taoist and Buddhist monks), 20

Tao-shih, 36

Tathāgata (Ja. Nyorai), 63

*Tathāgatagarbha* (doctrine of Buddha-nature), 62

Temples, 15, 25–28

Tendai Sage, 14 and 14n51

Tendai School, 21, 67

Tenmu, Emperor, 15, 19, 25

"Three paths," 59

Three Treasures, 46, 56, 63, 64; and Emperor Shōmu, 15 and 15n59; as theme of *Shokyō yōshū*, 36; offenses against, 41, 62; faith in, essential for leading good life, 57; wonder of, 84–91; defined, 89–90

Tōdai-ji (temple), 15, 23–24

Tokoyo no kuni (name for other world), 50

*Trikāya* (three bodies of Buddha), 88–89

*Uchigikishū* (Collection of Sermons), 43

Uematsu Shigeru, 42

Uji, Prince, 65

*Uji shūi monogatari* (Tales from the Later Gleanings of Uji), 43

"Unknown Passage of the Maeda Manuscript," 9–10, 11–14

Urashima no ko (legendary hero), 49

Usa Hachiman (deity), 28

Woman, as cosmic symbol, 68–76

Wu-t'ai, Mt., 39, 54

Yakushi (Buddha), 85

Yakushi-ji (temple), 3, 4, 7, 15, 24

Yama (lord of the dead), 52, 81–82, 87; and paradise and hell, 56–57, 58, 59, 60

Yanagita Kunio, 73

Yao, Emperor, 67, 77

Yellow Emperor (Huang Ti), 14n52, 77

*Yin* and *yang*, 47–48, 49

Yomi no kuni (name for other world), 50

Yoshino, Mt., 55

Yoshishige no Yasutane, 43

*Yu-hsien-k'u* (Chinese novelette), 49–50

Yuishiki School, 3, 4

Yūryaku, Emperor, 40, 54

*Zen'aku inga-kyō*, 60

Zenshu (monk), 13